THE AMERICAN INQUISITION 1945-1960

THE
AMERICAN
INQUISITION
1945-1960

CEDRIC BELFRAGE

The Bobbs-Merrill Company, Inc.
Indianapolis · New York

The Bobbs-Merrill Company, Inc.
Publishers: Indianapolis • New York

E743
.5
.B3

To W. E. B.
in happy memory
and to my children Sally, Nicolas and Anne
in not unreasonable hope

Augustus (B.C. 27—A.D. 14) was sensible that mankind is governed by names; nor was he deceived in his expectation that the senate and people would submit to slavery, provided they were respectfully assured that they still enjoyed their ancient freedoms.

Gibbon, *Decline & Fall of the Roman Empire*

Contents

Glossary
of Initial Abbreviations

AAAS	American Association for Advancement of Science
ABA	American Bar Association
ABC	Americans Battling Communism
ACLU	American Civil Liberties Union
ACPFB	American Committee for Protection of Foreign Born
ADA	Americans for Democratic Action
AEC	Atomic Energy Commission
AFL	American Federation of Labor
AFTRA	American Federation of Television & Radio Artists
ALP	American Labor Party
ALPD	American League for Peace & Democracy
AP	Associated Press
ASP	Arts, Sciences & Professions Committee
Cal Tech	California Institute of Technology
CBS	Columbia Broadcasting System
CIA	Central Intelligence Agency
CIO	Congress of Industrial Organizations
CP	Communist Party
CRC	Civil Rights Congress
DAR	Daughters of the American Revolution
ECLC	Emergency Civil Liberties Committee
FBI	Federal Bureau of Investigation
FCC	Federal Communications Commission
F. for R.	Fund for the Republic
HUAC	House Un-American Activities Committee
ICFTU	International Confederation of Free Trade Unions
ILWU	International Longshoremen's & Warehousemen's Union
IPR	Institute of Pacific Relations
IWO	International Workers Order

IWW	Industrial Workers of the World
JAFRC	Joint Anti-Fascist Refugee Committee
MIT	Massachusetts Institute of Technology
NAACP	National Association for Advancement of Colored People
NATO	North Atlantic Treaty Organization
NBC	National Broadcasting Company
NCASF	National Council of American-Soviet Friendship
NCCCA	National Council of Churches of Christ in America
NC-PAC	National Citizens Political Action Committee
NEA	National Education Association
NLRB	National Labor Relations Board
NLG	National Lawyers Guild
NMU	National Maritime Union
PP	Progressive Party
PU	Pension Union (Washington)
SACB	Subversive Activities Control Board
SCEF	Southern Conference Educational Fund
SCHW	Southern Conference for Human Welfare
SISS	Senate Internal Security Subcommittee
TU	Teachers Union (New York & Philadelphia)
UAW	United Automobile Workers
UE	United Electrical, Radio & Machine Workers
UN	United Nations
UNESCO	United Nations Educational, Scientific & Cultural Organization
UNRRA	United Nations Relief & Rehabilitation Administration
UP	United Press
USIS	United States Information Service
VALB	Veterans of the Abraham Lincoln Brigade
VFW	Veterans of Foreign Wars
VOA	Voice of America
WFTU	World Federation of Trade Unions
YCL	Young Communist League
YMCA	Young Men's Christian Association
YWCA	Young Women's Christian Association

Principal American Heresy Tribunals and Laws 1938-60*

Committee on Un-American Activities of the House of Representatives (HUAC)—1938

> Chairmen: Martin Dies (Texas) 1938–44; John S. Wood (Georgia) 1945–46; J. Parnell Thomas (New Jersey) 1947–48; Wood (Georgia) 1949–52; Harold H. Velde (Illinois) 1953–54; Francis E. Walter (Pennsylvania) 1955–60.

Loyalty Boards (nationwide for federal government employees under Truman Loyalty Order)—1947

Internal Security Subcommittee of the Senate Judiciary Committee (SISS)—1950
> Chairmen: Pat McCarran (Nevada, d. 1954); William E. Jenner (Indiana); James O. Eastland (Mississippi).

Subversive Activities Control Board (SACB)—1950
> Five full-time members (not Congressmen) appointed by President.

Immigration Department Boards (deportations)—1952

Permanent Subcommittee on Investigations of the Senate Committee on Government Operations
> Chairmen: Joseph R. McCarthy (Wisconsin) 1953–54; John L. McClellan (Arkansas) 1955–60.

* * *

Smith Act (1940) made it a crime "to knowingly or willfully advocate, abet, advise, or teach the duty, necessity, desirability, or propriety of overthrowing any government in the US by force and violence," or "to print, publish,

---

* Listing of all the tribunals set up by state and local legislative bodies and those for self-purging by specific government departments, industries, trade unions, citizens' organizations, etc., would be beyond the present author's limitations. A list of bodies which did not set up any form of inquisition would be shorter.

edit, issue, circulate, sell, distribute, or publicly display any written or printed matter advocating, advising, or teaching the duty, necessity, desirability, or propriety" of such overthrow. Also "to organize or help organize" or "to be or become a member of" any "society, group or assembly of persons who teach, advocate or encourage" such overthrow "knowing the purposes thereof." The original penalties of 10 years' imprisonment and $10,000 fine were halved after the war, doubled by Eisenhower in 1956. The law also required fingerprinting and registration of all aliens in the US, and made them deportable if they ever joined an overthrow-minded group.

Taft-Hartley Act (1947): a compendium of all classical restraints on trade unions. Injunctions to "cool off" or abort strikes; mass picketing and "secondary boycotts" banned; unions suable for "unfair labor practices"; closed shop abolished; employers authorized to interfere in employees' attempts to join a union, etc. The law's most publicized clause compelled all union officers to sign oaths that they were not Communists.

McCarran (Internal Security) Act (1950) set forth the thesis of a conspiracy "to establish a Communist totalitarian dictatorship in the countries throughout the world," and authorized concentration camps for emergency situations. It set up SACB (see above) to compel any organization found heretical to "register," disclosing its membership and financial affairs and labeling itself subversive on all its printed matter. Compound punishments were prescribed for each day of failure to register.

McCarran-Walter Act (1952): comprehensive law including and tightening previous restrictions on immigration and on aliens (resident and otherwise) in the US. Heavily reduced the proportion of immigrants from non-white countries. Removed deportation cases from the courts, the Immigration Service setting up its own boards unhampered by rules of evidence and procedure.

Preface

As these pages underwent final revision, America's "cold war" crusade against Communism had proceeded continuously for a quarter of a century; and at this rather late date in the resulting holocaust, the questioning of the crusade's credentials had developed into a veritable industry with a name—"historical revisionism." Thus the *New York Review of Books* (September 2, 1971) deals with nine re-evaluations of the cold war's origins. Some of the reviewed authors still insist on America's "good intentions"; the reviewer has more sympathy with "radical revisionists" who find the crusade to have been hypocritical, immoral and imperialistic from the outset.

The fact that some Americans saw this at the time—and what happened to them for saying so—is ignored by all "revisionists" or so distorted that they might better have ignored it. The domestic arm of the cold war was a calculated campaign to wash America's brain. The distortion of the reality of that campaign begins with the label now firmly and hygienically attached to it: "the McCarthy Era," referring to the late meteoric senator from Wisconsin. If any single American deserves his name on the label, implying fatherhood and rearing of the monster, it would be J. Edgar Hoover.

The few "revisionists" who purport to chronicle what was known as the American witch hunt have not found it possible to detach themselves from the Establishment viewpoint.* Yet without the victims' viewpoint the history of these years, the most decisive since America's revolution against England, is like a contemporary history of Germany or Russia without the concentration camps. We

---

* The author of a 500-page account of the Un-American Activities Committee (Walter Goodman, *The Committee*, Farrar, Straus & Giroux, New York, 1968), for example, finds no space for the perjury of government witnesses and its consequences. The book is described in a preface by Richard Rovere as an "indictment" of the committee by one who is "no less anti-Communist than Martin Dies [first committee chairman] or any of his successors." The text makes the latter claim—if not the former—redundant, and suggests that the study of American inquisiting has moved backwards since William Gellermann's *Martin Dies* (John Day, New York 1944), and August Ogden's *The Dies Committee* (Murray & Hester—Catholic University Press, Washington, D.C., 1946), both written when the inquisition was in its infancy and seemed about to expire.

leave it to the "revisionists" to consider the reasons for this scholarly lacuna, bearing in mind, if they will, the extent to which most Americans—and particularly the intelligentsia—shared responsibility for the follies recorded here.

This book is an attempt to chronicle the follies year by year and is, above all, a tribute to the resistance. It may seem presumptuous that one should undertake the task who cannot enter America to consult the mountainous research material, and must depend on the mail, interviews with travelers and an inadequate library. But the stuff of it is the sweat, laughter, tears, bones and guts of the writer and his American circle before he was deported.

In view of the chaos which the cold war has created in the English language, some advance semantic explanations are advisable, especially with regard to words used here with regrettable but necessary frequency.

I accept the Random House Dictionary's first definition of "inquisition": "An official investigation, esp. one of a political or religious nature, characterized by lack of regard for individual rights, prejudice on the part of the examiners, and recklessly cruel punishments." Being "esp. of a political or religious nature," it is essentially an investigation of thoughts rather than actions.

The same dictionary defines "heresy" as "opinion or doctrine at variance with the orthodox or accepted doctrine, esp. of a church or religious system"; and "religion" as "a specific fundamental set of beliefs and practices generally agreed upon by a number of persons or sects" (second definition), "*a deep conviction* of the validity of religious beliefs and practices" (fourth definition—emphasis added). I proceed here on the basis that both Americanism and Communism are religions.

"Communist" in these pages refers exclusively to persons who were publicly known as Communist Party members. "Heretic" in the American context embraces all persons who, whether Communists or not, were not deterred from an opinion or action because members of the proscribed cult shared in it. The inquisitor's function is to pursue all heretics, and the essence of heresy is refusal to admit that one was either conspiring or a "dupe" in forming the opinion or taking the action. Hence there is no accurate substitute for "heretic" and "heretical" in referring to the targets of inquisition.

Paid inquisitorial "familiars" in Spain "acquired notoriety in fact and in legend for the way in which they acted as a fifth column of informers and spies," although "the majority of denunciations were made by ordinary people, neighbors, traveling companions, acquaintances" (Kamen, *The Spanish Inquisition*). This corresponds with the American situation and I use the term specifically for the professional, as against the amateur, informer.

For the sake of convenience, and with apologies to purists, I have used "America, American" and "Russia, Russian" throughout for the USA and USSR and their inhabitants.

In a book teeming with organizations, I regret the inevitable welter of initials to designate these after the first reference. A glossary is provided from which the reader may refresh his memory.

With so large an array of persons involved on both sides, and so many investigations proceeding simultaneously, nothing like a full account of the inquisition up to 1960 is possible in a single volume. I have attempted no more than to present a continuity and relate it very briefly with world events. Various aspects need to be fleshed out in detailed studies, and if I have provided a helpful skeleton for this endeavor, my labors will have been worthwhile. I have mentioned as many victims as seemed viable short of producing a catalogue and regret having had to omit dozens whose heresies were equally gallant or perverse. As it is, the reader will often need to consult the index for full names and for identification of their owners from earlier references. In the selection of "cases," I have dealt briefly with more famous ones (about which good books are available) to give preference to barely known or forgotten ones which may be equally or more illustrative of the period.

A final word: I hope the reader will not think I have approached the American Inquisition with levity. On the contrary, I have tried to take it as seriously as it has taken itself, though I cannot claim to match it in solemnity. Despite their retrospectively ludicrous aspects, inquisitions are curtain raisers for massacres.

*   *   *

The most important single source of material for the book has been the *National Guardian,* and credit and deep appreciation are due to Elmer Bendiner, Lawrence Emery and other staff writers of the period when I was its editor, and especially to my colleague and comrade of then and now, James Aronson.

For the grant which made the undertaking economically viable, my thanks to the Louis M. Rabinowitz Foundation. For hard labor at the typewriter I am indebted to Catherine Sills, Sister Carmen Guadelupe Chavez, Monette Weinstone and Ann Levine, and to Jessica Fredricks whose stamina in typing, re-typing and indexing is beyond my power to praise adequately. My gratitude to professors H. H. Wilson and John Coatsworth and to Alex Crosby, Louis Melzack, Steve Nelson, Dr. David Prensky, Anthony Tillett and Celia Zitron, who read the manuscript at various stages and offered valuable criticism but are responsible for none of the errors. And to Mary for always being, as she should be, my severest critic.

C.B.
Cuernavaca, Mexico.

THE AMERICAN INQUISITION 1945-1960

PART ONE: FOUNDATIONS

Introduction
Christians, Judaizers, Witches, Etc.

"It is strange," writes a philosophy professor in 1969,* "that the critical events that I shall narrate should happen in America." His pioneer grandfather fought off Indians from a covered wagon, and the events he is to describe are his own nightmare years of battle against charges of heresy. He might have asked himself where else, in the modern world, they could have happened just as they did.

The professor is haunted by the America of Jefferson's noble phrase, which brought shiploads of pioneers from Europe, about "the safety with which error of opinion may be tolerated where reason is left free to combat it." Of modern America it might be more apt to paraphrase another Jeffersonian passage: When in the course of human events it becomes necessary for an established order to defend itself against doctrines which threaten it, inquisitions are instituted among men for that purpose. What is strange in America, in terms of thought control methods used elsewhere, is that the professor is alive and well to rub his eyes and publish his nightmare for those who may now be interested. But he has served his purpose. He was used by America's unique inquisition to frighten his good-hearted and nostalgic counterparts into orthodoxy at a moment of decisive re-definition of policy.

Thought control will become superfluous, and heresy nonexistent by defini-tion, only in a society which has been much discussed but never realized: one in which the whole population is the establishment, and citizens are valued by the extent to which they inform themselves, discuss and criticize. In societies con-stantly on the brink of war, loyalty must be imposed by one method or another. Italy and Germany chose "Fascism" which, having pronounced democracy deca-dent, could process the unorthodox physically behind walls without need for ex-planations or apologies. But Fascism flunked the acid test of war, and clearly a method that seems to have the sanction of God, Law and Democracy is preferable if it will work. A true inquisition—the method chosen by America—operates in the name of one or more of these, preferably all three.

The protagonists in an inquisition are people in power who aim to keep it, identifying the nation's best interests with their own; and citizens who, chal-

* Melvin Rader, *False Witness*, University of Washington Press, Seattle, 1969.

3

lenging the proclaimed orthodoxy, must be branded as outcasts by tribunals to prevent the challenge from spreading. A brief excursion into the history of inquisitions will show where parallels exist and where America has added its own distinctive touches.

Gibbon reminds us—and it is true of all inquisitions—that the persecution of Christians, when their faith was subversive, was a contest between two sets of deep convictions. The Christians' "faults were derived from an excess of virtue"; such a proconsul-inquisitor as the younger Pliny had "the most amiable and philosophic character"; and the orthodoxy-imposing emperor Trajan was "distinguished by the wisdom and justice of his general administration." Rome's imperial inquisition 18 centuries ago contrasted with America's in that Trajan barred anonymous evidence and sometimes executed a false accuser. The two coincided in a more essential aspect: Pliny reported to Trajan that he punished only followers of "this debased superstition" who refused to "curse the name of Christ [modern: socialism] which, it is said, those who are really Christians cannot be induced to do." Pursuing the similarities, we find Rome concluding that, since Christians understandably resorted to secrecy, "they only concealed what they would have blushed to disclose." Clandestine rites were imputed to them which, when they reached ascendancy, they would in turn impute to Jews up to the 20th century. They drank babies' blood as a prelude to "suitable entertainment in which intemperance served as a provocative to brutal lust," concluding the ceremony with "incestuous commerce of sisters and brothers, of sons and of mothers." In modern times socialism is hardly installed in one country before its devotees are accused of cannibalism and nationalizing women.

A cardinal feature of any inquisition, carried forward in Torquemada's Spain, is that the accused is presumed guilty unless he can prove innocence; and this he does by naming his accomplices as well as recanting. Spain's inquisitors were required to be expert in theology and law and capable of dignity and minimal humanity.* They operated their Holy Office as a monopoly, in contrast to the gaggle of competitive-cooperative tribunals befitting democratic America. Both inquisitions depended on penitent heretics for convincing accounts of their former friends' crimes. Both became targets for deprecations of their "excesses" by persons high in the establishment, who were in turn rebuked by zealots for "softness on Judaism" (Communism). Spain's liberals urged that torture be used in moderation, America's that their most famous inquisitor curb his zeal to inquisite practically everybody. In neither country was the excessive zeal punished by anything more than reproof and the requirement to retire. Pope Sixtus IV protested against condemnations "on the testimony of enemies, rivals, slaves and other lower and even less proper persons" in Spain's first inquisitorial years as did President Roosevelt in America's. Sixtus was blackmailed into withdrawing, Roosevelt became a posthumous traitor. The public can always use a scapegoat, and with some pres-

---

* "For this grave responsibility [as *visitadores* to supervise implementation of Indian protection laws in Spanish colonies] the Crown always chose trusted jurisconsults of maturity and standing, with a preference for inquisitors because of the rigorous and independent judgment that characterized them."—Ismael Sánchez Bella, *El Consejo de las Indias en el Siglo XVI* (University of Valladolid, 1970).

sure will accept those that its rulers provide. Waning enthusiasm for the Judaizer-hunt was revived when the J. Edgar Hoover of Spain, the Constable of Castile, discovered that Judaizers were behind the Comuneros' revolt of 1519–21. This verified the link (translated into modern parlance) between Jews and Communism.

The inquisition became a vested interest for an increasing number of Spaniards and accelerated by its own momentum. When Judaizers began to run out—though their underground activities never stopped in the mythology—the inquisitors substituted Illuminati, Erasmists and Lutherans. Investigators trailed merchants and seamen who might be carrying the Protestant Bible, the *Communist Manifesto* of the day; Protestants, "aliens" by definition and guilty of preaching sedition, were burned in public squares along with mountains of books. As with Communists in America (the supply of whom soon languished), it was neither necessary nor even desirable that plain citizens should know what these enemies of society believed. The public's memory was and remains conveniently short. Erasmus's humanist doctrines had been in high fashion not long before they were anathematized; a few decades before America anathematized Marxism, Marx was writing for the respectable New York *Tribune*. Yet we must note that Erasmus-influenced intellectuals, keeping their perceptions prudently indirect, managed to produce a golden age of art under their inquisition. America's culture disinte-grated and its intelligentsia surrendered almost in a body.

The only feature of Spain's inquisition which has lingered in general aware-ness is the forms of punishment. America does not parade heretics through the streets in *sanbenitos,* rarely submits them to physical torture if their skins are white, and never burns them alive except in remote areas like Korea, Vietnam and Latin America. The march of civilization is plain, although we must remem-ber that the cruelties Spain practiced on heretics were standard contemporary punishments, not an inquisitorial specialty. Punishment was the function of the secular arm after the inquisitors pronounced their verdict, as in America, but America has used two secular arms. One, the Law, imposed sentences beyond those prescribed for any civil crime except murder or (in the South) rape: up to 25 and 30 years' imprisonment and death. The second arm—the one that punished the great body of heretics—was the media. Their function was to ensure social and economic quarantine for the guilty by spreading word of the inquisitors' brand into every home: in America the inquisition did not have to provide weighty theo-logical arguments, merely appeal to the headline writers. The media do more effectively the work of the *sanbenito* in media-less Spain. They are a vital enough part of the modern inquisition to have given it a new dimension, so that one may speak of pre-media and post-media inquisitions.

In a final glance at Spain we note that, while every Spaniard was expected to inform on his family and friends, there was a rush of applicants for jobs as familiars, professional informers. The pay was meager, but the indirect benefits were great. As in America familiars were addicted to crime, and the job's main attraction was the protection afforded by inquisitors against the law. In 17th-century Aragon openings in the profession had to be curtailed to subdue outcries against a crime wave in which familiars were almost invariably involved. In 20th-century America the protection of familiars against prosecution became so notorious that the professional ranks had likewise to be drastically reduced.

Accepting the inquisition as an inevitable part of life, Spaniards devised crafty ways of avoiding it and left it to collapse by its own weight, which it took three and a half centuries to do. When it died Spain was one of the world's most backward countries and the establishment wondered if a little subversion might not have been a good thing. Meanwhile the institution had spread through Europe with witches as the threat to orderly society. The first alarums came from Roman Catholic theologians, but Protestant witch-roastings in Germany, France and Britain eventually outstripped Judaizer- and Protestant-roastings combined in Catholic Spain. German experts, with their basic handbook proving that witches flew, ate children and copulated with devils, roamed Europe to ensure that the conspirators' vileness was appreciated and that they were properly dispatched. An important element of witch-hunt lore—and judges failing to remember it could be burned as witches themselves—was that a "good witch" (modern: fellow traveler or anti-anti-Communist) might not be treated more leniently than a bad (modern: card-carrying) one; indeed one English expert found the former "a more horrible and detestable monster" than the latter, deserving "a thousand deaths." The custom crossed the ocean to Massachusetts Bay Colony after England stopped burning heretics and adopted a Bill of Rights—an alarming document to the elite and ecclesiastics who alone had rights in the colony. A "stupendous growth of witches" having been detected by the learned theologian Cotton Mather, a tribunal was set up in Salem, 20 nobodies were hanged or pressed to death, hundreds of suspects were jailed, and the inevitable informer network took shape. Mather warned of an even more stupendous proliferation of "Sadducees" who, while not bewitched themselves, endangered society as much or more by doubting the devil's power to enter a body and create a witch. But Sadducees proving to be the majority, America's first inquisition, the smallest in history, was smothered before the sparks could catch.

It ended on a touching note: Samuel Sewall, one of the tribunal judges and as gentle and wise a man as any Spanish inquisitor, publicly confessing his shame on an officially proclaimed Day of Fast and Repentance. He and his colleagues had only been trying to serve society by maintaining a decent awe for its institutions, but their zeal had got the better of them. Two deposits remained in New England soil: the seeds of Sewall—to give flowers of science and literature in the 19th century—and the Mather family's corpses which would fertilize toadstools in the 20th. Precedents for future inquisitions were set, and the fog of fear did not dissipate quickly. One tribunal judge had ruled that even if the accused brought the whole town to deny he consorted with witches, this would be no proof since there was testimony that he did. Three years after Sewall's act of contrition, Boston printers dared not set in type Robert Calef's book exposing the fraud: it had to be published in London, and President Increase Mather of Harvard ordered copies of it to be burned. It portrayed the witches' accusers as a "parcel of possessed, distracted or lying Wenches and Vile Varlets" who had since identified themselves as such by their "Manifest Lives, Whordoms, Incest, etc."

* * *

Within a man's lifetime from the burning of Calef's book, the popular Thomas Jefferson proclaimed that all men and all ideas had equal right of access to the marketplace, and that citizens' duties included the overthrow of abusive authority. By now the colonies had a well-formed Establishment* of people who lived like gentlemen with no theoretical objection to others doing likewise but authentic doubts as to who would then do the work. The Establishment was playing with fire: Jefferson's words were plainly heretical, yet without them men could not be persuaded to die to free its commercial operations from English chains. Since their author was a slave owner (though he would end by freeing his slaves),** the words need not be taken altogether seriously; and they would always be subject to interpretation by clever lawyers. Public demand required them to be partially written into law in America's Bill of Rights; but with revolutionary fervor cooling as after any bloodbath, the French lent propaganda aid for the re-imposition of discipline by the excessive (but judiciously exaggerated) amount of bloodshed in their revolution. The idea was then planted which was to become dogma for more and more Americans: that one revolution was proper for America but no other nation can be trusted with any. Along with it went the general theory of "aliens," especially "atheist aliens," as the core of a permanent conspiracy against the American way of life. In this concept—the only indigenous Americans being Indians, whom the colonists were methodically slaughtering—aliens were members of families who immigrated later than one's own. Negroes, most of whom arrived earlier than most whites, were excluded as irrelevant.

In the first use of this formula for American patriotism, the conspiracy was directed from France. Led by Voltaire and his atheist friends, it included anonymous Illuminati, members of that impalpable cabal which had done some service to Spanish inquisitors. No American had ever met an Illuminatus, but word was spread that they practiced free love and cannibalism and had infiltrated everywhere. Roman Catholics and Freemasons were also involved in the oddly assorted French plot. Quakers, pressed to be intolerant of Catholics, split into two groups— those who were persecuted because they refused, and those who became wealthy and followed developing Establishment trends in targets of abuse. In effect the targets were always witches, though the word was out of service. The answer was

---

* The term "Establishment" throughout this book signifies the American "governing class" as defined by G. William Demhoff in *Who Rules America?* (Prentice Hall-Spectrum, Englewood Cliffs, N.J., 1967): "A social upper class which owns a disproportionate amount of a country's wealth, receives a disproportionate amount of a country's yearly income, and contributes a disproportionate number of its members to the controlling institutions and key decision-making groups in the country." Estimating that it consists of under .5% of the population, Demhoff notes that it constantly gains cohesion and power by intermarriage and interlocking corporate directorships, capturing decisive government positions and financially dominating the armed forces. It drops some old members, enlists some trusted new ones, and has internal conflicts which it always resolves as a *sine qua non* for continuing to exist and dominate as a group.
** His intentions were thwarted in the case of a number of slaves, however. He explained to a friend that he was so in debt that if he freed the Negroes unable to move at once and earn a living, they would doubtless be attached for debts and sold—possibly into a much worse situation.

the alien and sedition laws, which put behind bars editors pleading for tolerance and inspired strong words from Congressman Edward Livingston:

"The country will swarm with informers, spies, delators, all the odious reptile tribe that breed in the sunshine of domestic power. The hour of the most unsuspected confidence, the intimacies of friendship, or the recesses of domestic retirement, afford no security. The companion whom you must trust, the friend in whom you must confide, the domestic who waits in your chamber, are all tempted to betray your imprudent or unguarded follies, to misrepresent your words, to convey them, distorted by calumny, to the secret tribunal where jealousy presides, where fear officiates as accuser, and suspicion is the only evidence that is heard."

With freedom on their lips and a seemingly unlimited frontier still to be developed by their brawn and brain, most Americans saw no need for such a distressing regime. The opposition was too highly placed, Jefferson's words too new and shining; and liberal experts in democracy congratulated themselves that the tripartite executive-legislative-judiciary division of powers had passed the test. Never, they were now confident, could a privileged minority capture all three at the same time. The laws soon passed into the ashcan leaving the ten basic Constitutional amendments intact and Jefferson in the White House; but the two currents which would beat against each other through the generations were clearly in evidence. A substantial body of citizens would hold firm to its conviction that exotic groups plotted to destroy America. Two decades after Jefferson's triumph an apostate priest exposed a Roman Catholic plot to overthrow the government and establish Popery; a renegade Mason revealed that Freemasonry "belongs to the power of darkness, of iniquity, compounded of Judaism and heathenism"; and many listened, trembled, and reached for their Bibles and fowling pieces.

I

The Bolsheviki

The great heresy of the 20th century—socialism—was well rooted in America long before the end of the 19th, not only among the multitudes swarming in from Europe, but also among Americans of ancient stock. It was associated with a trade union movement which, increasingly confronted with violence in its fight against starvation wages and murderous work hours, tended increasingly to use whatever counterviolence was available to it. The gentry resorted to clubs and guns against strikers with the same virtuous glow that suffused their forefathers in church after a massacre of Indians; and this created a school in which many thwarted capitalists became socialists. To a substantial minority, who polled at the peak nearly a million votes for a socialist President, socialism made a simple kind of sense. If governments intervened to share the products more equitably, and competition for profit and luxury were subordinated to community incentives, human society might begin to distinguish itself from that of the jungle.

By one kind of reading, the Founding Fathers' documents about all men and ideas having equal rights seemed not heretical but eminently American; but the Establishment employed the best legal brains to winnow out and enthrone America's supremely sacred value: property. Thus capitalism was the essence of "democracy" and "democracy" was the proper word for it; thus socialism was earmarked "alien" from the outset, and immigrants who were neither Anglo-Saxon nor Protestant found themselves under automatic suspicion. No matter how many socialists believed (as most did) that they could gain power democratically, their determination to seize it violently became an article of faith for the respectable. In fact, no practical plan for seizing power is ever known to have been made in America. But the gentry took no chances, filling the movement with agents who reported what went on and stimulated whatever violent or divisive trends they found.

America's entry into the first all-European holocaust lent new specificity to the doctrine of socialist alienness. Since democracy itself was proclaimed to be at stake in the slaughter of Germans, and socialists were prominent among those who denied this and declined to cooperate, socialists were "pro-German" regardless of ancestral or other connection with the land of Karl Marx. When "Preparedness Day" parades became de rigueur in 1916 two notoriously non-Teutonic socialists, Tom Mooney and Warren Billings, were sentenced to death (commuted to life imprisonment) for bombing one in San Francisco.* In New York, a general on the Board of Education demanded that "treason in the high schools be punished," and an investigation conducted by Assistant Schools Superintendent John Tildsley led to the firing of three teachers who were lukewarm to the war. The New York

---

* Fifty years later they were rehabilitated—posthumously in Mooney's case—by The New York *Times:* a reviewer of a history of the case concluded that its title, *Frame-Up,* was an "understatement."

Teachers Union's effort to reinstate them brought charges that the whole union membership was "working in harmony with German propaganda."

Espionage and sedition laws were passed to deal with "pro-Germans" and immigrants from Germany; and to protect them against abuses in or out of jail, "philosophical anarchist" Roger Baldwin—himself a victim—joined with pacifist-socialist clergymen Norman Thomas and John Haynes Holmes to form the first "civil rights" committee. But the expeditionary force had hardly reached Europe when the Russians overthrew capitalism, repudiated the Tsar's debts, and quit the war. They were elected by Establishment acclamation to fill the Germans' temporary role, and laws already on the books nicely fitted the new situation. Russian immigrants were in any case better cast than German since, coming from the homeland of the pogrom, they were heavily weighted with Jews who were aliens twice over. The socialist heresy, stemming originally from the brains of two Prussians and some Frenchmen, now became Russian; and socialists became "Bolsheviki," a word meaning "the majority" in Russian but loud with detestable overtones in English. As soon as the war ended Germans would be welcome to join mob attacks on Bolsheviki, who might be anything from actual Russians or sympathizers with the Russian revolution to pacifists or starving, protesting coal miners.

The war also raised a problem in black for the Establishment. When Negroes began to assert themselves soon after ceasing to be slaves, they had been held down by semi-ritual murders, castrations and electoral juggleries for which sanction was found in the Bible. Lynchings, recorded around the turn of the century at the rate of three or four a week, became too commonplace to report in many Dixie areas. A decade before America decided to fight Germany, 59 of these subcitizens had gathered to demand equal rights and justice in a manifesto that dotted the i's and crossed the t's. Their leader, W.E.B. DuBois, descended from a miscegenetic Huguenot in Massachusetts, was poor but privileged by his background to complete a liberal education: from the black Fisk University he went to study under William James at Harvard and then to German universities. Emerging with scholarship which few Anglo-Saxons could rival, he dedicated it to the race in which he was happy to be classified. Since 1903 he had challenged Negro leaders' proposals to buy peace by surrendering rights which were theirs on paper, and as a sociologist at Pennsylvania and Atlanta universities he had made embarrassingly comprehensive studies of black degradation. Against him and his brother militants stood not only the Establishment, but a rising black bourgeoisie ready to settle for subservience in return for respectability. Some of these, and some middle-class whites, were in the mixture that launched the National Association for Advancement of Colored People in 1910. But DuBois, editing its organ *The Crisis,* raised that journal's circulation to 100,000 in eight years by speaking his mind.

In 1917 hands were needed to forge and wield the sword of democracy, and paupers surged out of Dixie plantations in response to army and employers' appeals. Since both the army and the cities imposed the same discriminatory segregation to which Negroes were accustomed at home, and whites always had preference for factory jobs, tumults resulted. In Houston, Texas, 17 whites were killed and the courts ordered 19 Negroes hanged, 51 jailed for life. In East St. Louis, Illinois, where some 125 Negroes were killed, nine whites were jailed for five to fifteen years and 11 for one year. A later Congressional report described "scenes of horror" in East St. Louis "viewed with placid unconcern by thousands" while police "fled to safety" or joined the white mobs. Negroes, their dismal shacks put to the torch, were shot as they ran out; eyewitnesses described "a Negro child thrown into a burning building, bodies thrown into the morgue like so many dead hogs."

On the west coast, leaders of a general strike in Seattle—the first in US history—showed open sympathy for the Russian revolution; their mass trial for criminal anarchy in 1919 was followed by a patriotically murderous raid on a union hall by American Legionnaires. Among the indicted were two journalists: Harvey O'Connor, who had completed his education in the state's nightmarish logging camps, and Anna Louise Strong, a clergyman's daughter who had won her doctorate with a thesis on "Prayer from the Standpoint of Social Psychology."

On the national level a dedicated leadership was at hand to apply against Bolsheviki the laws drafted against Germans. For Attorney General A. Mitchell Palmer, about whose performance as Alien (German) Property Custodian scandalous rumors circulated, the uproar of a new heresy hunt was opportune. His 24-year-old lieutenant, J. Edgar Hoover, never allowed the Germans' enemy status to divert him from the pursuit of socialists; and now the infant Bureau of Investigation which he would lead to renown made its mark with a vast roundup of persons suspected of dodging the military draft—only a fraction of whom had actually done so. After Germany's defeat, Hoover was promoted to "study subversive activities" as head of the Bureau's General Intelligence Division. With an enthusiasm never and nowhere matched, he plunged into a crusade against "the most evil, monstrous conspiracy against man since time began." * Within two years he was credited with more dossiers, fingerprints, and agents within heretical groups than the Tsar's police at its peak.

In Congress, the Senate's Overman Committee investigating "The Brewing Industry and German Propaganda" switched smoothly into inquisiting apologists for Russia. Two of these, just back from Petrograd, were the irrefutably Anglo-Saxon Americans John Reed and Raymond Robins. A Florida boy who had found in the Yukon both God and enough gold to give him access to several Presidents, Robins had been sent in 1917 to make backdoor contact with Lenin on Washington's behalf. This he had undertaken with a family Bible in the margins of which he noted the fulfillment of scripture seen daily in Petrograd streets. He returned proclaiming that Lenin, whom he came to know well, should sit beside Jefferson, Lincoln, Jackson and Jesus in the pantheon of history. Before the inquisitors his connections and lineage availed no more than his Bible quotations and claim to possess an "American outdoor mind." Beer and Germans forgotten, the senators sent him back to his Florida estate with a mudpack of innuendos on his character.

During 1919 there was a crescendo of strikes and bombings; the Bureau, while unable to pinpoint the perpetrators, had proof that "emissaries of the Bolshevist leader Lenin had framed" the bombings. The American Legion was crying, "Deport Bolsheviki! Make America American!" and Palmer's and Hoover's men raided heretical haunts on a grand scale, bringing in more heretics than the

---

* Estimate of Hoover's view in 1919 by Don Whitehead in the FBI-sponsored book *The FBI Story* (Random House, New York, 1956).

jails could hold. Newspapers editorialized feverishly with a daily diet of such headlines as "REDS BOMB LABORATORY IN SECRET ROOM IN RUSSIAN'S HOUSE—DEADLY TNT DISCOVERED—50 BOTTLES & VIALS" (*Times*).* Little was reported about the beatings and tortures suffered by the captives and the destruction of their property. A Chicago "race riot" in July—ascribed by Negroes to lack of protection from bombs being tossed at them, and ending with 33 dead and 17 blacks indicted for riot and murder—was headlined "REDS PLOT TO STIR NEGROES TO RISE," "REDS ARE WORKING AMONG NEGROES—EVIDENCE IN POSSESSION OF GOVERNMENT." In coming decades, defense of the Negro would become the major identification mark of the heretic.

While Negroes thus took their special place on the inquisitorial stage, the *Times* discovered an "underground line via Mexico from Soviet Russia to the US" and the Immigration Service reported "anarchists . . . flocking here from Mexico at the rate of 100 a day." A Miss Rumel, a translator for the Lusk committee which was inquisiting suspect teachers in New York, made a headline: "SAYS 300,000 FINNS IN US ARE REDS." The committee agreed wholeheartedly with the Tildsley thesis that persons with "a destructive attitude towards the American economic order" were unfit to teach. A law to ensure their removal was passed in 1921 (but repealed in 1923), instructing school principals to report on each teacher's loyalty.

The Russians were busy resisting the 14-nation invasion to smash their revolution, and checking typhus and starvation intensified by capitalist blockade; but the *Times* man cabled from Riga: "REDS SEEK WAR WITH AMERICA," and the State Department predicted a Bolshevik campaign against India from bases in Turkestan. The mysterious double nature of the socialist state was becoming manifest: its people were ready to revolt for the right to be capitalists, but it was gearing for grandiose military adventures around the world. The explanation was that Russians were both hopelessly stupid and diabolically cunning.

The Palmer-Hoover raids climaxed at the turn of 1919–20 when 249 Russian immigrants, brought from scattered jails by "Red Specials," were shipped back whence they came. Wives and children seeking a last glimpse of their breadwinners fought a half-hour battle with police at the New York barge office. Hoover said he would send to Russia "as many more as may be necessary"—amounting, by 1921, to 550 more. An analysis of their backgrounds showed that the average one was in his 30s, married with citizen children, and a resident for 10 to 12 years. In heretical folklore the story lingered of an arrested anarchist's farewell words to America: asked by a judge, "Do you believe in free love?" she replied, "Do you believe in paying for it?"

American Marxists had broken from the Socialist party (whose Presidential candidate Debs was in jail under the Espionage Act) to form a pro-Russian Communist one, born and reared in compulsory semi-clandestinity. Detestation of Lenin's revolution and all its defenders became the hallmark of Social Democrats, led by Norman Thomas who would find little time from attacking Russia to promote socialism in America. From this point on, fragmentation, almost invariably based on emotional clashes about Russia, would be uninterrupted in the American

* The New York *Times* is hereinafter referred to as the *Times*.

Left, following the pattern of religious movements through history. The exception
for nearly 20 years was the American Civil Liberties Union which in 1920 grew
out of the war resisters' defense committee. Citizens assisting at its birth ranged
from social-reform intellectuals and slum settlement workers to Communists and
leaders of the ultra-militant Industrial Workers of the World. Although moving
in different political directions, they would hold together in defense of the Bill of
Rights under chairman Harry Ward, a former "do-gooder" in a Chicago slum
church who had become Christian Ethics professor at New York's Union Theo-
logical Seminary. His theology smelled of heresy as he kept extending his extra-
curricular activities, working with anyone for an agreed goal under conditions
precisely laid down. He had decided that Jesus and Socrates were alike revolutionaries whom society put to death for their heresies, and that a new order was
necessary, the war having merely readjusted the old one using "the formulae of
justice to work injustice."

Scattered socialists whom heretics had managed to elect were ousted, some
of them brought to trials where readings from the *Communist Manifesto* and
Bernard Shaw linked them with Russia. The Lusk committee's exposure of academic deviants inspired legislative demands for "investigation of Bolshevism at
the University of California" and elsewhere. There were protests from enough
college presidents, bishops and lawyers—and two Supreme Court justices—to remind patriots that the Bill of Rights had not been repealed.

Hoover marched on to become the world's most celebrated policeman while
Assistant Labor Secretary Louis F. Post, who had ordered 51 deportations, wrote:
"There was no conspiracy to overthrow the government, no evidence produced
which excused the action of the government. Any true American must blush."
Another inquisitor of the period who turned out to be a Sewall (the witch trial
judge who repented later) was the New York Education Board's Tildsley. He
would publicly apologize in 1936 for having been blinded by hysteria. He then
decided—and acted on the decision—that teachers' associations "should have the
courage to protest against any attempt to make teachers but loudspeakers for
other people's opinions."

Continuing to earn its subversive label by defending anyone who was
denied free speech or fraudulently or unconstitutionally tried, ACLU involved
distinguished Americans and multitudes around the world in a seven-year battle
for anarchists Sacco and Vanzetti. They were sentenced to die on murder charges
almost as clearly fictitious as those in the Mooney case; but they could have saved
themselves only by recanting their heresies, and they declined. During this campaign Tennessee made it a subversive crime to teach Darwinian evolution, and
ACLU provoked a test trial by promising to defend any teacher who would defy the
law. The trial brought world fame to the bold teacher John T. Scopes (who was
found guilty and fined $100), and to his defender Clarence Darrow, who was aided
by ACLU's Garfield Hays.* Mobs gathered from miles around to clamor outside

---

* Darrow's court opponent, ex-Presidential candidate William Jennings Bryan, believed
every word in the Bible including the whale's ingestion and regurgitation of Jonah. Becoming nervous under Darrow's scorn, he said: "I do not think about things I don't
think about." "Do you," asked Darrow, "think about things you do think about?" "Well,
sometimes," said Bryan.

the courthouse for Scopes's and Darrow's scalps in the name of Christian Americanism. To newspaper readers in foreign parts—and to many at home—the event pointed up a characteristic of Americans which had not been fully appreciated: a high gullibility about plots to overthrow their society.

II

The New Deal

and Jimmie Higgins

Eugene Debs often referred to a socialist named Jimmie Higgins who rang door-bells, sold party papers and passed out leaflets, argued with shopmates and neighbors or from soapboxes, painted banners, marched jubilantly, was blacklisted and beaten over the head on picket lines, swept out meeting halls, and when the hat was passed "emptied the frayed pockets of his shiny black suit." *

Aspects of Higgins's activity and milieu changed with time, but the type (male or female—the name was fictitious) has existed since long before the Russian revolution, wherever heretics were organized. He was moved by the need to be needed and by a blend of tough conviction and sentiment, an idealized vision of "the American people" who rebelled against British tyranny and of "the masses" who had been cheated out of the revolutionary fruits. It was their destiny to recover this patrimony through daily "struggle," and his duty to get the struggle moving on all fronts. But America's masses were unlike those of any other land, for they embraced all colors and cultures, and each immigrant group brought along ancestral prejudices which held it together and apart from the rest. The Higginsian way of life was distinguished by conscious efforts to break down these barriers.

After the Russian revolution the Communist Party inherited IWW's militancy without its anarchistic tendencies and grew into the largest force in the heretical movement.** Some Higginses joined it, involving themselves in tithed dues payments and weekly club meetings devoted to Marxist education and assignments for current campaigns. Some merely moved in its orbit because either unconditional subordination to its disciplined "line," or the semi-secrecy, was unattractive. Some joined and quit when their threshold of tolerance was passed. Among the latter, some became more passionately and enduringly hostile than if they had found their beloved in bed with the neighbor, directing their spleen at the leaders who, on the purported basis of democratic centralism, pronounced the line from Party headquarters on East 12th Street in New York. In fact the leaders varied from the intelligent and heroic—even saintly—to the talmudic and vulgarly opportunistic.

Higgins, however, whether or not he carried a Party card, accepted discipline on the principle that a fist is stronger than five separate fingers. As an organization man he respected the Party whatever his reservations. Hence the important thing about Higgins: he was the man the Establishment always had its eye on, and with good reason. The Party's deficiencies did not stop him from participating

* Ray Ginger, *The Bending Cross,* Rutgers University Press, New Brunswick, N.J., 1949.
** The Party (capital P) hereinafter refers to the Communist Party USA.

with like-minded comrades (a word that gave him pleasure to use) in causes he found irreproachable: prodding people to unite and act for higher wages, more leisure and facilities to enjoy it, lower prices, more and better schools, fewer half-wits and knaves in government, more justice; organizing publications and gatherings to curb discrimination, helping revolutionaries and refugees survive, prisoners get free, the sick get well, the workless get work. Since the political implications of such causes were as obnoxious to the gentry as the catacomb dwellers' and Judaizers' obstinacies were to Rome and Spain, Higgins was a fool. But any suggestion that he was religious, or that he had taken up the thin red line from the ancient "Just" and "Receivers of the Holy Spirit," drove him to fury. He spurned "religion" as the cause of all history's great bloodbaths. He lived as he did because something in his chemistry prevented him from living any other way.

But not all socialists were genuine Higginses; and the building of a viable Party out of America's medley of rebels called for rare character judgment—a quality not always conspicuous among active heretics. In 1925 the CP decided on a campaign to free the North Carolina lad Paul Crouch from Alcatraz penitentiary. Crouch had been sentenced to 40 years for treasonable activity as an army private in Hawaii. A rural Baptist minister's son who later claimed to have studied Marx on the farm since the age of 10, he had informed the Party's Young Workers Association by mail that he had "formed an Esperanto Association as a front for revolutionary activity" and was ready to launch a YWA branch in the army. The reply rashly encouraging this venture had been intercepted, and at his court-martial Pvt. Crouch explained: "I am in the habit of writing letters to my friends and imaginary persons, sometimes to kings and other foreign persons, in which I place myself in an imaginary position." While this failed to impress the army, it did not dilute the Party's vision of Crouch as a proletarian hero. Freed (for reasons never determined) after less than three years, he reached Party headquarters in triumph and was sent on to Moscow's Lenin School where comrades from many lands studied Marxism. According to an American teacher at the school he did little studying, and the Russians found his behavior so odd that after a few months they gave him money to go home. Nevertheless he was sent on tours for Party organizations and, later, to his native South as Party representative. Wherever he went he described to local Higginses the triumphs of the socialist state and the intimacies he had exchanged with its top people. Some comrades thought his tales on the tall side, but faith was reaffirmed in the genius of Lenin's successor, Stalin, and the evil of all "renegades and traitors" from Trotsky to the first Party leader Jay Lovestone, one of several apostates around whom "-ite" and "-ist" splinters had formed.

Higgins had welcomed the revolution in Russia, but subsequent developments placed him in a dilemma. Whatever he now tried to do in America, he was heckled from left as well as right about evil deeds attributed to Stalin. How much of this was true, the average Higgins had no direct means of knowing, but he saw certain indications. Capitalists—desperately after the slump of 1929—needed to expose the Russian system as even less humane than their own, and one Russophobe after another had been proved a liar. In any case Higgins was not consulted as to who should rule Russia and, as a convinced socialist, he reasoned that revolution was no garden party. Thus, even if some reports about Russia gave him uneasy moments, he tended to put on blinkers in a more or less conscious act of faith, as adherents of socially repudiated sects have ever done. As for the CP, it was assailed by liberals, Social Democrats, Trotskyists and ex-Russophiles as Stalin's accomplice in betraying socialism; but the conclusive argument for working in or with it was that Hoover devoted more agents and harassments to it than to all other groups. Clearly the Establishment saw it as the prime source of infection.

A decade after the Palmer-Hoover raids, the Establishment had genuine cause for alarm at the spread of heresy. Just when socialism seemed to be finding its feet in Russia, capitalism plunged into near-disaster, producing more hungry Americans than the international carnage produced corpses: a persuasive argument that the war resisters had been right after all. At the nadir of the slump in 1932–33, students were stirred into political awareness as they had not been before and would not be again for 30 years in America. At New York's City College and at Columbia University, where many students depended on shabbily paid jobs to stay in school and now lost even those, Higginses who would figure in later inquisitions emerged both from student bodies and from the younger faculty. Liberal and Social Problems clubs at City College joined in protests against militarization and suppression of free speech in schools, against the Mooney frame-up, the reign of terror in Kentucky coalfields, and Alabama's death sentence upon eight black "Scottsboro Boys" on the claim of two white prostitutes to have been raped. They circulated Marxist books, organized political study groups, listened to such heretical speakers as Scott Nearing, CP leader William Z. Foster, Joseph Starobin, William Mandel, Corliss Lamont and Theodore Draper. They held street-corner meetings (broken up by police with many arrests), demonstrated noisily against "Jingo Day" (the school's annual military parade), and "tried" the school president before an audience of 1,400 in a New York auditorium. The clubs were banned, their leaders and faculty "advisers" and dozens more troublemakers ousted from the school.* A campaign to reinstate them was supported by such intellectuals as Malcolm Cowley, Matthew Josephson, Waldo Frank, columnist Heywood Broun, and the ardent philosophy professor Sidney Hook who saw Communism as "not the negation of democracy but its fulfillment."**

On the weekend in 1933 when the capitalist debacle forced all banks to close, Matthew Josephson, biographer of America's "Robber Barons" whose prestige was at its lowest, had been musing about "the insane economic 'system' we live under." An unaffiliated liberal, he did not doubt capitalism's ability to survive but saw enough promise in Russia to send him back to Marx; and although unimpressed by Party leaders he had met, he saw nothing sinister in "fellow traveling" on issues of mutual concern.*** At a friend's home he confronted a large unkempt man who "screamed" at him that the next week would see "barricades in Union Square." When Josephson politely differed, the man cried: "Capi-

---

* For more details see Oakley C. Johnson (City College Liberal Club adviser in 1932–33), *Campus Battles for Freedom in the Thirties*, in *Centennial Review*, vol. XIV, no. 3, 1970.

** In an article, *Why I Am a Communist* (*Modern Monthly*, April 1934), to which Bertrand Russell replied in *Why I Am Not a Communist*.

*** See Josephson, *Infidel in the Temple*, Knopf, New York, 1967. In these frank reminiscences Josephson dismisses as eyewash the picture drawn by intellectual contemporaries, of "innocents and dupes manipulated by a few red Machiavellis" in the 30s.

talist tool! Spy!" Josephson offered to fight him but the host persuaded him to
leave. The host explained that Whittaker Chambers—the name he seemed to prefer among the many he used—either was or thought he was a Russian secret agent.
He usually carried a revolver in the conviction that Hoover's men trailed him night
and day (as they should logically have done, but apparently never did). Many who
knew him had had strange experiences: he had drawn a knife in an argument with
a poet, slashed his own and a magazine editor's wrists in a Dostoievskian blood-
brother ritual, hung a Hitler portrait on his wall as "protective coloring," and told
everyone he was either a Communist or a spy or both.

In addition to the above, capitalism was capable of acting sanely within
the framework of its apparent insanity. Although it would later become clear
that nothing except escalation of government military orders to private industry
could halt unemployment, boost buying power and thus save the system, Franklin
Roosevelt's pump-priming and welfare-state policies meanwhile kept the ship
afloat. His New Deal established regulatory commissions for industry and agriculture, projects to employ the starving, Social Security, and a National Labor
Relations Board requiring employers to negotiate with employees rather than beat,
blacklist and shoot them.

In Germany, Adolf Hitler execrated Soviet Russia and promised dehumanization, torture and death to heretics in his and his capitalists' path; he amplified
the definition to include in effect all who placed human considerations above their
country's rulers—an infection which Jews, from peddlers to millionaires, carried
in their bloodstream. His re-institutionalization of torture—surprising to all Americans except blacks, who had been subjected to it for centuries—would be emulated
throughout the civilized world in the following decade; but in the 30s all respectable establishments were shocked. In America, the literate but popular President Roosevelt moved to recognize Russia as a fact of life and to rescue capitalism
with no more, and possibly less, than normal state violence.

The New Deal consolidated itself with a landslide vote in 1936. For Higgins
this was an administration which recognized the grievances of the downtrodden,
exchanged ambassadors with Russia and at least opened up the dialogue about
systems. Cooperation with it fitted the Communist International's line of a Popular Front against Fascism, and became—after strenuous opposition—the platform
of the Party under its Kansan leader Earl Browder. The average Higgins followed
along, seeing a fresh slim chance of winning socialism by legal means: a pleasant
prospect, for he was essentially a gentle fellow. Party ranks were swelled by thousands who, not being of the class that must live with violence, would have joined
no group advocating it; but now it became grounds for expulsion. Heretics, generally with superior qualifications, obtained jobs in New Deal agencies wherever
the hiring policy was non-inquisitorial. They were far from thinking the New
Deal was socialism, as most of the gentry decided it was, but were happy to work
on any progressive team. The New Deal in fact offered heretics new scope on all
fronts. In its name—although the danger to life and limb continued—they could
act for freedom of speech and organization and against legal frame-ups and police
and employer terror. Lifelong nonjoiners flocked into the Party orbit in the American League Against War & Fascism (later, for Peace & Democracy). Thus the
New Deal on the one hand, and Hitler's concentration camps on the other, helped

to build a CP membership approaching six figures and to bring many hundreds of thousands (at one point possibly a million) Americans into heresy as members or collaborators of organizations that were Party-sponsored or contained active Communists.

One of the Higginses created by Hitler was Lee Fuhr, a health education student at Columbia Teachers College, who discovered that she was Jewish, a fact her mother had concealed from her. The League Against War & Fascism was her ideological graduation from a wretched childhood and from a course in the realities of violence as a textile millhand in a strike. Later, deciding that serious anti-Fascists were Communists, she attended a workers' school and found "family, shelter, security" in the Party. Fate provided her with a roommate, a Vassar graduate and the first leisure-class product she had known, who nagged for admission into the League: "Aren't all the best people in it, North Shore Chicago, Philadelphia Main Line, Back Bay Boston?" Beween shopping expeditions for outrageous hats, the questions of bony, love-starved Elizabeth Bentley ran on until Lee relented and Elizabeth took her chatter and millinery to the homes of the League's best people. Then the question: "I'm a descendant of American revolutionaries, so don't you see I must work for a Communist America?"

Although the factory girls' phrase, "Cheezit, here comes the stool pigeon," haunted Lee at her roommate's approach, she reported on Elizabeth to her Party club. They called her a "proletarian snob" for her misgivings, and Elizabeth launched into Party life with a zeal for the horizontal aspects unmatched by care with her diaphragm. On top of other duties, Lee twice held her hand while she had abortions. Soon Elizabeth was combing wider fields, and a day came when she told Lee: "I think I can serve the Party best by spying for it." Lee replied in astonishment: "*I* think you just don't want to work, only dramatize yourself." Elizabeth now skipped meetings and talked darkly of "important things" she was doing with "top Party people." When she confessed that she had finally found a man to love her, Lee said: "That's all you wanted. Don't give me that line about spying." *

Then Elizabeth went out of Lee's mind. As a volunteer nurse, Lee was among the 3,300 Higginses who left America to try to stop the Fascist rebellion in Spain. Another American who answered the call was Steve Nelson. Like countless others from unpronounceable areas, Nelson had acquired his new name on arrival as a husky lad from Yugoslavia. He became the typical American worker except that he read books till sleep overcame him, and channeled anger into heresy. Joining the Party because "its morality and philosophy made sense," he successfully recruited fellow Slavs but found them no more disposed than other groups to accept Stalin as an oracle. When Madrid was besieged in 1936, André Malraux and Louis Fischer passionately appealed for Americans to go to the aid of the Spanish Republic; Nelson and Joe Dallet, a trusted Ohio Communist, already had passports stamped "not valid for Spain" in their pockets as they listened. Their boat was met at Cherbourg by Dallet's wife Kitty, a biologist from whom he had separated and who was studying in London. Kitty, as she would later tell inquisitors, had "walked away" from the Party, but she admired Joe's action and they fell back in love, enjoying a second honeymoon in Paris while the volunteers awaited

---

* This is Lee Fuhr's version; for Bentley's, see p. 45.

marching orders. She wanted to accompany them to Spain but Nelson vetoed it, since others could not take wives along and an exception could not be made for Joe. Communists with organizing experience would be called to responsible positions in the International Brigades.

They crossed the mountains to the battlefront after a spell in a French jail for trying to make it by boat, and were appointed political commissars in this new kind of army, Dallet in a battalion commanded by New York Communist Robert Thompson. Their business was the morale of men varying in political maturity, and the first order of it was to fight better than anyone else. Nelson's debut was a May Day pep talk connecting the war with the struggles of steel, auto and rubber workers in America. The Americans threw their battle songs into the pot with those of their polyglot *compañeros,* knew hunger and pain, exultation and despair, and in one of the war's great battles helped take the Ebro bastion Belchite. Moments after that victory Nelson was hit in the face and thigh by a church-tower sniper. He lay in hospital among dying poets, coal miners and farm hands, but recovered enough to be sent as Brigades representative to Moscow's 20th revolutionary celebration.

Kitty Dallet met him in Paris. Swathed in bandages, he had to tell her that Joe had just been killed in action. She clung to Nelson for consolation through the days of waiting for his Russian visa, and was still in deep shock when he left. He hoped he had persuaded her to drop the idea of going to Spain; she should return home to finish her biology studies. When she took his advice and won a Berkeley research fellowship at the end of 1938, she found Nelson there: the Party had posted him to San Francisco as district chairman and he was beginning to raise a family.

With Hitler helping Spanish Fascists overthrow Spain's elected government while Russia sent it weapons, and with every luminary of German culture going into exile or torture, American intellectuals now inclined toward tolerance or sympathy for Russia. A minority retained their purity in the Establishment's eyes with an unfailing supply of evidence that Stalin enforced socialism (or whatever it was) more cruelly than Hitler enforced Fascism: their estimates of the Russian prison-camp population soared into eight figures. Stalin had, in fact, begun arresting "enemies of the people" on a grandiose scale and physically as well as mentally abusing them to extort confessions. Yet most intellectuals saw a qualitative difference between Russia's social, industrial and diplomatic goals and policies and Germany's proclaimed revolt against humanity. They also saw that they could not come out against Fascism without landing in bed with Jimmie Higgins, who was working day and night to convince his neighbors that Hitler wanted war, that Stalin did not, and that apathy could make the new style of Fascist hell "happen here." But many an intellectual managed to swallow this fear. The New Deal was providing outlets for writers and artists who wanted to communicate with Americans about American realities, and the novelty of bringing culture to a host of previously unexposed citizens was exciting. The ideas they expounded, though seldom explicitly socialistic, smelled of heresy and sometimes caused a scandal. For example, Rockefeller Center commissioned Diego Rivera and the rising American painter Ben Shahn to do a mural and promptly destroyed it as subversive. (Shahn had made his heresy apparent in a series of 24 furious paintings about the Sacco-

Vanzetti affair.) Nevertheless it was the exponents of social upheaval that had
the floor in New Deal America rather than escapists or the Russophobes polarized
around *New Leader* and the literary journal *Partisan Review* which moved in 1938
from heresy to "anti-Stalinism." A "committed" theatre influenced by Brecht,
Toller, Shaw and O'Casey drew successful dramatists into its orbit. Pete Seeger,
Woody Guthrie, Earl Robinson and other young heretics composed defiant and
ribald trade union songs and revived American folksong in concerts which not
only drew crowds but afforded an indigenous, humorful ritual for the movement.
New York and Los Angeles show people aired political issues with song and dance
in "socially conscious" musicals. Despite Marxist solemnities, humor continued
to travel with heresy as it had traditionally done in America. The art of subversion
through laughter had its sophisticated practitioners in Dorothy Parker, Donald
Ogden Stewart and Robert Benchley, and a grass-roots one in Oscar Ameringer,
socialist editor of Oklahoma City's *American Guardian.*

San Francisco had been a nest of subversion ever since the Mooney-Billings
frame-up and especially since the victorious general strike of 1934. After one of
the last meetings there for Spain, the chief speaker came up to Nelson and said:
"I'm going to marry a good friend of yours . . . Kitty." He was Robert Oppenheimer, a physics professor regarded as an outstanding man at Berkeley. Nelson
"hardly knew the difference between physics and mathematics" but knew Oppenheimer as a man who, despite his affluent family and educational background, gave
both time and money to the movement. Oppenheimer was one of many around the
universities who both taught and acted on the principle that the mature man
must pursue truth wherever it led. Their heresies took various forms and they did
not conceal them. Harvard, for example, had its literature professor F. O. Matthiessen who spread the anarchistic doctrines of Whitman, Emerson and Thoreau, and
its observatory director Harlow Shapley who devoted more time to anti-Fascist
activities than was normal for a stargazer. Massachusetts Institute of Technology
brought mathematician Dirk Struik from Holland and found itself harboring an
outspoken Marxist. Educational reform programs at St. John's College and the
University of Chicago reflected the challenging ideas of Alexander Meiklejohn, a
Scottish worker's son who had become a legendary figure in his profession, opening mental shutters and arousing conservative wrath at Brown, Amherst and Wisconsin. Meiklejohn left no doubt in his *What Does America Mean?* (1935) that
it did not mean to him what it meant to the Establishment; and University of
Chicago president Robert Hutchins made his own position clear by remarking:
"Meiklejohn men are identifiable because they think."

Clamoring simultaneously against Fascism and for bigger school budgets,
the New York Teachers Union was the educational field's chief nursery of heretics
under the leadership of Bella Dodd, an ex-Catholic Communist who would leave
the post only to become a Party official. Hundreds of the teachers drawn into TU,
and many of her students at Hunter College, joined the Party under the influence
of her brilliant mind, handsome appearance and magnificent voice which were
also not without effect on New York legislators. The union had spent years under
harassment from one side by respectable trade unionists, from the other by school
authorities who objected to teachers having any union at all. While such an organization could sink roots in New York, union-minded teachers were summarily

dealt with wherever regional establishments had long decided who should learn what. In 1937 a Montana University president loyal to Anaconda Copper Corporation fired librarian-professor Philip Keeney. Already under suspicion for resisting book censorship, Keeney was involved in an attempt to organize the faculty. His wife Mary Jane backed him in a two-year court battle for professorial tenure rights. Like many pure-lineaged bourgeois in the Depression years, the Keeneys had progressed from Gibbon to Marx in re-examining their society. They had concluded that Americans were educated in "a social vacuum" and that salvation lay in free access to ideas. They were dismayed to recall that, in schools they attended during and after World War I, no teacher ever mentioned that Russia had had a revolution. Mrs. Keeney, however, had learned early of the existence of socialism through Debs' fortuitous presence in her hometown jail: his strong and pleasant personality had spread through the bars, causing even her loyal father to be "rather tolerant of socialists as people." In Montana the Keeneys won a victory that included the president's replacement, but the fight cost them all they had and Philip's near-death from nervous ulcers. "I fear," wrote Mary Jane as they took the Mayo Clinic's advice to seek a calmer atmosphere, "that the main victim of this storm may have been our sense of humor. We hope to regain it."

In the milieu where Joseph Gelders grew up, a sense of humor was harder for a sensitive person to cultivate. His German father had settled at the age of 14 in rural Alabama, surrounded by people farming worn-out land, without implements and sunk in debt. Joseph saw the terror which was the black sharecropper's extra burden, and the poor whites' participation in it which perpetuated the abjectness of both. He was skeptical about the postulate of the Dixie Establishment that white females stood in perpetual peril of rape by black males, and that this tendency must be curbed by selective lynchings.

While Birmingham grew into the South's coal and iron center, Gelders polished his education at MIT and returned from World War I to teach physics at Alabama University. He began early to search such authors as Bellamy and Steffens for clues to social conundrums. For example, anyone trying to organize black workers with white landed in jail, hospital or both, and he concluded that coal and iron company profits and racial myths were directly related. In 1934 he resigned to consult with seasoned Northern heretics about ways to explode the myths that held wages down and working hours up. As a native Alabaman he hoped to organize and protect other organizers with small danger, but soon after his return he was beaten and left for dead on a country road. His health permanently impaired, he went to Washington in 1937 to testify on Dixie violence before sympathetic senators including Hugo Black, soon to be a Supreme Court Justice. The Roosevelts and Agriculture Secretary (later Vice President) Wallace encouraged him, and soon afterwards he saw the Southern Conference for Human Welfare launched in Birmingham at a gathering attended by top New Dealers, clergymen, professors and newspaper editors, with North Carolina president Frank Graham in the chair. Policemen saw to it that the 1,200 black and white delegates sat on different sides of the hall, and noted the presence of a handful of Communists together with the fact that no one else seemed to mind. Among these was Paul Crouch, who was now moving about in a jalopy to palliate the isolation of the scanty Southern membership and spread the Party gospel, "Self-Determination of the Black Belt." * As a man from headquarters who could describe Russian marvels in a North Carolina accent, and as a serious sufferer from stomach ulcers, Crouch was welcomed by local comrades with awe and sympathy.

In the year of the Gelders beating, Anne, a teen-ager of "one of the South's first families," strove in Anniston, Alabama, to fit two pieces of her world together. She had won a school oratorical contest with a recitation of the Bill of Rights; and "one of the gentlest people I knew" had said to her: "You have to have a good lynching once in a while to keep the nigger in his place." Her way of resolving it would lead to stormy years at the side of Carl Braden, a working-class socialist's son whom she would marry. In Arkansas a year later, landlords captured a Tennessee-born Presbyterian minister, Claude Williams, and reduced him and a woman accompanying him to pulp with a mule harness. Heresy had infected him and he was helping organize whites and blacks into the Southern Tenant Farmers Union.

Meanwhile in the North the black heretics Richard Wright and Langston Hughes agitated in prose and verse about offenses against their people, of which the Scottsboro case became a grim symbol. Through predominantly CP efforts which kept most liberals out of the campaign, the case became known throughout America and millions of foreigners heard of Alabama for the first time. In Europe the Scottsboro story was spread by Paul Robeson, the most famous black American of the day. Treated contemptuously at Rutgers University where he was the only black student, Robeson had battled his way through to end as a Phi Beta Kappa and All-American footballer. He left America in the 20s and became a stage and concert idol in London, where he and his sociologist-Africanist wife Eslanda mingled freely with duchesses and Communists. His deepest impression abroad was a visit in 1934 to Russia with its mosaic of races and colors. "For the first time here," he wrote from Moscow, "I, the son of a slave, walk this earth in complete human dignity." The same thing had impressed DuBois on a visit in 1926 which left him wondering—but not for long—why American educators had so little to say about Marx. Robeson went to Spain to sing American, Russian, German, Jewish and Spanish songs for Republican troops. Coming home in 1939, he sang for Columbia Broadcasting System and around the country Earl Robinson's choral history of American protest, *Ballad for Americans*. He was a huge, gentle man with a cathedral-organ voice that ranged like his emotions from thunder to lullaby, transfiguring words that expressed the patriotism of Jimmie Higgins.

The theme of the hour was "organize"; few knew how to do it better than Communists, and for the first time they began to believe they carried weight in America. The greatest eruptions since World War I followed the break of eight international unions from the placid AFL. Two million strong within six months, the new Congress of Industrial Organizations quickly earned the "Communist" label as its auto, rubber and other workers held factories under siege to compel employer compliance with New Deal laws. The drive against such stubborn industrialists as Henry Ford, the darling of Hitler's American admirers, could not have succeeded without dedicated Higginses. Even in less violent sectors such as

* This line, based on a predominantly black-populated area covering several states, had no appeal for Negroes until put forward under black auspices three decades later.

the garment trades, CIO unions formed and trained security squads to defend their members against police and employers' hired toughs—a judicious move which would produce much inquisitorial folklore about a "CP goon squad." Police and their cohorts had little trouble detecting Communists' presence by the militancy and catholicity of their approach: wherever, for example, no racial strings were attached to membership, there was a Red in the woodpile. The decisive CIO leaders were in fact using heretics with canny determination to permit no challenge to their own power. With dues collections enabling them to draw corporation-director salaries, they saw that American-style success was just as achievable in their field as any other. None saw more clearly the value of temporary trafficking with heresy than young Walter Reuther of the Auto Workers (UAW). Having once worked in Russia, sending fervent reports of the land with "no bosses" signed "Yours for a Soviet America," he would soon become America's most admired purger of labor heretics as president of UAW and then of CIO. On the other hand many leaders of CIO-affiliated unions were open Communists, and others, like the Seamen's Joseph Curran and Transport's Michael Quill (who had risen from a New York subway pick-and-shovel gang), were as ready as Harry Bridges of the West Coast Longshoremen (ILWU) to seek Communist advice and found it often worked.*

Bridges had come to San Francisco from Australia, and proof that he was a Communist could legally send him back there. His brawny longshoremen, a consortium of races and colors with a predominance of Irish Catholics, ignored or emulated his heresies after he led two bloody strikes—which he had handsome offers to settle—to victory. His motives were suspicious, for he continued to live as modestly as his members. He was among the first to accustom himself to a retinue of government and private detectives wherever he went, the opening of his mail and tapping of his phone. His behavior contrasted with that of New York's Joseph Ryan and Ryan's Seattle ally Dave Beck, wealthy leaders of eastern long-shoremen and of the Teamsters Union, who had tried to stop the strikes.

After denunciations by loyal Congressmen and the American Legion, the Justice Department's Immigration Service summoned Bridges to a deportation hearing in 1939 but staged it carelessly. The two able heretics who conducted his defense, San Francisco's Richard Gladstein and Barnard graduate Carol King, convinced the examiner, Harvard Law School Dean Landis, that the prosecution's costly array of witnesses were all liars and many were knaves. This became so obvious that Immigration's clumsiness embarrassed some of the local gentry. In humorous vein, Bridges confessed to talking with Communists and thinking that they probably did more good than harm. Landis knew of no law against either and could not believe that a foreign-born labor leader so shrewd as Bridges would risk joining the Party even if he wanted to. The prosecution offered selections from Marxist texts, a student of which might be moved to consider the possibilities of violent overthrow. Landis listened restively and seemed grateful when a Stanford professor testified about Marx and Engels for the defense. "Whatever else one may

* "Labor experts" in the media all wrote of Curran and Quill as if they were beyond doubt CP members. The evidence suggests that Quill probably was and Curran probably was not.

think of these gentlemen," he said, "they possessed intelligence"; and the notion that they would have counseled violence in such an overwhelmingly capitalist-minded society was "too ridiculous to warrant consideration."

The hearing only succeeded in adding the professor and Landis to the suspect list, and some months later the House would pass America's first law calling for a named person's deportation. To dispel the Senate's blushes about its crude unconstitutionality, Bridges's name was omitted from a substitute law making participation with any "overthrow" group a deportable offense. This would enable Immigration to start afresh, and a more carefully-chosen examiner found Bridges guilty after hearing 7,724 pages of the same or similar evidence. Bridges would spend the war years pursued by Hoover's men, with one hand entangled in court rulings and overrulings while the other speeded supplies to the battlefronts.*

While CIO's honeymoon with heresy lasted it had a handful of defenders in Congress representing scattered constituencies where New Deal partisanship was especially strong. Like the two Communists on New York's City Council, Benjamin Davis and Peter Cacchione, their heretical stance guaranteed them an early return to private life. Jerry O'Connell of Montana who pitted himself against Anaconda, and John Bernard of Minnesota who cast a lonely vote against the Spanish arms embargo and paid a visit to besieged Madrid, were shot down in 1938 after one term. The exception was an Italian carpenter's son representing a predominantly Negro and Puerto Rican slum district in New York. A protege of New York's popular Republican Mayor La Guardia, Vito Marcantonio grew so steadily in political skill and his constituents' confidence that it would take 14 years and exotic gerrymandering to oust him, his heresies unscathed. In the amount of money spent to get rid of him, Marcantonio topped the national list with Bridges. But as a native citizen Marcantonio, who also consorted and counseled with Communists, was theoretically privileged to do so.

There was a considerable drift of heretical writers, actors and others from New York to Hollywood, where they hoped to breathe some life into the most important and most moronic of the mass media. They found the iron law of "box-office" almost impossible to penetrate but were able to launch a Hollywood Anti-Nazi League and a Spanish Republican committee whose rallies, due to the presence of celebrities, drew large audiences and contributions. Tales began to circulate of Communist club meetings where such activities were planned beside kidney-shaped swimming pools with butlers serving highballs. Hard as this was

---

* In a *New Yorker* interview published in October 1941, Bridges described to St. Clair McKelway a month of "fun with the FBI" at the Edison (New York) Hotel with two of Hoover's men eavesdropping in the next room. Quickly spotting them, Bridges made a telephone rendezvous with "the big shot, the Number One," and they followed him as he left the hotel; he dodged them and trailed them to the FBI office in Foley Square. ("They never seem to suspect that *they* are being followed.") He rented binoculars and a room in a neighboring hotel from which, while he hatched lurid and imaginary plots in his Edison room and the eavesdroppers noted it all down, his friends could watch the performance. Expecting the agents to be interested in his wastebasket, he obtained waste paper from a used-furniture dealer's office, tore it small, and observed them from across the street laboriously piecing it together. "I still," he told McKelway, "have the microphone which they put in my telephone box at the Edison."

to credit, it would later be confirmed by apostates and agents within the Los Angeles Party. The city "Red Squad's" William Kimple would relate how, by opening a gas station with liberal credit for comrades, he won such confidence that he became membership secretary. Keeping duplicates of all membership books, the industrious policeman was passing along the names as they joined. He performed this task strictly along the line of duty and found the comrades on the whole to be good fellows.

Most challenging to the inquisitors' punitive ingenuity would be the case of Charles Chaplin. A product of London slums and a pioneer in the medium that suddenly spoke to all the world simultaneously, he was America's greatest success story and for some two decades the most famous living man. Faces lit up everywhere at the name of the splay-footed tramp who turned tables on pompous cops; and thoughts turned affectionately to a land where an immigrant who invited it to laugh at itself, and who universalized the humanity of the wretched, was crowned with wealth. He could indulge every whim and most enjoyed the yearning of monarchs and celebrities to meet him, no matter if the name was Einstein or Hearst. To the non-inquisitorial eye it was plain that politics belonged among Chaplin's hobbies along with sex adventures and playing the organ. But as the inquisition began taking hold, his choice of friends would deepen the suspicions aroused by his films. The orthodox found more heretical than hilarious his *Modern Times* satire on the dehumanization of people in the mass production of objects; and he could not resist ending his *Great Dictator*—produced before active hostility to Hitler was approved—with an anti-Fascist declamation. Years later he would show his remoteness from organized politics by recalling that at the time he knew nothing about "the horrors of German concentration camps," otherwise he could not have "made fun of the Nazis' homicidal insanity." He was merely "determined to ridicule their mystic bilge about a pure-blooded race." But agents assigned to watch Chaplin found him to be spending too much time with Hanns Eisler, Feuchtwanger,* Einstein, Thomas Mann, Brecht and other émigré heretics. His American circle included Theodore Dreiser, John Garfield, Clifford Odets, Anti-Nazi League president Donald Ogden Stewart and his wife Ella Winter, Robert Oppenheimer and John Howard Lawson—all profusely cited in the postwar cleanup. Suspicion would become certainty during the war when Chaplin, who never spoke at mass meetings, addressed a San Francisco audience as "comrades" in appealing for Russian War Relief, and joined Marcantonio and Quill by telephoned speech demanding a second European front at a New York rally. He told "comrades" that "democracy will live or die on Russian battlefields" and warned of "enslavement to Nazi ideology" if Hitler won. As he would describe the sequel, he suddenly stopped being "invited to weekends in opulent country houses" and

* Of the exiled German intellectuals who settled around Hollywood in prewar and war years, Feuchtwanger was best able to resign himself to remaining there. A Jew who wrote about his own people (his novels sold 50,000,000 copies in 40 languages), he was one of the first Germans to sound the alarm against Hitler; the Germans ordered his execution when they invaded France, and he escaped disguised as a woman. Thomas Mann urged him to return to Germany after the war, but he replied: "The political climate here is terrible, but the climate is good, and I remain optimistic that man will advance toward reason." He died in Santa Monica in 1958.

the media began transforming him from hero to scoundrel. His uninhibited sexual habits would provide a timely scandal, bringing him twice to trial (with a possible 20-year sentence) on a former bedfellow's claim that he fathered her child. If the morals charge could not destroy him, patriots' fury at his "un-Americanism"—he never even became a citizen—would make his life in America intolerable.

III

The Holy Office

As we have seen, the New Deal at home and the march of Fascism abroad brought the American "joining" tradition to a peak; and most of the organizations that Americans joined were tinged with heresy. An old and regional one like the New York Teachers Union could enlist its 10,000th member by 1939. A new one like the National Lawyers Guild (1937) could achieve rapid solidity, and a Southern Conference for Human Welfare, to promote Negroes to full citizenship, could be born under distinguished patronage in the heart of Alabama. Membership of the International Workers Order, a heretics' breeding-ground sponsoring choirs, children's camps and cooperative insurance, rose into six figures. Circulations of the *Daily Worker,* the Yiddish *Morning Freiheit, New Masses* and other Party-line journals soared higher than their sponsors once dared to hope; and by 1940 some New York journalists would persuade Chicago philanthropist Marshall Field that a heretically oriented daily (*PM*) without advertisements—compensated for by doubling the prevalent newspaper price—could be economically viable.

To the surprise of no one, all these developments inflamed the flag-draped paranoia which was another part of America's tradition. A "Western" government's adoption of the Semitic blood-pollution mystique, and blending of this into a battlecry against the great heresy, drew covert or open admiration from frustrated Americans. "Progressive" organizations and cultural trends were tirelessly exposed as Russian-inspired by the American Legion, Veterans of Foreign Wars, Daughters of the American Revolution and kindred patriots; the National Association of Manufacturers and Chambers of Commerce supplied ammunition and the media used it generously. By 1938, despite the President's open lack of enthusiasm, the mood had been created for a Congressional inquisition, to be conducted by a Texan with appropriate views on Negroes, Jews and heretics in general.

In view of America's seminal scrolls (enshrining all Anglo-Saxon precedents of equality under the law, of an accused person's rights and even the right of revolution) an American inquisition had to be of a special kind. For one thing, an overt note of anti-Semitism would not do, if only because of its value as a propaganda theme against Russia while its German manifestation was soft-pedaled. (In fact Russia, once the world capital of the cult, had been first to make it a crime and in 20 revolutionary years had reduced it well below the American level; but there as everywhere it was a persistent weed.) America's thought-control device was the committee of elected legislators. There had been sporadic precedents since Russia was cast as Satan: the Overman and Lusk committees, the inquiry in 1930 by Rep. Hamilton Fish into Russia's trading agency in New York and Muscovite penetration of schools. The climate had been unpropitious for Fish who, however, would point with pride decades later to having chaired "the first Committee to Investigate Communist Activities." At the time a fellow Congressman wondered why, in view of the many Americans starving, an inquiry into "what is wrong with our industrial and economic system" would not be more useful, but granted that "it is easier to go witch hunting" to "shift the minds of the people from the great economic problems." When Hitler began preaching the gospel of Aryan blood across the oceans, Rep. Dickstein inspired a committee which investigated for a few months the source of American anti-Semites' funds, then let the matter drop.

The objects of the inquisitorial committee as it developed were to expose deviants in a democratic way: formally set up to obtain information for the framing of laws, it imposed no punishment except confinement to a quarantine of public obloquy. In the most basic sense, a deviant was one who had at any time been willing to do something for nothing—the earmark of a Higgins. By spreading fear among persons who might otherwise participate, heretical organizations would be immobilized or destroyed. Persons subpenaed to appear before the committee were accuser X and accused Y, but both were "witnesses" and pocketed the same honorarium for their trouble (X's other emoluments were none of the committee's business). It was not a court of law and hence did not need to observe the proprieties of one. If Y ended in jail, this was the affair of the secular arm, and in any event he never went there for the crime that brought him the subpena. The crime was perjury or "contempt of Congress" at the hearing itself, the latter being committed by balking at any related question after "opening up an area" by answering one. Y's least painful alternative was generally silence on what became known as "the $64 question" * and all that followed it, although with expert legal advice and louder voice than the chairman's he might succeed in dodging long enough to make a positive statement, his only consolation. The media ensured that he would walk with a mark of Cain, while X left the tribunal with a halo of potential market value.

The difference between the orthodoxy defended by the democratic committee and by the Roman Catholic Holy Office was more apparent than real. Just as almost every Spaniard or Italian believed in God, almost every American believed in Liberty: it was a question of definition, and those claiming expertise had the last word. The Holy Office condemned persons who doubted that God told the sun to move eternally around the earth and Satan to preside over furnaces beneath, or that Jesus was a blond anti-Semite resulting from miraculous birth. The committee condemned those who doubted the eternal joys of competition to sell and acquire objects, and the devilship of Marx, Lenin and their disciples.

In America as in Spain the public, once alerted to the peril to the social fabric, got the kind of inquisition it was persuaded to want. Yet squeamishness about inquisitions was still widespread and was reflected in the caliber of those drawn to undertake the work. Any resemblance to Solon became increasingly coincidental among Congressmen under the system of two barely distinguishable parties vying for the spoils of office. Committee candidates tended to belong to the bleakest category of all: products of unidentifiable law schools, elected through shabby political machines by communities where the majority, because its skin was dark or it could not pay the poll tax, was kept from voting. Plunged into national

---

* "Are you or have you ever been a member of (a heretical group)?"

and world affairs, these politicians continued drawing their inspiration from the interests and homely prejudices of businessmen who elected them. But the inquisition promised publicity and professional success, and they strove to compensate by zeal for their lack of the theology which lent elegance to their Spanish predecessors' work.

The committee of 1938 was empowered by Congress to investigate any "activity" deemed to be "un-American." The public being as hazy about Fascism as about Communism, the mandate was appropriately vague. With every irreconcilable and apprehendable German now under Gestapo treatment, and Jews fleeing in all directions as Hitler lunched off Austria and dined off Czechoslovakia, most Americans seemed to think Fascism more worthy of the House Un-American Activities Committee's attention. Liberal groups blessed its investigations on the assumption that it shared this view. They tried to avoid inferences from its inclusion of John Rankin, Congress's most candid anti-Semite representing 2% of the electorate of Tupelo, Mississippi, and from the praise showered upon it by every crusader against Jewry from coast to coast. Dickstein turned hostile as soon as the committee showed its disinterest in his favorite subject, but he had played out his role and no one was listening. Doubts about the elements to be investigated were dispelled by chief inquisitor Martin Dies, who had discovered that Fascism and Communism were identical twins tearing at each other's throats to hoodwink their ultimate prey, Christian America. The doctrine was hard for those who had read *Mein Kampf* and *Das Kapital* to digest, but few Americans had and Dies could hardly have been one of them. In labeling Hitler a Marxist, Dies was a move ahead of earlier semanticists who had labeled Stalin a Fascist.

In his inquisitorial work Dies proceeded from the ancient principle of contamination, propounding the modern anathema "fellow traveler" for persons guilty of heresy by contact. Since there were Communists in nearly all the organizations for welfare and justice which Americans were joining, material for applying the principle was abundant. Often Communists were the prime movers, but Dies undertook to show that, wherever they were present, they dominated the group. In many cases they did, for reasons stemming from the nature of Jimmie Higgins: he knew what he wanted and why, and was never a passive member of anything he joined. Higginses might be a small minority, but by participation in meetings when others stayed home they could form a large enough caucus to swing a vote on policy. They rarely identified themselves as Communists or Party collaborators on the sober ground that they would join the unemployed if they did. Other groups within an organization could have done the same but, except for some Roman Catholics in CIO, they lacked the necessary fervor, discipline and unconcern about personal gain.

The picture now to be built up was of Communists drawing "dupes" into their own organizations and conspiring to take over organizations formed by others. How many non-Communist adherents of popular organizations were dupes in the sense of not knowing Communists were involved, no one tried to determine accurately. The Party's viewpoint was that if it was intriguing, it did so to defeat the intrigues of Fascists, and that the exit door was open for members differing with any organization's policies. In some organizations Communists intrigued to an extent that would recoil disastrously in legitimate charges of dishonesty. Their

most successful fellow-traveler groups were those in which they acted most frankly
and with most consideration for their associates' views.

The top priority for exposure in 1938 was the CIO sitdown-strike conspiracy,
especially in UAW; and after a quiet day hearing leaders of Hitler's German-
American Bund, Dies's HUAC turned to "probing" (the headline writer's word
now yoked to "red") CIO. The heresy of Bridges, Curran, Quill (who was thrown
out of the chamber) and others was established by calling a spokesman for the
rival AFL to assert it and undercover agents to confirm that these serpents consorted with Communists. Names great and small cascaded into the record, and the
media cooperated energetically. The well known fact that several unions had Communist leaders was dramatized as "infiltration" into the labor movement. The
precedent was being laid down that Communists never joined anything, not even
the army, but infiltrated it.

The New Deal cultural projects, which had enabled artists to eat and made
their work available to the poor, were then exposed as a "hotbed" and caused to
vanish.* This laid foundations for Dies's doctrine of complicity in the plot by
President and Mrs. Roosevelt, Interior and Labor Secretaries Ickes and Perkins, Agriculture Secretary Henry Wallace and other New Deal luminaries masquerading
as capitalists. The representative of 17,000 rural Texans was keenly aware that "the
majority of followers and disciples of Marx deny they are Communists or socialists," and smelled the presence of many in "high government positions." **

Dies's nose did not deceive him, but it failed to identify the most pungent
of plots which, according to his postwar successors, was going on right beneath
it while he droned the $64 question to comparatively unnewsworthy heretics. A
possible explanation is that the plot that was to be so generously banner-headlined
never existed. Two facts, however, seem reasonably certain with regard to Washington heretical activities in the late 30s: some government employees were members or friends of the CP, and Julian Wadleigh, a lowly State Department man, met
with Whittaker Chambers to give him Department documents. Beyond this the
mass of postwar testimony about a spy ring funneling secrets to Russia affords little
clarity since, throughout the years when the ring was allegedly in high gear in
Hoover's and Dies's backyard, no one was ever caught funneling.

The inquisition would pinpoint as Communists some young lawyer-proteges
of Henry Wallace—Lee Pressman, Nathan Witt, John Abt and Alger Hiss—who
moved into other good positions after Wallace fired them under pressure. Chambers would identify as a Party club, inquisitorially known as a "cell," gatherings
attended by these four at the home of Henry Collins, a heretical New Deal official
who shared with Hiss the hobby of studying birds. But since Hiss (rising steadily
in the State Department) left no heretical footprints on the public record, and
Pressman (the group's only postwar penitent) would assert that he was a Com-

---

* A *Scribner's Commentator* writer in 1940 called the defunct Federal Theatre Project
"the most exciting experiment in the last 50 years of the American theatre; through it
54,960 performances were given before nearly 27,000,000 people." However, Dies exposed 26 of the 924 plays it produced as heretical. Some renown was won by assistant
inquisitor Starnes (Alabama) for his question about a play by Christopher Marlowe:
"Is (or was) he a Communist?" Whichever tense Starnes actually used—the record is
unclear—it was a good question.
** *More Snakes Than I Can Kill*, by Martin Dies, *Liberty* magazine, January 1940.

munist but never knew Hiss as one, the nature of the gatherings remained obscure. The Russophobia and Germanophilia of some officials with whom the participants worked would have been one likely topic for discussion.

What was Chambers's business in Washington? Collecting documents for the Russians, Chambers would say after prolonged insistence to the contrary. Who gave them to him? Wadleigh—unconnected with the Collins group, admiring Hiss from afar as a Department paragon—alone would admit doing so. Having "suddenly decided to offer my services to the Communists" in the 30s, Wadleigh had been asked for material on Germany and Japan and the threat they posed to Russia. As a courier he had been provided with "Carl," a "plump little man with an air of great importance" and a rich Muscovite accent who turned out to be Chambers. Wadleigh delivered "400 to 500" documents up to the end of 1938, when Chambers said he had decided to "become a bourgeois," Moscow having marked him for liquidation as a Trotskyist. Their last rendezvous followed a "desperate" phone call from Chambers: "Do you want me to starve?" Wadleigh gave him $20 and lived in dread until Chambers, after labeling Hiss a spy, belatedly "remembered" Wadleigh.

The important point in 1948 would be to demonstrate that Hiss supplied the contents of a pumpkin then unveiled by Chambers. The pumpkin would become a foundation stone of the inquisition and lift to the Presidency the obscure inquisitor whom Chambers led to it at dead of night.

IV

The Pact and

the Strange Alliance

Sixteen hundred survivors of the Abraham Lincoln Brigade returned in 1939 from offering their bodies against the violent overthrow of the Spanish government. They found that they headed the list of Americans proclaimed to be plotting the violent overthrow of their own government.* Their concern for democracy must be fraudulent unless (as few were willing to do) they joined John Dewey, Bertrand Russell, and such reformed heretics as Max Eastman, James Burnham, Eugene Lyons, Louis Fischer and Sidney Hook in denouncing Russia.

Pressure mounted daily to accept Stalin as a satanic yardstick for any judgment or activity in America. Intellectuals had overwhelmingly "taken sides against Fascism" in 1938; many had since taken cover, yet as late as May 1939 a denunciation of Hitler without mentioning Stalin was signed by far more than a Dewey- and Hook-sponsored manifesto equally condemning both.

The cynical "Axis" slaughters in Ethiopia, China and Spain had convinced Stalin that only Russo-Franco-Anglo-American collective security could stop the rampage. Hitler's invasions of Austria and Czechoslovakia, as Fascism won the day in Spain, confirmed this view; but the capitalist democracies still yawned, and Russia acted upon its frequently dropped hint that if they were bored by its proposals it would see to its own security. Its [Molotov-Ribbentrop] nonaggression pact with Germany abruptly turned the tables. The capitalist democracies had sought to maneuver themselves into a neutral stance in a Russo-German war, and instead Russia had achieved this posture in a German war against France and England.

The Pact created an ideal inquisitorial climate for two years. Intellectuals led a precipitate flight of citizens tainted by heretical contacts or praise of Russia. Like Protestant Irishmen on the subject of the Pope, Americans failing to see Stalin as the fount of all evil forfeited their last right to be heard on any subject. The "alliance" confirmed Dies's thesis that Stalin and Hitler were both "high priests of Marxism," although Hitler "disguised" his version "under the name of Nazism." "The real issue," as Dies wrote, was "between Americanism on the

---

*Thirty years later (*Journal of American History*, October 1967) the possibility that American volunteers did not go to Spain "to make the world safe for Joseph Stalin" was explored by a California Institute of Technology historian. The average volunteer, he found on analysis, was a trade unionist "conditioned . . . by the spread of union-smashing totalitarianism abroad"; and since Hitler and Mussolini had joined in Franco's rebellion, "many Americans felt the time had come to make a real stand against Fascism." Ethnically they were "as much a melange as the US itself," descended from pioneers, slaves and recent immigrants, and by and large they were not Party "war-horses." This information had been available for three decades from the surviving volunteers who had, however, been treated as criminals since their return and were not always easy to reach.

one hand and alienism on the other"; but the Pact had defined alienism more clearly, establishing Stalin's satanic ascendancy. Dies exposed Earl Browder as an infringer of passport regulations, and the Kansan CP leader was jailed until after Russia became America's ally. Harry Ward was among the next to be probed. More confident than ever of his Christian ethics, Ward spread it in all directions, becoming active in the National Council of American-Soviet Friendship and Committee for Protection of Foreign Born and chairman of ALPD as well as ACLU. Another of his activities was the Methodist Federation for Social Action, one of several heretical churchmen's groups which flourished under the New Deal. Their views on the church's role in society were variously reflected in publications which would also come under scrutiny, such as Dorothy Day's *Catholic Worker* (pacifism, direct charity to derelicts, "the more property becomes common, the more it becomes holy") and Guy Shipler's *Churchman,* the oldest church publication in America.

In February 1940, the Justice Department raised the national temperature by storming ten Detroit homes at 5 a.m., arresting the occupants without warrants and jailing them; bail was set as high as $20,000. They were charged under a law of 1818 with recruiting volunteers for Spain. Dies proceeded to send committee henchmen with police escorts to search offices of the Party and IWO. They returned with a truckload of evidence; a judge ordered Dies to return it, which he respectfully did after an all-night photostating session.

He then inaugurated what became known as the "contempt mill," requesting Party officials to name their members and having them locked up for contempt after they declined. Dies applied it with pioneer crudeness—the committee was supposed to "cite" the victim through a routine Congressional vote and leave the jailing to a court—but some experts regarded the device itself as the greatest inquisitorial innovation since the thumbscrew. On pain of jail for contempt, a heretic could not admit any membership without naming his accomplices, who would be the next candidates for the mill. On pain of jail for perjury, he could not even deny his own membership, for familiars were generally on hand to swear the contrary. At the same time all formulas for not answering had been hedged about with hazards. The first Constitutional amendment barring infringements of free speech and association seemed the obvious one to invoke for silence, but had doubtful value long before the Hollywood Ten affair effectively suspended it in 1947. The Fifth, under which the suspect could not be compelled to testify against himself, was a priceless formula for convicting him in the eyes of the public, for in order to avoid endangering his friends, he had to plead self-protection as his sole concern. While he gradually became versed in the correct method of not answering questions and not going to jail, he had no alternative (from the media-eye view) to making either a knave or a fool of himself.

Later in 1940 Dies summoned Hollywood personalities who were suspected of contributing funds for Spain and against Hitler. The answers from Fredric March, Florence Eldridge, James Cagney, Luise Rainer, Humphrey Bogart and some others were less than satisfactory, but they had been warned. Mindful of the need to show concern about Fascists, Dies had previously subpenaed the well known anti-Semite William Dudley Pelley. Pelley assured the committee he had nothing against Jews, and threw in a "God bless this committee" and a "Splendid,

splendid" to assistant inquisitor Parnell Thomas before going on his way. When
the Herrenvolk began obliterating West Europeans in the style perfected in Spain,
and set London afire preparatory to the *Fahrt Gegen England,* Dies did not lose
heart. He detected rampant heresies in Mexico, pushed bills for wholesale deportation of socialist-minded aliens and proved in an amply documented book that
Communists planned to sabotage American industry. Congress was so impressed
that it gave him $150,000 for 1941, with six contrary votes including Marcantonio
and the still querulous Dickstein.

Bookish Americans were distressed by Dies's methods and ideology, but pressures from every side began to give them the haunted expression that would characterize the postwar intelligentsia. Two former leaders of the conspiracy confirmed
all that Dies said about it with shocking details: Benjamin Gitlow (who, before
going to jail in Hoover's 1919 roundup, had vowed eternal fealty to "CP principles") in the book *I Confess,* and the more sophisticated Jay Lovestone, now a
heresy specialist for the CP's bitter enemy, labor leader David Dubinsky. Roosevelt
stopped scolding Dies and columnist Walter Lippmann wrote that, although
HUAC "violated American morality," it was "attacking a formidable evil, cannot
be abolished and must be continued." Loyal to capitalism as only a reformed socialist could be, Lippmann had and normally exercised a special license from the
Establishment to rebuke its follies and impudicities. Hoover's Detroit raid produced a press slur on the FBI's "publicity-mad chief," but his reputation for alert-
ness and legality continued to rise. By June 1940 only Marcantonio and three
colleagues were prepared to oppose a new version of the Alien and Sedition Laws
offered by Virginia's Rep. Howard W. Smith. Prescribing ten years in jail for
advocates of violent overthrow, the Smith Act could be interpreted to mean either
Communists (who did not advocate this but were notorious for conspiring to do
so) or Fascists who were practicing it wholesale. The same penalty was fixed for
members of any overthrow-advocating group even if they did not themselves advocate it, but no one noticed this clause which for years would lie dormant. The
federal heresy law was quickly outdone by various states.

In the months following the German-Russian pact, the inquisition scored
its greatest breakthrough on the liberal front. The liberal-heretic alliance in ACLU
was still held together by Ward, although the complexion of ACLU's board would
have startled Sacco and Vanzetti. Now mainly consisting of lawyers and intellectuals, it included Morris Ernst, one-time workers' champion and crusader against
censorship who had since served as Hoover's personal attorney. Deepening confusion in ACLU—already indicated in 1938 by its statement *Why We Defend Free
Speech for Nazis, Fascists & Communists*—became manifest when the Ford Motor
Company warned its employees not to join UAW, devised new intimidations, and
was told to desist by NLRB. After internal recriminations ACLU rebuked NLRB
for interfering with Ford's freedom of speech. Dies was not satisfied and, when
familiars had formally identified ACLU as heretical, demanded its prosecution for
not registering as a foreign agency. But Ernst, accompanied by ACLU counsel
Garfield Hays, paid a call on Dies and suddenly the heat was off.

ACLU declared itself "wholly unconcerned with movements abroad and
with foreign governments," but its resistance was brief to the pressure inside its
board to condemn Russia. Ward had to resign after a resolution to join the in-

quisition was approved, over many protests including Arthur Garfield Hays's. The resolution barred from ACLU office all "supporters of totalitarian dictatorship in any country," specifying "the Communist Party, the German-American Bund and others." Roger Baldwin gave Ward a resignation party with a sentimentally inscribed iced cake and a gift of a traveling bag.

The board then put its lone Communist, Elizabeth Gurley Flynn, on trial with John Holmes in the chair. A veteran scarred from labor battles since before World War I, she defended both Russia and the traditional ACLU limitation to America and insisted that a Communist had as much business defending American liberties as a capitalist or a philosophical anarchist like Baldwin. But the thesis was now being solidly laid down that, whereas anyone else could defend liberty while pledged to a party's principles, and that party might (as was Norman Thomas's) be affiliated to an International, a Communist or non-denouncer of Communism *ipso facto* wore a foreign strait jacket. Corliss Lamont, a banker's son who lectured and wrote about Russia, recalled at the trial that in more heretical days Thomas's Socialist party had expelled chairman Holmes for not following its line: apparently Socialists also imposed discipline.

But since Flynn's politics had always been public knowledge, and her ACLU colleagues never before objected, the accused at the trial was in fact the CP, still pro-Russian after the traitorous Pact. Some liberals in the ACLU orbit objected that the Pact had nothing to do with American liberties and the purge made ACLU "seem like a fellow-traveler of the Dies Committee." A California bishop joined Alexander Meiklejohn in suggesting that ACLU should only bar members guilty of "concrete or verifiable" disloyalty, and that if the board could not "learn to deal with each other by rational, free discussion" it was idle for them to recommend democratic conduct to others. A. F. Whitney of the Railroad Trainmen's Brotherhood, one of the last labor men on the national committee, wrote: "It seems that one Adolf Hitler entered into a compact with Soviet Russia, and out of that arose the principal basis for the action against Miss Flynn. Apparently Hitler's crusade to save the world from 'Communism' has been taken up by ACLU . . . I hope I have not yet reached the point where the actions or policies of Hitler and Russia control my thinking." *

---

* The author sent a questionnaire to Board and National Committee members of the prewar ACLU, asking how they feel now about the Flynn purge; few replied, most of them being dead. Ernst, an advocate late in 1968 of "vigorous prosecution of the Vietnam war," wrote: "Although I would defend the right of Miss Flynn to urge the abandonment of the First Amendment, I still believe that a person who does not believe in the right of free speech, free press and due process should not sit on a Board of Directors whose main purpose is to spread those gospels. I assume you agree that a pronounced bigot should not be chosen to direct the affairs of an anti-bigotry society." Board member Spofford, editor of the Episcopalian weekly *Witness,* wrote that he was "on Miss Flynn's side throughout" although he voted for her expulsion on the explicit ground that "that is the only way it could get to the National Committee." He continued: "The red-baiting continued after this Flynn trial. First they tried to prevent [Abraham] Isserman and me from being reelected as directors. This dragged on for weeks and finally went to the dean of Columbia Law School for an opinion. He found in our favor but we later resigned because the whole business was a waste of time."

None of these views could prevail in the 1940 climate. The ACLU purge was historic in establishing a loyalty oath, and the precedent of guilt by association, in America's citadel of free speech and due process. It set the stage for the exclusion of heretics, by mass consent, from Constitutional rights. New York legislators meanwhile resumed the inquiry into academic heresy. Roman Catholics protested City College's appointment of the "leading anti-Christian" Bertrand Russell to teach philosophy;* and "ungodly and un-American traditions" in schools were investigated, along with New York's "financial ability to support education," by a committee chaired by Rep. Frederic Coudert, a former Tsarist government lawyer championing the Hitler-collaborationist regime in conquered France. Coudert had presented a bill to cut school budgets, and TU was, as ever, the liveliest force pressing to raise them. Most of the summoned TU members being Jewish, the Christian keynote assured the probe of anti-Semitic support. Coudert opened the public proceedings by having TU's lawyer ejected so that the naming of Communist teachers by a loyal colleague could be orderly. TU's president refused to produce his membership list and a court order to seize it was issued. The media demoted war news for banner-headlines: "100 ON COLLEGE FACULTY HERE BRANDED AS RED"; "RIOTOUS REDS RAIDED CLASSES, COWED PUPILS"; "GIDEONSE [Brooklyn College president] CHARTS RED PURGE." City and Brooklyn colleges fired over 30 teachers and education boards several more, and TU leader Morris Schappes was charged with perjury and jailed.

All this was happening on the eve of America's entry into the war as Russia's ally. The CP was as blind as Dies to what impended, and both would have to pay for it. After Hitler's blitzkrieg turned westward, the Party had continued its line that the war was a capitalist squabble which France and England had brought on themselves, and that as long as Russia stayed out America should do likewise. Such was the position in which Party theoreticians, ignoring the constant change-

---

The Board minority opposing the purge consisted of Corliss Lamont, *Common Sense* editor Alfred Bingham, Labor Research Association secretary Robert W. Dunn, and lawyers Osmond Fraenkel, Nathan Greene, Arthur Garfield Hays, Abraham Isserman and Dorothy Kenyon. The "17 liberals" who appealed to ACLU to rescind the purge included Franz Boas, Theodore Dreiser, Henry Hunt of the US Department of Interior, Robert Lynd, Carey McWilliams, the Rev. A. T. Mollegan, I. F. Stone, MIT professor Fayette Taylor, and James Wechsler.
    For full account of this episode see *The Trial of Elizabeth Gurley Flynn by the ACLU*, edited by Corliss Lamont (Horizon, New York, 1968).

* Russell's appointment was canceled after Roman Catholic patriots exposed him as "lecherous, salacious, libidinous, venerous, erotomaniac, aphroditous, atheistic, irreverent, narrowminded, bigoted and untruthful." He told the author in 1956, however, that he thought the sixth charge was simply "aphrodisiac." Reminiscing then about his earlier experience teaching in California, he recalled "the terror in the commonroom when a lecturer who defended migratory workers' rights to organize was suddenly dismissed as 'incompetent.'" In New York, he said, "not one New Dealer supported me. I concluded that liberty does not exist for the average American, and was rather astonished by the lack of protest."

process rooted in their own scripture, impaled Higgins just when the Establishment was concluding that Hitler must be stopped. The Party now found itself in bed with Republicans, who would soon abandon "isolationism" but at this point advertised in the *Worker* for the votes of heretical "isolationists." No policy of the CP would be more effectively cited, in proof of its Marxist treason, than its un-Marxist peacemongering up to the invasion of Russia. The fact that a much more solid body of citizens opposed entry into the war for love not of Russia but of Germany was soon forgotten. Even the abrupt change in June 1941, could not heal Party leaders of their fatal rigidity. Just after the invasion, the first prosecutions under the Smith Act were begun in Minneapolis. The targets were not Communists but Trotskyists. The Trotskyist *Militant* featured the indictments on the same page with the headline, "FOR UNCONDITIONAL DEFENSE OF THE SOVIET UNION." The Communist Party, which had clamored its objections to the Smith Act, applauded the Justice Department.*

But 1940–41 was the last good heresy-hunting season for some years, for Germany—with its Japanese allies, who treacherously dropped on Pearl Harbor the old iron America had long been shipping to them—was again a greater peril than Russia. There was no alternative to a pact with the devil, a logical and unexceptionable step when taken by Washington. Two embarrassments now confronted Dies. He became the German radio's favorite source to show that America had succumbed to the Red plague, and the War Department (which could do no less under the circumstances) listed "important differences" between Russia and Germany, dealing a blow to the "Marxist twin" theory. The Department described Germany's rulers as "not interested in improving the lot of ordinary people, only in war, plunder and world power," whereas "the Soviet idea is that the dictatorship must serve the people; no 'master race' idea, all people considered equal." To "build a better, happier country" Russia had "constantly improved working conditions" and raised school attendance by 400–800% while Berlin authorities were "ruthlessly destroying labor unions, turning their own people into slave laborers" and cutting the number of students by half. "Never before in history," the Department would add in 1944, "has a nation waged so unforgivably pitiless and cowardly a war against civilians . . . The mass slaughter of innocents, inhuman torture, compulsory prostitution, starvation of entire provinces are crimes which can never be explained away. Lidice and many other cities desolated by the insane murder of every inhabitant will never be forgotten."**

By 1942 pillars of the Establishment were heading the sponsor list of Russian War Relief, and a four-star general was bringing an emotional message from Gen. Douglas MacArthur to a Red Army celebration organized by heretics. In all decisive circles there was a moratorium on estimates of how many Russians Stalin had jailed, killed or driven to suicide. The Republicans' 1940 Presidential candidate, Wendell Willkie, accepted a brief from ACPFB to defend a Communist leader threatened with deportation, and ended by persuading the Supreme Court to declare that Communists as such were neither advocates of violence nor foreign agents, and that Party membership or office did not prove disloyalty. (This

* All 18 defendants were convicted and served their full jail terms, the Supreme Court declining to review the case.
** See 1950 Fever Chart, p. 128.

evanescent ruling so encouraged the Party that it abolished itself in 1944, assuming the label "Political Association" until normalcy returned in 1945.) Willkie assailed the jailing of Browder, co-sponsored with CIO a pro-Russian rally at Madison Square Garden, and in his book *One World* praised Russia's "effective society" and "real, deep, bitter hatred of Fascism." America "must work with Russia after the war," he wrote, and clean its own house of "domestic imperialism" and "smug racial superiority . . . Our boasting and our big talk leave Asia cold. Men and women in Russia and China and in the Middle East are . . . coming to know that many of the decisions about the future of the world lie in their hands. And they intend that these decisions shall leave the people of each nation free from foreign domination." * *One World* sold two million copies, but Willkie died on the eve of the permanent inquisition and could not be called to account.

Disappointed in his prediction that Germany would overrun Russia within a month, Dies had to suspend formal tribunals for the duration but never let the inquisitorial torch go out. He protested wartime price controls and the assignment of Russian sympathizers to key war jobs, and continued exposing red-tinged intellectuals, of whom he found 35 (one of them a nudist) in Henry Wallace's Board of Economic Warfare.** He warned of Muscovite elements in the Federal Communications Commission which monitored and reported the frequent quotations from Dies on Hitler's radio. After the Red Army began driving the Germans back across the thousand-square-mile cemetery they had created, Establishment publications impugned his judgment and timing. Dies countered with an evocation in Congress of "our boys fighting and dying to preserve" a system in which their leaders did not "believe." He named 39 more "radicals and crackpots" in government employ who should convince Congress that they believed in capitalism or be sacked.

With Russians dying by millions and Americans by thousands to thwart the same Herrenvolk, Dies was fated to pass from the scene unhonored by his countrymen. His arch-enemy CIO paid up enough poll taxes in his constituency to ensure his defeat, and he withdrew his candidacy for reelection in 1944. Even so, he might not have lost his place in inquisitorial history had not Joseph McCarthy captured the world's imagination after the war and lent his name to the entire inquisition. He lacked McCarthy's ingenuity in framing have-you-stopped-beating-

---

* Apparently no one told Willkie that months before America and England agreed to open the long-delayed second front in France, both were planning to resume the sabotage activities against socialism which they began in 1917. As three London *Sunday Times* men have recorded (*The Philby Conspiracy*, New American Library, New York, 1969), a British Intelligence unit for "operations against the Russians" was formed in the spring of 1944 and had a staff of 100 by the war's end. The Russians knew about it— and, as the authors put it, it "further confirmed all their paranoia about the West"— because their agent Philby, a socialist masquerading as a Fascist, was put in charge of the unit.

** Dies unmasked BEW economist Maurice Parmalee, a Vermont missionary's son, not only as a visitor to Russia and critic of capitalism but as author of a book "advocating nudism in office and factory" with "35 obscene photographs." Parmalee's works also included *Inebriety in Boston.* Dies could not prevent him from getting and holding another government job (unconnected with the war), and after retirement at 69 he survived unclad for 17 more years, having prudently moved to Florida. He agreed with his nephew that it was "too cold to be a nudist in Vermont."

your-wife-yes-or-no questions to suspects who admitted nothing. Yet considering the forces against him—a negative Administration, lukewarm intellectuals, the alliance of his country with Satan himself—his record is distinguished: it was he who set all the basic precedents. No successor had a sharper eye for promising inquisitorial talent. Robert Stripling, whom he brought from Texas as a clerk, soon earned his spurs as a detector of CIO heresy and went on to probe Hiss and win the tribute from inquisitor Mundt: "The best committee lawyer of modern times." When ex-ALPD chairman J. B. Matthews emerged as a penitent, bringing with him an enormous list of former associates and unimpeachable documentation which he had himself helped to write, Dies hired as research director the man whom familiars would later recognize as dean of their profession.* Matthews enabled him to pinpoint 563 heretical government employees on the ALPD mailing list alone—far more than McCarthy at his zenith would enumerate. Dies helped to oust Michigan's governor Frank Murphy who declined to suppress CIO sit-downs with troops. He exposed Minnesota's governor Elmer Benson as a heretic by producing a photo of him with a Communist official, and harried Labor Secretary Frances Perkins into moving against Harry Bridges.

In short, Harold Ickes did Dies less than justice in calling him "the outstanding zany of our generation." He could have done no better in his last years when bestialities of a kind then regarded as shocking were being committed all over Europe, and exigencies of the war made it impossible to conceal that Germans were committing them. Only after several postwar years would the combined efforts of government, media and inquisitors transfer the onus of bestiality in retrospect to the Russian account, allowing that it must be shared by "the Nazis"—a race happily extinct and replaced by loyal democrats.

*   *   *

America inevitably entered its second war against Germany with a confusing ideology for those required to fight it. Missouri Senator Harry Truman had just been applauded for hoping that the Russians and Germans would kill as many of each other as possible; and now here was Russia on the team to save democracy, which for good Americans was another word for capitalism. In all German-invaded countries notoriously subversive elements were leading resistance to the foe while loyal capitalists collaborated with him and redoubled their denunciations of Russia.

Skeptical as they might be about American leaders' genuflections toward Russia, heretics hoped that, through exposure to Fascist techniques in fighting the war, the anti-Fascist alliance might become a reality in peace. For Germany was spreading far beyond its frontiers the doctrine that heretics and sub-Menschen who had no value as slaves must be exterminated, and removing all limits from its definitions of heresy and contaminated bloodstreams. Apart from the military slaughter, the German establishment perfected the most advanced methods of the day (if crude by later standards) of destroying superfluous or inconvenient human beings

---

* Matthews, holder of a Wilmore (Kentucky) theology diploma, later wrote the neglected treasure house of inquisitorial theory, *The Trojan Horse in America,* by Martin Dies. His own work, *Odyssey of a Fellow Traveler* (1938), was among the first literary confessions by ex-heretics. Both books provided Hitler's associate, Goebbels, with useful material.

from sucklings to great-grandmothers. Its *Einsatzgruppen* moved across Poland into Russia with mobile extermination plants for Jews, Communists, gypsies or Freemasons encountered enroute, while regiments of prisoners of war were either shot in captivity or left within barbed wire to die of exposure and starvation.* Attractive sub-Mensch females could be temporarily saved as public conveniences for Aryan lust. Slaves were locked into boxcars to be shipped westward for use by German industrialists until they expired from exhaustion. Other trainloads steamed eastward and northward to corpse factories in Poland, where the industrialists were invited to extract whatever labor-value the cargoes represented pending liquidation. Managed by Dachau-trained experts, the corpse factories not only set production records unprecedented in any military operation, but showed handsome profits in jewelry, personal effects, gold teeth and human hair, which returned to Germany in the same trains. With its ultramodern gas chamber accommodating 2,000 persons at a time, the Auschwitz factory alone turned out 2,500,000 corpses over three years, apart from the half million whose deaths were attributed by medical attendants to disease and starvation. The 50,000 supervisors of the various "camps," including recruits from the ancient pogrom centers of Rumania, Hungary and the Ukraine, found the work on the whole rewarding although Auschwitz's commandant later confessed that it made him "no longer happy." The problem never solved in that pre-atomic era was corpse disposal—a task assigned to those about to become corpses themselves: they did not burn well in such quantity, and it was difficult to dig large enough pits.

The new thought-control dimension added by Germany did not surprise American heretics. They had long since seen it as no mere Hitlerian vagary, but an infection which any nation might catch under similar circumstances; thus what had to be defeated was not Germany but the Fascist way of thinking. This view of the situation did not, however, spread very far: it remained heretical although not immediately punishable, and disgust for Fascism was pronounced "premature" if displayed before Pearl Harbor, the approved date. Those who had been premature, or who now showed over-enthusiasm for the government's stated ideology, confronted obstacles on seeking to contribute to the war effort. Men with talents which they could only contribute as officers were blocked from commissions, and enlisters in the ranks might find themselves washing bottles far from the action. Yet one Negro finally got a merchant ship to command in 1942 (he had held a master's certificate since 1919)** and Robert Thompson, the Communist who had been seriously wounded in Spain, rose to sergeant's rank and won a DSC for gallantry in the Pacific. Thompson was recommended for a commission, but the convenient discovery that he had become tubercular in New Guinea brought his discharge on a pension.

Woody Guthrie was one of many heretics who entered the most dangerous of the services, the Merchant Marine, taking arms to the battlefronts: between

---

* In their study *The Incomparable Crime* (Heinemann, London, 1967) Manvell and Fraenkel reckon 3,700,000 as the "most conservative" figure for Russian POW's murdered in captivity. Of the 2,000,000-odd German POW's held by Russia, 1,800,000 returned home after the war. Altogether, about six Russians died from the war for every German.
** See Hugh Mulzac, *A Star to Steer By* (7 Seas Books, Berlin, 1965).

torpedoings, he strummed his guitar and dreamed and wrote for the *Worker* about "one big union" after the great victory over Fascism.* A few heretics infiltrated "sensitive" war agencies and noted the oddity of the anti-Fascist alliance: almost no information was exchanged with the Russians in either direction. Among these were William Remington (Naval Intelligence), newly graduated economist married to a Communist's daughter; Julius Rosenberg (Signal Corps), a slum-born child of Russian immigrants whose wife Ethel, soon after Stalingrad, interrupted her Civil Defense work to give him a son; and Julius's college classmate Morton Sobell (designing radar apparatus). The army drafted Ethel's maladroit brother David Greenglass and put him in the student machine shop at Los Alamos. Hoover's attention had not been called to this later notorious circle, and he had other business: for example, recruiting Matthew Cvetic and Joseph Mazzei (Pittsburgh) and Herbert Philbrick (Boston) to watch unions, the Party and Party-infiltrated win-the-war groups.

To Trotskyist derision about the "working-class vanguard," Communists in factories outdid CIO leaders in zeal for a no-strike and wage-freeze pledge. In Hollywood, producer Jack Warner summoned his top scenarist Howard Koch to adapt for the screen a Russophile book by America's millionaire ex-ambassador in Moscow.** Warner said it was "practically an order" from Roosevelt, who had told him the war effort needed such a film. Meanwhile Mississippi senator and plantation-owner James Eastland and New York lawyers Irving Kaufman and Irving Saypol labored for the standing in the political and professional arenas which would fit them for high inquisitorial destiny after the war. Joseph McCarthy, a Wisconsin judge recently reproved for impropriety by his state's Supreme Court, took a Marine commission mainly involving desk work which won him the self-devised sobriquet "Tail-gunner Joe" and a Purple Heart for falling down a ship's companionway.

Various intellectuals thought about the problem of peace with confidence or dread. Howard Fast, a young novelist concerned with dramatizing social heroes and martyrs, saw Communism as the future: in 1943, while working for the Office of War Information, he eulogized Thomas Paine in a book and joined the Party. Arthur Miller, seeing his first play produced on Broadway in 1944, sought in heretical company for answers to the global and domestic Fascist challenge. The militant and much-jailed pacifist A. J. Muste, true to his conviction that violence would never solve anything, spent the war defending conscientious objectors and proclaimed: "If I can't love Hitler, I can't love anybody." DuBois, now well into his seventies, planned a postwar Negro education project and an African liberation congress and remained both businesslike and cheerful. "I am especially glad," he wrote, "for the divine gift of laughter; it has made the world human and lovable, despite all its pain and wrong." C. Wright Mills, a Texan sociologist, brooded at the University of Maryland about democracy's future in huge, complex, wealth-dominated America. Corporation lawyer John Foster Dulles worried about his clients' German interests and led churchmen in debates on a Christian peace. In-

* Woody Guthrie, *Born to Win*, Macmillan, New York, 1965.
** Joseph E. Davies, *Mission to Moscow*, Simon & Schuster, New York, 1941.

vestment banker James Forrestal, Under Secretary and later Secretary of the Navy, feared for the booming arms industry after peace broke out and formed the National Security Industrial Association to protect it. Sidney Hook entered a brief lull in his final and irrevocable mission of exposing Russia, and Dwight MacDonald, an ex-heretic disillusioned in turn by Stalin, Trotsky and Marx, foretold in his journal *Politics* America's doom from joining in the war. *Time-Life* publisher Henry Luce outlined the postwar "American Century"; Wallace, now Vice President, limned the "Century of the Common Man" with the peace formula "a daily glass of milk for all." *

For the future of the human species, the giant drama between the Volga and Berlin was matched in importance by events in China, although these were scantily publicized. Back in the 30s America had had its first reports on the epic of Mao Tse-tung's Red Army from Anna Louise Strong (who settled in Moscow after the Seattle disturbances of 1919); from Agnes Smedley, a Coloradan miner's daughter who had been jailed in New York for precocious dedication to colored peoples, and from Edgar Snow. Orientalist professor Owen Lattimore had later reached Mao's fastness in north China and written with respect but less partisanship for Mao's philosophical range and attention to detail, his "fire and passion" and ability to "discuss complicated subjects without a single cliche." All four had reported on Mao's strivings to make President Chiang Kai-shek fight China's Japanese invaders rather than his own starving people. Lattimore, most concerned about the danger of civil war to the American stake in China, had continued pressing for white powers to face unalterable realities: if they did, he believed, Chiang might compromise with Mao and still retain leadership. Lattimore's initial report was suppressed by the London *Times* for which he wrote it, but journals of the Institute of Pacific Relations had given him an outlet. IPR was an American-based organization financed by Rockefeller (who made vast profits from oil sales to China) and semi-governmentally sponsored by Britain, France, Japan, the Philippines, Australia, Canada, America and Russia.

Now Lattimore shouldered the burden in China of advising Chiang, who wanted two wars—against Japan and his own Communists—at once but frankly preferred the latter. Meanwhile American leaders were grateful to IPR experts, such as England's Sir John Pratt and Canada's Herbert Norman, for their realistic analyses of war and peace complexities across the Pacific. The distance was small between them and IPR's left wing (including America's wealthiest and most generous heretic, Frederick Vanderbilt Field), whose independent journal *Amerasia* was firmly hostile to Chiang. Field, Smedley and a few others did their utmost to keep America from forgetting that Mao's China and Russia would also demand to be heard on postwar arrangements.

---

* Luce asked Americans "to accept wholeheartedly our duty and our opportunity as the most powerful and vital nation . . . to exert upon the world the full impact of our influence, for such purposes as we see fit and by such means as we see fit" (*Life,* February 17, 1941). The origin of Wallace's much-mocked phrase was a semi-humorous remark he made to Russian ambassador Litvinov's wife, that the war was "to make sure that everyone in the world gets a quart of milk a day"—to which she replied: "Yes, even half a pint."

In the US Treasury lights burned late in the offices of Henry Morgenthau and Harry Dexter White, working on postwar economic policies for Germany. Ardent New Dealers both, the banker's son and his assistant believed that only Germany's wholesale denazification and military and industrial disarmament could bring peace to the world. White's zeal to find money for public works, Social Security and the unemployed, together with his premature anti-Fascism, had long since brought his mail and telephone under Hoover's observation. Early in the war he had protested against American firms continuing to do business with Germany through Swiss banks; later his partial responsibility for the "Morgenthau Plan" deepened Hoover's suspicions that he was a Russian agent. As it happened, the Russians thought the plan too drastic to be effective, but Hoover did not ask their opinion.

Six months after Stalingrad, Alexander Meiklejohn posed the impending peace as a "tragic question." A believer in religion if not in the prevailing view of what it was, he found "new hope" in China, "new vision" in Russia, and "the human spirit, weary of selfishness, of cunning, of self-deceiving aggressiveness, trying to break loose" everywhere. But just when "humanity has something to do together"—to abolish the increasingly barbaric war system—he saw the English-speaking nations "culturally disintegrating." They portrayed themselves as "the democracies" fighting "the dictatorships" to restore reasonableness, but "the distinction between reason and violence has been blurred or destroyed," he wrote in the *Nation*. He suggested that "the democracies" stop "trying to solve our dilemmas by abolishing our scruples" and holding back the new world which "has long seemed powerless to be born." He pleaded for "regarding the interests of any other person as of equal importance with one's own" and asked: "Can we organize a world society on the principle of human brotherhood? I am sure that we can at least try."

Out west the production of an atom bomb occupied Oppenheimer, who had married Kitty Dallet and disappeared with several physicist colleagues—where or for what, Steve Nelson had no idea. Their progress was agonizingly watched by Einstein, from whose discoveries British, American, Russian, French, Swedish and German scientists had developed atomic theory. Einstein had long dreamed of how the atom could help create an abundant, socialist world. Now a fugitive from Hitler pursuing his research at Princeton, he agreed with his friend Thomas Mann and other fellow exiles that if the Bomb was possible, Hitler must not make it first.

Years later Oppenheimer would talk to inquisitors for days about everyone he knew before and during the bomb project at Los Alamos, the highlight being a chat in 1942 with a friend whom he finally identified as his French professor-colleague at Berkeley, Haakon Chevalier. Chevalier remarked on that occasion that another scientist had said he had means of getting information to Russia; Oppenheimer replied that this was "terrible" or "treasonous"; Chevalier agreed, and the matter was dropped. This conversation would be blazed around the world, ruining Chevalier and inspiring his public contempt for the physicist who had been his friend. Oppenheimer's problem after he renounced heresy was to explain why he put scientists on his team for their qualifications, regardless of their politics. Yet nothing emerged to show that any of them gave anything to the Russians: indeed the security atmosphere on the project was such that they thought twice before making the most innocent remark among themselves. What did emerge was that heretics teemed in Oppenheimer's circle. Hoover can hardly not have had dossiers on at least some of the bomb-project scientists, but fortunately for the project its security was not in his hands. Brains of a rare type being necessary, Military Intelligence officers mastered their natural suspicions of the intellectual; and Oppenheimer may even have suggested to them that scientists allergic to Fascism were more likely to complete the Bomb on fever-pitch schedule.

As the time approaches to obliterate Hiroshima, we pause to note happenings west of the Los Alamos, New Mexico, Bomb project. In Pasadena, Cal Tech's top scientist Linus Pauling causes a neighborly stir as a "Jap-lover" by employing a Japanese gardener when hatred of Japan is mandatory. Pauling, among other things, is doing secret work on rockets, for which contribution President Truman will give him a Medal of Merit. In Santa Monica one of the age's great playwrights sits with Charles Laughton (who will play the part) writing the English version of his play *Galileo Galilei*. Perhaps scenting the breeze in the war's final months, he changes the emphasis on Galileo's famous recantation before papal inquisitors. Formerly interpreting it as a wise move so that the scientist could continue his work, Bertolt Brecht makes Galileo tell a pupil that, no matter how important the work, a recanting intellectual is a criminal betrayer of his responsibilities. Brecht has landed in the Hollywood area along with his composer-partner Hanns Eisler and other Germans nauseated by the Hitler regime. Eisler's revolutionary brother Gerhardt is in New York under strange circumstances, denouncing Hitler in the German-language press, acting as a volunteer warden for air-raids that never come, and with less than no interest in becoming an American.

Working in San Francisco for the same cause as Oppenheimer, Nelson's problems were comparatively trivial, but one of them calls for mention. The drain of Party men into war service had caused a leadership shortage, and Crouch, who had moved west seeking a war job after being relieved of his functions in Dixie, was elected chairman of the Oakland group. The comrades soon began complaining of his Marxist ineptitude: his reading seemed to consist mainly of the *World Almanac,* and he devoted much time to playing the jukebox in a bar and staring at the wall. Everyone was sorry for him and his wife because of their son doomed by hemophilia; Nelson and others donated blood and visited them with toys and gifts; but inevitably the comrades voted to oust him. They continued chipping in for medical expenses until Crouch drifted away, out of Nelson's ken for several years.

As for the wartime activities of Elizabeth Bentley, the only available evidence is her autobiography in the soap-opera genre, *Out of Bondage* (1949), in which sex and suspense predominate over probability. The book has documentary value as an example of what, in the postwar inquisitorial era, became the popular concept of high-level Russian spying on its ally. The romantic partner whom she announced to Lee Fuhr, here identified as "master-spy" Golos, died in 1943 without saying or being asked to say a word; Bentley vanished from Lee's orbit after Lee went to Spain. Her perhaps naive comment today is: "When I recall how we all laughed at Elizabeth saying she wanted to be a spy, I can't help doubting if she ever was one." As appraised by Lee in retrospect, Bentley was "a love-starved nymphomaniac—a tragic creature." *

Bentley was of the school of penitents who, after joining the inquisition, mixed a certain nostalgia with venom for her former comrades. In *Out of Bondage* it is Lee who harps on Elizabeth's revolutionary ancestors to lure her into the Party; nevertheless, Lee's unselfishness "reminds me of my mother" and the comrades at "warm, homelike" club meetings are "generous and genuinely kind, really mature." Later it will be a Christian act to betray them (after "shivering with sudden uncontrollable fear" at the thought), because they are "no longer individuals but robots." By "selling them down the river" Bentley will restore them to "normal life, free of any further entanglements." She is caught in the informer's dilemma of justifying both her heresy and her apostasy to a public that needs its heroes and villains plainly marked.

Bentley's villains are presumably the same "top Party people" with whom she told Lee she was doing "important things." They include a Riverside Drive lesbian who plots to rape and murder her, a wealthy Lithuanian with "bright-green eyes," the Party's "cheap, tawdry" leader Browder, and various Russians with "deep-set eyes and high Slavic cheekbones" or "short, fattish, with shrewd cold eyes." Finally the Russians convince her that the movement is "completely rotten" by offering her fur coats and the Order of the Red Star over caviar, oyster and lobster dinners ("I contented myself with a cup of coffee . . . he eyed me savagely.").

Such alarming encounters are counterbalanced by "Yasha" Golos. Like all the other eccentrics he belongs to "the dreaded Russian Secret Police," who "ruthlessly disposed of anyone who threatened their safety." But his eyes are "startlingly blue," his mouth "very much like my mother's"; and, as he teaches her the rudiments of spying and underground security, "I quite suddenly found myself in his arms." The romance blossoms although he tells her that by underground rules "we are forbidden to fall in love." The security measures include tying a thread around her secret-document trunk "so I would know if they had been tampered with," reporting to Yasha "via a third party and using a pay phone," and never going to his apartment; Yasha, however, is constantly in hers (he dies there as Elizabeth murmurs, "Without you I am nothing"), and Julius Rosenberg announces himself as "Julius" on her phone while everyone else uses aliases. Yasha, so far under-

---

* Between her return from Spain and the end of the World War, Lee Fuhr was invited three times to tell FBI men whom she knew and what they and she thought, and she kept losing jobs after visits to her employers by Hoover's agents. She had not rejoined the Party because of "disappointment with the leaders" but, retaining the "faith in mankind" which drew her to it, worked for the defeat of Fascism with Lincoln Brigade veterans and other groups.

When Bentley's reminiscences began serial publication in 1948, starring Lee as the instrument of her political seduction, Lee would not have recognized the plump face in the newspaper but for the baroque hat topping the smile. The press said that Lee would be subpenaed for a heresy trial in which Elizabeth was a government witness. Lee told the author in 1969: "I was willing to testify—I still didn't know enough to be scared of the US Government. But the defense lawyer in the case said, 'They'll frame you—get lost.' My ex-husband threatened to take my child if I didn't cooperate with the FBI. So I took the lawyer's advice and left my country forever." She is now a citizen of Mexico.

ground that when attending "top Communist meetings" he "sat behind a black-curtain so that he wouldn't be seen," tells her: "I am never sure whether my wires are tapped." As Hoover later made clear, Golos need not have worried.

Bentley's chief role is collecting documents for Yasha and the Russians from Americans employed by the government. When Yasha is sick she substitutes as a "contact" with *Daily Worker* managing editor Louis Budenz—both using aliases—at a bar-and-grill near his office. Apparently Budenz is one Party official with whom one can sit without an intervening curtain, but since he has no government documents the purpose of their furtive contact remains a mystery. When Yasha is dead, Elizabeth calls at CP headquarters under her usual alias and Browder, in the corridor outside his office which "undoubtedly the FBI has wired," coins a new name for her as a "foolproof means of communication." The Russians now decide that after Yasha's death her apartment "must be under FBI surveillance" and she must leave it; no one has suggested that this might have been the case when Yasha was alive and sleeping there. As the truth dawns that she and Yasha have been "just pawns," a "tall, dark, athletic-looking" FBI man knocks at her door: "he memorized every detail of my appearance" while asking routine questions, and "departed reluctantly . . . I found myself thinking about the FBI agent . . . he looked very nice . . . his eyes interested me." The new love angle does not develop as expected. Its object is America, which "frail though [its] system was, was the one bulwark against the growing power of Communism" and whose "clean-cut" manhood the agent typifies. After a "quiet peaceful church" scene "trying to pray" for strength, Elizabeth takes the plunge, noting how "unfailingly courteous" Hoover's men are in contrast to the Russians who "despite their superficial arrogance, cringed like whipped dogs."

Good soap operas are based however remotely on life, and at least three elements in Elizabeth's seem authentic. Whatever information they may or may not have given her, her Washington contacts were a fairly complete list of heretics hired by the New Deal. Stalin's diplomats, in or out of quotes, were always distinguished by rich and voracious appetites. And the extent of Hoover's expertise in his lifelong Russian spy-hunt is accurately implied, although of course not stated since the book was written under his wing and he must have thought it flattered him.

The only established facts about Golos are that he was a small red-haired Communist who had grown old in the movement and ran the Russian tour-agency affiliate World Tourists. During the war the agency shipped food parcels to Russia where Leningraders, for example, were receiving a quarter-slice of black bread a day under German siege. That Golos would have sent any useful information he could get along with the food is no more to be doubted than his cohabitation with Bentley. Yet Hoover, for whom any communication to the ally was treason, was too indifferent to Golos to tap his phone or find out where he slept—for when Bentley told him her story in 1945 it all came as a surprise. This was especially odd since Golos had been convicted as an unregistered Russian agent and let off with a fine at the height of prewar hostility toward Russia in 1940—at which time the Attorney General suggested that he was spying for Moscow.

A few conclusions can be ventured. With regard to Russian intelligence operations—all the allies continued spying on each other throughout the war, even when they pretended to share information—Bentley's account strains credulity far more than Len Deighton's novels which only purport to be well-researched fiction. The nature of the work draws lunatics and blackguards into any intelligence service, and Russia presumably had its quota of these along with brilliant operators like Kim Philby. Bentley adopted the thesis, standard since Lenin's day, that Bolsheviki were at the same time boorish as yokels and subtle as Machiavelli. Amateurs basing themselves on probabilities must, however, wonder how the socialist fatherland survived if its intelligence service was run as Bentley depicts it.

The US Communist Party is another story. Always short of skilled leadership and manpower, never able to decide whether it was open or clandestine and trying to be both at once, its fumbling efforts at "security" brought it nothing but headaches. It would be out of character if some members or peripheral heretics, objecting to the denial of information to the country most threatened by the common enemy, did not contact Party headquarters as a logical avenue for passing it along when official channels were blocked. And on the Party's record, we cannot rule out as impossible that it made go-betweens of such obvious suspects for counterintelligence as the convicted Russian agent Golos, the Dostoievskian paranoiac Chambers, and the whimsically hatted chatterbox Bentley. Yet if it did so, Party security in this case was at least more effective than the vigilance of Hoover, whom Congress had instructed in 1941 to investigate all federally employed heretics. In any case it became an all-American credo that these three and their contacts spent years spying for Russia unmolested by Hoover, and that Hoover was at the same time America's stoutest bulwark against Russian spies.*

If confidential information was indeed shared with the ally who was bearing the brunt of the war, those who question that this called for retribution in jail or electric chair are guilty of naivete. It was incumbent upon patriots to understand that the alliance was one of convenience, no more destined to continue than the War Department's praise of Russian strivings for a "better, happier country." Such acts were treason against the enduring policy of the Establishment, of which a new bastion now emerged: the device produced by heretical scientists at Los Alamos.

The problem of corpse disposal did not arise at Hiroshima and Nagasaki: those cities were obliterated with one bomb apiece soon after the death of Roosevelt, who called with his last breath for peoples to stop killing each other to settle their differences.

---

* The author has been able to obtain only one meager clue concerning Bentley as she was at the height of her dramatic career. A woman accustomed to frank exchanges with fellow-heretics met her in a New York restaurant during the war and relates: "She spent the whole lunch talking about the servant problem. As she didn't have any servants, I thought she must be crazy."

PART TWO:
THE INQUISITION
INSTITUTIONALIZED

V

1945-47: The Islamic Horde

Whether any appreciable part of the Establishment took seriously Roosevelt's and Willkie's admonitions about its postwar behavior, we do not know. The distinguished advocates of less American smugness and more amiability preceded Hitler to the grave; the precedent of literate political leaders was cut off by replacing Roosevelt's heir-apparent Wallace with Harry Truman; and the Establishment coolly undertook to assert itself in its own home as the essential corollary to its global destiny. The course taken had been charted since before America entered the war by voices that proved decisive. It was the natural course for men secure in the knowledge that liberty of acquisition was God's highest mandate and that they were the chosen.

Communists had attributed other intentions to them in a rash of wartime sentimentality, but the Establishment was never sentimental. The condition in which the war left the world made Luce's "American Century" dream irresistibly attractive. All rival capitalist nations were physically disabled and deeply in hock, and Russia was a shambles of broken cities, installations and bodies.* America's dead numbered some 5% of its surplus labor in the preceding peacetime decade. The war had brought an unprecedented boom to its industries and banks. Not an ounce of TNT had fallen on it, and it had airbases around the world plus the exclusive Bomb.

Furthermore the "socialistic" New Deal experience had revealed what seemed to be the key to slump-free capitalism: industry's partnership with government to produce death-dealing devices. The costs of these soared as they became more ingenious, and full employment was assured along with pyramiding profits since the products, unlike hospitals, houses and dams, became obsolete as soon as they were made. More than trivial use of the resulting super-arsenal might never be necessary, but the possession of it was a decisive factor in the "cold war" master plan. It would compel the Russians to spend on arms what they needed for reconstruction, prevent them from modernizing the extended backward area now under their influence, and at the same time subdue any reluctance of other "free world" countries to be occupied by friendly American troops.

To induce citizen cooperation in what would now be called the "Fair Deal," a menace to America even more threatening than the extinct Fascist one was

* D. F. Fleming in *The Cold War and Its Origins* (Doubleday, New York, 1961), the best American-eye view of world events since 1917, cites the following as wrecked or eliminated in Russia: 15 cities, 1,135 coal mines, 2,800 churches, 2,890 machine and tractor stations, 3,000 oil wells, 10,000 power stations, 31,850 industries, 40,000 hospitals, 43,000 libraries, 44,000 theatres, 56,000 miles of highway and 65,000 of railroad, 71,710 towns and villages, 84,000 schools, 98,000 collective farms, 181,000,000 head of farm livestock and at least 20 million people. In 1959 the London *Times* estimated Russian war dead at 10,000,000 combatants, 15,000,000 civilians, 20,000,000 unborn babies and infants.

promptly needed. The actual menace—which should indeed not be underestimated—was to the Establishment and its economic system: for if with their war-won prestige the Russians were left in peace to concentrate on human needs, a society might emerge to entice humanity away from capitalist virtue. Yet this was hardly enough to arouse enthusiasm for heightened war preparations just as peace broke out; and the crisis presented to the public was that devastated Russia planned a blitz against the prepotent, atom-armed "West" at any moment. This thesis was at once as implausible and as successful as Germany's Jewish plot against civilization. Unable to believe that anyone could have invented it, the public was soon so convinced that persons in authority could suggest the opposite and be scornfully discredited.

Above all, since the free world must include the part of Germany where capitalism had been saved, memories of days when Germans were bestial and Russians gallant must be expunged. "War crime" trials of Hitler's chief surviving colleagues were unavoidable, but reversal of the world-wide loathing for Germans was the supreme test of America's skilled semanticists. Three effective lines of approach were (1) the fixed label "Nazi" for wartime and prewar Germans (implication: a race by that name invaded Germany in 1933 and was now being replaced by the former inhabitants); (2) stress on the Jewish, and disregard of the politically heretical, share in German holocausts (implication: Jews as such being no threat to any establishment, the holocausts were the sole responsibility of a lunatic); (3) reversal of common-usage war and prewar terms such as "fifth column," "Munich," "quisling," to connote Communist instead of capitalist betrayals. In the war's last months public-relations men gained a head start from the fact that Russians, millions of whose wives and daughters had been enslaved or assigned to brothels by the Herrenvolk, frequently penetrated German ladies without asking permission in the advance toward Berlin. Outrages to German grandmothers, for whom the Reds were reported showing a peculiar fascination,* re-ignited embers of sympathy for the inventors of the corpse factory. It was a helpful antidote to the Germans' reassertion, just before leaving France, of their exterminative prowess as earlier manifest at Lidice and elsewhere. At Oradour they had left no grandmothers to complain. After the male villagers were machine gunned, the females and children were roasted inside their church.**

An overdue public-relations task was to remove the "Robber Baron" tarnish from the American capitalist and his ideals. At the same time doubts that an inquisitorial America could be squared with the Founding Fathers must be stilled. Such doubts would hamper the work of HUAC which had been made a fixture six months before Hitler's departure for Valhalla, and following a "while our boys fight and die" speech by the Representative from Tupelo, Mississippi. John Rankin was especially concerned about the "tarantula" of Hollywood where "loathsome paintings" hung in the home of the "seducer of white girls" Chaplin. Liberals

---

* Allusions to this quirk of the Russian character, as an argument against defrosting relations with Moscow, persisted for years in American media. See page 218.
** Lammerding, the commanding general in this exploit, was one of some 1,000 "war criminals" convicted by postwar French courts but still surviving comfortably in West Germany in 1970. While the French sentenced him to the guillotine, he was prospering as a Düsseldorf businessman; he died in bed in January, 1971.

hoped for the best, for if (as a New York *Post* writer pointed out) Congress was "genuinely concerned over possible threats to our constitutional form of government," it had only to "pack the committee with members with a reasonable, national attitude." Such Congressmen as might have answered to this description were, however, no more interested than before in becoming inquisitors.

As HUAC got back into business weeks before the war's end, Hoover supplied ammunition for a preliminary headline salvo: "FBI SEIZES SIX AS SPIES, TWO IN STATE DEPARTMENT," "ARREST OF SIX REVEALS REDS GOT US SECRETS." A night raid on the journal *Amerasia* had produced Far Eastern documents properly belonging in State Department files. The editor had been seen with Browder, "a Chinese Communist" and two Department men named Larsen and Service. The "*Amerasia*-IPR case" (the two were easily "linked" through Frederick Field and Lattimore who were active in both) was to linger on for years as a bastion of cold-war mythology.

But 1945 was a year of inquisitorial retooling while wartime eulogists of Russia adjusted to going into reverse. For example, New York's Democratic organization, dreamily endorsing for re-election Communist Councilman Davis who would soon be sentenced to jail for "conspiring to advocate," had to be sharply brought to its senses. Hoover arranged the firing from "sensitive" jobs of scattered minor heretics such as Signal Corps engineer Rosenberg, who vainly denied being a Communist; but many could still get work elsewhere. At about the time when Rosenberg was seeking paltry capital to start a machineshop business, Hiss (who was to share top heretical notoriety with him and his wife) reached the peak of his career at Yalta, looming behind Roosevelt in what would be exposed as the great betrayal to Stalin. During the summer Bentley and Budenz both repented of their bar-and-grill assignations in marathon sessions with FBI men, enriching the dossiers with hundreds of spy names. The ousting of Browder by his CP associates for guessing wrong about postwar perspectives created the new Marxist deviation of "Browderism" and a promising new lode of ex-Communist familiars.

A few heretics in the forces occupying Germany applied themselves to replacing Fascists with surviving anti-Fascists, in the simplistic view that Commander-in-Chief Eisenhower's orders to that effect were meant to be obeyed. As later in Japan, the decisive occupying elements were uniformed bankers and businessmen who, making swift contact with their German brethren, explained why a future without the 11,000,000 slave laborers provided by Hitler need not be wholly bleak. Truman returned from his Potsdam meeting with Stalin making bluff references to "Uncle Joe," but America was beginning to assert its priority in deciding the future of every country up to the Russian border. The August atomization of Hiroshima put forward the wordless argument on which this claim was based, but which the Russians—whose land army commanded anyone's respect—declined to accept. They maintained that they too had the right to security and to decide what kind of governments should emerge in countries they had occupied.

On the eve of the birth of the United Nations in San Francisco, Truman was receptive to Forrestal's suggestion that it was "now or never" for a "showdown" with Uncle Joe. The second-generation multimillionaire Averell Harriman, America's wartime ambassador in Moscow, was in equally combative mood:

he felt (as Forrestal would note in his diary) that "Hitler's greatest crime" had been "opening the gates of east Europe to Asia." Forrestal was in fact proposing the delivery of a mongoloid monster in San Francisco, Russo-American cooperation being the semen and egg of UN conception. Yet with hopes lifted by the world parliament's existence, many heretics sought posts in it and its branch organizations such as UNRRA—a short-lived enterprise for aiding Fascist-wrecked countries without profit to the source of aid. International organizations of women, students, journalists, etc., born out of the anti-Fascist friendliness of the war, became UN affiliates structured to bridge the capitalist-socialist gulf in peacetime. Under the two systems trade unions, for example, had different functions but similar basic concerns, and the latter were to be the preoccupation of the World Federation (WFTU) which CIO joined in August. The International Union of Students had originated in London in November 1941, in honor of 137 young Czechs massacred by the Germans in Prague; after the war its members cooperated on such projects as building a "peace road" in Yugoslavia. But the membership of all UN-affiliated organizations being predominantly capitalist, their capacity to function depended primarily on capitalist compromise.

At home heretics had little time to start anything new, but Pete Seeger, Guthrie and other pioneers of the folk-song revival formed People's Songs on capital consisting of "conviction that the world is worth saving and we can do it with songs." Guthrie continued using a guitar inscribed with the out-of-date slogan, "This Machine Kills Fascists." Soon their vision of a "singing labor movement" was dispelled by a labor hierarchy alert to their dangerous thoughts, and they were confined to singing and passing the hat in schools and summer camps and at heretical gatherings. Among volunteers who helped run the People's Songs office was an eager, waggish young newcomer to the CP, Harvey Matusow, who won a trip to Puerto Rico for record *Worker* sales. Many of the songs would become worldwide hits, but the group would expire under inquisitorial pressure in 1949, the same year in which CIO blew up Guthrie's "one big union" dream.

A month after Japan surrendered, heretics greeted a rainbowlike false dawn with Justice Murphy's decision finding Harry Bridges undeportable. The former governor of Michigan whom Dies had denounced for CIO-pampering said for the Supreme Court that Bridges had merely "dared exercise that freedom which belongs to a human being," and that the "relentless crusade" against him might "stand forever as a monument to man's intolerance of man." There was no proof that either he or the Party wanted to overthrow the government, and whether he was a Communist or not, "American doctrine" forbade punishment for guilt by association. Murphy noted that the case involved "the liberties of 3,500,000 other aliens" many of whom, "like many of our forebears, were driven from the original homeland by bigoted authorities." These unseasonable remarks made it impossible, despite patriotic outcries, to block citizenship for Bridges. For heretics the decision seemed to promise an end to political deportations, perhaps even to the need for ACPFB, the most active organization in that field. In the years when it defended anti-Fascists against deportation to probable death, ACPFB had enjoyed the sponsorship of John Dewey, Archibald MacLeish and various Congressmen, and had once been "greeted" by Eisenhower; but the Bridges decision could not turn back the clock now that all anti-Fascists were to be identified with Communism.

Nevertheless the mass of heretics, while aware of the strong opposing trend, remained hopeful that Roosevelt's tolerant philosophy would prevail. Sponsors or friends of organizations based on New Deal ideas, such as the National Citizens' Political Action and the Arts, Sciences and Professions committees, included liberal journalists, unreconstructed senators, professors from top universities, CIO leaders, show-business celebrities, hundreds of businessmen in the non-lethal sector, and notables of the Roosevelt circle from members of his cabinet to his widow and two of his sons. An unprecedented situation for Higginses was that they had, in Wallace, a man to back who had been one step from the Presidency. With obvious lack of enthusiasm, Truman had retained as Secretary of Commerce the New Dealer who thought Hottentots should have access to milk. Yet Wallace, a well-to-do farm-journal publisher and hybrid-corn expert, had no interest in socialism: he merely saw the American Century policy as an impractical formula for saving capitalism. He and his respectable backers were convinced that "progressive capitalism" could end hunger and war, coexist with Russia, and remain satisfactorily profitable at the same time, and that all this could become America's policy through citizens' pressure upon the reigning Democratic party. Obsessed with the problem's technical aspects, which he knew to be capable of ready solution, Wallace was slow to grasp that the Establishment had already decided the issue another way. Yet the signs were certainly confusing. In November of 1945 Eisenhower was saying that Russia "wants to be friends," and Assistant Secretary of State Dean Acheson, a Groton-Yale-Harvard product barely tainted by the New Deal, was speaking without embarrassment at an American-Soviet Friendship rally.

HUAC reaped a poor harvest from its *Amerasia* spy-probe but laid some useful precedents. Canada arrested 22 persons named as wartime spies by a defecting Russian diplomat; and although efforts to link the *Amerasia* suspects with them came to naught, scare-headlined stories about the "case" served to warn 'China hands' in or out of the State Department that pleas of objectivity would not clear them of suspicion for their lukewarmness to Chiang.

No inquisitor had yet turned up with the makings of a Dies. J. B. Matthews had left with his mentor to use his subversive letterhead collection as a consultant to union-haunted industrialists. Robert Stripling, who through the war had shared Matthews's House Office Building suite with dossier cabinets bulging into the corridors, had been drafted into the army. Ernie Adamson, a lawyer from somewhere in Georgia—the same state as chairman John S. Wood—was conducting much of the work by correspondence. Adamson frankly informed the National Committee to Combat Anti-Semitism, sponsored by CIO leader Philip Murray, Ickes, Thomas Mann and various bishops, that he disapproved of its attempt to "control the thoughts of American citizens." "I should like," he wrote to the Federation for Constitutional Liberties, "to send an investigator to take a look at your books and records, to determine whether the organization is engaged in subversive activities." Of his many requests to "be good enough to send me a list of your officers," the most publicized (because he expressed the same thought to columnist Drew Pearson) was addressed to Veterans Against Discrimination, which had "referred to democracy several times" in its literature. "I wonder," he asked in his letter, "if you are aware that this country was not organized as a democracy?" The thought that this was what the war had been about haunted Pearson and others. Adamson invited radio stations whose commentators criticized the committee too much, and Russia too little, to send him copies of their scripts. The committee also introduced a law to make foreign-language journals translate their copy so inquisitors could know what they were saying. But press freedom was an essential trapping of inquisitorial America, and publishers of opinion-molding journals frowned on this overt interference. The prescription for un-American foreign-language publications, to be applied when the inquisition gathered more steam, was deportation of their editors for personal heresy.

A further reminder by inquisitor John E. Rankin of the Russian custom of indiscriminate rape assured HUAC of a $125,000 budget for 1946. Rankin had clarified HUAC ideology by recalling that "after all, the Ku Klux Klan is an American institution; our job is to investigate foreign isms and alien organizations." Courteous questioning of anti-Semite Gerald Smith added such show-business names as Orson Welles, Ingrid Bergman, Eddie Cantor and Frank Sinatra to the list of citizens who would need to clear their skirts.

When Adamson's correspondence with radio stations and sponsors removed eight commentators from the air, the committee's power began to show. In the case of organizations obviously involving Communists, action followed closely on the postman's heels. By the fall of 1946 HUAC had fed into the contempt mill George Marshall of the Civil Rights Congress, the Rev. Richard Morford of NCASF, and nine leaders of the Joint Anti-Fascist Refugee Committee (relief for Spanish Republican survivors) including novelist Howard Fast and Edward Barsky, a New York surgeon who had saved many heretical lives as head of a hospital near Madrid. Declining to give names, they would end with three- and six-month jail terms. Also questioned was the Rev. Stephen Fritchman, editor of the Unitarian *Christian Register,* formerly of the Unitarian Fellowship for Social Justice: he was not jailed but the Unitarian headquarters fired him. Corliss Lamont, a well-known non-Communist who remained chairman of NCASF until 1946, was started through the mill but would fight all the way and stop one station short of the terminus, at the point of indictment in 1954. CRC (specializing in legal defense of Negroes) had three board members—Robeson, the Rev. Charles Hill of Detroit, and Harry Ward—who defied the inquisitors with equal success, although its executive secretary William Patterson would end in jail. Robeson graced the question as to whether he was a Communist with a reply—in the negative—for the last time in 1946.

Truman's invitation to Churchill to make the cold war official, in a speech in rural Missouri expounding Anglo-Saxon virtue and the criminality "behind the Iron Curtain" (the new term for socialism), was excellent showmanship; but a native son on closer terms with God, and less notorious for the consumption of whisky and costly cigars, was needed to develop America's cold-war ideology. Foster Dulles seemed to have been prepared by a higher destiny for this critical hour. The early habit of attending his father's church four times each Sunday had inculcated in him a love of God and fellow man which, as an American in and out of public affairs since World War I, had predominantly emerged in the form of solicitude for Germany. By the 30s he was head of America's biggest corporation law firm and a director of 15 corporations, mostly with German interests which continued to flourish; he represented Hitler's favorite Berlin bank and had a partner on its board. Dulles also flourished, possessing a yacht, servants and cars, a New York seaside place, an island in Lake Ontario, a cellarful of Montrachet, a wardrobeful of Brooks Bros. suits, and a quietly appointed East 91st Street house with six telephones and an elevator. His unfailing ability to match all this on the ideological plane, praising his "forebears [who] trained their moral muscles with puritanism and austerity," drew the admiration of his peers. At a League of Nations "peaceful change" discussion in Hitler's fourth year, uncharitability toward Germany again aroused his indignation. Finally he had become the acknowledged expert on peace for the World Council of Churches and for foundations set up, just before World War I, by Carnegie and Rockefeller to promote amity and well-being. As such, his supreme concern was that the peace be Christian: it could only endure if built on knowledge that "there is a God." Since Americans knew this more profoundly than anyone, they were called upon for leadership, and must exercise it without "material self-seeking, hatred and vengefulness."

Early in 1945 Dulles's brother and partner Allen, in Switzerland for American intelligence, discussed with German emissaries an arrangement for a more Christian peace than could be expected if Berlin fell to the Red Army. The effort failed, but Foster Dulles worked tirelessly from the day of surrender to show the Germans that America forgave them. Six months after Churchill's Iron Curtain speech, Dulles began to clothe America's cold-war ideology in more appropriate formulations. "Ten centuries have rolled by," he said, since the last time "the so-called Christian world was challenged by an alien faith. Now the accumulated civilization of those centuries is faced with another challenge . . . Soviet Communism [whose] official creed is an abstruse materialism." The previous challenge to which he referred was that of Islam. Hitler's challenge, after all, had been purely military and his creed, if materialistic, was never abstruse.

If Dulles's approach had any flaw, it was in ignoring the world's second largest Jewish population; but Jews close to the Establishment adapted well to their inclusion among Christendom's defenders against an alien faith. Other Jewish Americans sided with Wallace who, just when Dulles was evoking the neo-Islamic peril, caused a scandal at an NC-PAC rally to back Democratic electoral candidates. An undercover FBI agent detected 20,000 assorted heretics in Madison Square Garden applauding Truman's Secretary of Commerce. Resuming normal peacetime activities, Dixie mobs had lynched several Negroes who left the army with the notion that they could vote in elections; and Wallace cited the latest of these ceremonies to illustrate his point that "hatred breeds hatred" and makes war inevitable. He submitted that America must eliminate its own racism before it could talk to others about peace, and that in any case it had as little business in East European politics as Russia did in Mexican. The Russians would socialize their occupied lands whether America liked it or not, and "the tougher we get, the tougher they'll get." UN should control all A-Bombs and strategic airbases and be used, as its charter laid down, as an avenue to compromise, friendly competition, and joint help to backward countries.

At a moment when the American Legion's national commander was already clamoring to "aim an atomic rocket at Moscow," such sentiments inevitably got Wallace fired from the cabinet and cued the media to unmask him as "the man who wants to give Russia our secrets." On his first evening in the political wilderness he urged Americans to use their common sense about "pro-Russian" labels and think about the alternatives posed by Willkie: One World or none.

Republican gains in the 1946 elections, which put into Congress future inquisitors McCarthy and Richard Nixon, stimulated the contest between the parties for leadership in the crisis. Nixon had won the seat of mildly liberal Rep. H. Jerry Voorhis in a campaign featuring systematic phone calls to Voorhis's supporters: "This is a friend. I want you to know that Voorhis is a Communist." *
In a gesture symbolizing America's unity in face of peril, Truman appointed the Republican Foster Dulles as foreign-policy adviser to Secretary of State George Marshall, with special functions concerning Germany. Dulles opened 1947 with a rebuke of Russia's immorality in establishing "people's democracy" in its agreed-upon security sphere, and Acheson now saw the "chasm" between Russia and America to be "unbridgable." The wherewithal to suppress nationalist pretensions was speeded to colonial areas, and America began spending $1,000,000 a day to save Hitler's monarchist sympathizers from Greeks who resisted the Germans and survived. Greece was coupled with Turkey in a Truman doctrine of unilateral military aid which, ignoring UN Charter, in effect banned all further revolutions against capitalism anywhere. In the same month Truman ordered tests for two million federal employees to prove that they liked capitalism and always had.

Dulles was the man of the hour because he so deeply understood the Americans' need for reassurance that God approved their policies: the cold war and its attendant inquisition could not have been sold to the public by a naked statement that America declined to occupy the same world with socialism. Of the "four freedoms" enunciated for purposes of the war, freedom of worship had won the widest popularity, and the most telling of cold-war arguments was that Russians found in a kneeling position were arrested and probably purged. Stalin, however, was far less concerned with churchgoers than with good Communists who might threaten him politically. He was accelerating an extensive purge which did not even exist in Russian media, in contrast with the American method under which physical punishment was rare and fear was spread through the sensational publicizing of each case. Each country was imposing thought control according to its own tradition, and under the mass-fear stimuli the two programs fed upon each other.

Whether or how much Stalin's sanguinary tendencies were exacerbated by having to deal with Dulles, always so ready with moral garments in which to dress political realities, we can only guess. But the successes of the Dulles diplomatic style exceeded all the Establishment's hopes. Under unrelenting Christian-

* William Costello (journalist and later ambassador to Trinidad), *Facts About Nixon*, Viking, New York, 1960.

atomic pressure in its years of recovery, the area under Stalin's control continued unimpressive to the average American and increasingly harder for Higgins to defend as a paragon of socialism. Meanwhile in America the cold war fixed a "Stalinist" label on all who—whatever their views about Stalin—did not publicly abuse him and his country; heretical zealots condemned with equal violence all who found evil as well as good in the socialist world; and thus politically aware Americans rushed toward total polarization. It was not so much what they were that mattered as what they seemed to others in the drama, what the others needed them to be. The persistent Higgins was a Quixote in thinking he could row against so furious a tide.

VI

1946-47: The Manila Envelope

Despite their Montana heresies Philip and Mary Jane Keeney had both obtained confidential war jobs, he under poet Archibald MacLeish at the Library of Congress, she under Wallace at the Board of Economic Warfare. After the war both got occupation assignments and diplomatic passports. Philip's passport for Japan, where he was to be proconsul MacArthur's Libraries Officer, took longer because someone accused him of excessive hiring of Negroes; but his assurances that he had no plans to overthrow the government were finally accepted.

Mary Jane went to edit documents for an economic team in Germany. When she returned, she brought a manila envelope. She "proceeded" from the pier to a Greenwich Village apartment and then to a restaurant, where she was "observed passing the envelope to an individual suspected of being engaged in Soviet espionage." The individual later gave the envelope to Alexander Trachtenberg of International Publishers, "advising" the Communist publisher of Marx that a "contact" had "managed to bring in an important will furnished by a political deputy who had been shot by the Germans."

The observer of all this in March 1946 was "Confidential Informant T-I." Mrs. Keeney had stepped off the boat into the "investigative" world of J. Edgar Hoover, in which people were "individuals" and "subjects," friends and acquaintances were "contacts," and one "advised" and "proceeded" rather than told and went. Only after years of mysterious frustrations did she have an opportunity to explain what was in the envelope: a book by a French resistance hero, completed on the eve of his execution by the Germans, commonly known in France as "Gabriel Péri's Testament." The individual, a linguist friend, had asked her to bring him a copy for possible translation, and he had submitted the project to Trachtenberg.

In the next months Confidential Informants T-8, T-21 and T-22 and various "special agents" built up a dossier on the Keeneys of which Hoover could be, and was, proud: in 1949 he would permit HUAC to publish excerpts. The source of inquisitors' information was customarily kept secret, especially when it was Hoover. Over the years, the agents were able to advise, the Keeneys had been seen at Spanish Republican meetings, "active in the Washington Cooperative Bookshop, an outlet for Communist propaganda," and "personally introduced" to Browder. "Among their numerous contacts" were a Russian journalist "believed to be in the USSR," two New Deal officials named Silvermaster and Ullmann "reported as primary functionaries in Soviet espionage activities," and Haakon Chevalier "who has previously been mentioned as having been a contact of one Eltenton, who was involved in an attempt to secure atomic information." Their "most flagrant contact" was Gerhardt Eisler whom they had "entertained in their home after having met him at a banquet."

Guilty of these charges, if not responsible for the embroidery, the Keeneys were unaware that they had been made but were caught in the inquisition's impalpable net. Mary Jane had planned to join Philip in Tokyo, but in April 1947 she was refused a passport just as he was being fired and sent home, to the grief of Japanese librarians whose affection he had won. No reason was given for either action. Although the experience re-inflamed Philip's ulcers, he set to work on a universal library-service plan for submission to European, Latin American and African librarians. This aroused such interest in Czechoslovakia that he planned to go there and help implement it. His passport application rejected, he tried in vain to board a ship with an identity certificate. Mary Jane became a UN document editor in 1948 and was assigned to the General Assembly in Paris, but even in that capacity she was refused a passport. They had become prisoners in their own land, awaiting the inquisitorial summons which would finally come in 1949. HUAC would then ask if Philip had not "attended" Tokyo's May Day parade in 1946 (he confessed to watching it from his office window). Mary Jane, upon "evaluation" of the manila envelope episode, would be found to have "placed herself in the category of a Communist Party courier."

"Cases" like the Keeneys' multiplied Hoover's dossiers and openings for typists, agents, and fingerprint, handwriting and eavesdropping technicians in his offices across the land. His record of not catching spies has blinded some critics to the true function of an enterprise which, soon after the war, compared in magnitude with a giant corporation. The task was to spread all possible fear and mutual suspicion among heretics, and it was efficiently performed. The deployment of undercover agents in the heretical community, timing and spacing their emergence as tribunal familiars so as to keep comrades eyeing each other for signs of perfidy, alone called for skill above the average policeman's. The CP, for example, expelled some of its best members under the nervous delusion that independent thinking indicated unreliability, whereas Hoover logically instructed his informers to agree 200% with Party Headquarters. Hoover also used Negroes effectively, because a comrade even hinting that black men were agents risked expulsion as a "white chauvinist." The Justice Department and its Bureau also had to decide carefully, on the basis of the fear-potential to others, which heretic to select for the full treatment and when.

Hoover's agents, always in pairs like nuns and with one to cajole and one to threaten, visited suspects at offices or homes in tireless pursuit of names; and one or two such visits often frightened the subject away from any further contamination, whereas the unfrightened were demonstrable Higginses. The insistence on friends' names soon became more psychological than practical, for Hoover already had most of them from other sources; but name-giving was the symbolic act of self-abuse, assuring the subject's future loyalty. The phone-tapping was likewise mainly psychological. Even Hoover's bloated staff could not have processed the data from every heretic's phone, but the knowledge of his eavesdropping expertise made heretics act as if all walls had ears. They began using such furtive double-talk to each other as to betray themselves by that alone.

For the average American in this rising temperature, only one conclusion was possible from the disclosures about who contacted whom: all these people were filching American secrets. The whodunit-fed public showed a gluttonous appetite for spy sensations and no signs of indigestion. If the Establishment had any fears that Hoover's and HUAC's cuisine might prove too rich, they quickly vanished; rather was it to be feared that some spy revelation might dull the appetite by too closely resembling the probable. This was the period when Chambers was expanding his charges against Hiss (which he had peddled in vain ever since 1939), Budenz was well embarked upon the 3,000 hours he would give to listing names, and Bentley was identifying over 80 spies and "couriers." Among those named by both Bentley and Chambers was Dexter White, whose appointment by Truman in 1946 to represent America on the International Monetary Fund would be used for years as a political "soft-on-Communism" football.

All their charges related to the war and prewar periods, and although the Bureau would work on them for years no one on the Bentley-Budenz-Chambers lists was ever convicted of spying. But the Russians may well have been enchanted by America's melodramatic edifice as it soared skyward, diverting attention from their professional agents to heretics who had no access to strategic secrets but whose views had become proof that they were spies. With respect to the Bomb, the Russians were fully capable of making their own, but expert data on America's production had long been flowing to them from two agents who came to America with flawless credentials from London. Exiled German physicist Klaus Fuchs had been shown everything at Los Alamos in 1945, and British embassy official Donald Maclean sat on the Combined Policy Committee in Washington and had an unrestricted pass to the Atomic Energy Commission building there. By 1949 Russian agent Philby, head of British Intelligence's Soviet division, would be participating in Washington's most secret cold-war conclaves. These were perhaps not Moscow's only men so advantageously positioned while the media pyramided the CP's "underground spy apparatus."

Of the three famous spy-namers in this early period, Budenz would be the only one to stay the course. The exalting of its familiars' virtue and sanity for public consumption is a perennial problem for an inquisition, especially where (as was unavoidable in America) they are subject to cross-examination if the case should go to court; but whereas Bentley showed low resistance to alcohol and Chambers had a long history of psychosis, the only skeleton in Budenz's closet was a minor case of bigamy. After a decade in the Party he had returned fervently to his Indiana family's faith and been rewarded with a professorship at a Roman Catholic university. He was an expert on all aspects of the conspiracy from China to Marxists texts, buttressing his credibility with frequent references to God. At first, he coincided with Chambers in identifying the head of the underground apparatus as "J. Peters," a "short, pudgy" Hungarian with twelve aliases who "loved mystery stories." * But just before HUAC's chairmanship fell to Parnell Thomas in January 1947, Budenz told the committee that the master-spy was Gerhardt Eisler.

Thomas—who now had Stripling back as Committee counsel—lost no time in summoning Eisler to explain what he was doing in America. The professional Austro-German revolutionary, a small man easily moved to sarcasm or umbrage,

---

* Still fascinated by "J. Peters" ten years later, Senate inquisitors determined his name to be Goldberger; but he had long since passed out of reach, having "accepted voluntary departure" in what must have been a major Immigration Service blunder. The inquisi-

said that this was what he wished someone would explain to him. He had been stuck there for seven years and, finally getting an exit permit to return to Germany, had been arrested on the eve of sailing. The relevant background was that he had been working for the Spanish government at the time of its overthrow, had landed in a French camp and escaped a whisker ahead of the Herrenvolk with the necessary American transit visa and a Mexican entry permit. To obtain the former—since the Germans killed Communists of any nationality and the Americans permitted only native-born ones on their soil—he had regretfully denied his creed. Had he not done so, he would long since have been mixed among the ashes in Buchenwald. But the Americans had barred him from proceeding to his Mexican destination and he had made the best of it through the war, consorting, working, and indulging his favorite vice—poker—with American fellow heretics. Names please? Eisler would not give them; and Thomas after producing Eisler's sister to describe him as "the perfect terrorist type," cited him for not answering some questions after answering others—the crime of contempt. In July 1947 a judge sentenced him to a year in jail. Eisler settled down for the long process of court appeals, broadcasting acid jests about a country which punished revolutionaries for what they did not say and which deported alien Communists but insisted on keeping him.

Although Eisler continued contacting his usual contacts, the trial led to no further disclosures about the apparatus. For Thomas, there was an obvious lead to Gerhardt's musician brother Hanns and Hanns's playwriting partner Brecht, who were at large in Hollywood and known to be contacting Chaplin. For one thing, Brecht might provide a clue to the Communism of Christopher Marlowe, one of whose plays he had adapted. Brecht's and Hanns Eisler's HUAC appearances made a fitting curtain raiser to the Hollywood Ten session. The dossier showed that Eleanor Roosevelt, who moved in "egghead" circles where the two Germans had a certain prestige, had helped Hanns stay in America despite Hoover's exposure of him as a Communist. Stripling's formulation at the hearing, "the Karl Marx of Communism in the musical field," was the best that HUAC could do with Hanns. He was "allowed voluntary departure" (i.e., paid his own fare) in 1948; his brother would depart less conventionally in 1949.

Thomas and Stripling learned quickly how to spell Brecht's name, but were disconcerted by his rudimentary English and flat denial—the only one vouchsafed by the Hollywood heretics—that he was ever a Communist. This did not seem to jibe with his admission that he "of course" had studied Marx; but no familiar was on hand to place him at a Party gathering, and since he answered all questions both perjury and contempt were ruled out. Brecht had created figures not dissimilar to his inquisitors in his savage burlesques of dollar capitalism, but was hard put to get their wave length and had to struggle along through an interpreter who knew German but not much English. Linguistic was piled on political confusion as Stripling confronted him with excerpts from translated texts attributed to Bertolt Brecht:

---

torial data on him might have suggested that he was the Comintern's representative in America when that organization existed, but a reliable Party source is emphatic that he was not: "He was an official dealing with administrative questions." He did, however, "write a terrible book which the government used against the Party."

STRIPLING: I would like to ask Mr. Brecht whether or not he wrote a poem, a song, rather, entitled "Forward, We've Not Forgotten."

McDOWELL (assistant inquisitor): Forward, what?

BRECHT: I can't think of that. The English title may be the reason.

STRIPLING: Would you translate it for him into German.

(Interpreter does so.)

BRECHT: Oh, now I know, yes. (...)

STRIPLING (reads): "Forward, we've not forgotten our strength in the fights we've won;/ No matter what may threaten, forward, not forgotten how strong we are as one;/ Only these our hands now acting, built the road, the walls, the towers. All the world is of our making. What of it can we call ours?/ Forward, March on to the tower, through the city, by land the world; (...)/ We shall free the world of shadow; every shop and every room, every road and every meadow. All the world will be our own."

Did you write that, Mr. Brecht?

BRECHT: No, I wrote a German poem, but that is very different from this. (Laughter)

Brecht wanted to speak of his long efforts with others against Fascism, but Thomas interrupted: "We are not interested in any works that he might have written advocating the overthrow of Germany or the government there." After ten minutes of badinage about the translation of a song title "You must be ready to take over," which Stripling read four times and Brecht maintained should be "You must take the lead," Thomas moaned: "I cannot understand the interpreter any more than I can the witness." *

Thomas Mann joined with a retired bishop and California's former Immigration and Housing Commissioner Carey McWilliams in a committee to defend Gerhardt Eisler, and Chaplin and Pauling protested the harassment of Hanns. Harry Cain, a war-hero senator from the state of Washington who was dabbling in the inquisition, demanded Chaplin's instant deportation for "almost treasonably" asking "the self-admitted Communist Picasso" to organize French protests. For Chaplin, who had been found guilty of fathering a bastard and barely avoided jail, the sands of America were fast running out. Hoover's men had been constantly visiting him since the war to ask, "Did you really say 'Comrades'?" and to be told that Chaplin knew too little about Communism to discuss it with such experts. Now HUAC decided to summon him but had second thoughts—perhaps, Chaplin later suggested, because it leaked out that he planned to appear in his "little tramp" guise and "burlesque the burlesque." He forfeited the last claim to sympathy with his *Monsieur Verdoux* portrayal of a loving husband and father who murders wealthy widows to support his family, and who explains to the judge that he has merely applied on a small scale the rules of a jungle society. Patriots picketed the New York theatre with signs, "Chaplin's a Fellow Traveler," "Send

* For full text of the encounter with Thomas and Stripling in October 1947 see Frederic Ewen's *Bertolt Brecht, His Life, His Art and His Times* (Citadel, New York, 1968). Ewen, a popular English literature professor at Brooklyn College, walked the same plank as Brecht a few years later; he invoked the Fifth and immediately entered the ghetto. "I have been driven from the field of my life's activity," he said, "by the shameless persecution of freedom of thought and speech now disgracing my country."

Chaplin to Russia," and, there being no more American bookings, he withdrew the film.

In a land where names rocket onto front pages to dwell there and pass into the void, none shines brighter nor vanishes faster than the inquisitor's; but Parnell Thomas, the only inquisitor dropped from *Who's Who* during his lifetime, lingers in memory if only for the same reason: he went to jail. In 1936 the New Jersey lawyer-assemblyman had remarked to a reporter, as they observed an unemployed demonstration from a window: "Going after reds is going to make me." His maiden speeches in Congress argued for a fire-prevention stamp and the naming of a battleship after his state, but in 1938 he found his vocation on the Dies Committee and in 1947 he became chief inquisitor. His illiteracy met professional standards but his damp, forlorn appearance and lack of charisma presented a public-relations problem, which *Time* solved with the adjective "Pickwickian."

As a Republican, Thomas saw a double duty to expose Democratic New Deal heresy. While he lasted, he showed understanding that publicity was the inquisition's lifeblood and sound judgment as to what would produce it. Scientists were a rich field, not only because they were privy to mass-annihilation data, but because the mass media always enjoyed the discomfiture of eggheads. An Ernie Adamsonian inquiry revealed that some of the top ones "admit communication with persons outside the US"; and Thomas, noting that it was "entirely possible" they were spies, threw himself into the battle for army control of atomic energy.

From the nest of heresy in which the Bomb had been born, Thomas picked Edward Condon who had worked with Oppenheimer and also knew radar and rocket secrets, and whom the Democrats had made chief of the government research organization National Bureau of Standards. Along with Oppenheimer, Einstein, Pauling and others he had founded the *Bulletin of the Atomic Scientists* which, while frigid toward Communists, was equally so toward the inquisition. He had obtained the Bureau of Standards post through Wallace and was a contact of Shapley, the Harvard astronomer and chairman of ASP* who shouted "Fascist!" at Rankin when summoned for inquisition in December 1946. Hoover's dossier showed that Condon had sponsored a dinner for SCHW; his wife was a Slavic literature expert born in a country about to fall into the Communist maw, Czechoslovakia; and there was a "link" through her to an alleged heretic in the State Department (who would soon be fired and commit suicide). Apparently Condon agreed with Einstein that it was better to exchange scientific information than to blow up the world, for both belonged to an American-Soviet Science Society as long as such an organization could exist. He had even invited Russians to his office.

After promising in two magazine articles, *Russia Grabs Our Inventions* and *Reds in Our Atom-Bomb Plants,* to investigate Condon, Thomas issued a report on this "weakest link in our national security" and left unanswered Condon's pleas to be heard. The phrase delighted the media and became as firmly welded to Condon as "The Pause That Refreshes" to Coca-Cola. Condon's family celebrated each anniversary of the report as National Weak Link Day while he awaited an opportunity to face an inquisitor. But his eagerness to defend himself minimized his

* Also president at the time of the American Association for the Advancement of Science.

suitability as a tribunal witness, and the Pentagon and Congress hesitated to burn at the stake a brain so amply stocked with lethal know-how.

Oppenheimer, the mother-hen of the atomic heretics' nest, broke in 1946 with his last heretical connection, ASP. He had not complained (as many colleagues did) against the incineration of Hiroshimans as a warning to Russia when Japan was already suing for peace, nor against the army's attempt to control atomic energy. He struggled through the post-Hiroshima months on a Washington team developing an "international atom-control plan" which Russia would clearly not accept,* and retired gratefully to pursue pure science at Princeton. By 1949 he would be receiving eulogies from *Life* with pictures of him, Kitty and the children on his New Jersey manor; but he had lost one religion without gaining another, as his lukewarmness toward the H-Bomb showed. In contrast, Einstein expressed public disgust in 1946 for the split atom having fallen into the hands of patriots fascinated by its power to kill. It had "changed everything save our modes of thinking," wrote the obstinate old man, "and thus we drift toward unparalleled catastrophe." Again repudiating capitalism as the producer of depressions, wasted labor and "the crippling of social consciousness," Einstein earned the fatal epithet "sincere friend of Russia" in a *Pravda* article criticizing his advocacy of World Government. Matthews already had him down as a sponsor of 32 "Communist fronts."

Until McCarthy investigated the army, no probe would win such headlines as Thomas's of ten Hollywood writers and directors.** Television was taking first place among the media, and this star-spangled spectacular was watched by millions. "We are going," said Thomas, "to continue to expose, and if you will just sit around here every day this week you will see more exposure and more spotlighting of Communists than you have ever seen before." The testimony by Ginger Rogers's mother that her girl had been asked to say in a film, "Share and share alike, that's democracy"—"which I think is definitely Communist propaganda"—remains an inquisitorial classic. Her evidence of a Russian plot in the movie colony was reinforced by Ronald Reagan (later Governor of California and White House aspirant), Mickey Mouse's progenitor Walt Disney, Adolphe Menjou (who defined a Communist as one who enjoyed listening to Robeson), and Gary Cooper (who was not sure what Communists were but disliked them).

The apparent object of the probe was to show that Hollywood heretics were infiltrating un-American ideas into films. This could hardly be shown, for it could only have occurred over the bodies of the producers, who controlled all that went on the screen. But the producers were so alarmed by the publicity and its danger to business that they earnestly pledged new precautions to avoid un-Americanism in the future. Those who had made films showing a War Department view of the Russian ally began seeking "red spy" scripts to appease inquisitors and prove their

---

* The Russians rejected the "Baruch Plan" not only because it abolished the agreed cornerstone of the UN, Security Council unanimity, leaving atomic control in the hands of the capitalist majority. They also saw as futile disarmament proposals that left out germ warfare and other mass-destruction methods. They still took this position after they began making A-Bombs in 1949.

** Alvah Bessie, Herbert Biberman, Lester Cole, Edward Dmytryk, Ring Lardner Jr., John Howard Lawson, Albert Maltz, Samuel Ornitz, Adrian Scott, and Dalton Trumbo.

loyalty. Producer Warner went further and came to tell Thomas that screenwriter Koch, whom he had begged to do the *Mission to Moscow* adaptation, was a Communist so addicted to infiltrating subversion into scripts that Warner had had to fire him.*

A total of 19 had been subpenaed for the Hollywood session, but after the experience with Brecht, Thomas postponed the appointments of those who seemed likely to answer the $64 question. This group (including Koch, directors William Wyler and John Huston, and actors Humphrey and Lauren Bacall Bogart) had in fact urged the ten to talk freely, but the ten had insisted that it was time to test the First Amendment once and for all. The best the Bogart group could do was fly to Washington and publicly condemn the proceedings. But the media had no space for them and they subsided as the ten contempt citations confronted all film people with the new reality: there would be no work for anyone charged with heresy unless he abjured it and named his friends. For the ten the punishment would be jail and professional ghetto; for the unsummoned but still impenitent, like Koch, the ghetto. Koch's name still adorned Hollywood ASP letterheads, and the price asked for his de-ghettoization would be an admission that ASP was a Russian plot. Thus the inquisition ensured that no such doctrines as premature anti-Nazism could again be offered to the public under film-celebrity auspices, and that the richest single source of heretical funds was cut off. A new watchdog of show-business heresy in 1947 was the publication *Counterattack*, launched by three FBI alumni who saw solid possibilities in inquisitorial private enterprise.

The ten would end in jail for claiming that the First Amendment entitled them not to tell Thomas whether they were Communists. Trumbo, while waiting for the Supreme Court to reject the appeal, would contend in his pamphlet *Time of the Toad* that America was "surrendering its mind," having "become simply against something." "Whatever the enemy does," he wrote, "we mustn't do. Each morning we observe the drift of the wind out of the Don Basin. At lunchtime we test the temperature of the Siberian wilderness. At night we are canny with the moon, for it shines also upon the domes of Moscow." Another victim would write in the *Saturday Evening Post* fourteen years later that if he had not objected to the compulsion and inescapable naming of others, his answer to the $64 question would have been yes. He was the son and namesake of humorist Ring Lardner, descended from America's early revolutionary gentry, a talented writer like his two brothers of whom one had volunteered and died in Spain. Earning at 31 an income several times larger than Thomas's, he had to sell his recently bought beach home at a big loss on an advertisement: "Owner going to jail." Before he went he explained to journalist Andrews:** "If I am a [CP] member, I would be exposing myself to the bigotry and inspired hysteria which is forcing all left-of-center groups into a semi-secret status;" if not, "I would be exposing other men to the same bigotry and blacklist by contributing to the precedent that all non-Communists must so declare themselves in order to isolate the actual offenders ... Further, it would be clear to everyone, including me, that I had purged myself

---

* Koch's explanation was simpler: producer Goldwyn had wanted his services (before the subpenas) and paid Warner $25,000 for Koch's contract.
** Bert Andrews, *Washington Witch Hunt*, Random House, New York, 1948.

in order to please my past and prospective employers." Slow to grasp that ideas had become a crime, Lardner had invoked the First Amendment because he was constantly interrupted from the chair and "not allowed to reply in my own way." When he managed to say, "I could answer but I would hate myself in the morning," Thomas had banged the gavel and shouted, "Leave the witness chair—sergeant, take the witness away." In his *Post* article Lardner recalled having found "thoughtful, witty and generally stimulating men and women" in the CP along with "bores and unstable characters."

No more concerned than Thomas as to whether the ten were Party members—for proofs of heresy were abundant—the media showed no sympathy for them. The dwindling nonconformist press concentrated on the farcical aspects but only made its own guilt more clear, since everyone else took the conspiracy so seriously.* The general public was unaware that the ten were not sent to jail for Party membership but for contempt of Thomas, who was to join them there for adding innocent relatives to his Congressional payroll. ASP, which had already organized a four-day "Thought-Control Conference" in Hollywood in July, assembled a thousand heretics in a New York hotel as the hearings began. In a cable mentioning the Sermon on the Mount, Wallace told them: "You must destroy the un-American committee at the polls and in the courts, or it will destroy many of the foundations of democracy and Christianity." Two lawyers, Robert Kenny and John Rogge, suggested to the gathering that since HUAC was acting unconstitutionally the ten should defy it or simply decline to appear. Rogge was a former Assistant US Attorney General, recently fired after a mission to Germany to document connections between Hitler's agents and various Congressmen. Kenny, Attorney General of California in the administration that freed Mooney and Billings, was beginning as attorney for some of the ten a long period of service to accused heretics. Most of yesterday's ASP sponsors were as conspicuous by their absence as was the press.

In the American political context the prosecution of the current Torquemada just when the inquisition needed prestige, for an offense hardly rare among Congressmen, was less startling than it might seem. The two parties' contest for the spoils of office continued normally through the national crisis, and the Democrats—still in power although their rivals had gained a Congressional majority—seized the opportunity to silence a Republican who constantly exposed their lineage from the traitorous Roosevelt. Thomas's downfall was scantily reported and the inquisition showed its strength by not even being shaken. The important thing was that his conduct as an inquisitor had not been impugned.

Lardner and his Hollywood colleague Lester Cole would tell after their jail year, 1950–51, of a substantial posterior which they espied protruding from a hencoop in the Danbury penitentiary. The attached head slowly emerged, identi-

* Nearly 20 years later the Los Angeles *Times,* formerly among the journals most thirsty for heretical blood, published a cool article about the grotesqueries of the affair. It mocked the patriots who testified for HUAC and traced the victims' fate on Hollywood's blacklist after they left jail. Forgetting the Dies Committee of 1938, the writer described heresy as having been so "chic" in prewar Hollywood that one had to join the Party to be "in."

fying the whole as J. Parnell Thomas. Lardner had been assigned to the administration office, Cole to the gardens, and Thomas's duties consisted of removing the chickens' ejectamenta. There followed the kind of frank exchange peculiar to men in varied walks of life who have fallen afoul of the law. For a moment it seemed as if, after all, America had not yet lost its sense of humor.

VII

1947: "I Am Not

and Have Never Been"

Two years after the hurrahs for the Red Army died away, the Communist conspiracy was being presented to America on a giant screen. The recurrence of national paranoia in America every 20-odd years is a familiar theme, but this outburst would differ from all others. The inquisition was now institutionalized, to be run by a bureaucracy with speedy access at all levels to the media and to electronic dossiers.

Most citizens accepted the likelihood of a third world war, and all classes resigned themselves to possible combing of their pasts for suspicious words, actions and contacts. Swearing loyalty to the flag became a nationwide trend. The decisive impulse for this came from a US Chamber of Commerce brochure in January 1947. The Chamber's view of the crisis, inspiring one of Nixon's first Congressional speeches, coupled heretics in government with the New Deal's "cynical betrayal" at Yalta. The brochure proposed that the CP be outlawed. The American Legion and DAR were pressing for this step but it was hardly serious, the CP being the domestic cold war's foundation stone without which Hoover would have been practically out of business.

Truman's Loyalty Order in March expanded the inquisition from a committee to an all-government enterprise. The order required 2,200,000 persons on the federal payroll to swear that they never directly or indirectly associated with any of 78 organizations listed by Attorney General Clark, and to take the consequences of slips of memory. "Organizations" included publications, the reading of which at any time must be denied under oath or explained with the full ritual of penitence. Perhaps one of every 100 Americans might at some time have had some connection—or known someone who had—with one of the proscribed groups or journals; only a handful of the other 99 had ever heard of them, except for the CP which had become the nation's most publicized organization. The connection could have been giving a dollar or signing a petition.

A "screening" apparatus for which Congress allotted $11,000,000 opened the widest opportunities yet for citizens of inquisitorial bent. Invited to come and speak freely about any deviant acquaintance, they could rely on the government's absolute discretion: not even the person they named would ever learn their identity nor what they had said about him. As Eric Goldman told it nine years later in his *Rendezvous with Destiny*, "liberals shuddered"; but the stage was set with a judicious eye on their gooseflesh. Truman assured the two million that it was being done "to safeguard their rights," and set up a commission to "study civil rights" which would call in October for "a rebirth of freedom." Meanwhile the choice for first recipient of a jail term for perjuriously pledging loyalty fell on

Rhodes scholar Carl Marzani, whose father had emigrated from Italy to avoid pledging loyalty to Mussolini. Now making films for United Electrical Workers, Marzani had taken an Intelligence job in the war but, with the understanding of officials who needed his services and could not otherwise obtain them, had denied previous heresies. He was left to face the dilemma substantially alone, the intelligentsia being as aware as the involved officials that any word for him would kill their own careers. He would have three years in which to compile, from hygienic sources available in the prison library, a book on the origins of the cold war.*

The last organized move against loyalty oaths, which the public soon accepted as part of the scenery, would be a lawsuit against Attorney General Clark in 1949 by 26 post office workers. They were among 7,600 suspects engaged in sorting and delivering mail. A year after the first firing (June 1947) of persons showing up red in the ideological litmus tests, a respectable firm published a book about it. In *Washington Witch Hunt,* journalist Bert Andrews related the experience of a State Department man, "Mr. Blank," who was suspected of "association with representatives of foreign powers." FBI men had trailed Blank and he had ended up before the Department's loyalty testers: they said this was his opportunity to make a statement. About what? "Delve," they said, "in your mind into some of the factors that have gone into your career." He swore he belonged to nothing.

"Well, just go ahead and spill your feelings about all the things that you think might have been involved."

Blank delved and spilled that he once edited a pamphlet on the high cost of milk, and once had a neighbor who worked for Russian War Relief. He hastened to add that he was "completely in accord with what our government has been doing" and "working night and day for it." The testers' faces remained impassive. "Gentlemen," he cried, "I don't know what to talk about. I mean, I am . . ."

When liberal Elmer Davis suggested on the air that the Blank case made America "ridiculous in the eyes of the world," Truman assured reporters that "there will be no witch hunt." Secretary of State Marshall accorded Blank and other suspects the privilege of resigning. Still jobless eight months later, Blank was mortgaged to the hilt to feed his family. By then Department security chief Robinson—"the scion of an old and fine family" (Andrews)—who had fired Blank, was trying to account to the testers for an item in his own dossier: the possession of a heretical second cousin. This time Marshall demanded "fairness and decency"; Assistant Secretary Peurifoy was "quite frankly, disturbed," and Robinson was returned to his desk to continue purging his colleagues. Andrews sportingly offered Hoover space to rebut the charge that his Bureau, which supplied the "derogatory information" but would not disclose it, was acting "reprehensibly." On the contrary, Hoover explained, it was performing its Loyalty Order duties with constant care to "prevent injustice," checking each federal employee against its 105,000,000 sets of fingerprints. As an example, Hoover cited the case of a man alleged to have distributed heretical literature: "We assigned the matter to the field for investigation. It was established that the person engaged in Communist activities, although having the same name, was not the Federal employee."

* *We Can Be Friends* (Topical Books, New York, 1952).

As these watch-dog boards proliferated, loyalty-testing created far more employment than it cut off. Up to mid-1948, when Truman stretched his order to cover employees of industries filling military contracts, 438 persons would resign rather than sign; only a few hundred would ever be fired under the program, but thousands barely survived the ordeal and remained under a shadow of fear. Some who confessed to a past fall from grace would implore inquisitors to believe that their motives were never socialistic. A *Yale Law Journal* writer (March 1952) cited an "elderly lady" who, having "belonged to organizations for helping the Negro," was "completely panicked and became violently ill" at the misinterpretation of her "strictly Christian" ideals. A man was investigated on a neighbor's report of having seen him and others through the window, sitting on the floor and singing songs in a strange language. The neighbor logically concluded that "since Communists were strange and the scene observed was strange, the two elements must be identical"; the man finally persuaded his inquisitors that it was a Zionist ritual. Another man ("as it happened, always an anti-Communist") lost his job on a "charge that he was once a member of a sport team that included a Communist." Among questions used to test loyalty were whether the suspects ever listened to Hanns Eisler's music, or read Fast's novels, or were "extremists about civil liberties." On rare occasions the wording of the FBI report on the suspect—although never the informant's identity—came to light. One such, on a highly paid government employee of 15 years' standing, included the passage: "That the informant was present when the employee advocated the CP line, such as favoring peace and civil liberties . . . Another informant reportedly advised that while informant didn't have any concrete specific pertinent information reflecting adversely on the employee's loyalty, informant is of the opinion that employee's convictions concerning equal rights for all races and classes extend slightly beyond the normal feelings of the average individual."

Hoover's staff already faced a heavy backlog in "processing" names from heretical journals' subscriber lists (available through the post office) and from petitions, circulated through the years and now dug up, to put this heretic on the ballot or free that one from jail. The new Niagara of names pouring in from loyalty boards, running FBI men off their feet in the effort to visit them all and keep dossiers up-to-date, put the inquisitorial Parkinson's law into full operation. Journal subscribers and organization memberships were naturally declining, but as Hoover explained in his annual requests for a higher budget, subversiveness rose as more work was done by more people to reduce it. A fall in membership only heightened the danger, for it was a conspirator's very nature when the heat was on to pretend that he had stopped conspiring. Hence the continual need for more agents and informers to gather names from still wider circles.

Local testing enthusiasts did not rely on the federal program but set up their own. For example, Detroit's mayor installed a three-man board upon discovery by the press of a plot to "poison the water supply and take over." The oath vogue involved special headaches for the army after the draft was reintroduced, and for the growing number of scientists whose work was connected with war production. Any scientist who ever offered milk to a stray cat might be betraying secrets; and inquisitors, having no clue as to what was or might be of security importance, decided that everything was. The morale of scientists, at a loss to know whom they could talk to about what, sank to an all-time low just when the Pentagon most needed them.

The domestic and foreign cold wars continued to synchronize as the Taft-Hartley labor law emerged in June, along with the Marshall Plan named after the Secretary of State. The Plan, sending dollars after friendly occupation troops to crippled capitalist* nations, put UNRRA in an unmarked grave and completed the West Europeans' transformation into junior American Century partners. The law, imposing heavy controls on unions including loyalty certificates for all their officeholders, united AFL and CIO in angry denunciation. Truman was able to remind them that Congress had passed it over his veto, and the clamor subsided with dawning realization that selected labor leaders would also be promoted to Century partnership. To share in the benefits they were required only to purge their ranks of heretics who, after all, were a thorn in their flesh. The government had indicted Minneapolis UAW leader Harold Christoffel for perjury in denying Budenz's assertion that he was a Communist, but it would be happy to leave the inquisitorial chore to the unions. Unions declining the invitation exposed themselves to a joint government-AFL-CIO onslaught. By September even Curran was showing unaccustomed fealty to the flag, and rumblings of dissension between Quill (who had charged Truman with "treason" in 1946) and the CP began to be heard.

In October Parnell Thomas issued a report on SCHW which inspired carping analysis in the *Law Review* published at Harvard, a university deeming itself so aloof that it refused to fire Harlow Shapley. SCHW was getting distinguished Southerners to host and sponsor Wallace, and again importuning Congress to apply the Constitution to Dixie elections. Professor Walter Gellhorn admitted that .4% of the delegates of SCHW's founding conference in 1938 had been Communists, but doubted that they could have "manipulated" the conference and denied that Thomas had proved Party control of the organization by any recognized standards of law. This was painfully obvious, but SCHW expired within months of the report, which inquisitors would still be using two decades later as a manual on the subversiveness of skin-color-blind groups. Even if some of the 1938 delegates were dupes of a "most deviously camouflaged plot," Thomas showed that many of them had records littered with heresies. Some had expressed concern about Mooney, others had given money to Russian War Relief, and the chairman had "urged freedom for Browder" and defeat for Franco. The Alabaman New Dealers Clifford and Virginia Durr and Aubrey Williams had almost as long a history of heretical contacts as Joseph Gelders,** and SCHW's present administra-

---

* Marshall Plan aid was offered to socialist nations but was rejected—in Czechoslovakia's case, under pressure from Moscow—because of its obvious political strings. Russia had asked and been promised a stringless rehabilitation loan from America but had never received it. A cardinal object of the Plan was to swing votes away from the Communist parties of France and Italy, then enjoying peak popularity.

** Gelders had risen to master sergeant as an army electronics teacher during the war and then became an assistant professor at Davis, California. His last heresy was resigning rather than sign the university loyalty oath. He died soon afterwards, partly (his relatives say) from long-term effects of the beating [for biracial labor organizing activities in the 30s—see Part One, Chapter II]. In 1969 three draft-age grandsons named after him were declining to join in the massacre of Vietnamese.

tor James Dombrowski and chairman Clark Foreman had each published a book, one on *Early Days of Christian Socialism,* the other on *The New Internationalism* (in which two Communists were quoted "sympathetically"). Dombrowski, along with 450 professors, bishops and others, had defended Communists' right to exist and was a co-founder of Myles Horton's Highlander Folk School in rural Tennessee where copies of the *Worker* had been seen.

The report convinced Gellhorn that HUAC was "either intolerably incompetent or designedly intent upon publicizing misinformation," but he missed the point. The object was to scare away "dupes" who still thought a cause more important than the company one kept in working for it. What Gellhorn missed was quickly grasped by most SCHW sponsors including Florida's senator, Claude Pepper, who had chatted with Stalin in 1945 and was "proudly presenting" Wallace as Roosevelt's spiritual heir. Although the report blandly misquoted him, Pepper had indeed suggested that the cold war was unnecessary, and now he vanished from the heretical scene apologizing obsequiously—but still not enough to survive in the Senate.

SCHW sponsors fell away in shoals, leaving the isolated rump to struggle on in the affiliated Southern Conference Educational Fund. Aubrey Williams, former National Youth Administration chief who had been rejected for a new government job in 1945, accepted SCEF's chairmanship and returned to Alabama to edit the weekly *Southern Farm & Home.* His paper thrived and took 15 years of inquisitorial effort to kill. Clifford Durr had to resign as Federal Communications Commissioner early in 1948 after he had defended purged radio commentators and his wife had accepted the northern Virginia chairmanship of Wallace's Progressive Party.* Indignation at HUAC's efforts came oddly—and by definition, ineffectually—from the self-flagellating ACLU, which found that Thomas was "exposing red plots that did not exist." The job done on SCHW was timely since Dixie had reopened the lynching season, and mild liberals were also protesting about Mississippi's death sentence on the Negro Willie McGee and about the gouging of a black veteran's eyes for refusing to move to the back of a North Carolina bus.

But HUAC, as we have seen, was becoming a mere section of the inquisition. A Detroit Congressman undertook an independent crusade against "red art termites" infecting the public with their canvases. Rep. George Dondero had a record of loyal attitudes based on his experience with aggressive auto workers. On the eve of Pearl Harbor he had pointed out that not the Axis but "the trend of socialism and Communism threatens destruction of our form of government"—

---

* The Durrs continued fattening their dossiers wherever they went. In the summer of 1948 (along with O. John Rogge, radio writer Norman Corwin, the *Nation's* Freda Kirchwey, and Otto Nathan representing his friend Einstein) they attended a peace congress in Poland. In 1949 Durr participated in the Waldorf-Astoria conference (see chapter XI) and, as president of the heretical NLG, assailed thought-control and guilt-by-association laws before a Senate committee. (He was not thrown from the room as was the next witness, Arthur Schutzer of Marcantonio's American Labor Party, but the two senators present showed their feelings by carrying on a private causerie as he spoke.) In 1950 in Denver, where Durr took a job as counsel for the National Farmers Union, his wife caused a scandal by signing an international peace appeal at the request of DuBois. They returned, uncontrite but broke, to Alabama where Mrs. Durr was observed in another disreputable scene—shaking hands with a Negro.

a form which, he added, "was never democracy—democracy is mob rule." He had ascribed France's collapse in 1940 to "the 40-hour week." His vigilance had been turned to art by the State Department's purchase, for a touring exhibition, of 79 canvases by Americans whose thoughts had not even been tested. Secretary Marshall perceived the error and had the collection disposed of as army surplus.

The inquisition of teachers was logically resumed, and New York was more than ever the place to begin: its Teachers Union leader was soon to find peace of mind in a monsignor's arms ("We both knelt before a statue of Our Lady") and knew all the names. The hundreds of heretics who had known Bella Dodd through the years were flabbergasted by the change in her: their unanimous view, according to a contemporary on the Hunter College faculty, had been that "if you can't trust Bella, you can't trust anyone." But for TU members and students whom she had influenced she was a time bomb now that she was beginning to recognize Communism as "the most reactionary backward step in history" and everything her Party did, from supporting Spain to leadership of the union itself, as sinister. She never claimed to have been a spy but (in her later book of confessions) took a Bentleyan stance toward her former comrades. They were "warm-hearted people like myself" but had "moved like thieves in the night to disrupt this country" in their support of the war. She had picked the high-school French teacher Rose Russell as her union successor because of Russell's "human approach." She herself had developed her "deepest loyalty" to the Party after the Russo-German pact and had remained "completely involved" through the war; but it had been revealed to her that the better schools, playgrounds and teacher conditions for which the union fought would not "cure a sick soul" since "God is the cure for godlessness." She was shy to appear publicly as an informer but would finally "recognize that in the best sense of the word to 'inform' means to educate." Her confessions showed that, always needing a Church, she had found the Roman Catholic one (with its inscrutable God to blame for the blood it shed) better than the Communist one which had to explain all its sins.

Ex-heretics employed to expose their former comrades in the media were becoming an important arm of the inquisition. The Hearst papers had two— Howard Rushmore and George Sokolsky—in addition to the formerly New Dealish columnist Westbrook Pegler, who suffered more from dyspepsia than contrition. The Scripps-Howard chain picked Frederick Woltman. As Pittsburgh ACLU leader in the 20s, Woltman had been jailed for defending repressed coal miners by police who insisted he was "in the pay of Lenin," and fired from Pittsburgh University where he was a philosophy instructor. Now he won the Pulitzer Prize for unmasking his unrepentant friends. On the air, the most handsomely recompensed detectors of plots were Fulton Lewis, Jr., and Walter Winchell. Heretics found that libel actions against these experts were as fatal as answering HUAC questions. Moving now into education, the Chicago *Tribune's* man found Harvard, Yale and Princeton to be "infected with pedagogic termites," and Woltman joined the Brooklyn *Tablet,* a journal traditionally lauding Roman Catholic anti-Semites, in promoting a Board of Education trial of a suspect teacher. Like most teachers probed over the next years, this one was Jewish and a partisan of Negro, Puerto Rican and other minority-group children. Firings began on the university level with Lyman Bradley, German department head at New York University, who was en route to jail for not naming his JAFRC associates to HUAC. To tackle the problem in Washington and California, legislatures of those states set up the Canwell and Tenney committees. State Senator Jack Tenney, an ex-heretic noted for his song "Mexicali Rose" and the dictum "Communists and people from Hollywood are the same thing," was pushing 15 bills affecting education, one of which would ban all "politically controversial subjects." Not all states moved as fast, but the effect was visible at teacher institutes held in the fall. National and world issues were gingerly avoided, and University of Illinois education professor John DeBoer saw written across the gatherings "in large letters the word FEAR."

Schools began to ban tainted literature from their libraries: Fast's *Citizen Tom Paine* in New York and Detroit, the *Nation* (a weekly still portraying New Deal ideas as respectable, and earning its own anathema for its refusal to anathematize all Communists) in Newark, Arthur Miller's anti-anti-Semitic novel *Focus* in the Bronx. Miller stood at the crossroads with respect to heretical contacts and behavior. While his Broadway success *All My Sons* promised fame and fortune, he aroused new doubts by attending the production of one of his plays at a youth festival in Prague. An Oregon high-school principal declined to remove from his shelves John Steinbeck's *Grapes of Wrath* (destitute migratory workers) and Lillian Smith's *Strange Fruit* (lynching) and was forced to resign. Protests across the country were few and faintly heard. The clearest dissident voice was that of 75-year-old Alexander Meiklejohn. After a half-century of studying Anglo-Saxon democratic precedents, he still insisted that the Bill of Rights meant self rule by a people fully exposed to all arguments. He regarded as spurious the current rationalization for curbing those rights—that there was a "clear and present danger." The more dangerous the times, he believed, the more criticism was needed.

With some hedging on the "clear and present danger" thesis the University of Chicago's Robert M. Hutchins, Columbia University historian Henry Commager, Harvard's Zechariah Chafee and Supreme Court Justices Douglas and Black all supported Meiklejohn's position. For Thomas Mann, now an American, the issue was colored by the specter which had exiled him but permanently cured his allergy to politics. When millions were staking their lives for "a freer, juster world" he had predicted that they would not get it if America, "unmindful of its own revolutionary traditions, allied itself with a has-been order to subdue every revolutionary tendency." He had seen "irrational fear of socialism drive so many into the arms of Fascism"; yet he remained hopeful for a country where he could say so and stay out of jail.

While these sages advanced the open mind as the key to peace, Bertrand Russell was proposing in the *Times* that the Russians be threatened with atomization if they continued rejecting America's Bomb-control plan. Even if West Europe had to be destroyed as a result, wrote the British pacifist, "I think war would be worthwhile. Communism must be wiped out, and world government must be established."* The Russians correctly scouted America's intention of carrying out this now-familiar threat but had other worries. For clandestine insertions of sand into the machinery of socialism, America was putting final touches to the most

---

* In 1956 Russell described this to the author as "the worst thing I ever said and I am sorry I did. It wasn't that I wanted a war or to reform the Russian regime—they have the right to whatever regime they like—but to preserve the peace of the world." In the

grandiose "black" project in history, the Central Intelligence Agency, of which Allen Dulles would soon emerge as director. His record with wartime Intelligence was less than brilliant, but with Russia now the enemy and Germany the ally, and with a secret budget many times more lavish, he was expected to do well. He had learned black intelligence arts from the British, who owed much of their success to stringent laws against divulging any hint of such activities in print.

In America the ingrained public-relations tradition—the urge to publicize what was done, sometimes before it was done—produced an aberration with which the British never had to cope. Within a year Foster Dulles was telling an audience in New York's Waldorf-Astoria Hotel about "Operation X" in which (according to *U.S. News & World Report*) "strongarm squads would be formed under American guidance" and "assassination would be encouraged." By October of 1948 an organization named Common Cause Inc. would be presenting to the press a Russian "vouched for by high American officials" who had assassinated "several hundred Stalinists." For the first time black intelligence had moved into the public-relations field.* The generals resented its infringement on their lethal prerogatives; military experts reflected this in press slurs on its efficiency; and it must needs defend its use of the vast but unspecified sums it received from taxpayers. *Times* expert Hanson Baldwin, for example, wrote of "a year of fiascos" by "young and exuberant intelligence officers making contacts almost openly with anti-Communist leaders" in socialist territory. When the Russians protested in the UN that America was financing terrorism and that they were catching Dulles's agents right and left, "Operation X" was declared to be a myth. But at least America simplified Moscow's intelligence and counter-intelligence problems. Much of what it needed to know could be learned by subscribing for the right publications.

At a time when America had openly forgotten its agreements with regard to Germany, all this no doubt helped push Stalin's paranoia into the chronic stage. Communists showing traces of spontaneous thought and leadership were sent by trainloads to Siberian camps, along with surviving soldiers who had allowed themselves to be surrounded and captured in the war's initial defeats. On the principle that blind loyalty to Russia was more than ever the test of a true socialist, and that he was Russia, Stalin began treating East European socialist governments with a ruthless hand and placed Communist parties under closer supervision in a "Cominform" version of the old Comintern. The American Party, by not joining, failed to dispel the general belief that it never moved except after a call from the Kremlin. One outstanding argument, however, kept alive Higginsian faith in Russia. Visi-

---

interim he had drastically changed his views on America and decided that after the "absolute nightmare" under Stalin, Russia was "getting better; they have let out thousands of political prisoners although for years they have been saying there weren't any . . . In any case we've got to cooperate with them whether we like it or not."

* America continues to perform the feat of running a secret agency which is strenuously publicized. This in 1971 the public was informed that "between 150 and 175 agents stationed in Laos" were running the invasion of that country (purportedly by South Vietnamese) "because the 1962 Geneva agreement on the neutrality of Laos, barring foreign countries from playing a military role, led the US to turn over its assistance to the agency with the greatest experience in undercover activities." Details of this "undercover role" filled a complete column in the *Times* (March 11, 1971).

tors there reported a passionate but logical yearning to avoid a resumption of the bloodbath at any cost short of endangering the socialist state's security. Every Russian, and every Communist throughout the world, was crying "Peace!" and building organizations to bolster it. Free-world spokesmen, however, easily dismissed this as a sample of Russia's well-documented Machiavellianism.

Among the last American politicians to praise "Stalin's peace proposals" with impunity was Wisconsin's senator-elect Joe McCarthy in December 1946. Public figures with liberal hairs on their jackets, such as Adlai Stevenson (then on America's UN delegation) and Acheson, had warned months earlier of Stalin's poised steam roller. The implications of the Truman Doctrine purportedly designed to thwart it were at first "downright frightening" to liberals (Goldman), but they swallowed their tremors on the basis that Russia broke more agreements than America and that this indicated aggressiveness. Heresy tainted intellectuals of the Hitler period turned to sanitary themes or found pressing engagements elsewhere. On a Russian tour in 1947 Steinbeck found no signs of military preparations and the people all wanting to stay friendly with America, but he soon dropped the subject. Hemingway, who once spread defiance of Fascism from inside besieged Madrid, would now be observed from time to time in an African jungle or studying bullfights in re-medievalized Spain.

Yet Nobel Peace Prize judges were still able to find a genuine American recipient in the Quakers' American Friends Service Committee led by Clarence Pickett. Pickett's obstinacy stood out against the uproar in church circles about Yugoslavia's jailing of its Cardinal Stepinac for wartime collaboration with the Germans. Yugoslavia invited American clergy to see for themselves whether it was persecuting religion; but the delegates who went to inspect the situation (Tennessee's Claude Williams, Brooklyn's William Melish and *Churchman* editor Guy Emery Shipler) were too heretical for their report to find space in the media.* Archbishop Cushing of Boston called the report "infamous and monstrous," and a clergyman-headed "Friends of Democracy Inc." pronounced the *Churchman* to have become so "involved with the CP line" as to be beyond the pale.

Norman Thomas was as persuaded as Bertrand Russell that civilization depended on obliterating Russia—which he found as Fascist as Hitler's Germany "except for racism"—if less specific about the means. In the spring of 1947 he asked how Wallace could possibly be unaware of the Red Army's and the Communist movement's determination to seize the world. Wallace, conceding that Russia's tactics differed little from "the tactics of others," insisted that it could not be expected to do everything America wanted and that peace depended on compromise. In Britain, Sweden and France, and then to large American audiences, he kept talking about a kind of peace which was remote from Establishment calculations. The caliber of his sponsorship in Hollywood** and the fervor he aroused in cities like Detroit, where over 50,000 paraded to hear him on Labor Day, were dis-

---

* Williams privately reported that after visiting numerous churches all filled with the devout, he discovered the country's excellent plum brandy and felt he owed it a higher duty.
** Barred from the Hollywood Bowl and the University of California campus, Wallace spoke to an overflow audience of 30,000 in Los Angeles's Gilmore Stadium. Among his active sponsors at the time, or speakers or fund-donors at the meeting, were Katharine

turbing and mob attacks on his meetings began that fall. In November he headed
for Dixie, where few heard him since he refused to address segregated audiences.
On December 29 he announced his Presidential candidacy for a new third party
against Truman and New York's Governor Thomas E. Dewey, who cited his "gang-
buster" record as qualification for heading the free-world crusade.

Truman made Forrestal his Defense Secretary in that month as a reminder
that his party had equally if not more dedicated crusaders. Acheson endured a
sweatbox ordeal to persuade the Senate Foreign Relations Committee that he, one
of the Marshall Plan's and Truman Doctrine's chief architects, had enough aversion to socialism to preside over the State Department. He had come somewhat
late to the feast and was accused of friendliness with Hiss, now qualifying to become America's top scoundrel. Having (as Elmer Davis later wrote) "the mis-
fortune of being a gentleman and a Christian," Acheson told the senators: "He
and I became friends and we have remained friends." It was the last occasion when
an American could take such a position without the roof falling in, and perhaps
the action for which posterity would remember Acheson. He began his term of
office by forging the NATO alliance of anti-socialist "Atlantic" regimes regardless of geography, involving (as he promised the Senate it would not) the permanent presence of American armies in Western Europe.

Hepburn, José Ferrer, Paul Draper, Zero Mostel, Lillian Hellman, Canada Lee, Uta
Hagen, Robeson, Chaplin, Edward G. Robinson, Dorothy Parker, John Garfield, Hedy
LaMarr, Frank Tuttle, Budd Schulberg and Paul Henreid. Pauling was a speaker at Los
Angeles, and California's ex-Attorney General Kenny (NLG president in 1946) chaired
the meeting.

VIII

1948: Henry A. Stalin

Wallace's Presidential candidacy on a platform reflecting the UN Charter, just when peaceful socialist-capitalist coexistence was the motif of all Communist parties, presented an obvious line to the Establishment. It was not the Party that was supporting him; he was supporting the Party and hence was Stalin's tool. The same applied to all who joined forces with him, from Minnesota's New Deal governor Benson to Pete Seeger, who sang at the Progressive Party's founding convention; from Robeson and DuBois to Iowan farm-journal publisher Fred Stover; from UE president Albert Fitzgerald to Yugoslav-immigrant author Louis Adamic. A partisan of Tito who was now beginning to quarrel with Stalin (but inquisitors had no time for fine distinctions), Adamic showed his colors by publishing a "Slavic-American friend's" remark to him at the convention: "I have been a US citizen for 28 years, but this is the first time I really feel I am an American, that I belong, that this is my country and I can exercise my responsibility toward it."

Such appraisals, in direct negation of what the media had to say, could only appear in a journal like *National Guardian* to which three heretical ex-film critics, James Aronson, Cedric Belfrage and John McManus, gave birth in 1948. Out of some 1,800 commercial dailies, two and a quarter published Wallace's viewpoints fully and without distortion.* The two were the New York *Star,* a successor to the recently defunct *PM* which had tried to stay alive without advertising, and the *Gazette and Daily* published in York, Pennsylvania, by wealthy Pennsylvania Dutchman Josiah Gitt. Gitt compounded the heresy of becoming state PP chairman by printing a trial-run *National Guardian* without charge. The one-quarter was Ted Thackrey, whose wife published the New York *Post* and allowed him to write positively about Wallace in an otherwise hostile setting: the political split soon led to divorce as in many other such families.

The 3,240 convention delegates with their unprecedented representation of minority groups greeted Wallace rapturously although there was an uneasy feeling that, behind the words, the fire for "the common man" burned less deeply than in other PP leaders. He called for a progressive capitalism which would "stop the creation of fear" and "place human rights above property rights" instead of escalating war preparations far into the billions. For many delegates he was asking for a miracle, but he clearly did not think so and it was theoretically viable in the American context. He resisted pressure (which did not come from the CP) to advocate minimal nationalization, and also to condemn "totalitarianism of the Left no less than of the Right," a phrase to which liberals attributed talismanic properties.

---

* For documentation of media treatment of the Wallace campaign and the media's role throughout these years, see James Aronson, *The Press and the Cold War,* Bobbs-Merrill, Indianapolis-New York, 1970.

Norman Thomas, himself a Presidential candidate who would get 140,000 votes, labeled Wallace "a Communist captive preaching peace by blind appeasement." For UAW president Walter Reuther, Wallace was "a lost soul used by Communists . . . a tool of Soviet policy." Reuther had shown genius in eliminating competitors for union leadership—all of whom had voted to bar Communists from office—by labeling them red. Combining this maneuver with fiery militancy and a flair for publicity, he drew compliments from intellectuals for an "anti-Stalinism" which was "never vulgar."

The intelligentsia overwhelmingly adopted the Establishment line on the PP's origins or kept quiet. In fact there had been prolonged Party conclaves as to whether to back Wallace, and the decision had been made under the delusion that CIO could be induced to lead the parade. But Dwight MacDonald and Arthur Schlesinger, Jr., easily fricasseed these conclaves with excerpts from *Pravda* into proof that Moscow hatched the conspiracy, while Budenz revealed that the Party had not only had Wallace "in custody" ever since his return from Moscow in 1944, but had chosen Frederick Field to be his puppet Secretary of State. Mac-Donald, unable to shake off his gloomy mood about America, had ceased to believe in anything except that whatever might benefit Russia must be attacked. He proved in articles, radio talks and a book that Wallace, in addition to being a Kremlin footman, was a racist and lacked moral courage.

The actual PP pattern was that Wallace often made major decisions without consulting his advisers, most of whom were on the heresy's most nearly respectable fringe. He insisted against staff advice on using leftist phrases and talking too much about Russia, and chided his chief speech writer (no Communist, but accused of reddening up the speeches) as "too conservative, always holding me back." Communists in PP clubs varied their behavior from steam-roller attempts at domination to patient attention to contrary views; clubs where the latter prevailed were invariably more successful. Sometimes Communists became "a terrific pain in the neck" trying to use the Progressive Party as a recruiting ground for their own.*

A state PP in which Communists played a particularly small role was Massachusetts, although Herbert Philbrick, Boston's clean-cut Communist-for-the-FBI since early war years, had another version which would lift him to eminence. An $18-a-week door-to-door salesman when he began reporting from the inside on anti-Fascist groups, he had continued a poor earner from regular jobs but his living standards had risen. He would later claim to have been "one of the six top YCL leaders in the New England states," a CP "executive" and "chairman of leaflet production" who "went from cell to cell leading educational discussions," but

---

*Quoted from the three-volume PP history *Gideon's Army* by Curtis MacDougall, Northwestern University journalism professor and PP senatorial candidate in Illinois. MacDougall weighed meticulously the evidence that the Party fathered the PP and found it "weak." He examined the party's errors, raised "might-have-been" questions, and gave a detailed campaign-year account leading to dim conclusions about American electoral democracy. This case study of a third-party challenge is indispensable for students of the electoral system but few know it exists. MacDougall spent three years researching and writing it and after 36 publishers rejected it, it was issued in 1965 by the heretical firm of (Carl) Marzani & Munsell—a guarantee of its going virtually unnoticed.

ex-comrades could only remember him as an efficient, if torpid, mimeographer.*
Beginners' Marxist classes which the "leader of educational discussions" began
attending shortly before he surfaced were a good source of fellow students' names,
and Philbrick attended in 1948 a discussion of "world events in the light of
Lenin's *State and Revolution*" led by MIT mathematician Dirk J. Struik.

The Struik evening would figure prominently in Philbrick's early testimony
along with Wallace's visit to Boston: as an assistant advertising man for a theatre
company, Philbrick was one of a PP committee to revise Wallace's speech draft.
The revisions were necessary because Wallace included too much about Russia
and too little about such prosy issues as rising prices and the St. Lawrence Seaway.
It ended as one of Wallace's milder speeches, but no committee member could
recall Philbrick offering any suggestions.

At one point in the campaign Wallace called CP support a liability which
would cost him four million votes; but the sole alternative to accepting it was to
conduct his own inquisition, turning the co-existential essence of the movement
into a mockery. The core issue which he thought he could bring to the voters was
whether America would even discuss compromise with Russia, but the decision
that it would not was already taken and both of the traditional parties had been so
advised. In 1948 the word "peace" unprefaced by expletives against Stalin was an
instant identification of heretics, who futilely argued that Russia was the country
with which peace must be made and that they were not in a position to decide who
should govern it.

A June opinion poll predicted 10,000,000 PP votes, but by convention time
there was no chance of electing a Progressive dogcatcher. Intellectuals crowded into
the sternly Russophobe Fair Deal organization, Americans for Democratic Action.
Black leaders switched from praise to loyal reproof of the candidate who was
pelted with eggs in Dixie for refusing to countenance police-segregated audiences,
and of the only party making a national fuss about the special law-and-order system for blacks.** Negroes who supported Wallace spoke for themselves rather
than for organizations. DuBois found Wallace "the one man worthy of [Negro]
support" although his chances were "about nil . . . At least we can let the country
and the nations know that there are people in the US who are not stupid, who are
not to be bought with graft and fooled with lies." Soon afterwards the increasingly
cautious NAACP, for which he had been working again since 1944, fired DuBois
for "insubordination." When the "father of African liberation" (as young leaders

---

* One, who would be arrested for "anarchy" after Philbrick named him, reminisced:
"I can say from first hand that to put him in any office was the equivalent of abolishing
that office. He would do absolutely nothing except occasionally cut a stencil. There were
weeks at a time when we did not even see him"—weeks when, as he would reveal, he was
compiling almost continuous reports for Hoover on Bostonian heretics.
** In Georgia during 1948 Rosa Ingram and her two sharecropper sons, who had defended her against a white landlord's assault, were jailed for life; Amy Mallard, after
identifying the white murderer of her husband, was herself arrested while the murderer
was acquitted. In Martinsville, Virginia, seven young Negroes were jailed for rape (sentenced to death May 1949). Trenton, N.J., sentenced six Negro lads to death for a murder they could not have committed. Mississippi sentenced McGee to death for rape for
the third time since 1945, and an apparently white man to five years for "miscegena-
tion" (he married a white girl but had a Negro grandmother).

in that continent began calling him) joined Robeson in a Council on African Affairs, the Council's secretary complained of red infiltration and the Attorney General added it to his list. The few SCHW-SCEF race-equalitarians who had defied the inquisition stuck with Wallace although Aubrey Williams implored him from Alabama to "repudiate those New York sharpies." Even if Williams was referring to some but not all Communists, he asked the impossible. A new party needed millions of signatures merely to go on the ballot, and only the CP could mobilize the Higginses to plod from door to door collecting them.

The rout of liberals who had hailed Wallace as a savior in 1946–47, when he was saying the same things as in 1948, was undignified but understandable. The Establishment barrage thundered from every side. Bernard Shaw wasted his time advising Americans from England, through the purged and audienceless radio commentator Johannes Steel, that "Wallace is the only candidate who can do something about the international situation because he knows something about it." This might have been true if his global experience under Roosevelt had not been turned into contrary myths by a bombardment of facts fit for patriots. His visit to China in 1944, when he had successfully recommended more aid to Chiang and replacement of American officials who despised the man, became a "sellout of Chiang to the Communists." Budenz exposed his claim to have called on Stalin in that year to speed victory in the war: it was now firmly in the mythology that Wallace had "given the atom" to Russia. Somehow he had also become a partner with the Treasury's Morgenthau and Dexter White in their plot to "pastoralize Germany" to prevent further aggressions. There could be no blacker charge in the year of America's supreme Christian gesture toward Germany—the reprieve of Buchenwald commander Koch's wife Ilse, who outdid any Krafft-Ebing specimen by constructing lampshades from the skin of inmates she considered bedworthy.

When Wallace spoke at the PP convention, the costliest exercise in reversing German and Russian war roles had been begun with the food airlift to gallant Berliners. Left by lack of a peace treaty as a hippogriffic island in Russian's occupation zone, West Berlin was a perfect stage for this melodrama. America had but to issue a separate currency for its segment of the half-capitalist, half-socialist city to force the Russians into "blockading" or facing an economic madhouse. The fact that the blockaded Berliners were West Berliners, and that the part of Germany occupied by "the Allies" was West Germany, struck a wholesome note in itself. After the unfortunate Koch interregnum the Germany that had been saved for capitalism was once more securely "Western" along with America, England and France, as against "Eastern" or "Asiatic" Russia and its cohorts. "Europe" was now the capitalist part of that continent, the remainder of it being "the Iron Curtain." This included not only eastern Germany but Czechoslovakia, where the Communist Party (the country's largest) bloodlessly took power in February. To Wallace both the socialization of Czechoslovakia and the Russians' response to the Berlin currency issue seemed logical and inevitable if regrettable; but each attempt to explain this to a public yearning for black and white formulations made him easier to portray as Stalin's accomplice. A political simplicist's vocabulary had been popularized and Wallace was not even using it.

No one whose economy remotely depended on the Establishment could support Wallace with impunity. That this included labor leaders was made clear by the perjury conviction in March of Wallaceite UAW leader Harold Christoffel, whom a Senate committee including John Kennedy had tenaciously bullied for swearing he was not a Communist.* In the same month Michael Quill, whom black familiar Manning Johnson had "identified as a Communist," fell in behind Truman along with Joseph Curran, A. F. Whitney and earlier converts, leaving a foolhardy few like Harry Bridges and Albert J. Fitzgerald to beat against the tide with "woolly-minded Wallace." The CIO fired Bridges from its North California directorship and was ready to oust all affiliated unions refusing to repudiate the new party. Bridges's union was the exception in being able to flourish under the pressure and purges: in September it staged another waterfront strike which won demands after a nine-week struggle. But organized labor was becoming a qualitatively different element in society. With only fragments of it in his camp, Wallace headed not a movement but a congeries of individual heretics whom inquisitors would pick off one by one.

HUAC had entered the year with a $200,000 budget, and in the Senate Nevada's Pat McCarran and Mississippi's James Eastland began displaying their qualifications for inquisitor-in-chief. In April a bill fathered by inquisitors Karl Mundt and Nixon passed the House under which a new body, the Subversive Activities Control Board, would require heretical groups to "register" as traitors. Nixon, the House's coming man, would have the credit for this advanced legislation stolen from him when it emerged in 1950 as the McCarran Act. In July a New York grand jury ended a year's probe of Bentley's and Budenz's spy lists, finding no provable spies but indicting the 12 top CP leaders under the Smith Act. Then Chambers, his memory refreshed by Nixon, began to recall that he had known Hiss in the 30s not only as a Communist but as a spy; and Foster Dulles, who had appointed Hiss director of the Carnegie Endowment for International Peace in 1946, promptly demanded his resignation. The lifelong habit of prying in wastepaper baskets and "collecting and creating suspects, secretly appraising and tagging them for possible use"** stood the "senior editor of *Time*"—as he had now become —in good stead. Among his other recollections was that 63-year-old, white-haired Communist and Bryn Mawr graduate Grace Hutchins had been threatening his life ever since he went bourgeois.

Bentley (now earning modest fees for "I was a Russian spy" lectures at Catholic academies) and Budenz captured front pages by publicly naming their spies to House and Senate inquisitors. Most of those named were active Wallaceites. Appearing in a burst of BLONDE SPY QUEEN, SECRET CELL and APPARATUS headlines, Bentley felt a "terrible sadness" watching "my old comrades as they testified." With "flash-bulbs popping, newsreel cameras grinding, and television!" this changed to "a great cleansing anger" as she perceived that

---

*Christoffel had led strikes at Wisconsin's Allis-Chalmers plants in 1941 and again in 1946–47. Kennedy, a freshman in Congress, led the demand for Christoffel's conviction and upbraided the Supreme Court for reversing it on a technicality; Christoffel was retried and jailed. In his first decade in politics, the future President strayed once from the pro-inquisitorial path when he opposed the McCarran-Walter Act in 1952. He helped Nixon's and Smathers' campaigns to keep liberals Helen Gahagan Douglas and Claude Pepper out of the Senate, and adopted a consistently friendly or neutral stance toward McCarthy.

**Meyer Zeligs, *Friendship and Fratricide*, Viking, New York, 1967.

they were all "spiritually dead" while "I am alive." The word "spiritual" was not entirely appropriate. One of her spies, Dexter White, was removed from pillory to cemetery and inquisitorial mythology by a heart attack after his HUAC appearance.* Another, William Remington, sued Bentley for libel, won an out-of-court settlement, and paid a higher price than Hiss for denying a familiar's accusation: he would be jailed for perjury and battered to death by a fellow convict. Three others—former New Deal officials John J. Abt, Charles Kramer and Lee Pressman, who had joined Wallace's general staff—became notorious "Fifth amendment Communists" overnight after defying the inquisitors' $64 question. No one, however, had yet called Wallace's top organizer, C. B. Baldwin, a Communist. (Among hundreds consigned to the economic ghetto by loyalty boards that summer was Veterans' Administration employee James Kutcher, both of whose legs had been blown off in the war. A committee headed by Meiklejohn would fight the case for years but, since Kutcher was a Trotskyist, the CP ignored it.)

In a resumed onslaught on TU, headlines were captured by Board of Education inquisitor George A. Timone, an admirer of Franco. The union having supported the extinct republic, it seemed as if the Spanish war were being resumed on another front. With Hoover's and other agents prowling the schools for heretical data, and the media exposing academic "rats' nests," only in one other state—California—were organized teachers still taking anti-cold war positions, and their AFL union expelled them in 1948 after a HUAC probe. HUAC held its second Los Angeles hearings of the year with a third of the subpenas issued to leading Wallaceites. (Their party had "followed every twist and turn of the CP line with mechanical precision . . . an American tool of the international Communist conspiracy.") On election eve Hoover's men, in another smooth dawn raid on homes, marched six Los Angeles Wallaceites to jail in handcuffs to await a grand jury inquisition. Parnell Thomas, facing embezzlement charges which did not prevent his reelection to Congress, returned to his spy-scientist theme by linking a "Scientist X" with Steve Nelson, now back in Pittsburgh as CP organizer.

Through all this, Wallace continued to quote the War Department view of Russia which many hearers thought he had invented. When he was booed and vilified he would mutter: *"American* people—I don't understand it." His innocence about the price of consorting with Communists was a political marvel, only explainable by the puritanical remoteness of his personality. The violence used against PP campaigners left him calm, although it reduced to near-hysteria some who accompanied him around the country. There was but one murder, that of Charleston, South Carolina, Wallaceite leader Robert New by a fellow Maritime

---

* White appeared before HUAC at his own request, already a sick man from a first heart attack. Afforded the rare privilege of enlarging upon his credo, he told the inquisitors (and was applauded by spectators) that he believed in freedom of religion, speech, thought, criticism and movement and of "choice of one's own representatives in government, untrammeled by machine guns or secret police. I am opposed to arbitrary and unwarranted use of power or authority from whatever source or against any individual or group. Those are the principles I have worked for . . . have been prepared in the past to fight for and am prepared at any time to defend with my life if need be." After his death three days later, his wife was visited by FBI men and by New Hampshire Attorney General Louis C. Wyman, who had a search warrant and departed with a collection of her personal letters as well as White's papers.

Union member who cut "the Communist nigger-lover's" jugular vein with a ten-inch knife. After explaining that New was a "despicable, slick, slimy Communist prowling the waterfront" the patriot got a mild sentence but, upon emerging, was returned to jail for assaulting two small girls. MacDougall was stoned in Illinois; four women were kidnapped and beaten in Georgia; a campaigner was kidnapped, beaten and head-shaved with a penknife in Pontiac, Michigan. Vice Presidential candidate Glen Taylor, a senator from Idaho, was overpowered and hauled to jail for trying to enter a Birmingham church by the "Colored" door. Wallace's greeting in Pennsylvania and Idaho took the form of hurled farm produce as in Dixie.

Meetings at Yale, Louisiana State and other universities were broken up by egg-throwing students crying "Sieg Heil!" and other curious slogans, while police raided a Wallaceite students' meeting in a Chicago apartment and arrested participants. Meeting halls were denied in scores of places and Wallaceite teachers, clergymen and industrial workers were fired or forced to resign by hundreds. Rockwell Kent, artist, carpenter, architect, writer, world traveler and IWO president, running a sideline dairy in Ausable Forks, New York, presented the dairy to two employees when the customers boycotted his milk. In Nebraska such heat was applied by unions that Wallaceite members "years later paled and trembled" recalling it to MacDougall. Detectives openly took fund-givers' names at meetings and the media published full lists of Wallace petition-signers. A Binghamton, New York, judge said he would bar custody of any child to Wallaceite parents. Guardians of the law saw no more reason to protect Wallaceites than gangsters: as Detroit's police commissioner put it, they "ought to be either shot, thrown out of the country or put in jail." Perhaps he was a subscriber to *Look*, which in an August *Could Reds Seize Detroit?* picture-story depicted masked subversives mowing down telephone-exchange girls, radio announcers and power-station attendants and blowing up children on bridges. In El Paso a German Jewish refugee hosted Wallace, who would not stay in segregated hotels, just as new Nazi-style assaults on heretics were reported from West Berlin. "There's nowhere to flee to now," she said to him, "so I'll stay and fight it out here with you."

As the campaign drew to a close, the year's marathon inquisition ground on in Seattle. It focused on the University of Washington, the Pension Union which had led a west coast clamor for "a fair deal for senior citizens," and the Commonwealth Federation, a New Deal hangover which had managed to elect and re-elect heretic Hugh Delacy as a Democrat to Congress. The labor empire of the Teamsters Union's Dave Beck, built by methods widely compared with gang leader Capone's in the same period, had its seat in Seattle and the local Establishment had reached a constructive alliance with him against heretics who were a nuisance to both. To symbolize his acceptance as a gentleman and a scholar he had been invited to join the governing board of the university, where a probe of the faculty was deemed overdue.*

Attorneys and other interrupters were thrown out of the initial hearing by the state legislature's [Albert F.] Canwell committee, which was new at the plot-exposing game but imported national experts to brush in the background. Letter-

* In 1962 Beck would be sent to jail for embezzlement and tax evasion.

head-collector J. B. Matthews named Edward Condon, Linus Pauling, F. O. Mathiessen, political science professor Frederick Schuman, and "idle rich" Frederick Field and Corliss Lamont as Wallaceite "top fellow travelers" in a comprehensive list headed by Einstein. For good measure he threw in Oppenheimer, now a stranger to heretical circles, and Eisenhower: the general, as president of Columbia University, helped the conspiracy by "accepting funds from Poland." Matthews had "5,000 teachers in my files" and cited the "aliases" (anglicizations of difficult foreign names) of certain Communists to show that they were conspiring. Coming to local cases, he estimated the Methodist Church of the Pacific Northwest to be "just a tool." Howard Rushmore, the ex-*Worker* film critic from South Dakota, poignantly described the murder of Trotsky in 1940 and testified that Communists were now spying, sabotaging and engaging in immoralities throughout the land. George Hewitt, an ex-Communist employed by Chiang's Washington lobbyist, the China-trading merchant Alfred Kohlberg, pinpointed philosophy professor Melvin Rader as a Party member to whom he had taught Marxism at a secret New York school in 1938. He had gifts of memory which few familiars, and no one present at the probe, could match. The secret school earned exotic headlines while repentant faculty members informed on their colleagues at a more mundane level. University of Washington president Dr. Raymond B. Allen beamed gratitude on them and on the committee for its unfailing courtesy.

After the legislative inquisitors had cited for contempt each professor who would not say if he was a Communist (Rader persuasively insisted he had never been, and seemed to be off the hook), the university's tenure committee borrowed their robes and got answers. Herbert Phillips (philosophy) and Joseph Butterworth (old English) told the academic tribunal that they were, Ralph Gundlach (psychology) that he was not, others that they had been but had differed with the Party and left it. The academics needed still more testimony from experts about the global conspiracy, and brought familiars Benjamin Gitlow (who had just published a sequel to *I Confess*) and Zack Kornfeder (a Lenin School graduate once on the Party's national committee) to provide it in 30 trial sessions lasting from October to December. Residing 3,000 miles away, and having been expelled from the CP in 1929 and 1934 respectively, Gitlow and Kornfelder had little to say about the matters and defendants before the tribunal but much about the un-Americanism of Marxist texts cited in evidence. For the defense, former Harvard economics teacher Paul Sweezy was permitted to try to explain what Marx was talking about. Gundlach's protestations were frankly disbelieved: he could not, for example, deny organizing forums for JAFRC, which, the prosecution pointed out, made him subversive, incompetent and dishonest. He was fired without out severance pay along with Phillips and Butterworth, on the principle that "Moscow party-line discipline for any extended time" precluded any possibility of "teaching the truth."

The affair effectively strangled organized heresy in Washington, including unions not controlled by Beck; but a unique development showed that coordination between eastern and western inquisitors was still weak. At the insistence of Rader, who had never left the state in 1938 and was determined to prove his innocence of Communism, the local prosecutor issued a warrant for George Hewitt's arrest for perjury. But Hewitt, already helpful in jailing Carl Marzani, was needed to clarify the treason of Hiss amongst others, and he was whisked to New York before the warrant could be served. Requests for his extradition brought no word from New York except that Hewitt had denied being Hewitt, and that a law firm close to ACLU would fight his extradition as a "civil liberties" case. The unorthodox extradition hearing, finally held in mid-1949, was characterized by ringing affirmations of liberty and tirades against the red peril by all attorneys and the judge. The civil-liberties attorneys called Manning Johnson, who had just been caught in flagrant perjury in a deportation case, to confirm Rader's presence at the secret school. The judge reasoned that mere issuance of the warrant against the obvious patriot Hewitt showed Washington state to be a hive of Communists: to return Hewitt there would be "slaughter," and Rader was the one who should be tried.

By now Rader had abundant proofs that he was at a resort in his own state when Hewitt and Johnson placed him in New York, but lacked one document: the resort guest register had "disappeared." Fifteen months after Hewitt's first testimony Rader would convince President Allen of his innocence and receive "exoneration." State Sen. Canwell would admit that his agents had abducted the guest register which showed Hewitt to be a liar; asked what had become of it, he would say: "Much of the reports went through my fireplace."* Hewitt was hospitalized for "aphasia" soon after the hearing while Gundlach, Phillips, Butterworth and their families entered the wilderness of teachers forbidden to teach. They would not be lonely, for seven more university professors had been fired for heresy by the end of 1948. They continued their heresies and found other sources of food and raiment. For some years Phillips, the most impenitent, could only obtain work as a laborer. But he barnstormed schools around the country talking about the academic inquisition, passing the hat for expenses while his wife took in sewing to maintain the home.

The media hailed the election results as "a resounding defeat for Stalin" who, as was now well known, had been running for the Presidency disguised as an Iowa capitalist. Another version of Moscow's attitude came from Mrs. Durr on her return from the Polish peace congress. Russian delegate Ilya Ehrenburg had said to her there: "What is the Progressive Party? Nothing! The great USSR cannot pay attention to a few weak liberals who represent nobody and nothing!"** It was of no concern to the Establishment whether Truman or Dewey won, but Dewey lost by being too rigid and obvious. There was a hint in his voice of what

---

*Washington voters retired Canwell from the legislature, and the state inquisition expired because of legislators' quarrels as to how and by whom it should be run. According to Rader, Canwell set himself up under a McCarthy portrait in a private-enterprise "American Intelligence Service," combining dossier service with a *Vigilante* newsletter and sale of John Birch Society books. He continued aiming at the University of Washington which, being "located within the strategic invasion path of Russia," Communists made "great efforts to colonize." Johnson's career continued prospering until 1956 when the Supreme Court described him as "completely untrustworthy."
** Mrs. Durr reported Ehrenburg as adding, when New York Communist Joseph Starobin joined the conversation: "What is the Communist Party in the USA? Nothing! Whom does it represent? Nobody! Bah! Take all the Communists, all the Progressives, all the liberals in the USA and put them together, and what do you have? Nothing!"

America was going to get, while Truman, who was committed to and would deliver the same things, promised a cornucopia of peace, joy and abundance for all
except Communists. Voters once inclining toward Wallace had flocked to Truman's banner on the basis that he might mean some of it and that he was at
least electable. Wallace's million-odd ballots were 2.4% of the popular vote compared with 27% and 16% for previous third-party challenges in 1912 and 1924.
The scattered handful of precincts where he won were predominantly Negro, Latin
American and Jewish, and the only Wallaceite elected was Vito Marcantonio of
the PP-affiliated American Labor Party with his long-built-up following.

After the election 18,000 Progressives who had lost little of their enthusiasm filled Madison Square Garden to cheer Wallace and Britain's "Red Dean" of
Canterbury, the Very Reverend Hewlett Johnson. The Dean, commenting on the
complaint of the British minister to Rumania that three detectives followed him
everywhere, said: "In America *four* detectives followed me and slept outside my
door in the Waldorf-Astoria."

Many in Wallace's circle based their optimism on the conviction that another economic crisis was around the corner, and that the miseries of unemployment would overcome fear of voting for peace. "The only way capitalism can
survive," Wallace himself wrote in November, "is to go all-out on one-world
trade." This was old-fashioned thinking in light of the American Century's ingenious slump insurance. By the end of the year 6,000,000 Americans were producing war materials, and, with Forrestal asking for 1949 a military budget almost
double that of 1948, the number kept soaring along with corporation profits.
Yet resistance to the measures against Wallace showed that the heresy had not
been whittled down enough for comfort. It was still too prevalent among Anglo-
Saxons whose ancestors arrived in or shortly after the *Mayflower,* and among scientists, artists, doctors and others whose professions lent prestige and some immunity to economic pressures. Stubborn elements ranged from trade unionists
to aggressive peacemongers of the old feminist school and from black preachers to
small businessmen. The Wallaceites' ability to conduct a Presidential campaign
without going bankrupt testified not only to Higginsian devotion but to deviations
in an excessive minority of moneyed citizens. Three- and four-figure donations had
cascaded into Wallace's treasury in response to a Ritz-Carlton lunch appeal by
Lillian Hellman, who herself chipped in $1,000. Anita McCormick Blaine, the
harvester magnate's 82-year-old daughter who would still have $41,364,236.05
when she died in 1954, had always been on tap for pressing debts. Her contributions expressed her belief in peace and brotherhood and her distaste for "cousin
Bertie" McCormick, who used his share of the patrimony to publish the jingoistic
Chicago *Tribune.*

All in all, the results were no reason to slacken the inquisition but rather
to intensify it. As Truman settled back in his chair, the courts confirmed Marzani's
sentence and the right of Metropolitan Life Insurance to bar Negroes from its
Stuyvesant Town housing project in New York. An election-month incident in
Georgia was too routine to attract attention: a white jury's acquittal of the murderer of the county's only Negro who tried to vote. "He had been fairly warned
not to try," the sheriff explained. HUAC issued a *100 Things You Should Know
about Communism and Religion* brochure describing infiltration into churches by

such heretics as Claude Williams. Whittaker Chambers produced caches of microfilm and State Department papers from a pumpkin and a dumb-waiter shaft, putting Nixon on his way to the White House and Hiss to jail in a flourish of spy headlines.

There were prewar documents said to be in Hiss's and Dexter White's handwriting but nothing to show how or for what purpose Chambers got them, or why, once having them, he simply hid them. Julian Wadleigh, who presumably had supplied at least some, and who had been startled by Chambers's denunciation of such a "very moderate New Dealer" as Hiss, figured in the scandal as an afterthought. He was the last member of the spy apparatus whom Chambers would name, in time for the government to use him for the conviction of Hiss. In the media, HUAC's probe—and the subsequent perjury trials—of Hiss developed into a contest between Hiss and Chambers as to which was the greater perjurer, with Chambers constantly adapting his recollections and Hiss at first denying, then admitting, that he had met Chambers. After Chambers testified that Hiss once told him of seeing a prothonotary warbler, Nixon brought off the coup that put this rare bird into bigger inquisitorial headlines than anything except the pumpkin: casually getting Hiss to say he had seen one. The media cooperated in presenting this as damning evidence that the two men had been on intimate terms.*

The Hiss case had transcendent importance because (to borrow Spanish terminology) he and his wife, who was said to have Judaized along with him, were of purest Castilian blood; he had lofty connections and a brilliant career in the ascendant. Furthermore his presence at Yalta provided endless ammunition for guilt-by-association innuendos on the highest level. It was clear to all that if Hiss could be convicted, anyone could be.

In the Christmas shopping season, when Hiss-Chambers headlines had raised national blood-pressure higher than at any time since Pearl Harbor, the Hisses' Washington friend, Lawrence Duggan, "jumped or fell" from a 16th-floor window. Two Education Board emissaries appeared out of a snowstorm at the Staten

---

* For a detailed analysis of Chambers from early paranoid symptoms to his mysterious death in 1961 (which may or may not have been suicide), the reader is referred to psychiatrist Zeligs's *Friendship and Fratricide*. Zeligs brings out how many aspects of Chambers's personality—homosexual guilt feelings, self-destruction drive, resentment at not being liked, etc.,—were beyond the public's comprehension at the time of the famous "case." Alger and Priscilla Hiss's kindness to Chambers and initial inability to recall him fit logically into their pattern of sheltering stray creatures who came to their door and who sometimes had to be bedded on the floor. Even after Hiss sued Chambers for libel in calling him a Communist in September 1948, Chambers on deep reflection repeated his assertion that he never knew any spies; when he produced his documents to prove the reverse, most of them were dated after he said he turned against the Party (for which he now claimed that he and the "Hiss cell" had done their spying). Of the case's many aspects which remain obscure, one is the political philosophy of Hiss, who never declared his views on socialism nor left traces of being a socialist. The aspect most clearly brought out by Zeligs is that Chambers was a prodigious perjurer by any standards. Few of his less brainy and reputable colleagues equaled him, but no familiar's perjury against a heretic was ever punished. But as former British Lord Chancellor Earl Jowitt conservatively put it in his book on the case, the American climate at the time was "inimical to a calm and dispassionate hearing."

Island school where Minnie Gutride, widow of a Spanish war volunteer, was teaching. She decided to avoid the summons to come and be probed by turning on the gas that night in her lonely apartment. On Christmas night Roosevelt's Under Secretary of State Sumner Welles wandered from his home and was found partially frozen after a night in the snow. He explained on recovery that he had had insomnia since his friend Duggan's death—a remark assuring him instant obscurity in view of Duggan's contacts with Hiss.

IX

1948-49: The Pink Clambake

For all the progress that had been made toward paralyzing the intelligentsia, nothing seemed to remove the smell of roasting children from the nostrils of Hitler's most illustrious gifts to America, Albert Einstein and Thomas Mann. Their belief that the tide could yet be turned rallied morale for more defiance. Scientists were first to respond to Einstein's appeal in April 1948, through ASP's Shapley, for "a strong counterattack" against "the people in power in Washington pushing systematically toward preventive war." America having rejected two Moscow proposals to negotiate an end to cold-war escalations, Einstein modified his previous view that Russia was equally responsible for the tension. Yet he could see no barrier to an understanding that made any sense. Peace was universally desired; America's democratic institutions were being undermined but were "still alive"; and intellectuals had "the duty to see to it that our people's political aspirations gain influence and become dominant while there is still time."

Mann, supporting a Committee for the First Amendment after the Hollywood Ten affair, publicly addressed himself to the inquisitors: since they permitted no elaboration of a denial that one was a Communist, "I have the honor to expose myself as a hostile witness." He told an intellectuals' group in June that he disliked dictatorships and cultural regimentation but "I appreciate the attraction Communism has for the starving and oppressed who have come to know that their misery is unnecessary; who care little or nothing about political liberty, but to whom bread and economic security means all." In the "investigations, defamations and official espionage" to enforce unity based on hatred of Russia, he saw America becoming "something dangerously close to a police state . . . working consistently, and with a sort of clumsy Machiavellianism, in the interest of all that is retrograde and rotten." The same applied to foreign policy: the American-sponsored regime in Greece, for example, was mass-murdering hostages in "outrages which have no parallel, say, in Czechoslovakia." The excuse for such policies was that Russia wanted—as America did—to surround itself with friendly states.

Only three years had passed since Roosevelt said: "The work, my friends, is peace. More than an end of this war—an end to the beginning of all wars: yes, an end forever to this impractical, unrealistic settlement of differences between governments by the mass killing of people." Mann asked: "Was that subversive?" and answered, "Why, yes. The word peace might get you on the Attorney General's blacklist provided you are not yet on it."

The purge especially distressing Mann and Einstein was that of books and of teachers whose views on Franco and similar themes differed from Timone's. An Einstein-headed protest had enlisted some 5,000 university professors and administrators who would still sign the same document as a DuBois, a Matthiessen, a Gundlach, a MacDougall, Temple University's Barrows Dunham and Cornell's Philip Morrison. But a National Education Association statement made clear how remote they were from the spirit of the times, as formulated by a commission on which Harvard and Columbia presidents James Conant and Dwight Eisenhower were invited to sit. The commission found that "the continued threat of war requires a basic psychological reorientation for the American people as a whole" and that, in a time of "need for healthy young people to wear uniforms," education should be "an instrument of national policy." The "Threat of Totalitarianism" (socialism) should only be taught by people who disliked it. While there must be no "careless, unjust" denunciations, "Communists" (by Jansenian definition, anyone so accused who did not confess and inform) were unfit to teach anything. The exclusion of Communists was the very essence of academic freedom since they, unable by their enslavement to teach objectively, were the ones who violated it.

This was what Sidney Hook had been proclaiming ever since his repentance and now definitively set forth in the *Times*. The *Times* permitted Meiklejohn to argue in rebuttal that Communists did not accept their beliefs because they were Party members, but joined the Party because they had the beliefs. The University of Washington probe had shown that Communists resigned from the Party when their and its ideas diverged; how, asked Meiklejohn, could they do this "if as charged they were incapable of free and independent thinking? Slaves do not resign." Meanwhile, as Meiklejohn saw it, the purges were putting every teacher on notice that "if in his search for truth he finds the policies of the American CP to be wise, and acts on that belief, he will be dismissed."

But in the same month (March 1949) New York decreed in the Feinberg law that, heretical classroom propaganda being "frequently so subtle as to escape detection," the loyalty oath already imposed on teachers was not enough. Schools must report continuously on each teacher's loyalty, including anything he might say or write off the premises. In short, teachers must fall in line with the national trend by informing on each other. Most educators found it an unhappy echo of Germany in 1933, but few dared join the court fight against it organized by TU and ALP. Meanwhile Oregon State College had fired two Wallaceite professors; one, a chemist, had "gone right down the Party line" by suggesting that his colleagues study the theories of Stalin's pet geneticist Lysenko before reaching conclusions about them. There were objections to this purge from Pauling and a few other non-admirers of Lysenko. In Illinois a state probe of infiltration into Roosevelt University and the University of Chicago, with Matthews and Rushmore as expert identifiers of subversive professors, made less headway due to the uncooperativeness of presidents Edward J. Sparling and Robert Hutchins. One inquisitor there brought out that to win recruits Communists were using sex, a phenomenon which "plays a hearty role on the campus" but which evidently could not be suppressed.

These were some of the events taking place on the eve of ASP's "Cultural and Scientific Conference for World Peace" which climaxed the Einstein-Mann initiative at the end of March 1949. Others included the release in Japan of all "class A war criminals" except for seven already hanged, and in France of the collaborationist minister who had arranged the shipment of French Jews for extermination; and the death sentence on Greek resistance hero Manolis Glezos who had rashly torn Hitler's swastika from the Acropolis. Iran staged a mass roundup and trial of the Middle East's largest Left party after a military coup attributed to the CIA. CIO quit WFTU with appropriate comments on Russian unions, to help set up the free-world labor federation ICFTU in June; and on the basis of a survey by Dubinsky, who had long since perceived the indispensability of capitalism to a prosperous labor movement, America persuaded the UN to put "Soviet slave labor" on its agenda. Russia countered with documentation of free-world slavery and peonage in South Africa, Saudi Arabia, Latin America, Texas (Mexicans) and the state of Georgia (Negro chain gangs).

Russia overtook and surpassed America in spy paranoia by arresting Anna Louise Strong as a Washington agent; Hungary sentenced its Cardinal Mindszenty to life imprisonment for plotting a coup with Americans; Bulgaria tried 15 Protestant clergymen for treason; and the US army tried a number of Czechs in Munich on secret spy charges. From Tokyo, proconsul MacArthur denounced Agnes Smedley and journalist Gunther Stein ("a German Jew who seems to have become a British citizen") as "traitors to [pre-Pearl Harbor] Japan" who were probably still "busy with their trade" of spying for Russia. Smedley called MacArthur a liar and challenged him to repeat his statements publicly so she could sue him for libel. MacArthur did not oblige.

Strong was put over the Polish border after four days' questioning in Moscow; before she flew into New York, media which had blacklisted her for years were cabling to name her price for stories unmasking Russia. At the airport she told a vociferous mass of newsmen that everyone made mistakes and she would say nothing to exacerbate cold-war hysteria, for which she held her interrogators' employers chiefly responsible. To repeated shouts of "Did the Russian secret police mistreat you?" she replied: "No one has mistreated me the way you are doing tonight." Loyal to the paranoia *à la russe,* Communist friends of two and three decades avoided her; and the *Worker,* abruptly terminating a serialization of her latest book, compiled evidence that she had always been an agent in its midst. She moved into the ghetto's ghetto but told her story in the *National Guardian* whose correspondent she had been in Moscow. (The most pertinent Communist comment came from Gerhardt Eisler: "Russia charged her with spying, jailed her for four days and threw her out. Why won't America throw me out?") She found a haven in Los Angeles's First Unitarian Church, whose middle-class liberal congregation had recently picked the Rev. Stephen H. Fritchman as its minister. Fritchman was beginning to scandalize the community, but not his flock, with sermons and public forums on perilously down-to-earth themes, and the church was becoming a refuge and nursery of unbigoted heretics.

While the American Medical Association raised $3,000,000 to educate the public against health insurance, Rep. George Dondero resumed his exposure of red art. He could now identify "dadaism, futurism, constructionism, surrealism, cubism, expressionism and abstractionism" as "weapons of destruction [of] our cultural heritage." At the same time he honored Dwight MacDonald by readings in Congress from MacDonald's *Politics* on the subject of Stalinist infiltrators into American forces occupying Germany. In the art world he demanded a purge by "loyal clean-minded artists," naming galleries, museums, painters and critics as accomplices in the plot. No one pointed out that he was following the Moscow line.

Overlapping spy sensations and cold-war think-pieces left virtually no space in the media for Americans wanting to express repugnance for such developments. A typical protest letter to a heretical journal ended: "Please omit my name. My job is at stake." ACLU lawyer Garfield Hays had to resort to the *National Guardian* to comment on the forthcoming Communist leaders' trials: "Nobody seriously believes that Communists really advocate, in the sense of incitement, the overthrow of the government." Headlines were copious, however, for the launching of a campaign to cleanse Brooklyn's Holy Trinity Church of its rector, John Melish, whose son and assistant rector William was chairman of NCASF. The *Times* found three inches on page 17 of one edition for a press conference to publicize the Dixie-style death sentence on six black Trentonians. Three weeks before the peace conference at New York's Waldorf-Astoria Hotel, the arrest of Justice Department employee Judith Coplon again freshened the spy melodrama with mammoth headlines.

The Einstein and Mann prestige helped ASP to enlist as peace-conference sponsors some 550 scientists, writers, film and theatre luminaries, artists, architects, educators, musicians, physicians and other professionals. They comprised almost all the Americans left in *Who's Who* (most were of that status) who thought they could peacefully inhabit the same world with socialists, and who were either still unaware of the danger of saying so in heretical company or aware and ready to face it. There were few turndowns of the sponsor invitation, for almost all cultural personalities had by now shown their colors: Steinbeck had become a staunch Russophobe, and Hemingway had put a wall of daiquiris between himself and anything political. (Steinbeck would die exhorting America to kill more Vietnamese; Hemingway would kill himself.) Such press formulations as "US 'PINK COMINFORM' WILL HUDDLE IN LUXURY" and "A let's-all-love-Russia clambake" scared off a handful of sponsors who had accepted. In "unswerving devotion to freedom of information" the State Department underlined the conference's un-Western nature by granting visas to 21 Iron Curtain delegates and denying them to all but one in capitalist Europe. Hook won media popularity with exposés of Stalin's hand in ASP, issued from an Americans for Intellectual Freedom bureau which he set up at the Waldorf-Astoria. Nehru, Shaw, Anderson-Nexö, O'Casey, Michael Redgrave, Diego Rivera and Casals sent friendly messages to chairman Harlow Shapley; John Dewey, Dos Passos and T. S. Eliot sent them to Hook. Small attention was paid to the Chicago *Daily News's* hint that AIF was a State Department creation.

Sidewalk picketers cried, "God Save America!" "Hallelujah!" "Kill the red killers!"; women kneeled in prayer with banners inviting Russian delegate Shostakovich to "jump out of the window." An American Legion commander marshaling pickets warned that the conference might be "a center for the exchange of important military information," and HUAC assured him it would be kept "under constant surveillance." Three Canadian delegates were arrested at the opening dinner and two of them sent home. Despite all this, thousands more than the capacity of the hall tried to get in. "We've got to be careful, you know," said Shapley opening the conference. "We've been classified as part of a 'peace offensive' by those who regard peace as offensive." Accustomed to looking outward toward millions of miles, and backward billions of years, Shapley had a modest yet warm view of *homo sapiens*. If individuals could adjust their sense of proportion about their importance, he saw hope for the species.

Dwight MacDonald, novelist Mary McCarthy and poet Robert Lowell sat in the audience awaiting an opportunity to expose Russia's lack of intellectual freedom. They would best be afforded it by Stalin Prize novelist A. A. Fadeyev, who eulogized his fatherland in the stuffed-shirt style of a government official. *Saturday Review* editor Norman Cousins almost matched Fadeyev in encomiums for his own country, exhorting Russian delegates to "tell the folks at home" about America's "absence of tyranny, of every arbitrary invasion of the rights of man." The "near-violence" outside the hotel was due, he explained, to "the auspices under which this conference is being held . . . a small political group which owes its primary allegiance to an outside government . . . without standing and without honor in its own country." This somewhat confused the Russians: they would no doubt have preferred to be guests of an Establishment group but, with no such invitation forthcoming, had made the best of ASP.

Most of the American participants were less than rhapsodic about either country but knew and said more about the shortcomings of their own. Several scientists disparaged Russia's deification of Lysenko, Shapley coupling it with America's own "massive self-righteousness." Political science professor Frederick Schuman* saw America and Russia as equally blinded by paranoia to the fact that no one could win World War III: both were trying to avoid their problems by inquisitions instead of examining their consciences and building "substantive democracy." World War II bacteriological-warfare expert Theodor Rosebury, discussing the techniques that had turned war into genocide, submitted that while Russia was far from blameless it did not "threaten us either in its words or in its deeds as did—and still does—the corruption, depravity and anti-humanism of Fascism."

Other participants, impatient with Russian-American recriminations, thought racism and hunger more fitting themes for a discussion about ending war. British crystallographer J. D. Bernal (who was denied a visa) contributed a practical paper on planning for abundance. Indian mathematician D. D. Kosambi, the only Asian delegate, said: "While talking about peace you are already engaged in waging war on a considerable part of the world's population and against democracy . . . The countries I come from suffer from hunger [which] twists and warps and corrodes the mind and soul of human beings . . . Even the atomic bomb should be no more horrible than year after year, generation after generation having your mind filled with no other thought than that of food . . . One of the first things I heard here was that a million bags of potatoes had been dumped into the ocean . . . You are using a far more terrible means of warfare than the bacteriological or the atomic."

F. O. Matthiessen, Harvard's Christian socialist whom Hoover's men were dogging at the time, told the writers' panel that Americans had "a legacy to share with the world, to be proud of, to ask the world to share with us," the humane

---

* Schuman had been involved in the FCC monitoring of Hitler's radio which brought to light the Nazi affection for Dies; he was probed during the war. The probe resulted in his accomplice Robert Morss Lovett—an old Chicago colleague of Harry Ward and former secretary to the Virgin Islands government—having to return to teaching English at the University of Chicago.

internationalism and principled courage of Emerson, Thoreau, Melville and Whitman. Ex-*New Yorker* contributor Richard Boyer said "as an American Communist" that the Emersonian responsibility to one's conscience was the essence of his Party and cited Thoreau's exhortation "to be men first and Americans only at a late and convenient hour." Norman Mailer saw both Russia and America "moving toward state capitalism" and found peace conferences "absurd" although he was on this one's sponsor list: "until you have a decent equitable socialism you can have no peace at all . . . The only way socialism can be achieved is through revolution and I see no revolutionary spirit today." A participant and realistic chronicler of the Japanese-American carnage in the Pacific, Mailer was falling into black misanthropy after a brief sojourn in PP circles.

The difficulties of being friendly were aired in the fine arts panel by *Times* music critic Olin Downes, who complained that Americans called him a Moscow tool for praising Russian music while Russians attacked him for criticizing Shostakovich's Seventh Symphony. Aaron Copland, seeing little chance for art in a world of "men who have lost faith," regretted Russia's cold-war-induced hostility to Western music and recalled the recent funeral of the American-Soviet Music Society: it had arranged a tour for two Ukrainian singers who, ordered to register as agents of a foreign power or leave, promptly left. Shostakovich described Russia's mushroom growth of musical activity, especially in Soviet Asia which had neither an orchestra, a chorus nor an opera house 30 years ago. His slap at Stravinsky's "scorn for the broad mass" roused a man in the audience to ask if he agreed with Kremlin condemnation of "practically the whole Western musical production of the last 20 years"; Shostakovich partly did and partly didn't. Playwright Clifford Odets called on artists to reject the "solitary view" to which "a sick inhuman world" was pushing them and emulate Whitman by "reaching out to the healthy world of the people." Quoting from a prophetic prewar speech about the American Century by the Industrial Conference Board's Dr. Virgil Jordan,* he denounced "idiots again prowling the dynamite dumps of the world with lighted matches in their grasping hands."

Under the shadow of the Feinberg law, citizens already far gone in heresy predominated among participants in the education panel: DuBois, Rose Russell, Chicago's DeBoer, the three fired professors from Seattle. "The right to educate for peace is being denied or threatened," said DuBois, praising Harvard, Chicago and other universities for their coldness to the inquisition. "But teachers must know that conformity now will not save them. Only open, aggressive participation in the war program will provide safety from the inquisitors." In the screen-radio-

---

* The prescient Dr. Jordan in his December 1940 speech to investment bankers said that "whatever the outcome, America has embarked upon a career of imperialism both in world affairs and in every other aspect of her life . . . At best England will become a junior partner in a new Anglo-Saxon imperialism . . . Southward in our hemisphere and westward in the Pacific the path of empire takes its way, and in modern terms of economic power as well as political prestige, the sceptre passes to the US. . . . From the pages of British experience we know some of the things that the white man's burden may mean when we assume it . . . the immense effort and vast sacrifices which any great destiny demands if it is to be fulfilled . . . The vast effort and expenditure involved in our defense program are . . . necessary to fulfill the responsibilities and realize the opportunities of our imperial destiny."

press panel Clifford Durr said that, since it was now technically possible for all men to communicate with each other, the question was what they said, whether they "informed and educated or confused and degraded." Russian film director N. Gerasimov said that every country was making films of both kinds but that in Russia "the call for war has never yet sounded, nor will it" in any film, play, radio program, speech or newspaper. Journalist I. F. Stone accused America's mass media of "daily drumming home war, hate and fear" and of "hearty cooperation with the government to make peace seem unpalatable," but reproached Russia for paranoid press policies which only "helped our warmongers and hatemongers." He noted that the *Times* had objected to the labeling of Agnes Smedley as a spy and wondered which Russian paper would do the same with Anna Louise Strong.

Two retired bishops, a rabbi, a New York Episcopalian rector and British philosopher Olaf Stapledon joined Shipler in seeking areas of agreement between Marxism and Judeo-Christianity. A bishop said that Communism "by its despotic use of power becomes a cloak for men of ambition and for imperialism"; Rabbi Louis Newman thought the prevention of war such an "over-arching challenge" that the slogans of all religious people should be "Come and let us reason together," "Hath not one God created us all?" Astonished by a New York taxi driver's remark that "there's got to be another war and the sooner the better," Olaf Stapledon told the panel: "In my England there are one or two misguided people like Lord [Bertrand] Russell, but no one else would say such a thing." In America he saw a "Christian passion for brotherhood" wrestling against the "proverbial licentiousness and ruthlessness" of the business world. Russia had a "sacred value" in human solidarity just as did America in individuality, and if the original generous temper of the revolution had been perverted the West was partly responsible. The conflict had become a religious one, yet it arose from lack of clear religious consciousness on either side. "In the West there is far more religious doctrine than religious perception . . ."

Lillian Hellman, who blamed both powers for the crisis, seemed to speak for most of the gathering when she said: "It no longer matters whose fault it is. It matters that this game be stopped. Only four years ago millions upon millions of people died, yet today men talk of death and war as they talk of going to dinner. He who has seen a war and plans another must be either a villain or a madman. This group of intellectuals can do no worse than statesmen. We want to declare that there still are men and women in the world who do not think it dangerous or radical to declare themselves for the continuation of life . . . We place ourselves among those who wish to live, think and breathe, to eat and play and raise their children, among the millions who want to be a little use and have a little pleasure and bear a little sorrow and die a little death, close to someone who has loved them in decency and in peace."

Such sentimentalities failed to move MacDonald and his friends from seeking to bring the conference down to what interested them: Stalin's cultural censorship and purge of artists. They showed themselves better informed than any American peacemonger present, and whatever the Russian delegates knew about the purges, they were clearly not going to say it. The ardent Communist Howard Fast reminded the conference that Washington had censored it by denying visas to delegates from abroad, and that he and other American writers were about to go to jail for their beliefs. This left MacDonald more than one-up in the game since Fast could not complain of American writers being liquidated.

The conference provided an up-to-date guide to influential citizens who had not yet learned that consorters with Communists were Communists; and the combined efforts of federal and local probers, blacklisters, familiars and free-world intellectuals would see to it that no such gathering occurred again until the third year of America's war in Vietnam. Presence at the Waldorf-Astoria in March 1949 became almost as black a mark in a dossier as presence in the wrong part of Spain between 1936 and 1938. The despair which was aroused in some participants and sponsors culminated in the suicide of 48-year-old Matthiessen: he would jump from a high window in April 1950 leaving a note: "I am doing what I must do to be true to my beliefs and my profession." * The conference passed a resolution calling substantially for the Russo-American cultural agreement which the governments would sign a decade later.

For years heretics in various countries would be broadcasting invitations to peace congresses, but from America only heretics would respond—until they were banned from traveling. The Waldorf-Astoria affair was followed by one in Paris, with Picasso, Ehrenburg, [Gyorgy] Lukacs, [J. D.] Bernal, Robeson and DuBois among the participants from 60 countries. Its one noteworthy aspect for American media was Robeson's speech, published in many colorful variations, in which he called it "unthinkable" for Negroes "to go to war in the interests of those who have oppressed us for generations." A "counter-conference" was organized in Paris by the tireless Hook, with James Farrell, Richard Wright, Sartre, Camus and Carlo Levi. The four last-named withdrew beforehand, Wright and Sartre deciding on second thoughts that while Russia suppressed true liberty, America was no "paradise of democratic liberties" either. If (as Paris gossip had it) the State Department sponsored the project, delegates' insistence on denouncing American inquisitions and imperialism in addition to Russian prison camps may have caused some embarrassment.

For his Paris heresy, Robeson's passport was canceled. During the years when he was grounded in America, his voice, reverberating from millions of phonographs and radios, would more than ever symbolize "the other America" in socialist countries. The artist himself—unable to get a commercial engagement in a barn—became the exclusive property of the American ghetto.

The Waldorf-Astoria resolution was worse than subversive: like the doctrine of the Hollywood Anti-Nazi League, it was premature. There was a right and a wrong year to advocate cultural coexistence with Russia and none was more wrong than 1949. After the Muscovites went home from their confusing week in New York, America, with six more months to go of atomic suzerainty, reached the height of its resolve not to give a Russian so much as the time of day. If the MacDonald sect of Russophobes was still not beyond public confrontation with Stalinists and their dupes, almost everyone else unreservedly accepted the inquisitorial view that the time for words with them was over.

---

* Years after the circumstances of his suicide were forgotten, a *Times* critic would call Matthiessen "the greatest 20th-century rediscoverer of our literary past."

Fever Chart

1948-49

Scene: Loyalty Board hearing of M., Brooklyn Navy Yard sheetmetal worker.

LOYALTY BOARD MEMBER: What book clubs do you subscribe to?

M: The Book Find Club.

LBM: Does Feuchtwanger write for them? Does Dreiser contribute? Some of their writers adhere to the Communist Party line, did you know that? They weave doctrine into a story.

M: I ain't that much of a genius. I read the words, not the weaving.

Scene: Loyalty Board hearing of C., Negro hospital attendant.

LOYALTY BOARD MEMBER: As I understand it, Mr. C is before this board like an accused person would be before a jury in a criminal case.

C's ATTORNEY: The veterans' hospital is not an atom-bomb plant. This employee is not dealing with secrets but with mops, pails, bedpans, linens. I submit that there cannot be any possible security consideration for not letting him know the basis of the charges. I would like to ask why you don't bring in the FBI agent to testify as to what he knows.

LBM: Because we are not required to do so. (To C) I understand you fought for repeal of Executive Order 9835 under which the board is proceeding. Why?

C (Explains that whole union membership opposes it.)

LBM: Are you opposed to the government getting rid of disloyal people?

C: No, I am not opposed.

LBM: Then why do you want 9835 repealed?

C: Because we felt that when a Negro started fighting against discrimination this order would be brought against him . . .

LBM (interrupting): It appears to me that while you are criticizing the Loyalty Board proceedings that you are overlooking what might have happened in Russia where the Communist Party takes its orders from. Had he been found to be a member of some subversive group in Russia he wouldn't be confronted by a Loyalty Board. He would face a firing squad.

(C is found guilty and fired.)

Scene: Press conference by State Department visa chief Herve L'Heureux on immigrants' admissibility to America under Displaced Persons program.

L'HEUREUX: Under normal immigration laws there is nothing that would exclude a Nazi or a Fascist.

REPORTER: They [Nazis] are not considered to be in violation of the rule against admitting persons holding views regarding overthrow of the government by force and violence?

L'HEUREUX: I don't think so. At least, we have never determined that . . . Well, there may be an individual case of a person who was a Nazi who also believes in the overthrow of government by force. But I don't think we have ever concluded that the Nazi party agreed that it is for the overthrow of government by force.

REPORTER: This is sort of astonishing to some of us. We assumed they set out to overthrow governments.

US News & World Report (August 1949), after setting forth detailed plans for atomization of Russia:

"War scare is having to be drummed up again to excite interest in a gift of arms to other nations. War talk is artificial, phony, but it is regarded as necessary to get Congress stirred up enough to produce a favorable vote."

Scene: Senate joint committee hearing on foreign military aid program. Wallace and DuBois have asked and been permitted to testify.

WALLACE: This program proposes to repeat our tragic mistakes in China, placing the same emphasis on arms to the exclusion of the people's needs for social reform. There is an lternative policy—agreeing to live in the same world with Russia. We must come to the Russians with a plan for world-wide development and reconstruction within the UN framework, resting solidly on economic self-interest. The two great problems of our age are first, our own abundance; second, the world's poverty.

DUBOIS: Why in God's name do we want to control the earth? We want to rule Russia and we cannot rule Alabama. We who hate "niggers" and "darkies" propose to control a world full of colored people. We are daily being pushed into a third world war on the assumption that we are sole possessors of Truth and Right and are able to pound our ideas into the world's head by brute force. What hinders us from beginning to reason now before we fight? We are afraid . . .

Music critic Olin Downes reviews 1948:

"When the record is written it will not be flattering to the 'liberal' intellectuals of America . . . Was it that they simply could not dream of taking off their coats and taking the tomatoes and rotten eggs, the abuses and indignities that would be the penalty for honesty and forthright action? It was safer to break the faith which they had long and politely professed."

Scene: Senate Judiciary Committee hearing on Mundt-Nixon anti-heretic bill. C. B. Baldwin testifies on behalf of Progressive Party.

SENATOR EASTLAND: Are you now or have you ever been a member of the Communist Party?

BALDWIN: I would be glad to take the oath of allegiance to the United States and I would particularly want the Fourteenth and Fifteenth Amendments included.* I doubt whether you would take such an oath with a clear conscience.

EASTLAND: (Signals to police to remove Baldwin.)

BALDWIN: For fifteen years you have fought every measure that would have helped the Negro people.

* Citizenship rights not to be abridged; equal rights for white and black.

EASTLAND: You're a god-damned son of a bitch and a god-damned liar!
(Baldwin is rushed from the room.)

$2,000 *Times* ad inserted by Ferris Booth, former Guaranty Trust Company vice president, after Russia explodes its first Bomb:

"GOD IS ONLY DEFENSE AGAINST A-BOMB . . . We must take steps to bolster and aggressively aid Confucianism as a bulwark against Communism."

Scene: Hopkins (Minnesota) home of E. R. Shopp, father of newly elected "Miss America."

REPORTER: Mr. Shopp, your daughter is quoted from Europe as saying that American girls are man-crazy and falsies are an abomination. "Every girl must be true to herself," she said.

SHOPP: Bebe would never say such things! They are the words of some red over there!

Scene: A Brooklyn apartment. Police have opened up a 6-by-3-feet recess in which Paul Makushak has interred himself for ten years, and explained to him the pleasures of circulating in the free world.

MAKUSHAK: It's no good being out. I'd rather go back where I was.

X

1949: "I Appreciate
Your Permission To Weep"

Beginning in mid-1947, a New York grand jury spent 12 months of weekdays listening to Elizabeth Bentley and other familiars who had pinpointed Russian spies, and then to the spies. After Hoover's men had visited hundreds of thousands of the spies' contacts, 12 Party leaders were indicted.* The charge was not spying but "conspiracy to advocate the overthrow of the government by force and violence."

The Smith Act trial at Foley Square initiated a nationwide series over the next years. Far from being an obstacle to the government, the Act's patent unconstitutionality multiplied the agony of the victims, plunging them into a murk of unreality and spinning out their ordeal into ever costlier months and years. Together with deportation, Subversive Activities Control Board (from 1950), Taft-Hartley, Loyalty Board and assorted hearings, the trials compelled heretics to run at furious speed in a vain attempt to stay in the same place. The argument that they did not "advocate force and violence" was doomed in advance, for the government was ready to prove that they did, with scores of familiars and countless excerpts from Marxist texts. Committees proved it—or anything else that was required—simply by framing a question to which they knew there would be no reply. As an added precaution the court always charged "conspiracy." This ancient British device was useful in cases where it had been decided to jail someone for his politics, but proof that he actually did anything might appear weak. He was then accused of talking about doing something, which the law rated as a more serious offense, and innocence of which was beyond proof.

But justice was abundantly seen to be done, for the machinery of higher-court appeals was available to the humblest citizen provided he had the money and lived long enough. The bills became astronomical as heretics invoked and re-invoked the Founding Fathers to discredit the proceedings; meanwhile, they had to bleed every possible source for fines and bail which eventually might or might not be refunded. The fund-raising task left an organization little or no time for its constituted functions; and when a favorable decision finally came, the organization would be decimated if not bankrupt and the question more or less academic.

Since the public believed in American justice, and the Communists wanted to show they were as American as anyone else, they and their lawyers—who set the defense trend for peripheral heretics—did not consider the IWW approach that capitalist justice for socialists was a charade. The best of the lawyers they could

---

* Party chairman William Foster was "severed" from the trial due to ill health. The defendants were Eugene Dennis, John Williamson, Jack Stachel, Robert Thompson, ex-New York Councilman Benjamin Davis, Henry Winston, John Gates, Irving Potash, Gil Green, Carl Winter and Gus Hall.

get (Harry Sacher, George Crockett and Richard Gladstein in the 1949 trial; Frank Donner, John McTernan, John Abt, Nathan Witt and Vincent Hallinan in later ones) were able men and ready to accept the financial and other sacrifices involved. But they were heretics themselves, a fact of which judges took full advantage; and the rare non-heretical lawyer who was available generally charged fees far above his worth, on the ground that accepting such cases deprived him of hygienically lucrative briefs. On strategy, some lawyers urged taking the offensive with regard to what Communists believed. Others wanted to let the government present its version and then try to disprove it, relying finally on the right to be wrong, and these prevailed.

The Marxist thesis, familiar to political science students, was that state establishments tended to maintain themselves by increasing violence which, beyond a certain point, could only be met with counter-violence. The CP's position was that this point had been reached in the America of 1776 and the Russia of 1917 but not in the America of 1949. But if the defense believed that its strategy would at least make the courts a forum of public enlightenment about heretical ideas, it was sadly misjudging the loyalty of the media, which saw to it that this part of the 5,000,000 words of Foley Square testimony was ignored or buried. In the event, the public's boredom with the solemn and stupefying ritual was only exceeded, after a few weeks, by that of juries and defendants. The one question retaining a flicker of interest was the length of the sentences. These, at Foley Square, turned out to be five years and $10,000 fines for each conspirator except Robert Thompson, whose medal for fighting for America had to be weighed against his sin of fighting for Spain. For him a mere three years behind bars was deemed appropriate.

In the play *Fear and Misery in the Third Reich* (1939) Brecht makes the judge who must pass sentence on heretics say: "Understand, I am ready to do anything. I can decide this way or that way, just as they want me to, but I must know what they want. If one doesn't know that, there is no justice any longer." No such doubts assailed Judge Harold Medina, and the jurymen (whose selection alone had taken three months) were too paralyzed by Marxist readings to show resistance to what was wanted. The curtain rose in April in a patriotic setting as moblets attacked ASP and CP meetings in Baltimore and Pittsburgh, Congress raised Hoover's budget by $9,000,000, and Maryland decreed 20-year jail terms and $20,000 fines for teaching heresy "in any way" within its borders. Barnum's circus at Madison Square Garden dedicated itself, with a parade of elephants followed by girls stripping to red, white and blue bras and panties, "to the struggle to maintain our way of life against the menacing horde of aggressors."

After Budenz's week on the stand, interpreting each Marxist reading as an "Aesopian" mask for the conspiracy, the red-white-blue motif emerged on the bow tie of witness Philbrick. The surfacing patriot became an overnight celebrity with his account of eight years as a top Boston Communist,* and Boston newspapers combing their files for a picture were startled to find they had none. Nowhere in

---

* *I Led Three Lives* (McGraw-Hill, New York, 1952) described Philbrick's years "in the shadows where glances must be furtive . . . days of deception and guile, plotting every move . . . blind calls from telephone booths . . . hushed instructions hurriedly

their copious collections from picket lines, heretical gatherings, even war-bond rallies, did his face appear. But since Philbrick had been a Communist, it followed that everyone whom he contacted and who did not rebuff him was involved in the conspiracy. He had a wealth of names, and though few of the owners remembered him he would rarely slip into naming a total stranger. In his tribunal debut he created the clean-limbed impression which would characterize his work, saving most of the melodrama for newspaper columns, a book and a TV series. While he had seen no guns in heretical circles, he could attest to the comrades' secret studying of Moscow orders to start "armed insurrection when the time was ripe." He gave a graphic account of [Dirk J.] Struik's talk at the soiree in 1948: "A very broad summary of *State and Revolution* which covered the entire question of the state and revolution, and in his discussion he brought in a very complete discussion of current events, that is, the present world situation." Philbrick's presence at the PP session to rewrite Wallace's speech was proof enough that Wallace was a CP puppet, but Philbrick elaborated the point at some length, bringing in Matthiessen and others as conspirators to raise PP funds. To all this Medina listened gravely, the defendants dazedly. Perhaps, their lawyers tried to suggest, it had slipped Medina's mind that neither Struik, Wallace nor Matthiessen was a defendant.

Browder declined prosecutor John McGohey's invitation to testify for the government, but ex-Communists followed one another to the stand throughout the summer. Negro auto worker William Cummings recalled (as he would do before many tribunals) the Communists having taught that "American streets would have to run red with blood," and described recruiting three relatives into the Party to maintain his flow of names to Hoover. The procession of familiars brought home to the Party the extent to which its ranks had been penetrated, and it appointed John Lautner, a comrade of 20 years' standing, to take charge of Party security as well as the trial defense. The trial was hardly over when Lautner proved to be an agent himself.

Frank Sullivan tried in the *New Yorker* to poke fun at the trial, and at the cascade of new melodramas which pushed it into back pages after its blazing start. He found that life, as depicted by the media, had overtaken even a genius's power to lampoon. For the inquisition, however, the trial set two important precedents. One was the "Aesopian language" thesis which, proving that Communists never

---

given . . . sleepless nights and secret meetings on darkened street corners where automobiles drove up, swallowed me and whizzed away." He graduated to "super-secret meetings" conducted in "muffled voices" under "a single ceiling lamp" (one comrade had "markedly red" hair) to which, "cognizant of party instructions," he "wound [his] way up dark, narrow streets" and "slipped in" through a "dim hallway." In this Bostonian hideout he was taught about "the three classes of society" in language at first Aesopian ("but we understood") but moving into such "outright sedition" that "I almost dropped my pencil . . . I felt a paroxysm of excitement as I transcribed her words for . . . the Bureau." He prepared his FBI reports in a "secret, compactly equipped room behind the furnace" in his home, but comrades distrusted him and even "scrutinized [him] with binoculars." He logically concluded that this was "a mob movement of ruthless totalitarianism" and Marxism was "pap."

meant what they said or wrote, made it idle for them to cite their actual words.*
The other was that lawyers defending heretics were guilty of contempt if, in what
they thought to be the line of duty, they sought to confine a trial to the indictment
and to have normal rules of evidence enforced. Such rules were clearly inappli-
cable once the prosecution established that Communists did their conspiring in
secret—the burden of all the familiars' testimony. Early in the trial Medina graciously told defense lawyer George Crockett, who had broken into tears of frustration: "I make no objection to it, but I think it better that counsel refrain from
weeping in court." Crockett replied, "I appreciate your permission to weep."**
Subsequently Medina's scorn for the lawyers' efforts became unconcealed, and he
sent all five to jail along with their clients—a judgment which the Supreme Court
(Black and Douglas dissenting) would uphold. The others were Harry Sacher,
Abraham Isserman, Louis McCabe and Richard Gladstein. McGohey got an immediate federal judgeship and Medina, likewise regarded as a martyr to patriotic
duty, would shortly receive along with Foster Dulles an award from the wealthy
manufacturers' "Freedoms Foundation."

Two or three respectable journals criticized the verdict and sentences. In the
Catholic Worker, still tolerated by the church hierarchy, editor Dorothy Day
wrote: "Although rejecting atheism and materialism in Marxist and bourgeois
thought, we respect our Marxist brothers' freedom as a minority group and believe their rights have been violated . . . We extend to them our sympathy and
admiration for having followed their conscience."

While the affair still lingered on front pages, six young Negroes in Trenton
waited to be put to death, hopefully scanning newspapers for some word of their
plight. The disreputable CRC won a new trial for them and stirred enough fuss
about the condemned Mississippian McGee to delay his execution again. CRC
secretary William Patterson had warned McGee, the Trentonians and their frantic
families that acceptance of his help would brand their defense as a Communist
plot; but none other being offered, they were grateful for it. During later stages
of the Foley Square trial, policemen casually shot down two Negroes in Brooklyn,
clubbed another—a 77-year-old who moved too slowly to the rear of a bus—to death

---

* George Marion, a heretical chronicler of the trial, recalled the paper produced at the
Knave's trial in *Alice in Wonderland:* it was not in the Knave's handwriting, said the
White Rabbit, "and that's the queerest thing about it." The King concluded that "he
must have imitated someone else's hand . . . If you didn't sign it, that only makes matters
worse. You must have meant some mischief or else you'd have signed your name like
an honest man." The phrase tellingly introduced by Budenz at Foley Square seems to
have been taken from the preface to *Imperialism* where Lenin explains that, writing
in exile, he must use "that cursed Aesopian language" to get by the Tsarist censorship,
for example writing "Japan" when he means Russia.
** Although he saw no cause to repent his defense of Communists, Crockett would be
elected to a judgeship many years later by white and fellow-black voters in Detroit. A
storm broke around him in 1969 when, after a street battle in which a policeman was
killed, Crockett refused to detain 147 Negroes brought in under arrest. According to
the *Times* he was by then regarded as "the finest expert on the Constitution on the Detroit bench." Crockett commented: "I know from physical contact what it means when a
judge says one year, two years, three years. I don't want to wish it on any of my associates, but I think it would do them some good if they would spend some time in jail."
The *Times* preferred (in 1969) not to recall the details of Crockett's jail experience.

in Texas, and beat out the eyes of another who had sought (and been denied) treatment in a New York hospital. The seven jailed for rape in Martinsville (Virginia), and two more on extorted murder confessions in Greenville, North Carolina, were sentenced to death. White residents around Groveland, Florida, burned the homes of Negroes complaining about their work conditions, pursued them with cries of "Rape!" as they fled, captured four and killed one of them on the spot. Bloodhounds streaked after fleeing blacks following rape scares in Texas and South Carolina; and mobs attacked and bombed Negro homes in Los Angeles and Birmingham and later in Chicago. In Waukegan (Illinois), however, justice triumphed for a black American who had spent 26 years in jail for a rape that did not occur. He was freed and replaced in circulation with a compensation of $10. By September NAACP's Walter White was discussing in *Look* the possibility of Negroes bleaching the color out of their skin.

The third attempt to deport Bridges, beginning in May, set the stage for the CIO convention decision to investigate and expel all 11 affiliated unions which held out against the cold war. Most of them would pass out of existence. The deportation plank was now out for Communist labor leaders who were aliens, while those who were citizens resigned from the Party and signed the Taft-Hartley oath necessary to hold their posts—a procedure hardly taken seriously by inquisitors. CIO set up rival unions which raided heretical ones for members and beat up the recalcitrant, in smooth teamwork with inquisitors to "clean labor's house." NLRB required a workers' ballot as to which union should represent them, but in most cases the inquisitorial apparatus—including if need be a Committee visit to town at the strategic moment—could see that the loyal union won. AFL, meanwhile, was getting its first CIA money to break a strike (by French dock workers) abroad.

The response of ordinary citizens to the melodrama was indicated by a rural incident that summer, when Congressmen were considering the first bill for heretics' concentration camps. Learning of a plot by male, female and child heretics to hear Paul Robeson sing of peace and brotherhood in a quiet spot near Peekskill, New York, American Legionnaires mobilized local patriots to frustrate them with clubs, rocks and police and state-trooper support. The heretics refused to take warning from the first onslaught and organized a second concert with subversive war veterans forming a protective ring around the audience. The strategy of the patriots, among whom women and teen-agers abounded, was to line the only exit road after Robeson finished singing. Police formed a gauntlet through which concertgoers could be forced for the club-wielders' convenience, and in a polyphony of shattered car-windshields and cries of "Commies, nigger-lovers, kikes, string 'em up!" substantial casualties were inflicted: 145 injured, one almost totally blinded, two not quite killed. New York Governor Dewey appointed a committee which investigated the victims but brought no charges. Robeson promised to continue singing to anyone who dared listen and expressed confidence that America would not go Fascist. The Party, less confident, began setting up an understudy leadership. Selected members vanished from their haunts and altered their appearance against the possibility of all leaders being arrested.

It was an appropriate summer in which to open, in cooperation with the West German press, a campaign exposing anti-Semitism in Russia. In America,

Robeson read the signs correctly but the calendars of the inquisition's various arms had never been so full. Hoover daily brought to light new evidences of disloyalty: one citizen had written a thesis on "the New Deal in New Zealand," another received mail from Russia and spoke Yiddish, another was "a Progressive Party Negress." HUAC probed atom spies continuously from April to July, with prime headlines for exposing Steve Nelson's contacts with scientists who worked on the first Bomb.

Nelson paid too little heed to the Fifth-Amendment warnings of his attorney Emanuel Bloch and returned to Pittsburgh with a contempt citation for invoking it incorrectly.* But this would be the least of his problems in 1950. His blood-pressure was perhaps raised at the HUAC hearing by confrontation with Paul Crouch, who had turned up in Miami, begun naming names, and had much to tell. In 1927, he recalled, he had toured Red Army bases and inspected maneuvers as a guest of the late General Tukhachevsky, who had consulted him on Russian plans (written in English) to invade America. To remove any doubt about this reminiscence, which would help to jail, deport or ghettoize scores of American heretics, he had a photo of himself in Red Army uniform. Mrs. Crouch joined him to form the first husband-and-wife familiars' team. Crouch's sense of melodrama rivaled that of Bentley, who was numbering her days as a familiar by exposing her spies too impetuously—27 more in June, 37 in November—leaving no more for rainy days. One of them, heiress Louise Berman, a notorious wartime contactor of Nelson and Oppenheimer and of Russians in her work for San Francisco's American-Russian Institute, said enough (including a denial of spying) in two HUAC sessions to yield a contempt indictment for blocking other questions.** The nearest the Justice Department came to a conviction for spying was in the two trials (April, December) of its own employee Judith Coplon, who was not on Bentley's list. Coplon had been caught on what she said was a romantic rendezvous with a Russian, but Hoover fumbled the case by using wiretap evidence which the court felt it must reject.

Together with the Hiss trials (May 1949, January 1950), these cases were outstanding attractions for spy aficionados while CIA and FBI welcomed Philby into their councils as the West's top expert in black activities against socialism. Philby had been a Russian agent since 1933 but, as a crony of Ribbentrop with a medal for loyalty to Fascism personally presented by Franco, was above suspicion. In his tour of duty in Washington he appraised the "haughty dilettante" Allen Dulles as a "bumbling" performer compared with Russian counterparts and noted Hoover's undying resentment of CIA competition. His talks with the FBI "prima donna"—a man of "raging vanity" who seemed ever ready to sacrifice intelligence

---

* The trap had been set for all to see after a grand jury probe of Denver Communists in 1948, where the local CP's former treasurer, Mrs. Rogers, admitted having held that office but refused to identify her successor to whom she had turned over the records. The Supreme Court in 1951 would confirm her jail sentence for contempt on the ground that, by making the admission about herself, she had "waived the privilege" not to identify her associates.

** In a statement which HUAC would not hear but which she gave to the press with some results, the heiress supporter of heretical causes said: "If I had spent my money on yachts and jewels this Committee would not have bothered me . . . On the contrary, I might even have been appointed ambassador to some small or medium-sized duchy."

needs to advancing himself politically—were "extremely curious"; and Hoover's deputy was "astonishingly dense . . . he tried to convince me in all seriousness that Franklin Roosevelt was a Communist agent." Philby's main FBI contact was "a dreadful man" whose "favorite amusement was to play filthy records to women." At the time there was known to be a "leak" from the British embassy, and Hoover's men "put in an immense amount of work resulting in an immense amount of waste paper" to detect it. They produced a 15-page report on "a charlady with a Latvian grandmother" with details of her family, friends, private life and vacation habits. Philby joined in bi-national talks about sending agents into socialist areas where nationalist sentiment might be fanned against Moscow. The talks bogged down in acrimony because each government had its own "puppets" anxious to take over, but they were able to agree upon a joint operation in Albania. Subversion teams were air-dropped, sent over the Greek border and landed from submarines, but as one member who managed to escape said later, "the police were *always* there" to welcome them. Some 300 trained subverters were killed before the operation was abandoned in 1952. Philby would write that, while he never knew just what happened to the teams, he could make an informed guess.*

Hiss's first trial at Foley Square almost blotted from the media that of the 11 Communists which was proceeding simultaneously, and an incident on another floor of the court house passed unnoticed: the tag-end of the Gerhardt Eisler case, which had blazed into headlines three weeks earlier. Eisler had made his getaway and his wife, Hilde, who had promptly been caged on Ellis Island, was asking release on bail in an empty courtroom. The government demanded her confinement in case she should sail before arrangements could be made to deport her. Weary of America and of waiting for high courts to decide his fate, her husband had paid 25¢ to visit a Polish ship in New York harbor and remained sitting on a deckchair until a suitable moment to declare himself a stowaway. He spent the voyage reading [Harry] Hopkins's memoirs of Roosevelt, cabled CRC (provider of the $25,000 bail which he had forfeited) that he would refund the money from Germany, and in talks with passengers remarked that Americans "if they are decent—and many, many are—are the nicest people in the world." Policemen carried him bodily off the ship at Southampton on a request from Washington. The London magistrate rejected the application to extradite back to America a German enroute to his own country, and soon Eisler was functioning as East Germany's propaganda chief.**

The inquisition missed Eisler only briefly, promoting Hungarian-born Alexander Stevens to replace him as "top US underground agent." Stevens and IWO official Peter Harisiades, whose deportation to Greece would probably mean death, were among 135 heretics threatened at the time with being sent back whence they had come as children or teen-agers. Most of them had American wives and children and had lived in America for two to five decades; but having been too

---

* Kim Philby, *My Silent War*, Grove Press, New York, 1968.
** The *Batory* in which Eisler escaped, the only socialist passenger ship plying into an American port, was so harassed by American authorities that it soon gave up the struggle. Its crew members were questioned on arrival, barred from coming ashore if showing socialist taint, and encouraged to desert. The maritime convention to return deserters did not apply since America classified them as political refugees.

active in trade unions or subversive groups, they swelled the new population of
Ellis Island heading the other way. The inquisition had not only reversed the
westward human tide through the island but closed the golden door even for
short visits by aliens who could not prove lifelong devotion to capitalism. The
American Astronomical Society, faced with this problem and at a loss to influence the politics of colleagues abroad, withdrew its bid to host a world astron-
omers' conference.

Patriotic paranoia mounted in a steady action-reaction pattern behind both
curtains. On a flight to Prague from Warsaw, where he had been living since his
risky wartime service helping anti-Fascists escape from the Germans, the American Quaker Noel Field disappeared without trace in May. His wife and brother
went in search of him and likewise vanished. In short order he was a capitalist
spy for the Russians and—as a "Hiss circle" member when he worked for the
State Department before the war—a Communist spy for the Americans. Four
months later Hungary (where the Fields were being third-degreed in jail) tried
and executed its foreign minister Rajk and other top Communists for treason,
having extracted fictitious confessions on Stalin's orders. Top Bulgarian Communists were liquidated in November after a similar trial. The scorn of Trotskyists
and other heretics' heretics rose to a new pitch as the Party stoutly defended
Russian-style justice. At the same time American inquisitors, whose efforts in that
direction consistently failed, marveled at the open-trial confessions of non-existent
acts of treason.

In America the sweltering propaganda climate had so affected Defense Secretary Forrestal that by January 1949 he was reported to have a raw spot on his
head from scratching it. While staying with Harriman in Florida in April, he ran
from his room in pajamas (according to Drew Pearson) shouting that the Russians had invaded America and were after him. A month later he "jumped or fell"
from a window in a Washington hospital, where his case had baffled psychiatrists.
His demise briefly preceded that of former State Department employee Morton
Kent, who cut his throat after Hoover began dogging him.*

The situation of the American Century at this stage was that Russia declined to take fright at the Pentagon's mounting collection of annihilation devices, while $6 billion in American aid since 1945 proved too little to save capi-
talism in China. Chiang's men deserted by regiments to Mao. On Chinese streets
countless families expired whimpering in vain for alms, or for the price of a small
daughter's body; even a heavy bundle of money was worthless and the only good
business left was importing presses to print more banknotes. "You Americans,"
a Chinese merchant told a reporter, "seem to be concerned only about isms. What
we want is enough to eat." A professor released from one of the jammed jails
said: "I couldn't sleep for the screaming of the tortured."

The problem was, as financial columnist Sylvia Porter wrote, that "we are
now into our first business slump since 1938" with unemployment again rising
into millions. Huge loans to remote, unsuccessful anti-Communists were increasingly hard to get from Congress. America was producing a Niagara of wheat,

---

* Throughout the peak cold war years, mental wards became accustomed to three types
of paranoid fears: of "the Russians," "the Bomb," and "the FBI." The latter was most
difficult to treat since physicians could not rule out the possibility that it was rational.

cotton, eggs and milk products which, to maintain prices, the government had to stash in old anchored ships, quonset huts and caves. The question of this produce being eaten or worn did not arise since persons in need lacked money to pay for it. The surpluses would prove useful bait and control instruments for free-world alliances, but the only employment created was guarding caves where not-to-be-eaten food was stored. In California's San Joaquin Valley an argument had developed as to whether it was starvation or malnutrition of which 11 migrant workers' children died. One answer to the recession, suggested by Russia's first atomic detonation in September, was "civil defense" construction against the impending attack. Chicago *Tribune* publisher McCormick gave a lead by refashioning his building with a warning system, a "command post and nerve center," stockpiles of aspirin, and arrangements for the staff to shelter from radiation behind newsprint-roll barricades.

Civil defense would in fact find a place in the cold-war economy, but clearly the budget for costly weapons, which were its mainstay under the new philosophy, was still too modest. As Wallace observed, Congress was now "fundamentally owned" by builders of planes, battleships, tanks, and bombs, and with an intensified war-scare the appropriation could be doubled without seriously disturbing the public. At this moment timely cries of alarm came from Syngman Rhee, a Korean long resident in America who had been sent back with dollars and experts to preserve capitalism in the southern half of his country. He needed more massive aid to resist the socialist hordes north of the line drawn across Korea after the war. Rhee's point was underlined by multitudinous riots against the American occupiers of Japan, and Dulles and Acheson took up the cry for a shoring-up job in the Far East.

While the Korean crisis ripened, inquisitors noted that the largest single nest of heretics in America was UN headquarters in New York. Little could be done about the socialist-country delegations apart from restricting and following their movements; but the presence of Americans who had pledged loyalty to an alien body, and who as staff members could not be prevented from contacting Russians, cried out for probing. After a media buildup HUAC summoned UN document editor Mrs. Keeney to ask if she was a Communist and how she got the job. She said she was not, and that as an international civil servant she "couldn't discuss" the second point. Her ailing husband, who was also summoned and asked the $64 question, prudently invoked the Fifth.

The Senate probing committee headed by McCarran, which had already begun stealing HUAC's thunder with a Bentley spy session, moved in with charges of "red terror in UN" two days before HUAC issued its report on the manila-envelope incident. Enlightened at last by the report as to what started the harassment in 1946, Mrs. Keeney explained the envelope in a registered letter to the Senate's Millard Tydings Committee which the committee said it never received. UN Secretary-General Trygve Lie soon recovered from his initial shock and joined in the hunt: Americans on the staff found that guards were spying on them and rifling their desks at night. By the end of 1950 Lie would be ready to fire without explanation Mrs. Keeney and an "undisclosed number" of others. The Keeneys were back where they started in Montana before the war, faced with an exhausting battle—which they would again win—to establish the rights of job tenure.

After the "Ten" lesson, Hollywood was giving new assurances of loyalty with such films as *The Iron Curtain* and *The Red Menace* (showing an ex-GI's seduction by one Marxist Molly), although it complained that the public would not pay to see them. *The Iron Curtain* roused stormy scenes in a Paris theatre and had to be withdrawn there and as far east as the Punjab. The front on which heretics continued to be most vocal was education, but hardly an avenue remained for their protests. With no access to radio and TV networks, they spoke with muted voice through their own press which reached a maximum of one in 2,000 Americans. The last two births of heretical journals for several years occurred in May: Leo Huberman's and Paul Sweezy's *Monthly Review* and the *Compass*, a third and final effort to maintain a *PM*-style daily in New York, financed by Anita Blaine and edited by Ted Thackrey who had become odious to his wife and her New York *Post*. Taking the position that all heretical sects had the right to exist and that Russia's policies were not necessarily criminal and should be accurately reported, the newcomers' claims to have no party ties were treated with the same derision as *National Guardian's*. Einstein christened *Monthly Review* with a new plea for socialism after an admiral had proposed that, if he "doesn't like Americans, Einstein should go back where he came from." A Pentagon man reassured the public that secrets were being kept from this "poor security risk." An anonymous heretic commented that this was "like not telling God about Creation."

Opposition to the University of California's private inquisition initiated in June was strong enough to delay the showdown there for a year. The university required its faculty of 4,000 to sign am-not-and-have-never-been oaths based on state inquisitor Jack Tenney's list of 142 organizations and publications. At the NEA convention held in June, where it was reported that 22 states had adopted such oaths, the largest educational body first opposed them and then adopted the Hook principle as its policy. The 250 delegates were left speechless with the single exception of Rose Russell, who angered the chairman by opposing all inquisitions on the basis that "the target cannot be limited to Communists." The chair commented: "The lady who just spoke represents an organization that constantly follows the Communist Party line." When delegates opposing the resolution were asked to stand, five stood. Others told Russell afterwards that they agreed with her but dared not say so.

Thus the purge became official with guarantees that it would be democratic. Wholesale firing of teachers was ready to begin, but TU continued mobilizing protest against those already recorded: a Wallaceite Bible professor at Evansville Methodist, two "ultra-liberals" at Olivet, mathematics instructor Lee Lorch at New York City College, etc. Lorch had made himself notorious by leading a fight against the exclusion of Negroes from Stuyvesant Town where he and his family lived. He compounded his offense by lending his apartment to a black family after City College fired him, and when this came to the ears of his next employer, Penn State, he would again be unemployed. Teachers were heartened by the success of TU's lawsuit to have the Feinberg law ruled unconstitutional, and in a tribute to this decision Garfield Hays mocked the idea that the few Communist teachers were "such supermen" as to be able "in spite of overwhelming conflicting influences, to indoctrinate pupils without anyone's knowing it." Hays was premature.

A Bill of Rights conference in July managed to bring 1,300 delegates to New York from 33 states, but almost all were already marked heretics. A South Dakota newspaper editor assured himself a stormy return home by turning up to warn of "the danger of an American brand of Fascism." In a July report noting that "intolerance is not peculiar to Russian Communism," a Quaker group sparked by Clarence E. Pickett recalled that neither Christianity nor Islam, nor Catholicism nor Protestantism had been destroyed in past ideological struggles: capitalism and socialism, they said, likewise had no choice but coexistence. The Methodist general conference had urged Christians to "resist a mood of despair, a blind hatred, hysteria and hopelessness . . . seek to develop mutual understanding" with Russia.

Bicentennial Goethe celebrations in Aspen, Colorado, and in Germany moved Robert Hutchins and Thomas Mann to more defiance. Hutchins, advocating that Hoover should study Jefferson even if Goethe was too much for him, called for resistance to "the pressure on us to abandon thought, to cut ourselves off from other groups, and to conform without question to a line laid down we do not know where or by whom." Mann acted upon his consistent view that "anti-Bolshevism is the basic foolishness of our epoch" by attending the bicentennials in both German zones. He returned to launch a Committee for Peaceful Alternatives with Einstein, Pauling and Chicago's Negro bishop W. J. Walls, but his visit to West Germany seemed to have finally estranged him from his adopted country. America had handed over the trial of "war crimes" to German judges many of whom committed them; Hitler's aides and partners flourished on all sides, and a new Wehrmacht was being born to lead free Europe against Eastern barbarism.

The latest trial of Harry Bridges ran from November well into 1950 (81 days). The testimony of a battery of ex-Communists that Bridges had been, and probably still was, contained the standard quota of contradictions; but Judge George B. Harris found "the golden truth in the fiery crucible" of the proceedings. Bridges was guilty. In his twentieth appearance against heretics, Manning Johnson said that on the one hand he had seen Bridges elected to the Party national committee in New York in 1936, and on the other that he never met Bridges. Paul Crouch said he had also been present at the 1936 ceremony on a date when Bridges had documentary proof of being on the west coast. On the trial's first day Harris sentenced Bridges's defender Vincent Hallinan to six months for contempt. Among other signs of his Irish rebel descent, Hallinan described prosecution witnesses as "trained pet cobras" and/or criminals of record whom the government was paying up to $125 a week for the job; he estimated that the government had spent from two to three million dollars to "frame Bridges" over the years. In December he demanded the arrest of Johnson and Crouch for perjury, upon which two women were indicted for "blackmail involving sex" to intimidate one of the familiars.

Bridges, who yielded during the trial in signing the Taft-Hartley oath, admitted talking to Communists, favoring trade with what had now become "Red China," reading Marx and opposing Hitler. In nine days on the stand he covered every aspect of the heretic's eye-view in typically breezy style. But (as a Birch Society spokesman would put it 18 years later) Bridges had "been identified as a

Communist in sworn testimony by some 35 witnesses" and "holds a razor at the throat of our Far East defenses."

Be that as it might, another one-fifth of the world's population had fallen under the heresy, and radiation from the first un-American Bomb drifted across the stratosphere, as Bridges went on trial. Washington blamed Russia for the collapse of Chiang, whose last formula for victory was mass beheading of suspected heretics in the streets as Mao's armies approached. Smedley ascribed Mao's victory to Chinese ability to learn from "100 years of bloody struggle," and to "38 years of American stupidity."

Confirmation of Russia's Bomb brought the cry from the Catholic War Veterans' commander: "Either we destroy them in time or they will destroy our civilization." The *Wall Street Journal* found the public "conspicuously calm" in face of the Bomb while Congressmen "charged about" to determine who leaked America's prime secret. But an event in England gave the greatest stimulus yet to the domestic melodrama: the arrest and confession of Russian agent Klaus Fuchs.

PART THREE:
THE INQUISITION
RAMPANT

XI

1950: Tail-Gunner Joe

According to Richard Rovere,* Joseph McCarthy was seeking in January 1950 a gimmick to lift him out of three years' obscurity in the Senate: he considered an old-age-pension crusade and was only persuaded by a priest at a stag dinner party to become an inquisitor. It seems curious that so discerning an eye in so ambitious and grammarless a head would not have already spotted the inquisition as his road to success. Yet, as Rovere seems correct in pointing out, McCarthy's anti-Communism was not genuine: "He drilled Communism and saw it come up as a gusher, liked the gusher but would have liked any other just as well." His biographer, on the other hand, was a man committed since his conversion from heresy to the view that "only a Communist or an idiot could have denied that the Communist threat to the US was real and great." Playing the political game by ear, entering the holy office with a lack of decorum that amounted to sacrilege, the carefree Wisconsin lawyer was distasteful to the loyal intelligentsia, yet they owed him much. After it became the vogue to deplore inquisitorial "excess," it was the happy but inaccurate formulation "McCarthyism—McCarthy Era" that drew attention from their passivity when, years earlier, the foundation on which he built his fame was being laid.

The Senate already had a workmanlike inquisitor in plump, 74-year-old McCarran, who represented a state slightly less populated than greater York, Pennsylvania. His seat had been secured since 1933 by Nevada's gambling and mining barons; a few tens of thousands of votes ensured his constant re-election, and thus seniority had brought him the strategic Judiciary Committee chairmanship. He had appointed subcommittees to probe almost anyone who did not share his admiration for Franco and Chiang, and now he set up the Senate Internal Security Subcommittee which would consistently outshine HUAC. But without waiting for an invitation from McCarran or anyone else, McCarthy took the priestly hint and within a month had set up in business on his own.

"I have here in my hand," McCarthy told an assembly of West Virginia ladies, "a list" of scores of Communists currently in the State Department, whose number he would constantly vary through the next hectic weeks. The phrase, referring to papers he dug from a briefcase and waved ominously, became more famous than a toothpaste slogan along with his "Point of order" interruptions and questions beginning, "Isn't it a fact . . . ?" (Occasionally he would show some document to a reporter, unabashed by the fact that it never said what he said it said.) When all America was dying of suspense he named Johns Hopkins professor Owen Lattimore as "Hiss's boss in the State Department ring," the "top secret agent" responsible for "our loss of China." Lattimore's sin was that he had seen, correctly estimated, and politely but firmly warned about, Communist

* Richard Rovere, *Senator Joe McCarthy*, Harcourt Brace, New York, 1959.

strength in Asia; his advice—to relieve Asians of tyranny and corruption by backing liberal independence movements—had sometimes been asked by Washington but rarely acted upon. Of the few other names on McCarthy's State Department list which ever came to light, one was Mrs. Keeney who likewise was not in the Department.

Lattimore had hardly called McCarthy a "madman" before Budenz came forward to corroborate the senator; and who should know better than Budenz? McCarthy had chosen fruitfully in making the "loss of China" his first target. Textile manufacturer Alfred Kohlberg, Chiang's confidant and inventor of the "Kohlkerchief," became an ardent McCarthyite along with the journal he sponsored, *Plain Talk*. The Taiwan police could supply on demand names of Chinese heretics and their American friends; McCarthy could not always pronounce them but reeled them off to dazed, impressed fellow senators. Unfortunately Agnes Smedley was not available for the Asian master-conspirator role: ghettoized, penniless and in ailing health, she had moved to England and would die there in May after an operation from which "I don't care much if I recover." But she lived to see Mao's ragged millions take over their country, and her ashes went to Peking for burial in its revolutionary heroes' cemetery.

At the outset of McCarthy's short but dazzling career the Establishment's attitude, as reflected in the media, recalled that of the German gentry toward the early Hitler. The Establishment already permitted itself—especially in such club periodicals as the *Wall Street Journal* and *New Yorker*—moments of public levity at the harlequinades of its inquisitors. It could not do less to show its European junior partners that, within limits, it shared their dismay and contempt. McCarthy and his aides were the subject of brilliant jests by cartoonist Herblock* and of through-the-keyhole columns by Pearson and the Alsop brothers; he turned up in the likeness of a skunk in the comic strip *Pogo* and was treated with consistent disdain by Lippmann. Syndication of these features in editorially loyal journals was harmless and healthy in the American context. Yet the Establishment had decided to enforce conformity in a nation born in nonconformity, and if the necessary fear could only be created by contemptible persons and methods, so it must be. Just as the German establishment had found Streicher, Himmler, Goebbels and Rosenberg to be what the doctor ordered, so the American had learned empirically the value of a Rankin, a Hoover, a Hearst, a Hook. The clay it was molding responded better to inquisitorial and intellectual vulgarians and raw journalistic distortions than it would have done to anything that smacked of dignity or truth. Fear in some Establishment circles that McCarthy was excessively uncouth yielded to the conviction in others that here at last was the ideal inquisitor. This conviction had a short life, but for the time being the *Wall Street Journal* could afford to smile on both sides of its face.

McCarthy captured a mass public's affections by parading his illiteracy and penchant for obscenity as proof of American horse sense, by his authentic genius as a liar, and by his total disrespect ("There is no one too high") for sacred cows,

---

* Heretics often borrowed Herblock cartoons from respectable journals to lend force to the perennial plea to abolish the inquisition. A favorite one showed three inquisitors surrounding a man gagged and bound to a chair with a rope, with the legend: "All we want is the truth as we see it."

scholars and hereditary gentlemen. Reputable Americans were soon agitatedly recalling membership in the YMCA and Boy Scouts to assure him of their loyalty,
but even the Scouts were no longer immune. The feeling was now widespread
that since America needed an inquisition it must, as in all else, have the best; and
by every established standard McCarthy was pre-eminent. He did nothing his
predecessors had not done but did it with far more style, daring and noise. He
fell into place at the hour when the laborious exercise of washing the American
brain was ready to bear prime fruit. A psychiatrist diagnosed him as "a classical
paranoiac" without noting that he was a true reflection of the already induced
national paranoia. With equal solemnity it would later be adumbrated that, as the
man who made America's inquisition the butt of horrified derision around the
globe, he was a Communist secretly working for Stalin. There was the alternative
possibility that he was a man with a ghoulishly Barnumian sense of humor, enjoying the gullibility of the gaping crowd. If such was the case, it was a joke that
heretics might have shared had they come upon it in a book, but this was no book.

McCarthy talked almost pure nonsense at such roller-coaster speed that courtroom and parliamentary veterans gave up the struggle to bring any colloquy with
him down to earth. His flair for publicity rivaled that of Hoover, the inquisition's
everlasting father and permanent insurance figure. He wisely established friendship with Hoover on personal as well as dossier levels while labeling Acheson "the
Red Dean of Washington." His public enjoyed the removal of Acheson's stuffed
shirt and revered Hoover as their shelter from the stormy red blast. Hoover's personal tastes ran to Edgar Guest poetry, postage stamps and Tarzan, with a phobia
for McCarthy's favorite beverage, whisky; but the two men coincided on Communists and love of horse racing. What was for Hoover "the most evil, monstrous
conspiracy against man since time began" was for McCarthy "a conspiracy so immense, an infamy so black, as to dwarf any previous such venture in the history of
mankind." When vacationing with McCarthy in 1952, Hoover would tell the
press: "I've come to know him well officially and personally. I view him as a
friend and believe he so views me."

Journalistic familiars loved the inquisitor who embraced them with gusto,
poured highballs and "always had a hot story" meriting bigger headlines the more
outrageous it was. Dignified editors surrendered their front pages explaining that
it might be ridiculous but it was news. His lumping together of the Roosevelt
and Truman administrations as "20 years of treason" delighted his fellow-Repub-
licans in the Senate, but Congressmen of both parties who saw through him had
good reasons for not saying so. Long accustomed to the blackmail of Hoover who
always kept his dossiers on them up to date, they perceived that a new expert had
arisen in their midst who could ruin them with blank or meaningless sheets of
paper. No senator was more vulnerable than McCarthy on the score of petty
financial manipulations and personal misdemeanors, but he made it clear that
any attempted exposure was a "Communist smear" to be deftly turned against the
accuser. Maryland's scrupulously anti-Communist Millard Tydings, who inquired
into McCarthy's first "charges" and pronounced them bogus, was drowned at the
next elections beneath McCarthy-inspired forgeries linking him with Browder.

For Congressmen or commentators it was anyhow too late to point out
that the inquisitorial king was naked. It could not be done without exposing the

royal nudity ever since Dies, and almost all were implicated in the hoax. Eight Republican senators signed a manifesto for "security based on freedom"; the Washington *Post* protested that McCarthy's "terror" in the capital was no way to defeat "the cancerous evil of totalitarianism"; Acheson suggested that McCarthy was shattering the "American faith and unity" which alone could frustrate the Kremlin's designs. They merely bayed at the moon. As McCarthy became a world sensation, established men like Nixon perceived their own comparatively drab image but were in a worse position than anyone to belittle him. McCarran decided on a policy of warm support.

A Justice Department man testifying on budget requests said that 21,105 subversive cases were "pending" at the time, but that many "perfectly good" ones were unpursuable because "the sole witnesses are confidential informants" who were not ripe for exposure. Nevertheless the McCarthy stimulus brought to the surface more than enough familiars for probers' immediate needs. Matthew Cvetic, Hoover's undercover man in Pittsburgh since early war years, emerged from clandestinity to name "co-comrades who posed as clergymen, doctors, dentists, etc." Among his first names were a piano teacher and Joseph Mazzei, manager of a theatre showing Russian films, who would both turn out to be co-comrades for Hoover; but his banner-headlined testimony about subversive Slavs ghettoized scores of union men, identified Nelson as their red chieftain, and inspired Pittsburgh patriots to band together as "Americans Battling Communism"—the ABC of midcentury America. Cvetic's accounts of Party activity would run a gamut from its infiltration of Republican and Democratic ranks—with "the base objective to carry on these two objectives with the primary purpose of by subversion gaining control of the government"—to assassinations. A *Saturday Evening Post* man ghost-wrote them as a colorful serial, *I Was a Communist for the FBI*, which would sell book and film rights and enable Cvetic to introduce himself to inquisitors as "lecturer and author." After he exposed Moscow's hand behind their party, Pittsburgh Progressives photostated his indictment for beating his sister-in-law (putting her in hospital for some weeks) which had been nol-prossed shortly before Hoover recruited him. The photostats went to the press over the name of local PP director Alexander Wright, a veteran trade unionist who had himself been on Hoover's payroll for seven years but was not yet ready for surfacing. The *Worker's* publication of the counter-exposure, and of an appraisal of Cvetic by his estranged wife as "a sneak, liar and yellow coward," helped ABC to build him up as a hero. In March he brought to Washington for HUAC 80 pounds of documents unmasking New Dealers' support of the American Slav Congress before it was branded heretical. These were mysteriously lost in the hearing room before the culprits' names, which included several Congressmen still in office, could be recited.

John Lautner (as he would say later) was doing "a lot of soul-searching." Concluding that his lifelong associations had been "insidious," he prepared under Hoover's wing to "fight this conspiracy" as a government expert in nine Smith Act trials. The Party never seems to have discovered just when Lautner turned familiar. Harvey Matusow, the champion *Worker* salesman of 1946, who yearned for popularity but saw that "being a Communist wasn't popular any more," accepted a beginner's $70-a-month "expenses" to report to Hoover on his Party and People's Songs friends. Seeger sang at the funeral of People's Songs and would be excommunicated from TV networks in July. Hoover wanted "physical descriptions," and Matusow's opportunity to please him came with New York's annual May Day parade. Regretting that "an old war injury" prevented his marching with the comrades, Matusow "stood on the sidelines watching rank after rank carrying banners proclaiming slogans which I claimed to believe in . . . contingent upon contingent singing songs that I loved to sing. I had my camera . . . each of the 144 clicks of my shutter caught the face of a friend. Most of them recognized me and waved as I took their pictures . . . As I turned the film over to 'my' FBI agent, I had the childish sense of playing 'cops and robbers.' " *

Judges with New Deal hangovers continued to obstruct the inquisition here and there, but cooperation became more generous in the first McCarthy months. In March a higher court found New York's Feinberg law Constitutional after all. In April, Long Island's Episcopalian Bishop De Wolfe won judicial sympathy in his crusade to oust the Melishes from Holy Trinity Church, Brooklyn, but the judge still needed time to consider so delicate a matter as church democracy. De Wolfe had fired rector John for refusing to fire his assistant rector, son William; but the congregation liked the Melishes so well, especially for their development of community activities, that it voted out its pro-De Wolfe vestrymen and elected William as rector and John as rector emeritus. When De Wolfe ruled this out of order and the pulpit vacant, the flock had appointed William as their "acting minister" on a day-to-day basis, sending De Wolfe back to court to repeat his expostulations.

Bridges's five-year sentence for perjury was followed by ILWU's expulsion from CIO on the assurance of Quill—now a CIO vice president and president of its New York Council—that Bridges really was a Communist. His citizenship canceled, Bridges was primed for deportation on leaving prison. Defense lawyer Hallinan's charges of government subornation of perjury fell on stony ground and he ended up with his own jail term to serve, his personal assets impounded for alleged tax arrears. In the same month Matthiessen killed himself, the seven Martinsville Negroes' appeal against death was routinely rejected, and a Senate committee voted to probe homosexuals in government as security risks. In May and June the Hollywood Ten, the 11 JAFRC leaders and CRC's George Marshall, all of whom had expensively exhausted their rights of appeal, went to jail. NCASF's Morford would follow them in September. The inquisitors of whom they had been contemptuous were meanwhile handing out 39 similar citations in an exposure of an ILWU "red Pearl Harbor" plot in Hawaii. Using his standard arithmetic of CP membership multiplied by ten, Hoover now reckoned America's "potential fifth column," all of whom seemed candidates for jail, at 540,000. The Supreme Court had upheld the 22 convictions and at the same time endorsed the Taft-Hartley law with a minority reduced to one from the usual two or three. The solitary Justice Black still made no exceptions in declining to reject "the fundamental principle that beliefs are inviolate."

Remington was indicted for perjury, and an outburst by Roman Catholic Senator Dennis Chavez against Budenz ("he has been using the Cross as a club

* Harvey Matusow, *False Witness*, Cameron & Kahn, New York, 1955.

. . . using the Church which I revere as a cloak for un-American, un-Christian, dubious testimony") was slapped down by president Laurence J. McGinley of Fordham where Budenz was employed. Chavez, said McGinley on front pages, "posed as a Catholic" in calumniating "a Christian gentleman"; Fordham students responded by nominating Budenz as their "favorite personality." New York schools superintendent William Jansen had retained Budenz to confirm the subversiveness of eight teachers, all active union members, whom Jansen suspended without pay in mid-term. Of 9,665 University of California employees from professors to scrubwomen who were required to swear they had Never Been, 157 refused; two days before America went to war in Korea the board of regents, with Governor Earl Warren in the chair, unanimously agreed that they must be fired.

Although McCarthy's State Department rampage won him the lion's share of headlines, all official and unofficial inquisitorial bodies ran him stern competition. Tremors ran through media and show people as *Counterattack's* handbook *Red Channels* listed 151 of them who, unless they "proved anti-Communism by word or deed," should be prevented from contaminating airwaves, stage or screen. Among them were José Ferrer, critic Olin Downes, Edward G. Robinson, William Shirer, Orson Welles, Irwin Shaw, Hazel Scott, Howard K. Smith, Henry Morgan, Abe Burrows, Garson Kanin and stripteaser Gypsy Rose Lee. The criteria used by *Counterattack's* ex-FBI agents, which made them the national arbiters of blacklisting, included: "Reported as member of Freedom from Fear Committee," "Sponsor, national committee to combat anti-Semitism," "Author of Book Find Club selection." Their call for vigilance was taken up by columnist-broadcaster Ed Sullivan who applauded the jailing of "dangerous jerks," and by columnist Westbrook Pegler who agreed with Pennsylvania's Governor James H. Duff that Communists should be hanged. *Red Channels* not only became every radio-TV executive's and sponsor's vademecum but an adjunct to education. The Newark, New Jersey, schools superintendent, who a year previously had banned the *Nation* from school libraries, bought 60 copies for distribution as a "teacher's reference book." By this time smoke was beginning to rise from bonfires, often on remote river banks for privacy and convenience in ash disposal, of heretical literature sacrificed by owners who dared not keep it in their shelves.*

---

* The number of heretical books burned by their owners at the height of the inquisition is impossible to estimate but was considerable. Some heretics recalled, as they watched the flames, reports of similar scenes in occupied Russia a few years earlier. As Anatoly Kuznetsov would describe one such in Kiev, in *Babi Yar* (Dial, New York, 1967):
"It was cold, and the books got the stove well heated. All that was left, I remember, was the collected works of Pushkin. Pushkin was a *moskal,* a Russian, but he had lived a long time ago, and neither the Bolsheviks nor the Germans had condemned him. My mother's face was expressionless. I said: 'Don't take it to heart. Some day we'll have lots of books again.'
" 'Never have idiots spared books,' she said. 'Never . . . If you live, remember this: When books are burned it means things are bad, it means that violence, ignorance and fear are everywhere. And what is happening now? When a gang of degenerates burns books in the streets it is horrible, true, but it's not the worst thing that can happen. When each person in each house begins to burn his books, shaking with fear—.' "

These were secondary developments compared with two arrests made by Hoover's men in May and June. With a wealth of detail the eccentric Philadelphia chemist Harry Gold insisted to his captors that, although he never liked Communism and they paid him nothing, Russians had "groomed" him as a "courier" for Moscow agent Fuchs (now in a British jail) and to steal secrets ranging from the Bomb to a "soap-making technique." Ethel Rosenberg's dull-witted brother David Greenglass, whom Hoover knew to have committed "loyalty" perjury and purloined a lump of Los Alamos uranium, named Julius as his master spy and, later, Ethel as his accomplice. Clearly made for each other, Gold and Greenglass were deposited together in a privileged cell-less jail, a convenient spot to discuss how they could contribute to a spy melodrama involving the Rosenbergs whom Gold had not met. FBI men paid an early call at the Rosenbergs', took Julius to their office and told him what they said David said. Julius asked and was refused the favor of calling his brother-in-law a liar to his and their faces. He walked home and, after consulting lawyers, went on with his life as a struggling machine-shop operator, father and husband. Shadowed in this daily round for another month, during which he did nothing peculiar, he would finally be handcuffed and led away as he and Ethel were saying good night to their sons.

Since Hoover's men were now visiting all who ever knew Rosenberg and could be members of his "ring," it was a suitable time for his classmate Morton Sobell to leave on a long-planned family vacation in Mexico. Mexican press reports of Julius's arrest scared Sobell into laying a trail of assumed names in a futile effort (the family having no passports) to sail for Europe from a Caribbean port. He returned in soberer mood to end the vacation in a Mexico City flat he had rented under his own name. Again fortune smiled on the inquisition: one of the suspects visited by FBI agents, Sobell's wedding best man Max Elitcher, had been practically a member of the Sobell family but was now estranged; he also had a perjurious loyalty oath in his dossier. By coincidence, both Greenglass and Elitcher chose the newly repented heretic O. John Rogge as their lawyer to get them off the hook in return for information about conversations incapable of corroboration and incidents equally questionable.* After some years as an international peacemonger, Rogge had renewed amiable relations with his former employer, the Justice Department, and become American representative of Stalin's sworn enemy Tito. He was, as he would write later, on the road back to "belief in capitalism and opposition to Communism and to socialism as well."

In the broader background, even the exchange of American-Russian insults had stopped: unable to remove Chiang from behind the "China" plaque in the UN, Russia had abandoned the Security Council to the capitalists who dominated it anyway. It was a triumph for the Dulles school of geopolitics which had moved China from its traditional location to Chiang's island refuge, Taiwan, and

---

* The unlikelihood of the incidents described by Greenglass, Gold and Elitcher was quite persuasively documented by John Wexley in *The Judgment of Julius and Ethel Rosenberg* (Cameron & Kahn, New York, 1955) and by Walter & Miriam Schneir in *Invitation to an Inquest* (Doubleday, New York, 1965), to which the reader is referred for details. The first and more factually limited book on the subject was *The Atom Spy Hoax* by William A. Reuben (Action Books, New York, 1955).

Truman made Dulles his top foreign-policy adviser. So far as could be seen from the media, no one except Einstein was perturbed by the gathering momentum of the linked foreign and domestic cold wars. Mrs. Roosevelt gave him time on her radio program to call the cold war "a disastrous illusion" which had merely brought America "the concentration of tremendous financial power in the hands of the military, a growing police force, intimidation, indoctrination by radio, press and school." As if his dossier were not already large enough to discount his opinions, Einstein proceeded to accept TU's annual award for "distinguished service to education." Nobel laureate Thomas Mann was also earning new discredits by protesting the teacher inquisition, petitioning for the Hollywood Ten, and asking parole for Carl Marzani. The media had been closed to him and his kind who, though not suspected of being socialists, thought the subject which had become America's ogre should be quietly discussed rather than struck with a club. Leo Huberman tried in vain—his book being ignored—to explain what it was to Americans who "are told the exact opposite day in and day out." * At this point it was possible for young Americans to hear socialist economics expounded expertly and sympathetically by one professor, Huberman's associate Paul Baran, at one university. Moscow-born Baran was too critical of Stalin to get a Russian visa to visit his mother but, having been branded a Kremlin agent while on an American mission to Germany and Japan in 1945, had no passport to put it on. There were enough doubts about the brand for Stanford University to hire him, but, haunted to the end by inquisitors, he would become the American professor most shunned by his colleagues.

America's economic problem was to spend enough billions on preparations for a war which, now that the Russians had the Bomb, it had less intention than ever of fighting. But Russia's Bomb itself had opened up a wider horizon than publisher McCormick envisaged in his fortification of the Chicago *Tribune* building. "Making a place to hide from the A-Bomb is to cost billions," the candid *US News & World Report* reassured its businessman readership. "Planners are busy now deciding what to sell the country and how to sell it. They figure that they have hold of a program that, in years just ahead, can serve as a vast pump-priming enterprise in the event that armament, foreign aid and other government activities are not big enough to keep business at a high level." The nation must be ready to place itself beneath 12 inches of concrete (21 for factories) with "mines, caves, tunnels recommended" for war industries. Noting that as matters stood an atomic attack would "produce panic" and that "latest intelligence reports" indicated it might be imminent, the *Times* thought it would "not be possible to get a big and complex job done quickly without some very powerful stimulus . . . the one real stimulus that would do the job, of course, is fear." A gathering of west-coast mayors heard San Francisco's Mayor Elmer E. Robinson outline the prospects for an American Hiroshima, on the planners' "assumption that 20 cities would be bombed the first day and bombing would continue over a three-year period." Russian Bombs, he admitted, would "have an effect on the blood count, bone marrow and so on," but "the medical profession is studying the matter."

* Leo Huberman, *The Truth About Socialism*, Monthly Review Press, New York, 1950.

Such ruminations were temporarily submerged by a vaster pump-priming enterprise, "a made-to-order situation to keep business on a high level," as Air Force chief General Emmett O'Donnell would call the Korean War. America urgently needed to expend some of its stockpiled lethal devices in order to invest more billions in their replacement. But if expending them on Russia would have been unwise, their use on populations surrounding Russia and China would have educational value for the recipients at comparatively small risk of Russian reprisals. The time was more than ripe for America to step up its policing activities against heresy in Asia. Only where America had undertaken to supervise the police job was it being efficiently done—as in Greece, where some 100,000 heretics had been exterminated since the Germans left and some 30,000 more were in concentration camps. While the cleanup was making headway in the Philippines under American tutelage, in Malaya 100,000 British troops still pursued 4,000 guerrilleros through the jungle, sticking their heads on poles when caught but failing to unman the survivors. The French in Indochina had the advantage of German experts in their Foreign Legion to modernize torture techniques: as one German wrote home, "I get pleasure from beheading rebels—we either behead them or cripple them, beginning with fingers and ending with the head." Yet there was little beyond severed brown fingers, genitalia and heads to show for the ever dizzier sums America was paying the French to suppress Indochinese heresy.

Most Americans had never heard of Korea, and not one in 100 knew where it was; but it leaped into banner headlines as suddenly as had McCarthy, to share them with him until both disappeared together after four years. Emerging in 1945 from a long and ruthless Japanese police regime, the 25,000,000 Koreans had seen their country divided in half by palefaces speaking two different tongues; they yearned for unity and little cared what sort of regime gave it to them so long as it was Korean and anti-Japanese. But in trenches along the artificial frontier, Koreans had been put under a capitalist flag to face Koreans under a socialist flag, and there were constant flare-ups. American officials and generals jetted in and out via Tokyo and Taiwan explaining the advantages of salvation from Communism and depicting North Korea as a Russian slave state, while North Koreans depicted South Korea as a slave state of the Americans who had settled in Japan to inherit the mantle of Southeast Asia's policeman. In this climate Syngman Rhee, whom America had sent in to preside over South Korea, logically ignored northern proposals for discussions. Envisaging a "greater Korea" with slices of China and Russia, he exhorted his generous suppliers of arms and experts to let him attack the North, whose President had for years been a leader of anti-Japanese guerrillas. Since North Korea shared a frontier with Russia and Russia had the Bomb, many in Washington frowned on Rhee's proposal, especially after Rhee spoiled the picture of South Korea as a democracy: he was trounced at the polls (having failed, said North Koreans, to jail enough of his opponents) but continued on the throne.

Dulles, however, was not discouraged and paid a morale-building visit to Rhee's front-line trenches. Some days later word flashed to MacArthur's Tokyo headquarters that the South had attacked the North, but by morning edition-time

American media had firmly established that the North attacked the South. The question hardly needed argument, for North Korea was notoriously Stalin's property, and Stalin's belief in violence was as well known as America's repudiation of it.*

In any case it was Northern forces that began sweeping into Rhee's domain because, as they claimed, Rhee's corruption gave Southerners nothing to fight for. His soldiers emulated Chiang's so energetically that after two weeks the *Times* military columnist reported: "A large percentage of the South Korean army has disappeared." Rhee's American advisers were also trying to locate the South Korean legislature, whose members had shown with their heels their loyalty to Rhee. But Russia, by walking out of the UN, had set the stage for America to enter the fray with impeccable credentials. The war would be a "police action" for which the international peace organization would contribute its flag. America's crusaders soon recovered from their surprise on finding that there were no Russians to fight, only underfed little brown men with out-of-date weapons whom they christened "gooks."

For the sole benefit of already convinced heretics *National Guardian* and *Monthly Review,* and Marcantonio in Congress, appraised the imbroglio as a civil war, the natural consequence of Korea's partition, in which outsiders should not interfere. Hoover's men were systematically visiting *Guardian* readers to sketch the consequences "if your employer should learn that you read this Moscow propaganda": and to be seen with a *Worker* (naturally pro-North) was tantamount to carrying a sign, "Kindly beat me up and call the police." As in all fresh war situations, normally uncluttered brains succumbed to loyal intoxications. *Compass* columnist Stone wrote that to restore peace "the next step is up to the Russians" by countermanding the marching orders they gave North Korea; but the Russians had no orders to countermand. Henry Wallace belatedly grasped the flag, to concede on reflection that he really had been a Communist dupe in 1948. He was a political corpse whom nothing, not even his proposal to atomize North Korea, could revive; but his abject flight hung a further weight on heretical morale.**

American churches backed the crusade, but Bertrand Russell began reproving America's attempt to "cast out Satan by the help of Beelzebub." Irrepressible pacifists like A. J. Muste and Clarence Pickett sought to stop the slaughter, regardless of who began it, through an interdenominational Church Peace Mission. Despite the grandeur of the cause, young Americans showed the usual preference that someone else should die for it. The inquisition had complicated the work of military draft boards, for crusade candidates were required to swear non-

---

* For detailed background of America's involvement in Korea, see I. F. Stone, *Hidden History of the Korean War,* Monthly Review Press, New York, 1952.
** In a letter to *National Guardian* questioning Wallace's "confused chauvinism" in urging Progressives to "support the UN" in Korea, an impenitent heretic wrote: "I am reminded of the bartender who called upstairs to the owner of the bar, 'Shall I trust Jim Jones for a drink?' The owner called back, 'Has he had the drink?' 'Yes.' 'Then trust him.' " Wallace's defense of the war was his last appearance in the *Guardian;* after a few weeks his views were appearing in the ultra-Russophobe *New Leader,* whose benefactions from CIA would later come to light.

contamination by any of the Attorney General's listed organizations, now totaling 123. Most of the organizations were dead or dying, but *ex post facto* membership in one of them might offer a simple if painful escape hatch. The *Nation* found it odd that the Klan and kindred groups were not on the list, but a Pentagon spokesman explained: "After all, we have to take somebody into the army." As for those who might claim heretical contamination to avoid service, he told the *Nation* the army would accept them and "either keep them under surveillance or courtmartial them." One defense official "gave it as his personal and unofficial opinion that the Nazis had handled the problem correctly" by forming a Wehrmacht division of Germans from concentration camps. By the end of World War II "there wasn't one of 'em left."

By the end of the police action, some would still be left. But since the foe against whom patriots must rally was plainly colored red, this crusade promised even brighter inquisitorial weather than the first war against Germany. The timing of McCarthy and his priest had been brilliant.

Fever Chart

1950

Scene: Hollenburg, Texas (pop. 99) home of Mrs. Stapaules, the first home-steader's daughter. A Wichita editor interviews her about broadcaster Fulton Lewis's charges that she wrote hostile letters to "war-mongering" radio commentators:

MRS. S: Yes, I've been writing them for fifteen years. I monitor the radio for the Voice of Freedom.

EDITOR: Don't you know that has been called a Communist front organization?

MRS. S: Who said so? Isn't the former chairman of HUAC in jail? I shall continue writing protests against things I don't like. I believe in the principles of Christ. What's more, you can tell Lewis to go to hell.

(2-column Wichita *Beacon* headline next day: WOMAN ADMITS SHE WROTE PEACE LETTERS.)

Scene: Secretary-General Lie's office at UN on eve of Korean war. Newsmen question him about his just-ended global peace mission, including Moscow where he found an obsession for peace.

CHICAGO TRIBUNE REPORTER: Mr. Lie, are you or have you ever been a Communist?

LIE: You should not transfer this press conference down to that level. By God, I think there should be *some* respect for my integrity.

Philadelphia: Holmes Alexander writes in *Evening Bulletin.*

"Military chiefs dread even the remotest possibility of mediation in Korea. They need an extensive period in that bloody peninsula to pyramid what is re-alistically called 'bodies and guns.' They know that the more men in Korea, the more men and weapons Congress will authorize to services elsewhere. Warmon-gering may now be called the almost official Pentagon policy . . . It is time to stop yammering about reliance on the A-Bomb being a Maginot Line complex. The most effective weapon in the human arsenal will strike the enemy flush in his heartland."

Scene: Los Angeles.

C. D. JACKSON (publisher of Luce's *Fortune*): The American people should get over their complex about shooting.

REPORTER: But can the Russians be provoked into war?

JACKSON: I am frankly doubtful. But the consideration should be, can the mission be safely accomplished?

New York: *Wall Street Journal* editorializes in first days of war.

"We went into this shooting war to wage a political fight against the Russians. Today it looks like the shrewd Russians may simply ignore the challenge, neither backing down nor openly fighting. We may be drawn deeper into a war against the little man who wasn't there."

"The US is convinced that its sacred mission in life is salvation of the world at any cost. It is conceivable that this messianic complex has gone far enough. Nations with missions tend not to be appreciated in the long run even by their friends."

New York: DuBois writes in *National Guardian.*

"The basic cause of our insanity is that in our unprecedented organization of industry with its marvelous technique, the vast majority of mankind are sick, ignorant and starved while a few have more income than they can use. Proposals to solve this problem by socialism and Communism did not originate in Russia and will not end there. We think money-making is the great end of man; our whole ideology bows to this fantastic idea. War is a business immensely profitable to a few, but of measureless disaster and death of dreams to the many. In order to have war, big business must have hate, so its press asks you to hate Communists and, if not Communists, hate all who do not hate Communists. Its present plan to compel the world to adopt our philosophy and methods by force of arms is not only unreasonable in light of our failure, but impossible in itself. There is no possible chance for us to accomplish what Egypt, Persia, Greece, Rome, Britain and Hitler failed to do . . . But here in New York you can vote for peace—provided of course that your employer does not know it."

Scene: Los Angeles. General who trained South Korean army speaks to business executives on war manpower problem:

BRIGADIER GENERAL ROBERTS: Why could we not use Filipinos or Japanese? We could pay them as little as $5 a month and a bowl of rice a day. No fight, no rice. The Korean makes a good soldier though he may do a little stealing. They have come to like us Westerners in a way because we're somebody to steal from. It's my conviction that only as a last resort should white men be sent to Asia to fight.

Scene: Lidice, Illinois, town renamed in 1942 with an "eternal flame" monument to commemorate Lidice, Czechoslovakia, as "an everlasting reminder that tyranny will not destroy love of freedom or the courage to mention it."

REPORTER (finding monument lightless, crumbling and weed-grown—to residents): Do you know anything about it?

SUSAN HARRIS (age 9): Nobody ever told me why they put it there.

LUELLA WEEKS (housewife): I never saw any flame there. I heard there used to be, though.

Tampa, Florida: University president Elwood C. Nance speaks in praise of teachers' loyalty oath.

"I advocate that Americans learn all there is to know about how to kill, based on the law of the jungle, because it is the only law by which Russia and her satellites know how to live."

New York: Letter-to-the-editor from woman whose son just began school.

"After his third day I asked him what he had done that day. He sat down on his heels, curled his arms around his head and said: 'We learned to sit like this in case the windows break.' A few days later he came home with a tag around his neck bearing his name and address. He explained: 'That's if a war gets me in the street, people will know what my name is.' "

Scene: Reno, Nevada. The 105 employees of Brodsky's gambling saloon—dealers, B-girls, pit bosses, waitresses, janitors—are lined up before Murray Brodsky who exhibits a loyalty-oath form.

BRODSKY: All right, you guys. Either sign or get out.

GIRL WHO POSES NUDE IN CHAMPAGNE GLASS: Me too?

BRODSKY: Yeah, put your John Hancock here and don't argue.

(All sign. Manager of neighboring Harold's Club announces he will march his 600 employees behind a brass band to administer non-Communist oaths on courthouse steps.)

Hollywood: Dispatch to New York *Times*.

"Fear that a motion picture dealing with the life and exploits of Hiawatha might be regarded as Communist propaganda has caused Monogram Studio to shelve such a project. It was Hiawatha's efforts as a peacemaker among the warring Indian tribes of his day, which brought about the federation of five nations, that gave Monogram particular concern, according to a studio spokesman. These, it was decided, might cause the picture to be regarded as a message for peace and therefore helpful to present Communist designs."

XII

1950: "An Insane

Lunatic Asylum"

Up to June 24 the marks of heresy were those already set forth here: support of the New Deal or Republican Spain, old-fashioned union militancy, possession of Marxist books, skin color-blindness, nonrecognition of anti-Semites' or recognition of Communists' free-speech rights, premature aversion to Hitler, skepticism about Chiang's or postwar Germany's democracy; too little enthusiasm for World War II before June 1941, too much after that month; voting for Wallace, presence at the Waldorf-Astoria conference, etc. From June 25, any sign of sympathy for Koreans north of the 38th parallel became the decisive proof of disloyalty.

Auto workers administered rough justice to peacemongering colleagues in Los Angeles and Linden, New Jersey, and ejected eight from a Milwaukee factory, one with such force as to break his back. Stones crashed through suspicious residential windows in Houston, Pittsburgh, Philadelphia and Jackson Heights, New York. Female peacemongers were arrested in Burbank, Long Beach, Pasadena and Vancouver, Washington. In Philadelphia, which soon clocked 40 arrests, a judge held four mothers and grandmothers in $5,000 bail and advised them to "go back to Russia." Citizens were urged by Truman to report any suspicious neighbor to Hoover, by Hoover to watch out for "some peace groups and civil rights organizations," by radio patriots to help apprehend anyone who would "stab our boys in the back." Boston youths slugged distributors of anti-war leaflets and passed out their own: "White Gentiles, Awake! Down with the Communists, Hail America!" Ten Jewish groups exposed one peace petition in circulation—the Stockholm Appeal to destroy all A-Bombs, eventually signed by half a billion people around the world—as "a despicable divide-and-conquer tactic." The Los Angeles *Times* advised anyone who might be approached with a petition: "Don't punch him in the nose, Reds are used to that. Get his name and address and phone the FBI."

Arrested in the first weeks, Julius and Ethel Rosenberg would be told by the judge sentencing them to death that they were responsible for the war and consequent toll of American lives. The public readily accepted this since the Rosenbergs' marks over the years identified them as hard-core Jimmie Higginses. The logic was easily grasped: America could have atomized the North Koreans with its Bomb, but their Russian friends now had a Bomb with which to atomize the South Koreans. The killing would therefore have to be done "conventionally"; thus Americans too must die. Russians not being bright enough to produce the Bomb by themselves, some American must have given them the formula. And who should it have been but the little New York engineer and his wife with an FBI dossier and a collection box for Spanish war orphans in their home?

Inquisitorially if not legalistically speaking, the statements of the professed co-conspirators Greenglass and Gold—with embellishments by Bentley and other familiars who never met the Rosenbergs—were enough to fasten the guilt where it belonged. Julius had arranged for Greenglass to steal the secret and give it to Gold, who gave it to the Russians with *Kommunisticheskim privetom* from the Rosenberg family. It was no more necessary to explain to the public the point of this cunningly complex Los Alamos-Moscow transmission belt, or Gold's motives for participating, than to show that the Rosenbergs knew any Russians, that the secret existed, or that if it did Greenglass could have had access to it or made head or tail of it.* The Rosenbergs' significance was not alone that they had, in the time left from feeding and raising a family in their sparse apartment, clearly belonged to the Higgins tribe. In Hiss the inquisition had found its highly placed prototype victim *pour décourager les anglo-saxons;* now it had its human sacrifices to strike fear into heretics of exotic alien vintage. By arranging that all those who sent them to death should be Jewish, justice was seen to be done.

In Korea, where Rhee's Japanese-trained torturers gave the Americans lessons in dealing with heretics behind the lines, MacArthur pursued what he had called the "Mongol-Slav hordes of the East" across the North-South frontier in October with the slogan "Home by Christmas." This produced an early "peace scare": in the Establishment because it had hardly begun to expend its bursting arsenal, in Japan because supplying the crusaders refreshed its businessmen with a golden rain of dollars. The crusade had brought even more gratifying results for Chiang in Taiwan: an American fleet (without UN flags) was sent to protect him, and he saw hope that the police force might advance into China and restore his throne. While he remained a member of the UN "Big Four" representing "China," his 400,000 refugee troops (as an American newsman reported) "cluttered Taiwan engaging in robberies, depredations" and assorted brutalities. The crusade also raised hopes in the French, who were bogged down in Indochina despite all the largesse from Washington. Now that the Americans were in the area in full panoply of war, perhaps they would contribute some bodies to protect the investment.

In August Russia returned to the UN and Acheson, who had been "most vigorous of all" (Elmer Davis) in advising intervention in Korea, launched a campaign to bypass Russia's veto by transferring major issues to the General Assembly. MacArthur began re-militarizing Japan, the Senate voted a $100,000,000 loan to Hitler's surviving comrade-in-arms Franco, and Dulles called for Germany's rearmament as an equal free-world partner. "When you're fighting for your life," remarked Governor Dewey, "you don't ask if a man has got a little corruption under the table as long as he can fire a gun and keep American boys from being killed."

---

* Gold's motives would, however, be explained by Hoover in *Reader's Digest:* The Russians rewarded him with the Order of the Red Star, entitling him to free rides on Moscow subways.

Regarding Greenglass's capacity to grasp and transmit "the secret" should he have had access to it, his educational record showed that he had failed in eight out of eight papers in a simple engineering course. Nobel Prize physicist Harold Urey told Congressmen in 1946 that the bomb details would need 80–90 volumes of fine print which only a few experts would be able to read and understand.

Throughout the Far and Middle East, however, suspicions grew that (as the Lucknow *Herald* put it) America had "taken over seriously the white man's burden—all this talk of freedom of smaller countries is mere propaganda." Neutral and socialist UN members—who, had China been admitted, would have represented more than half of mankind—complained that the UN had been turned into a psychological warfare bureau for one member. Under the one-nation-one-vote system they were powerless against America and its pensioner governments, some of whose entire population could not fill any major city. But North Korea's ability to resist American land, air and sea power with obsolete guns astonished the world, and if anyone was losing prestige it was not socialism.

Each side soon began accusing the other of frightful atrocities. In the era of America's new "conventional" weapon, napalm, by which spruce airmen could convert people into inextinguishable jellied torches, the definition of the word had become relative like that of "democracy." The suggestion began to be heard that America had adopted Hitlerian concepts of mass slaughter, but there was a signal difference: true to the free-press tradition, American atrocities were reported by its own newsmen and sometimes published. Military draft chief General Hershey told the press that "what we need are more good young killers," and General Mark Clark said of a new crop of trainees: "We will make them ruthless—soldiers who will learn to kill the mad dogs who are shooting our wounded in Korea." Reports came to the breakfast table of gooks machine-gunned while trying to rescue their families from villages turned into bonfires, or excruciatingly tortured or forced to dig mass graves before being pumped with bullets; and of Tokyo mental wards filling up with GI's who could not stomach it. The performance of UN atrocities on the ground was generally ascribed to South Koreans, who were under American command but could not help not being Western. Orientation officers said it was all for democracy; American chaplains consoled the participants with benedictions and prayers, as German ones had consoled Hitler's *Einsatzgruppen* in Russia.

From Moscow *AP* reported, "One hears no criticism of the American people [nor] any suggestion that the USSR should go to war against the US"; but American schoolchildren were taking cover under desks in drills against a Russian atomic attack. New York's Sherry-Netherland Hotel offered Geiger-counter-equipped suites with the promise that maids and bellboys would stay at their posts till guests were out of danger. Kansas City's sheriff inspected surrounding quarries and found they could accommodate 840,000 souls. In the nervousness aroused by these precautions, a New York subway short circuit caused 1,000 passengers to stampede, and there were shrieks of "War! The Russians!" when sewer explosions blew off manhole covers in Brooklyn. Intellectuals adjusted their *Weltanschauungen* to the overseas and domestic imperatives of the crisis as readily as anyone, calling for an atomic ultimatum to Russia "in case of any further aggression." Navy Secretary Francis Matthews publicly urged "war to compel cooperation for peace . . . it would win us a proud title—we would become the first aggressors for peace." He was not referring to the police action. Arkansas Senator John L. McClellan advocated "firing the first shot [against Russia] in a war that would be inevitable" if Moscow would not cooperate on American terms. In a message of confidence that America could dominate all east Asians from its Pacific bases,

MacArthur addressed Veterans of Foreign Wars on "the pattern of oriental psychology"; Governor Dewey asked querulous Canadians to consider "the oriental mind of our persecutors."

The cool columnist Lippmann watched MacArthur approach the Chinese and Russian borders and wrote: "The President and his Secretary of State have lost control of US foreign policy." The Establishment had never meant to attack Russia or China, merely to threaten and throttle them. What it saw in Korea was summed up by the *Wall Street Journal:* the forerunner of "years and years of little wars and half wars." Lippmann reflected fears that the heady American Century wine had gone to the generals' heads. The same was beginning to be true of the inquisitors, from McCarthy and Hoover down to lesser lights and amateurs like Acheson, for everyone wanted to get into the act. The Establishment had started something with such high yields in publicity, cash and career advancement that it was hard to control. Acheson warned the public against entrapment by 82-year-old DuBois, who at a meeting in lawyer Rogge's home had accepted the chairmanship of a Peace Information Center to circulate petitions and reports on this perilous subject.

As New York's mayor William O'Dwyer sent 1,000 foot and mounted police to suppress a peace demonstration in Union Square, three members of a lawyers' delegation (including Emanuel Bloch, who had agreed to defend the Rosenbergs) and an accompanying *Compass* reporter returned in bandages from a weekend in Jackson, Mississippi, trying to intercede for McGee. They were greeted there with blackjacks, shouts of "Kill the bastards!" and a local newspaper editorial: "Why the hell go to Korea to shoot Communists when the hunting is good on home grounds?" In neighboring Kosciusko, which had followed Birmingham's lead in barring Communists from its territory, an editorial expressed puzzlement on one point: "There probably are not four people in Mississippi who could tell a Communist from a flying saucer." Thirteen hours before McGee was to die CRC won him another stay in Washington, but then William Patterson received one of his many invitations to be probed. He told Georgia Rep. H. L. Lanham that his state was ruled by "a lynch government," and Lanham raced around the hearing table with fist aimed at the witness crying: "You black son of a bitch!" Attendants averted the affray, calm was restored, and Patterson was cited for contempt.

Public-relations men were, however, fortunate in America's possession of black soldiers for democracy, who were featured in photos from the front. Young blacks experienced the novel sensation of being wanted by their country. The Negro press, maintaining a precarious existence by advertisements for hair straighteners and skin whiteners, played its part by glorifying black heroes in the advance across North Korea. One, a lieutenant, had led a group of engineers in destroying an entire city, burning enough rice to have fed its 150,000 ex-inhabitants for a year.

Four days after Ethel Rosenberg's capture the headline "A-SPY NABBED FLEEING US" announced the kidnaping of Sobell by Hoover's Mexican agents. He was beaten unconscious, rushed to the Texas border with his wife and children, and held in the standard A-spy bail of $100,000 on five charges of "conversations" with his classmate. Michael Rosenberg's "long agonized scream" over the phone, when Ethel told him of her arrest on the street, would echo in her head through three caged years. Yet, as government attorney Myles Lane told the press, but for her "perhaps we would not have the present situation in Korea"; and as a patriots' group explained in a *Times* advertisement, "those among us who defend Russia or Communism are traitors . . . American soldiers are dying . . ." Michael and Robert were handed over to Ethel's mother Tessie who, awed by the inquisition's power, would implore Ethel to emulate David by confessing whatever was required. The mother threatened to "dump them at the police station" if Bloch did not "get those brats out," and a Dickensian waifs' and strays' home was provided for them.

With "atomic" arrests and trials crowding each other for headlines, wholesome terror was not confined to the Rosenberg circle. Some heretics began to wonder if they had not indeed been involved in a dreadful plot. All felt themselves at the mercy of exhibitionists and psychopaths whose giddiest statements were accepted as *obiter dicta*. Ruth Greenglass was confidentially telling Rogge that her husband was subject to hysteria and talk of suicide and to "saying things were so, even if they were not." After his own trial in July, Gold testified at a series of prosecutions of people he named, all headlined as "A-spies." Gold was a sad little man, friendless since childhood except for his mother, apparently riddled with guilt and longing for expiation, glorying in his sudden release from obscurity. He held jurors agog with intimate details of "the hideous snarl that was my life," and explained later that they were fantasy: he had lied so much that it should have brought "steam out of my ears." In a quieter time some Americans would have wondered whether Gold was qualified as a spy for a girl scout troop, and what possible use the expert Fuchs could have had for him. In 1950 he was only slightly more outlandish than the pattern to which the public had been accustomed and was one of the most useful men the inquisition turned up. Once caught in the "red A-spy" net which he helped to spin, a heretic had only one way to escape: to say whatever was expected of him about himself and his friends and hope for a light sentence. The Pope of Rome himself could not prove he was not a spy and not a Communist; and Remington's perjury indictment in May, for denying he was either, provided the latest example of the alternative.

Legislatively the year reached its climax in September with passage of the McCarran Act in a setting of extraordinary inquisitorial activity. Congressional committees sat into the late hours asking fantastic questions and compelling heretics who would not name their friends to invoke the Fifth Amendment and pass into the ghetto. To date, 57 had been jailed for invoking the wrong amendment or doing it incorrectly. Some had lawyers to try to steer them through the inquisitorial maze, but these were almost always members of NLG which stood under HUAC stigmatization as "the Communists' legal bulwark." Border officials were alerted to turn Robeson back if he tried to leave. The machinery for deporting resident aliens, for heresies similar to those which held Robeson captive, moved into high gear in an Immigration Department hearing of Andrew Dmytryshyn, an official of IWO's Ukrainian branch. Most of the familiars introduced had never met him, but this was irrelevant since, as the Immigration attorney explained, "the primary issue in this case is the nature and character of IWO." One witness, who contradicted himself seven times in a day, testified that in 1920 and 1921 he had advocated violent overthrow in the streets of Boston. The relevance of this was that he had been an IWO member at the time.

Remarking that "anyone who speaks his opinion on Korea is in danger," Bridges watched jail doors close behind him. They opened again after an appeals court upheld his right to $25,000 bail, a decision "restoring my faith in the courts" for Hallinan but causing the government prosecutor to sigh, "God help America!" For the appeal he was preparing against the conviction, Hallinan had a 76-page deposition by one of the familiars in the case, a seaman with a criminal record, on the 13-year effort to deport Bridges with details of government intimidations and subornations.

In contrast to Bridges's men, Joseph Ryan's east-coast longshoremen showed their loyalty by declining to unload Russian crabmeat and furs from incoming Cunarders. The crabmeat, it developed, belonged to British traders who had re-exported it as too costly for British austerity, and American importers had already paid for the furs. Bridges's union backed both the war and his right to his opinion, but the Mine, Mill & Smelter Workers called for peace and was commended by the incorrigible Einstein. The labor hierarchies had no apologies for their full cooperation in the police action, which swelled their treasuries by multiplying jobs. At the same time they were critical of new, war-inspired heresy legislation until they were assured that loyal unions could share the profits of the crusade. Margin speculators had reaped up to 450% on their money in the last week of June alone; General Motors' annual profit rate was about to top $1,000,000,000, and unions had an equal privilege of buying and selling the magical paper.

In the first headlined action inspired by *Red Channels,* General Foods found a new Mrs. Aldrich for its "Aldrich Family" TV program. Although the former Mrs. Aldrich had been denying heresy for years—she insisted she thought the CP "vicious" and had not even voted for Wallace—General Foods could not risk contaminating loyal households with so "controversial" a performer. She was followed into the ghetto by Gypsy Rose Lee and by the black singer Hazel Scott who approved of the airwaves purge of "Communist infiltrators" but wanted it to be "orderly." The stripteaser's protests that she "abhorred totalitarianism whether red, brown or black" were in vain since she could not deny premature eagerness to see the brown defeated by the red; she had spoken for the Hollywood Anti-Nazi League and "greeted" Barsky on his return from Spain. Thousands had now been ghettoized by the loyalty-oath program (whose director ruefully confessed it had caught no spies), but a rare case of a heretic triumphing against it was reported from Torrance, California. A postman, fired by the loyalty board on anonymous allegations of "constantly pro-Russian sympathies," was able to identify his accuser as a neighbor who corresponded with Hoover and received from him lists of local suspects. The neighbor turned out to be illegally receiving an old-age pension, and to indulge an eccentric habit of lying on the public library floor and setting fire to the chairs. Unable to refute this, the board saw no alternative to letting the postman continue delivering mail, presumably under close observation.

After one August day when 27 bills and amendments against heresy were filed, Montana's aging senator James E. Murray described Congress as "an insane lunatic asylum." Truman told Congress that on the one hand "we must not be swept away by hysteria," and on the other that heresy control must be greatly and specifically extended. On another day, senators unanimously approved bills to exact death for peacetime spying and to exclude from America any suspicious alien including diplomats. By September the various bills, including a concentration-camp measure composed by senators Hubert Humphrey, Paul Douglas of Illinois, Herbert Lehman of New York and three more Fair Dealers, were wrapped up in the Internal Security Act named after inquisitor McCarran. Apart from "emergency" concentration camps, the Act provided for a Subversive Activities Control Board to order "registration," with names and relevant data, of groups it and the Attorney General found to be "Communist-action" or "Communist front." Heretics involved became liable to $10,000 fines and five years in jail for every day of not registering, and would commit a crime by applying for a passport. All this was based on the clear and present danger that "there exists a world Communist conspiracy which . . . is a world-wide revolutionary movement aiming to establish a Communist totalitarian dictatorship throughout the world by treachery, deceit, infiltration, sabotage, terrorism and any other means deemed necessary." In view of America's cold-war friends in Germany, Japan, Spain, South Africa, Latin America and elsewhere, citizens were left in no doubt that "totalitarian" meant "socialist."*

Senators voted overwhelmingly for the law—and a little less so to override Truman's veto of what he had done so much to encourage—with Fair Dealers performing a gavotte. John Kennedy joined Wayne Morse in sponsoring the concentration-camp amendment; James Fulbright voted to override the veto; Humphrey called the law a hoax, voted for it, then voted to uphold the veto. Liberals found the new inquisitorial charter too crude; the *Times* called it "self-defeating, diversionary, undiscriminating" while objections to the inquisition as such came from the usual muffled sources such as Pauling and Mann. Zechariah Chafee, seeing the law as the death knell of any free association, offered an arithmetical analysis of Hoover's estimate of Party strength. If the leading expert was correct in estimating 1/20 of 1% of the population to be Communists (who apparently were unarmed), "the odds are 1,999 to 1 in favor of free institutions . . . What can we do to prevent them from harming the other 99.95% of us who have on our side only city and state police, almost every newspaper and schoolteacher and professor and preacher, FBI, Army, Air Force and Navy, never forgetting the Marines?" America, he mused, had traveled a long way from Valley Forge; but "even if we no longer want to be the land of the free, at least let us be the home of the brave."

In November elections, Marcantonio was finally ousted by a Republican-Democrat anti-heresy coalition, and Nixon defeated Helen Gahagan Douglas, in whose record New Deal traces were detectable, for the Senate. Nixon had proven himself a model solon for the inquisitorial era, with a quieter technique than McCarthy's in exposing the treason of his opponents.** New York Progressives

---

* Surveying the Act after 20 years in operation, civil liberties lawyer Leonard Boudin would comment that it "contains more provisions held unconstitutional and unworkable [in major court decisions] than any statute in our history."
** According to Costello in *Facts About Nixon*, contributions for Douglas's defeat included $25,000 from Chiang, with whom the future President would make personal friends in Taiwan in 1953. He reassured Chiang that only over his own dead body would

had nominated DuBois for senator, and *National Guardian's* John T. McManus for governor, hoping not to win but to break through a few media curtains on the hustings. On his return from a Prague peace assembly DuBois confronted the Attorney General's invitation to register his Peace Center as a foreign agent; declining it, he prepared for trial while conducting his senatorial campaign. Court defense being a luxury the Center could not afford, it decided to dissolve itself; the Attorney General said it must register even if it did not exist. In campaign speeches DuBois enumerated the points of the credo which every American must now proclaim—and denounce neighbors who did not proclaim—and continued: "The mere statement of this creed shows its insanity. What can be done to bring this nation to its senses? Most people answer: Nothing. Just sit still, bend to the storm, if necessary lie and join the witch hunt, swear to God that never, never did you sympathize with Russian peasants' fight to be free, that you never in your life belonged to a liberal organization or had a friend who did, and if so you were deceived, deluded and a damned fool. But there are others who say: We can do something. That America needs no more cowards and liars. It needs honest men. And that honest citizens who are mistaken are infinitely more patriotic than scoundrels who follow the herd."

DuBois won 4% of the vote. He was not only a self-proclaimed traitor to inquisitorial America, but a black one, and "it was far more than I expected." He had passed into the ghetto politically, socially, and as a literary man, along with all other writers who proclaimed their heresies or mingled with publicans and sinners. Howard Fast was the only such writer who did not face professional frustration and penury as a result: while he had to publish his books himself in America, he sold by the millions in socialist countries and became such a hero of "the other America" that he would win the Stalin Prize in 1953. With rare exceptions, the phenomenon of heretical books under respectable imprints was about to disappear for a decade. The culminating scandal, involving Eugene Lyons, Elmer Davis and ex-*New Masses* editor Granville Hicks in a shrill *New Leader* controversy, followed disclosure that the chief editor of Lattimore's publishers (Little, Brown) was treasurer of the PP. The firm also published Fast and Carey McWilliams, who was about to enter the special twilight ghetto reserved for editors of the *Nation.* Lyons pointed out that chief editor Angus Cameron had been "one of the nation's most eminent fellow travelers for years"; that Lattimore's book of self-defense, *Ordeal by Slander,* had been "instantly snapped up by the equally pro-Soviet Book Find Club," and that Lattimore had "bought a half-interest in a Bethel, Vermont, property from Vilhjalmar Stefansson, a forthright pro-Communist."

The year's cultural highlight was the Cultural Freedom Congress appropriately held in West Berlin. Organized by converts from Russophilia who now basked in Washington's approval, it brought together early penitents like Hook with later ones like Reuther and Century-attuned intelligentsia from 19 other free-world lands. German ex-Communist Dr. Franz Borkenau presented a key-

---

America recognize the government of China. Eighteen years later he sent a secret emissary to Peking to request an invitation to visit Mao.

note exposition of the "meaninglessness" of socialism and capitalism in that day of "ebbing revolution" when destruction of Communism was the one great issue. German delegates' cheers for this reminded a British delegate, Nazi-era historian H. R. Trevor-Roper, uncomfortably of Hitler's Nuremberg rallies, but Hollywood actor Robert Montgomery focused attention back where it belonged: in the current showdown between "slavery and freedom," no artist could be neutral.

In tune with this philosophy New York's Board of Education banned TU and tried its president and secretary and six members. One of the eight was charged with being a Communist, others with insubordinately invoking the First Amendment, all with being under the Party's "iron discipline." In face of graphic disclosures by Budenz and Kornfeder, who related his own conspiratorial talks with Russians two decades previously, chairman Theodore Kiendl ruled irrelevant the accused's 162 years of impeccable service. A skillful all-heretic team—Rose Russell, Nathan Witt and Harold Cammer—had Yale Law School's Thomas Emerson and Sarah Lawrence College's Helen Lynd ready to testify as to the meaning of academic freedom, but this topic was "entirely irrelevant." Russell and Kiendl differed as to what was at issue in the trial: for him it was "potential commission of an act," for her it was "assumed potential commission of an act." Cammer said no court was competent to pass judgment on a doctrine, on books found in every university and library which had been "brought in by police spies as though they were loaded revolvers"; even if it were, the acceptance of Kornfeder and Budenz as expert interpreters was "an obscene spectacle." Kiendl nostalgically evoked Salem after Cammer asked a witness if he had any knowledge that the accused David Friedman "prefers the interest of a foreign country to the interests of our own":

Prosecution counsel: Objection.

Kiendl: Sustained.

Cammer: This is one of the exact specifications of the charges, sir. I am quoting the charges.

Kiendl: The fact that you could get a million people in New York to say that Mr Friedman never said such a thing to them would not disprove these charges.

Kiendl re-emphasized that no charge of doing anything was being made, and found all eight guilty.

The educational inquisition was now being tallied annually by the Harvard *Crimson.* The University of California's loyalty oath had resulted in some 200 faculty members refusing to sign, 37 resigning in protest, 47 offers of faculty appointments refused, 55 courses dropped from the curriculum. A Colorado Springs patriot, who was credited with preventing the appearance of Shostakovich to play the piano at Yale, was organizing pressure on Harvard to investigate 76 "reducators" there. The *Crimson* said Hoover was investigating everyone at Yale and Harvard but Hoover denied it. The Texas legislature, with one opposing vote, gave the University of Texas ten days to report whether it planned to fire a Veblenite economics professor who had called free enterprise "decadent." Cornell had fired a heretical librarian, Rutgers a teacher who fell under suspicion by "raising the salary question."

In Korea, MacArthur plunged on toward the Chinese frontier, and Truman, too late, flew to an island rendezvous to reason with him. MacArthur complained that his Air Force had so leveled North Korea that there were no more targets left. The Chinese poured across the Yalu River to drive the crusaders back. Thousands of Americans died in what at times resembled a rout, and MacArthur had to be fired. But the crusade on the home front was scoring new successes every day.

XIII

1951: The Touch

of Handcuffed Hands

While shiploads of white and black Americans moved into Korea to kill and be killed, raising corporation profits to all-time records, the death roll in the domestic orbit reached a modest peak. Patterson and his CRC mobilized 3,000 adherents to invade Richmond, Virginia, the seat of the Civil War fighters for slavery, and intercede for seven Negroes sentenced to die there. The woman who complained of rape by "13 or 14" blacks could identify none of those tried and convicted, but the executions were going ahead. A committee visited the governor, whom heretics around the world were plaguing with telegrams and phone calls as a result of CRC's agitation: he broke with precedent by addressing blacks as "Mister" in declining to show mercy. The invaders, mostly atheists, froze their extremities outside the Capitol in a 24-hour vigil proposed by a bishop, one of Richmond's few Negroes rash enough to participate. Seven black clergymen presided at a public protest funeral after the first two executions, and the vigil continued for an almost sleepless week. Challenging segregation in buses and eating places, the invaders spent thousands of nickels on random attempts to touch consciences over telephone wires; many whites came by night to give money surreptitiously. When all seven were dead the heretics went home—William Patterson to stand trial for objecting to an inquisitor calling him "black son of a bitch."

Pending the Supreme Court's reassembly to decline to intervene, Justice Douglas again extended McGee's stay in his Mississippi death cell. McGee's wife Rosalie toured northern states forming a committee; apart from the expatriate chanteuse Josephine Baker—on a visit home from France, where death sentences were more newsworthy—only already exposed heretics were available. Also raising complaints about the six condemned Trentonians, Baker was exposed as subversive by Walter Winchell, the alert Jewish broadcaster-columnist who had briefly criticized the inquisition as long as it remained too crudely anti-Semitic. Londoners interceding for McGee at the American Embassy were reassured by an official there: "McGee's trial was in the best American tradition." Mississippi orphaned Mrs. McGee's four children in May, Baker staying at her side to her man's final heartbeat.* Before the ceremony McGee told newsmen he had in fact

* Josephine Baker's visit home failed to change her mind about living in her native country. In St. Louis she publicly evoked memories of the pogrom against blacks which she saw there as a child. In Los Angeles, when police refused to arrest a man in a restaurant who said, "I won't stay in the same room with a nigger," she made a "citizen's arrest" and a scene. In New York she was refused service in the show people's rendezvous, the Stork Club. She rejected a Latin American concert tour when asked not to mention the grievances of US Negroes. Her personal contribution to the destruc-

been "forced" by his white accuser, who had cried "rape" when discovered. His lawyers knew it but dared not have him admit it, all cohabitations with black men being rape by Dixie definition. Loyal whites cheered outside the prison as a hearse bore the corpse away. "McGee," defiantly commented the Little Rock (Arkansas) Negro weekly *State Press,* "was guilty. His crime in America carries a penalty where there is no pardon or commutation: he was born a Negro." A right-wing Mexican journal, noting that "Abraham Lincoln's country" would not have wreaked this "monstrous" retribution if McGee's skin had been paler, weighed America's "absurd prejudices" against its "endless talk about the rights of the individual." Cocteau, Sartre, Camus, expatriate Richard Wright and distinguished Africans sponsored a protest rally in Paris, startling American visitors there who had never heard of McGee. McGee's last letter, circulated by his wife but ignored by the media, betrayed the un-American state of mind in which he went to his death: "Tell the people the real reason they going to take my life is to keep the Negro down. They can't do this if you and the children keep on fighting—Your truly husband."

In June the ninth Negro of the 1951 season was executed for rape in Louisiana; a mob's attempt to cheat the gallows by lynching him was thwarted just in time. Northern justice made amends by freeing four of the six Trentonians who had spent two and one-half years in the death house and had been tried three times. The third jury's verdict was welcome but puzzling to the black community: the four freed included the only two charged with performing the murder, and the two held—for participation in a conspiracy which the jury found did not occur—were the least illiterate and most combative. Bessie English, the sister of one of these, had sparked the CRC campaign but for which the case would have been hardly known. Her brother sickened in his cell while awaiting yet another trial, and would be returned to his family in a coffin.

Patterson's trial was one of several fear-spreading legal moves during the year when the first Party leaders went to jail. There was UE's Julius Emspak whose non-answers to inquisitors' questions had been incorrectly phrased: six months for contempt (March). There was William Remington—like Hiss, an egghead Anglo-Saxon product of the best schools—who had evidently begun to reform but still would not repent his youthful deviations with proper humility: two trials for challenging Bentley's word, three years for perjury. There was Dirk Struik, fired from MIT and indicted for "conspiring to teach the overthrow" of Massachusetts: he had refused to tell HUAC in July (but told the press later) that he was not a Communist and didn't know Philbrick, against Philbrick's testimony that he was and did. There was peacemonger DuBois—handcuffed, fingerprinted, searched for concealed weapons and indicted for not registering as a traitor, and brought to trial in November. Another abortive trial was that of heiress Louise Berman, whose right to invoke the Fifth Amendment before HUAC in 1948–49 was upheld. But Nelson, identifiable by any familiar as a top conspirator before,

tion of racist doctrines was a working-model UN of assorted children (Peruvian, Senegalese, Japanese, Korean, Finnish, French, French-born Jewish) whom she adopted and reared on her estate near Paris.

during and since Spain, was sentenced to 20 years at his sedition trial beginning in December.

The warning to lawyers not to defend heretics was re-emphasized soon after 17 more New York Communists faced indictments under the Smith Act. ACPFB's Abner Green, who had devoted himself to defending alien heretics since he left college, was jailed; Harry Sacher and Abraham Isserman, already sentenced to jail for contempt of Medina, were disbarred. Also jailed were three trustees of the CRC heretics' bail fund who would not name their contributors: Frederick Field, DuBois's Africanist colleague Alphaeus Hunton, and America's top detective-story writer Dashiell Hammett. The fund had lost $60,000 in bail money for four convicted Communists who failed to appear for imprisonment; for the seven who showed up, it had to find $110,000 in fines.

Above all there was the lesson taught to Higginses, especially those with children, by the Rosenberg-Sobell trial. Judge Irving R. Kaufman, who conducted it, was a loyal Jew educated at a Roman Catholic college where he won 99 out of 100 for "Christian doctrine." He took his sons regularly from his Park Avenue home to ball games and synagogue and was honored by the American Legion and Jewish War Veterans. He had recently embarked at 39 on a promising judicial career in the trial of Harry Gold's former employer for "obstructing justice" (an "A-spy" in the media) with Irving Saypol and Roy Cohn as prosecutors and Gold and Bentley as familiars. Having persuaded the public on that occasion that the Russians used Gold to assist Fuchs and were so backward that they must steal American formulas for soap, Kaufman, Saypol and Cohn were an apt team to demonstrate the Gold-Greenglass spy assignation "for Julius" in New Mexico five years previously. Saypol, who had prosecuted Coplon, Hiss and Remington, was as clearly top man in his field as 24-year-old Cohn, son of a New York judge, was its most promising youngster. The prosecutors showed acumen in announcing they would call atomic experts as witnesses; in charging "conspiracy to commit espionage," thus avoiding the need to corroborate the professed co-conspirators' narrations; and in portraying the Rosenbergs and Russian spy-techniques so improbably as to ensure mass acceptance, the only alternative conclusion being that the government hatched a frame-up on a brobdingnagian scale. Oppenheimer and Harold Urey were among 79 announced witnesses who were never called, but the bluff worked on defense lawyer Bloch and his assistant Gloria Agrin. Knowing no more about nuclear physics than defendants or jurymen, Bloch decided not to challenge the validity of the "secrets" and to concentrate on the Rosenbergs' innocence of transmitting them.

Apart from the Spanish refugee collection-box, the "exhibits" were sketches made by Greenglass of the most complicated device ever produced by scientists, two Jell-O box halves for spy-to-spy identification, and photostats of New Mexico hotel registration cards signed "Harry Gold." The sketches and Jell-O boxes were prepared especially for the trial (a fact passing almost unnoticed in the steamy atmosphere) and the cards, showing Russian spies' nimbleness in switching from aliases to their own names, were forgeries. A headline producer on a par with the Jell-O box (although a replica of it was not deemed necessary) was "a console table hollowed out for microfilming." By FBI oversight the table had not been removed from the Rosenbergs' home and had been mislaid. Its unique construction could only be described in court, but the public was no less equal to the task of imagining it than of picturing solemn, church-mouse-poor Julius as host to his spy friends in exotic night clubs.

Bloch, without experience of such trials but the best lawyer available and devoted to his clients, later apologized to them for his courtroom errors. He did not, however, think it had been an error to refuse to say if they were Communists. There were familiars to swear the contrary if they denied it (as Julius had already done in 1945), and an admission would have been futile unless they repented and gave names in the manner inquisitorially prescribed. Ethel and Julius assured Bloch that nothing any of them could say or do would have changed the outcome. Watching Kaufman outdo Medina in sarcasm and hostility on the bench, and Greenglass smile as he spoke the words to kill his sister ("Are you aware that you are smiling?" asked Bloch; "Not very," said Greenglass), they had known that America was trying them for heresy and there was only one way out. Neither they nor Sobell were prepared to take it. Sobell, facing his own Greenglass in Max Elitcher, decided not to testify at all although Elitcher's narration was uncorroborated even by custom-made exhibits. Not-guilty verdicts are rare in political trials; this one was no more a frame-up than any other.*

During this exposure of "how they stole our Bomb in 1945," Philby was still in Washington helping CIA plan subversive missions into Russia and forwarding the details to a Moscow reception committee. Philby read in the newspapers about the Rosenbergs but no one read about Philby, who was not only getting up-to-date information from the horse's mouth but was part of the horse. Locked in separate courthouse cells after the death sentence, Ethel sang "One Fine Day" in her small fine coloratura to keep up Julius's spirits, and Julius replied with "John Brown's Body." A marshal joined the prisoners' applause for Ethel and said to Julius: "You're a lowdown son-of-a-bitch but the luckiest man in the world—no man ever had a woman who loved him so much." In the wagon returning them to their respective jails, other prisoners moved aside so that Ethel and Julius could sit beside the male-female mesh partition and touch handcuffed hands.

More than a year later there would be a family reunion in Sing Sing death house, permitting them to see Michael and Robert and each other again. There was still hope of confessions involving bigger game—the ideal would have been a Nelson-Kitty Dallet-Oppenheimer ring in which the Rosenbergs could be demoted to pawns or dupes—and perhaps thoughts of the children would bring the parents to their senses. In the long interim of appeal formalities they were allowed to write each other one cell-to-cell letter a week, and Ethel had two visits from her mother urging that she "back up Davy's [Greenglass] story even if it was a

* Describing it as "the outstanding 'political' trial of this generation," *Columbia Law Review* left readers to decide the significance of the inverted commas. The most forthright editorial appeared in the Hearst press: "The importance of the trial cannot be minimized. Its findings disclosed in shuddering detail the Red cancer in the American body politic—a cancer which the government is now forced to obliterate in self-defense. The sentences indicate the scalpel which prosecutors can be expected to use in that operation."

lie." The pogrom background had done its work on Tessie Greenglass: she could not understand anyone refusing to cringe to save his own life. She would only see Ethel again in a coffin, but would eventually have David back.

Whatever deal Rogge thought he had made with the Justice Department, his pleas that other informers must not be discouraged, and the government should show it "respects the dignity of the individual," could not persuade Kaufman to give Greenglass less than 15 years. Greenglass had steeped himself publicly in guilt, and Kaufman's duty was to show that no deal was ever made. Rogge had played his role for the inquisition and would pass into limbo after the disaster of the DuBois trial. Kaufman passed sentence for the crime "worse than murder," which "caused the Communist aggression in Korea," after a week of sleepless nights and of seeking God's advice in the Park Avenue synagogue. The all-Jewishness of the inquisitorial team consoled liberals, but since every other headlined spy name except Hiss and Remington was Jewish, the sentences had the effect of stimulating anti-Semitism throughout America.

Kaufman entered the national pantheon and Saypol received a $28,000-a-year New York State Supreme Court judgeship. The style had been set for cold-war judges, but an old-fashioned few still held out. Sitting with two other appeals-court judges who disagreed with him, 79-year-old Learned Hand said that the way the Remington case was conducted by Saypol and Cohn reminded him of the Spanish inquisition. He did not mean it as a compliment. When a lower court decided that the CRC bail fund was an unacceptable source of bail for newly arrested Communists unless contributors were identified, it fell to Hand to review the matter. He told Saypol he must take the money "even if it was stolen," and brushed aside Saypol's alternative demand to raise it from $10,000 to $50,000 apiece. Bail had originally been set at up to $100,000 each for the 17 Communists captured in New York and 11 more subsequently in Los Angeles. Hand also rejected a similar multiplication of bail for the CRC fund's Hammett and Hunton, who were already behind bars. When Saypol indignantly questioned Hand's right to rule thus, Hand said: "That is the order of this court."

"I don't agree . . . ," began Saypol.

"I don't care whether you agree or not. I have made my order. I don't care to hear any more, sir."

"This is a terrible thing, an outrage!" cried Saypol.

The best that could be done was to enlist Treasury Department cooperation in slapping a $100,000 unpaid-tax lien on Hammett as he emerged to temporary liberty. On the same day Congress raised Hoover's budget by another $20,000,000. [Frederick] Field walked out of prison after three days into the arms of a Senate inquisition subpena-server, making an immediate appointment for questioning about the defunct IPR.

In general, however, the juridical situation was in hand. Only Black and Douglas disagreed with the Supreme Court's seal of approval on the first Smith Act convictions, Black still protesting that punishment had to be for doing something, not for "agreeing to assemble and to talk and publish certain ideas at a later date." Perhaps piqued by Black, the Justice Department charged the new Smith Act indictees with "overt acts." One "did leave 35 East 12th Street"; two others "did cause directives to be circulated"; another "did mail 50 envelopes."

CRC published the charges in a pamphlet, hoping someone might find them absurd, but no one read it. Douglas in his dissent wondered how the books from which Communists taught, all of which remained lawfully on library shelves, could be used to prove a crime. He belittled the danger since America's few Communists could "be picked up overnight in case of war with Russia."

Familiars, their profession endorsed with front-page dignity, flew tirelessly between courts and tribunals naming fellow conspirators and confirming the un-Americanism of Marxist literature. The smell of burning and decaying flesh, wafted from Korea, hung constructively over their labors: "Communists killing our boys over there" was always a tribunal keynote. Philbrick, now a "Red Underground" columnist for New York's *Herald Tribune*, surprised Massachusetts's 900-odd Communists with his portrayal of their plot to overthrow the Commonwealth. There was approximately one Communist in the state for every three policemen in Boston, but they "taught teenagers it would be necessary to gather arms" and "used lies, blackmail, bloodshed, murder—they wipe out people every day." Queried on this by lawyers Marcantonio and Abt at SACB's premiere hearing, Philbrick added the qualification that the Party "feels it would be very bad to conduct and hold open liquidation" in America.

Nearly all the reigning familiars, and a few obviously decrepit ones like Gitlow, helped SACB to determine that Communists were Communistic—an often stormy process taking a full year. The new inquisitors settled down fitfully to Crouch's evocation of himself mastering the *Communist Manifesto* and *Value, Price and Profit* as a Dixie farm boy and proceeding to "more serious works" at age 12. They indicated embarrassment when Manning Johnson, his perjuries ticked off by Marcantonio, said he would "lie 1,000 times if the interests of my government are at stake." Gitlow's statement that he not only reported on Communists to Hoover, but on SACB to McCarran (who considered himself its legal guardian), did not go down well. Kornfeder's refusal to stop yelling brought from the chairman a threat to resign and an outburst against prosecutors and fellow inquisitors who encouraged Kornfeder. This episode reminded Marcantonio of Italian Fascists who, on the eve of Mussolini's coup, "would march into courts, actually spit in the judge's eye and tell him there's a greater power than you." The evidence, however, was clear that the CP had urged recognition of Russia in 1924; and Marcantonio's listing of senators who urged the same thing at the same time was dismissed as a diversionary maneuver.

Suspects who had passed the first oath test were summoned back by loyalty boards with the tightening of the system. Under the new dispensation "reasonable ground for belief" of disloyalty gave place to "reasonable doubt" of loyalty as grounds for firing and ghettoizing. The oath vogue had inspired a California man to start a mail-order business in $1 oaths which persons who had not been asked to sign one could hang on the wall. Heretics recalled the "papers tied up in so many knots, and certain words or figures written on them," which Defoe recorded Londoners wearing to fend off the plague. So strictly was Los Angeles applying oath regulations that a three-year-old, who earned a $3 fee modeling for a junior-college art class, could not collect it without signing a denial that she proposed to overthrow the government. Since she could neither read nor write her parents were permitted to sign for her, but they protested that it was absurd so she got no fee.

In a handy *Guide to Subversive Organizations* HUAC alphabetized every heretical group since 1917 including defense committees for Mooney, Ethiopia (1935–36), Browder (1940, "cited as Communist") and Eisler; the Committee to Lift the Spanish Embargo (buried with the Spanish Republic); Commonwealth College, Arkansas (long since raided and closed, its library burned); the Communist Party of Panama (listed in two languages) and, among publications, the organ of the Hollywood Anti-Nazi League. James Eastland, now coming into prominence in McCarran's SISS, distinguished himself at a probe of Distributive Workers in Memphis by addressing their black president as "boy," telling union lawyer Victor Rabinowitz to "keep your mouth shut" and finally instructing attendants to "throw that damn scum out of here." An SISS familiar named as past heretics Canada's foreign minister Lester Pearson and UN spokesman Herbert Norman, stirring acid Canadian editorials about "contemptible attacks" in "the current Washington witch hunt." Norman, the familiar revealed, had belonged to "a CP student group in Cape Cod in 1939."

Yet HUAC and SISS were consistently eclipsed in the headlines by McCarthy, who chose as his target none less than Defense Secretary (ex-Secretary of State) George C. Marshall and compared him in the Senate with Macbeth wading in blood beyond the point of return. After delivering a third of his 60,000-word exposure of Marshall, McCarthy thoughtfully put the remainder in the Congressional Record so that senators would not "miss this evening's ball game." A further attempt to expose the champion exposer, by Connecticut's Senator William Benton in the fall, ended like the others. Benton, a multimillionaire encyclopedia tycoon, lost his seat at the next elections in face of McCarthy's irrefutable argument: the *Worker* proved that Communists hated McCarthy; Benton hated McCarthy; so what did that make Benton?

Budenz had another good year, inspiring such headlines as "BUDENZ REVEALS US REDS TOOK PLEDGE TO STALIN," "BUDENZ CAUTIONS OF PLOT IN PACIFIC," "US RED PROFS WELL ORGANIZED, BUDENZ ASSERTS," "LARGE GROUP OF REDS IN RADIO, BUDENZ SAYS." Having by his own statement earned a mere $25,000 as a professor since 1945—perhaps because he had so little time for those duties—his $70,000 earnings to date as a tribunal and literary familiar had stabilized his economy. Whenever a cry of alarm was needed on any front, Budenz could supply it. McCarran was reported flying into a rage when the Alsop brothers queried in their syndicated column a selection of Budenziana, especially the data on how Lattimore and Wallace "lost us China." All that came of this was a suggestion by liberal New York Senator Herbert Lehman—who could hardly have believed it would be implemented—that Budenz be investigated for perjury. McCarran summoned Budenz back to repeat his previous statements, and there the flurry ended.

Civil defense opened up not only business opportunities but another small inquisitorial branch, exposing persons who objected to atomic-attack drills or to their children ducking under desks in school and being dogtagged. A Los Angeles Health Department psychiatrist said: "If you find your youngsters playing war games and pretending to atom-bomb each other, you should encourage them." The Bronx Bureau of Attendance chief called "next to insane" parents hauled before him for keeping their seven-year-old out of school on drill days. A Los Angeles inventor advertised in his city's *Times:* "Protect yourself against atomic radiation. Be shielded from contamination and flash burns by the ATOMICAPE. Satisfaction guaranteed or money refunded."

McCarran exhaustively probed TV and radio with Rushmore as chief familiar, and the cooperation of *Counterattack* made 1951 a bumper year for show-business inquisiting. No radio-TV sponsor dared advertise his product with, nor any film producer hire, an actor, director, musician or stagehand whom *Counterattack* had not "cleared." It was credited with a collection of heretical letterheads, petitions and brochures surpassing Matthews's, exposing the supporters of more "fronts" than the Attorney General had unearthed. The health of two multi-billion-dollar businesses was at stake, and *Counterattack's* clearance fees and $24-a-year subscriptions were a trivial price to pay for thought readings of present and prospective employees. Competition stiffened in private-enterprise inquisiting as *Counterattack's* Vincent Hartnett launched his own "talent-consultant" business AWARE Inc., the American Legion card-indexed in Indianapolis all names mentioned undisagreeably in the *Worker* since 1940, and columnists Winchell, Jimmie Fidler (Hollywood), Victor Riesel (labor), Ed Sullivan, George Sokolsky, Pegler, Frederick Woltman and Philbrick vied to expose "Commies" and "pinkos." Unofficial probers developed a comradely competitiveness with the official holy office. They would chide it for overlooking certain heretics while cooperating with it in an endless chain of borrowed names. A said X had been or should have been named by B; B said X had been named by A; C said X had been named by A and B; and so on until X donned sackcloth or was economically and socially obliterated. The one whom no prober criticized was Hoover, spyless and inscrutable in his Bureau, whose utterances were "off the record" except on his annual transubstantiations in Congress to get more money.

Advertising agencies created a new employment field by appointing "security officers" to cooperate with all types of inquisitors on clearance duties. The Authors League "deplored" the probing and naming of its members while "fully understanding that under wartime conditions precautions have to be taken." Actors Equity, quietly resisting the Broadway theatre blacklist, passed resolutions condemning Fascism as well as Communism—a proof of insincerity which would not escape HUAC's attention. CBS, the pioneer network in all-employee loyalty oaths, assured customers it had "made Communist infiltration impossible." An attempted counter-counterattack by a Voice of Freedom Committee was exposed as a red plot, making its defense of anyone under fire a kiss of death. Some writers deprived of outlets accustomed themselves to living in penury, such as Dorothy Parker who—an anti-Nazi as indefatigable as she was premature—refused to give either HUAC or the press the time of day when probed for her beliefs. Other blacklisted screenwriters tried to bootleg scripts under false names. Even when this succeeded, they paid the bulk of their earnings in bribes and to front men who represented themselves as the author. One of dozens who discovered the producers' new machinery for clearing heretics was *Casablanca–Mission to Moscow* scenarist Howard Koch, a $50,000-a-script man reduced to furtive little checks for marginal TV work. A 15-minute call on a certain Hollywood lawyer could arrange everything painlessly, and Koch, whose money-making talents were not forgotten, was told he would have only to forswear heresy without naming anyone. When the lawyer mentioned the further formality of a payment of $7,500, Koch wondered who would get the money (he assumed some at least was for HUAC) but declined and, feeling bilious, decided to try his luck in Europe. Several more film heretics had had the same idea (Jules Dassin, Joseph Losey, Carl Foreman, Sam Wanamaker), but the inquisition pursued them, for their names on a film would bar it from the American market.

Show business produced a normal quota of tribunal repentants. The Hollywood Ten's Edward Dmytryk, fresh from jail, resumed film directing at $2,500 a week after adding 30 friends to HUAC dossiers. Actor Ferrer confessed to endorsing for City Councilman a Communist whom he "thought was a Democrat," promised not to be so careless again and urged that the Party be outlawed. Director Frank Tuttle traveled from Vienna to confess his "monstrous error" in being a Communist for ten years. Writer Budd Schulberg felt justified in naming ex-comrades because in 1940 they thought he had written an anti-Semitic novel and reproved him for it. He had so much to tell inquisitors that they ended imploring him to stop. Actor Larry Parks, little comprehending his inquisitors' firm resolve, gave a mild and reasonably accurate picture of Party life—he never noticed any plots—but pleaded to be allowed to "save that little bit of something that you live with." They mercifully closed the doors while he named 12 friends (resulting in 12 subpenas) before collapsing under doctors' care; but his halfhearted confession could not prevent the cancellation of his next production and a VFW call to boycott all his films. With 152 names writer Martin Berkeley set what was prematurely described as a record.* Actor John Garfield agreed with Ferrer that the Party should be outlawed, but added that he was never a Communist and never even knew one, an invitation to inquisitors to have him "checked for perjury." Actors Morris Carnovsky and J. Edward Bromberg, and writers Michael Wilson and Paul Jarrico, called the inquisition by name and defied it; the inquisitors remarked on the evident signs of Bromberg's heart condition of which his doctors had warned them. The Unitarian minister Fritchman, asked 68 questions about his "aiding and comforting" of Hollywood heretics, simply invoked the Fifth on all of them. (His congregation topped 1,000—a record—the following Sunday.) Canadian writer Reuben Ship engaged in this colloquy with Rep. Francis E. Walter, the ascendant inquisitor from Pennsylvania:

Ship: I think this committee is trying to make anybody who stands for peace out to be subversive. I think Jefferson said that if there is anyone among us who would dissolve this union, let him stand as a monument to the safety with which error of opinion can be tolerated.
Walter: Who do you think you're kidding?
Ship: Well, I'm not trying to kid Jefferson.

* According to Frank J. Donner, Matusow eventually named 216, Mary Markward 318, Cvetic and Barbara Hartle over 400 each, and the Los Angeles Red Squad's William Kimple over 1,000. But with the unique collection of membership books which he had acquired as Party secretary, Kimple was not called upon for the feats of memory which strained other familiars.

Coming to town like wizards who could cause swimming pools, butlers and yachts to vanish at a pass of the hand, the inquisitors brought unprecedented prosperity to Hollywood psychiatrists. Almost everyone had at some time fallen into conversation about topics other than dollars, dress, pugilistics and fornication, and had either said or heard something that might have been disloyal. The only sure shelter was to join the informers, but even the sick sensation which they normally aroused now called for agonizing reappraisal. Insofar as the habit of forming opinions could not be downed, at least they must not be expressed and above all not on the screen. A great silence fell over Hollywood and its products, briefly shattered during the inquisition's second 1951 visit by a hurtling glass against the wall of Chasen's restaurant. The glass landed near one of the latest name-givers, who at first thought he had been shot and was taken home prostrate. All the men around the bar, whence the missile apparently came, were questioned but could shed no light. No one, it was remarked later, thought of questioning the women. Hollywood's heretical community still existed although the Ten affair had produced seismic repercussions, not in economic despair alone, but in broken families and friendships. A talented actress tried to kill herself after her ex-husband, who had given names, sued successfully for custody of their child on the ground that she was unfit. A young writer with an airplane from more prosperous days headed out over the Pacific and was not seen again.

For those now proscribed from entertaining loyal America, there was work keeping up the spirits of their fellow ghetto residents. For this they were paid little or nothing, but discs and a popular but heretically owned New York night club brought occasional bounty to the blacklisted. Thus Seeger and his folk-singing "Weavers" enjoyed a year of prosperity despite Woltman's exposure of them as "in there pitching Commie propaganda." The Seeger family had found a Thoreauvian solution by building their own rural home for $700, which they could now equip with water and electricity. Woltman reminded good citizens that Seeger had performed for indicted Communists, for Wallace and at the funeral of the *Worker's* music critic, and had sung against war in the wrong periods. Yet if he could get them, Seeger could still fill the largest halls, mainly with heretics, but with some other desperadoes willing to face the inevitable picket lines and familiars in the audience. Perhaps there was some envy of the cheerfulness displayed by heretics at their cultural and social affairs—an increasingly rare phenomenon in loyal circles.

Production costs seemed to eliminate Hollywood heretics from practicing their craft, but Wilson and Jarrico and Hollywood Ten director Herbert Biberman passed the hat and filmed in New Mexico a story of the long Mine-Mill strike against copper corporations. The union's Mexican-American members were sufficiently immune to the joint government-CIO anathema to fight for 12 months and win almost all demands. *Salt of the Earth,* in which strikers and Mine-Mill organizer Clifford Jencks played themselves, depicted the revolution in family relations after the men were enjoined from picketing and the women and children faced tear gas and jail in their place. The film enterprise was harassed as part of a Mine-Mill-Moscow "copper plot" to strangle production for Korea, and inquisitors moved in, using the acolyte familiar Matusow to expose Jencks. Matusow perceived the importance, for success in his new field, of divulging names slowly and having "a specialty": his specialty was Youth. He soon achieved first-name terms with *Counterattack's* Kirkpatrick and a Hearst newspaper collaboration with Rushmore.

The film of Cvetic's *I Was a Communist for the FBI,* showing Nelson committing a murder, had its premiere in Pittsburgh in April after a gala parade marking Matthew Cvetic Day. Cvetic had another four years before it would be necessary to hospitalize him for mental sickness and alcoholism, but a wide range of citizens named by him, from a dishwasher to a symphony orchestra violinist, had been fired and 170 heretics had left town for good. The fever in the steel city, now blackening the sky with production for Korea, had risen steadily since the formation of Americans Battling Communism by Judge Michael Angelo Musmanno, who led the crusade basking in Cvetic's glory. The pair had raided and padlocked Nelson's office, carted the contents to a warehouse, and sworn out sedition charges against Nelson and two colleagues. HUAC having labeled Nelson an A-spy, this produced more than enough headlines to fulfill Musmanno's ambition of a State Supreme Court appointment.

With Musmanno and Cvetic (employed by ABC) as chief witnesses, Musmanno's nephew as a prosecutor, and a judge, Harry M. Montgomery who announced in court that he was an officer of ABC, Nelson's trial set new standards of inquisitorial justice. While testifying against Nelson in Montgomery's court, Musmanno commuted to and from his own where he and Cvetic were cooperating in disbarment proceedings against Nelson's lawyer Hyman Schlesinger. The only heretical lawyer left in town, Schlesinger was at the beginning of an 11-year-long ordeal. In June he was arrested at a Pittsburgh bus station and taken handcuffed to jail, where a guard assaulted him in Musmanno's presence. Since he could get no defense attorney, hearings by a "Committee on Offenses" of charges that he was a Communist would be continually postponed; the disbarment "recommendation" would not be filed until 1957, and still would not be confirmed for another two and one-half years.

Nelson's two colleagues were convicted, but multiple fractures from a car crash made an intermission necessary in his own case. The intermission was not uneventful. From his hospital bed Nelson managed to grab the wrist of a man who entered with a revolver announcing he would blow Nelson's brains out in ABC's behalf; attendants removed him after answering their patient's call with some delay. The hospital then made Nelson, still in a state of near-collapse, return home where he received a visit from Musmanno. As Musmanno described it in court to Judge Harry M. Montgomery, "Nelson tried to hit me with his crutch," to which Nelson rejoined: "When a rat invades my home I have a right to strike it." Turning to Musmanno, Nelson continued the courtroom colloquy: "You're a fine example for a Supreme Court Judge—you think you're Mussolini." "You fought in Spain?" asked Musmanno. "Yes, against Mussolini's troops." Still on crutches, Nelson had spent the night before his resumed trial perusing *Hints to New Lawyers,* having received from all 1,400 members of the state bar whom he approached either no reply or: "I don't want to be like Schlesinger." The Party was so pressed for lawyers that it could only send down one who, fresh from a cataract operation, could not read.

As his own defender Nelson perhaps overused the epithet "Fascist" for

Musmanno, an admirer of "the heroic work of the Fascisti in driving out Bolshevism" during law-school days in Italy. But the sick and unversed Communist had
a difficult adversary to cope with. A vulgar but able Quixote, Musmanno had
mounted his horse in a wide variety of crusades since his championship (along
with Mussolini) of Sacco and Vanzetti: against German corpse-producers, op-
pressors of widows, pornographers, flag-desecrators, above all Communists. He
had nearly all the makings of an eminent demagogue. His volubility and assurance in interpreting the exhibits removed from Nelson's office, which included
maps of Russia and Korea and literature trucked into court for a week, became the
talk of Pittsburgh. He could rattle off from memory 75 Marxist book titles of
which the gaping jurors had never heard, and readily decipher each excerpt he
selected to read. Through this scholarly marathon Nelson, to whom the prosecution had referred as an "A-spy" on the first day, could only keep interrupting: "I
didn't say it, not responsible," "I move for a mistrial," "Why don't you put it on
the scales and present it by the pound?" Nelson's disgust for the Korean police
action (which he "proudly admitted") was constantly stressed. Crouch took the
stand to confirm Nelson's violent tendencies and describe his own visits to Red
Army bases and consultation with Tukhachevsky on the plans to invade America.
Nelson somewhat unnerved Crouch by addressing him as "Mr. Stoolpigeon" in
questioning him about contradictions between his testimony now and at previous
tribunal appearances. Pleading to get some pills to avoid a heart attack, Crouch
was excused from telling the court where he lived since "my life would be in
danger from assassination by the defendant."

Cvetic, described by Nelson as "a degenerate, shifty-eyed barfly," wiped his
face with a handkerchief as he exposed Communist plans to "infiltrate basic industry" and accused Nelson of calling HUAC "goddamn bastards." Regarding the
murder incident in his film, he could not recall seeing any Communist commit a
murder, but Nelson had told him "there would be a liquidation of one-third of
the US population." He was oddly wedded to this arithmetic, having on previous
occasions quoted Nelson as telling him of a similar liquidation in China and of
a plan to "liquidate one-third of the population of Czechoslovakia." His record
of assault and abandoning his children made no more impression on the court
than the efforts of Nelson's witness, Marxist historian Herbert Aptheker, to correct Musmanno's interpretations of Communist theory; but when the time came
for a verdict, a juror named Roman was missing. On Nelson's demand to know
where he was, he was brought in by detectives. His eyes were purple, his nose
patched, his face painted with iodine, and the judge explained that Roman had
had a slight accident.

Nelson was expeditiously convicted and would be sent to a local bastille
with bags marked "To receive in 20 years" and bail set at $100,000. The bastille
barber, to whom Nelson mentioned the missing juror, said: "Oh, *that* son of a
bitch—a friend of mine knows him, he was on your side." The accident had occurred outside a bar where Roman, in his cups on the eve of the verdict, had
announced that he thought Nelson innocent. As Roman later told it to Nelson:
"Some goons beat the shit out of me when I left the bar and said, 'This'll teach
you how to vote.' I was jumpy when they came for me next day, a doctor gave me
an injection, and after that I don't know what happened."

Fever Chart

1951

Scene: House of Representatives.

SPEAKER: Is there objection to the present consideration of this bill (to prevent entry into US of certain giant snails)?

MR. RICH: Mr. Speaker, reserving the right to object, I would like to know whether the gentleman supporting this bill would not include, beside snails, Communists and radicals. If he did, then I think he would probably get a good bill . . . I wonder if the gentleman from North Carolina would not include Communists and radicals.

MR. COOLEY: I would not have any objection to that myself.

Scene: House of Representatives. A bill has been introduced to admit a half-Japanese child into America.

RANKIN (Mississippi): I intend to block this bill. The country is being flooded with un-American elements.

A CONGRESSMAN: But isn't the alien involved a three-year-old boy?

RANKIN: They all get some kind of excuse for bringing these people in here.

Scene: Houston, Texas. Immigration examiner testifies about a group of aliens applying for citizenship.

EXAMINER: Eighteen of them formerly belonged to the Hitler Youth and similar organizations.

JUDGE: Yes, but they have been thoroughly investigated. None has ever been a Communist or member of a Communist front organization, only Nazi and Fascist.

New York: Railroad Trainmen president speaks to national CIO convention.

"I have received and rejected an invitation to spend the summer at a Rumanian rest home. Perhaps these evil powers hoped to influence me with torture or drugs or hypnosis. Perhaps in some unimaginable way they hoped to enslave the president of a powerful union, enslave him so that he would return to these shores and carry out their murderous designs."

New York: Headlines in same day's *Times*.

RECORD ARMS BILL OF $61,103,856,030 VOTED BY SENATORS
SHORTAGES HALVE SCHOOL PROJECTS

Washington: Two correspondents sum up current dilemmas.

"PEACE MAY BE STALIN'S NEW SECRET WEAPON. Without Stalin as an enemy, the Administration's economic program of global and domestic spending would collapse."—Chicago *Tribune*.

"Waning war scare brings a letdown here and across the country. The Government doesn't know what to do about it. If they preach war is imminent, they may set the stage for a worse letdown later. But if the war drums are muffled, the arms effort will slow down."—*Wall Street Journal.*

Scene: Pittsburgh. A steel tycoon talks to a writer friend off the record.

TYCOON: I'm very depressed. Has this country gone crazy? You should see the stuff these factories are turning out. I come out of them sick at the stomach. The whole economy's tied up in it. I shouldn't be yelling, I'm getting my share. But if there's a war . . . well, I just want it stopped.

WRITER: Why don't you talk to your steel friends?

TYCOON: Listen, if I talked this way I'd be lynched before I got out of the room. They'd call me a Communist.

WRITER: But everyone knows you're a Republican.

TYCOON: You don't know Pittsburgh.

New York: Item in *Herald Tribune.*

"A web system would be used by underground Communists systematically to kill civilian defense officials during a Soviet air raid. Small groups of Reds in an organized network would—by various spiderlike ruses—entice a civilian defense warden into an open position where he could be garrotted with the 'cheese-cutter,' knifed, shot or run down by a vehicle. In the last month Communists have been instructed in the use of this system."

Los Angeles: A rear admiral speaks to the press.

"I have arranged for two million cups and containers to be stockpiled here in case of enemy-caused disaster. Enemy bomb attacks might disrupt water supplies, making dishwashing impossible."

Los Angeles: A millionaire carpet dealer talks about his new backyard shelter equipped with radio, phone, heating and Geiger counter.

"I personally don't think we'll be bombed. But I'm fortunate to have the money, and I like crazy things."

Hanover, New Hampshire: College paper, *The Dartmouth,* appraises new graduating class.

"We're more interested in Security (née Getting-Rich) than public service or someone else's minimum subsistence. We've stopped listening to the Other Side, ceased reading and thinking about it. Every man has his own Iron Curtain. We would much rather be safe and sure and successful than be called names or be accused of ideological heresy. We have neon teeth and a firm handshake, but no political guts or conviction. Both faculty and administration, shoulder to shoulder, arm in arm, have been 'walking reluctantly backward into the future.' "

New York: Advertisement in show-business weekly *Variety.*

"ANTICIPATING RED PROBE? Purge by doing timely farce on foibles of the comrades. Suitable for TV, pictures, single set, small cast. Offer open to non-suspects."

XIV

1951: The Piercing Shriek

Having reduced the gook population by some 3,000,000, and its own forces by 15,000 dead and 75,000 wounded, the crusade was stalemated at the point where it began a year previously. American generals sat down to truce talks wondering what to do next, while Dulles shored up the situation elsewhere. Franco agreed to provide some atomic bases on the 15th anniversary of his rebellion, and a "peace of God which passeth all understanding"—as Acheson phrased it in his concluding benediction—was signed with Japan. Moved to the brink of tears by this ceremony, which showed that "moral principles can be brought boldly and unashamedly into the arena of world affairs" provided there was "a common faith," Dulles pressed on with Germany's rearming as a sovereign ally.

Headlines such as "PEACE BID BRINGS SLUMP IN STOCKS," "COMMODITY FUTURES MOVE SHARPLY LOWER AS DROP IN SPENDING IS FEARED," suggested Establishment anxiety but the *Journal of Commerce* found it "unthinkable" that Korean truce talks meant a slash in war expenditures. All authorities agreed with Truman on the continued imminence of the Russian threat. "Korea is only an incident in a larger struggle—the fight must go on," said Marshall. Iran, Malaya and Indochina were "danger points that could set the world aflame," said War Mobilizer Charles E. Wilson. "We will be hit within the next six months to a year with a much tougher blow somewhere else," said Acheson. Taxpayers stopped trying to keep up with the soaring arms bill. In an October poll-sampling 38% guessed less than a tenth of the real figure and 34% simply did not know.

Nevertheless an Establishment minority expressed concern, as dividends poured in, that the military monster they created might prove to be like Frankenstein's. When time came to approve a 1952 arms bill 56 times greater than that of 1938, some senators wanted to add yet another $5 billion, but Illinois Fair Dealer Paul Douglas thought that a billion or so could be trimmed off. It was too bad, he said, that anyone suggesting such a thing was seen as some sort of Moscow agent. Hardly were the words uttered before Wyoming's Joseph O'Mahoney implied just that about Douglas, and the *Times* thus reported the ensuing scene: "Sen. Douglas, who had been spreading his hands in gestures of exasperated frustration . . . uttered a piercing shriek, put his hand against his head and rushed from the chamber . . . He returned within half an hour . . . looking fit to those in the galleries."

Draftees, although well schooled in "how bad Communism is," were confused as to why they should go to Korea to fight it when their generals were talking peace with the enemy. The *Times* education editor found half the students at an army indoctrination school asleep or stupefied in lectures on democracy. The dilemma was indicated by the *Wall Street Journal:* it thought Washington had provided insufficient evidence of "the probability of an imminent Soviet attack," but had to confess that "actually, military advisers and diplomats have no evidence of new Russian moves . . . Grim warnings from the Pentagon are largely propaganda."

Pending better public-relations coordination, *Saturday Evening Post's* Demaree Bess reported postponement of the "target year" for war against Russia from 1953 to 1954. The rival weekly *Colliers,* however, had the war planned for 1952 and would not budge its schedule. It recruited Robert Sherwood, J. B. Priestley, *Times* military expert Hanson Baldwin, *Christian Science Monitor* editor Erwin Canham, Winchell and Arthur Koestler to limn the anticipated events of that year in an October *War We Do Not Want* issue. Victory would come fast, and the subsequent de-warping of Muscovite souls would be slow but equally sure: Reuther and Stuart Chase would arrive to straighten out unions and economy, and Hattie Carnegie to stage a hat show in Dynamo Stadium. The cover—depicting a GI on guard against an "Occupied Russia" map, with a UN flag over "Moscow Occupation Headquarters"—inspired brisk sales in France where the UN's General Assembly was meeting at the time. France's obliteration in *Collier's* war was implied but not stated. A Paris commentator assured purchasers of the magazine that its contributors were "respected writers, not madmen or practical jokers." Ottawa's *Citizen* thought the magazine would "deepen misgivings about American instability and emotionalism . . . Not content with mass slaughterings they dream up atrocities. The sickening effect of these narrations is aggravated by self-righteous and sanctimonious attitudes."

The truce parley, reflecting the reality of Establishment cold-war policy, would last for nearly two years while bombs continued raining on North Koreans and Chinese—and for some months, even on their negotiators' lodgings. HUAC exposed the enemy's "peace offensive" as "the most dangerous hoax ever devised by the international Communist conspiracy." But GI's were still coming home in flag-draped crates, and lest it might occur to their families that the American team was stalling, care was taken to keep the trend of the parley from attendant newsmen. A sinister figure emerged in the person of Australian war correspondent Wilfred Burchett who, weary of the London *Times's* and *Express's* manipulations of his copy, had gone to report on Korea from the heretical side. At the end of each day's talks his loyal but newsless colleagues crowded about this "red mouthpiece" for some facts to send home, and thus shreds of information found their way into the media.

When it began to seem impossible to browbeat the North Koreans into giving Rhee more territory, a Pentagon report said the Chinese had murdered 2,513 police-action prisoners in cold blood; and Acheson described Chinese conduct to the UN in Paris as "so low it would take considerable improvement to raise it to the general level of barbarism." China was broadcasting alphabetical lists of all Americans it held, with photos of them fishing and playing football, which only such a journal as *National Guardian* would publish in America. Congressmen demanded atomization of the "sub-barbarians," but a request for proofs from America's reluctant allies brought a Pentagon disclaimer of the report. The atrocity which was undeniably being practiced on the prisoners was a systematic effort to brainwash them into heresy.

At home the *Times* had found "creeping paralysis" on 72 college campuses: "an apathy about current problems that borders almost on their deliberate exclusion" for fear of "being labeled pink or Communist." The University of California loyalty oath had been ruled unconstitutional after a stubborn campaign led by Pauling—a well known "Rooseveltian democrat," as he reminded two state inquisitions—but all heretics had already left the campus. Asked to write a pamphlet on some current problem, college students (as their teacher told the New York *Herald Tribune*) replied: "The FBI would get you," "I am looking for security, not trying to change anything."

NEA invited American Legion Commander Erle Cocke, who had just awarded his organization's Merit Medal to Franco, to address its July convention on the crimes of Communism; and New York's Board of Education hired lawyer Saul Moskoff to unmask more heretics and breed more informers among teachers. Moskoff summoned suspects to an inquisitorial bureau in Brooklyn where, never knowing who supplied it, they were confronted with data "channeled" by Schools Superintendent Jansen. "I always try," Moskoff would tell the Denver *Post*, "to get suspects to name more names." On July 4 a *Capital Times* reporter stood on a Madison (Wisconsin) street corner seeking signatures on a petition. The petition was the Declaration of Independence: of 112 passersby approached to sign it, 111 thought it subversive and refused. McCarthy exposed the experiment as "a typical Communist stunt" by editor William T. Evjue, who for a year had been trying to expose McCarthy. In a spirit of fair play NBC permitted Evjue to defend himself on the air against the charge of heresy, then called on McCarthy to repeat it.

In his cell Julius Rosenberg came upon the *Times's* annual July 4 facsimile of the Declaration, added his signature to the John Hancocks, and pinned it on the wall to keep him company. America's first death sentences on such charges, in what was officially peacetime, had been so effective that no one important seemed to have studied the trial record except Urey. Urey still did not know he had been announced as a government trial witness, but he told Kaufman in a letter that the sentences based on such dubious testimony "amazed and outraged" him; he thought Communists "unreliable generally" but objected to the punishment of anyone "unless they commit crimes." After a two-month search for an editor who would read the record, Bloch brought it in despair to *National Guardian*. With a 58,000 circulation and so deep in debt that it expected each issue to be the last, the paper began analyzing the trial under the headline "Is This the Dreyfus Case of Coldwar America?" The series brought a rain of small bills to keep the paper alive and start a Rosenberg defense committee. Higginses presented themselves with restored enthusiasm to run the committee, and French and British counterparts spread the word across the Atlantic. The committee printed the trial record and relied substantially upon it as campaign literature. "Read and be convinced" was easily said, but the inquisition had done its task well: mere possession of such a document was dangerous. The committee's Moscow origins were promptly exposed.

In September the much-"cited" author Louis Adamic was found in his New Jersey home with a rifle across his lap and a bullet through his head. His wallet contained a clipping headlined "ADAMIC RED SPY, WOMAN* CHARGES," his typewriter a sheet with only the words "Now is the time . . ." Budenz thought it "not unlikely" the Russians killed him. *Counterattack*-listed actress Mady Chris-

* Elizabeth Bentley.

tians died in October; no one seeing her in her "last months," Elmer Rice wrote, could "doubt that her death was hastened, if not actually caused" by the inquisition. The "death by political misadventure" (as described by his friend Odets) of actor Bromberg, alone in his room in London where he had somehow managed to retreat with his rheumatic heart, followed in December.

Culturally, the fall season more than justified the inquisitors' educational work on the intelligentsia. Publishers produced memoirs by Hitler's generals which were warmly reviewed on literary pages. One of these was being sympathetically filmed; another recalled how the author "turned in horror from the barbarous Red excesses" on the Russian front. A New York *Herald Tribune* critic hailed the "maturing" of novelist Truman Capote with a "story of some people who escape life's problems by living in a tree house." Mailer's *Barbary Shore* depicted a group of disillusioned and self-hating Americans indulging, along with a three-year-old girl, in freedom of indiscriminate obscenity; but Mailer would have to wait a few more years before he could write *fuck*.* A startling full-page review was accorded by the *Times,* which ignored 95% of such books, to Corliss Lamont's *Independent Mind* published by the heretical Horizon Press. "A fair hearing for Lamont," wrote the reviewer, "owes him the courtesy of presenting his own picture of his position," although his views (that Russian aggression and the national emergency were myths) were "so fantastic they are not even wrong; they enter a science-fiction universe of meta-wrongness." Perhaps there was still hope of repentance by the Morgan partner's son.

Little, Brown of Boston, one of the last publishers selecting books without political tests, announced that the resignation of its vice president and editor-in-chief had "no political implications." England was not keeping up with its ally's inquisitorial pace—it still permitted heretical artists to ply their trade without litmus tests, and even confessed spies to resume normal circulation after a few years in jail—and an unpleasant free-world situation threatened when Aberdeen students nominated Robeson for their university's Lord Rectorship. If elected (which he was not), Washington might have faced an official request from London to let the Lord Rector go. To urge loyalty to capitalism by nonaligned countries' artists, the CIA arranged a Cultural Freedom congress in Bombay which reformed heretics Stephen Spender, W. H. Auden, Ignazio Silone and Louis Fischer attended; and with the first snow came DuBois's turn before the inquisition.

Even with Marcantonio donating his legal services, DuBois and his four peacemongering colleagues needed $35,000 to defend themselves and mobilize what support could be had. If the case had to be appealed the costs would rise to about what the government was spending to jail him, which DuBois estimated at $100,000. Ghetto friends bought a suitable house for him and his newly married wife Shirley Graham, but his savings were meager and his income consisted of a $1,200 annual pension and occasional $25 checks for *National Guardian* articles. An 83rd birthday fund-raising dinner was planned at a New York hotel with a black university president and a rabbi as speakers. The speakers changed their minds; the hotel canceled the booking. Shifted to a Harlem night club, the affair

---

* Students of semantic jurisprudence will recall that America was led across this Rubicon on July 29, 1959, when Judge Frederick Van Pelt Bryan affirmed Grove Press's right to print the word in *Lady Chatterley's Lover.*

raised $6,500 with Robeson as speaker and support from Einstein and Mann and the Negroes Mary McLeod Bethune, Langston Hughes, and Domestic Relations Court Judge Hubert Delany. Hughes reminded the Chicago *Defender's* black readers that "the dean of Negro scholars, one of the leading men of our century" was known and read throughout Africa and Asia where he had been "an immeasurable influence for good upon young minds." DuBois, he wrote, "began before I was born to put reason above passion, tolerance above prejudice, wisdom above ignorance, cooperation above strife. At 83 he is still a wellspring of knowledge, a fountain of courage, a skyrocket for the great dreams of all mankind . . . Somebody in Washington wants to put Dr. DuBois in jail. Somebody in France wanted to put Voltaire in jail. Somebody in Franco's Spain sent Lorca to the firing squad. Somebody in Germany burned the books, drove Thomas Mann into exile and led their leading Jewish scholars to the gas chamber. Somebody in Greece gave Socrates the hemlock to drink. Somebody at Golgotha erected a cross and somebody drove the nails into the hands of Christ. Somebody spat upon His garments. No one remembers their names."

On two fund-raising journeys DuBois, long an observer of the "class structure development" * among his people, was not surprised by the coldness of well-to-do Negroes: they could not fathom a DuBois's or a Robeson's sacrifice of fame and wealth for a principle. ACLU counsel Hays said, "Personally I should have liked to help," but his organization felt otherwise. The standard white liberal response was, "You have nothing to fear if you are innocent." Twelve writers, expressing mingled indignation and disbelief, promised articles on the case which never appeared.

But the prosecution had been prepared deplorably. Although Hoover's men had visited "practically every person who had attended a Peace Center meeting," no familiar had been found to swear to seeing DuBois "emerge from the Kremlin with a bag of gold." Judge James McGuire took the unusual position that guilt must be proved by something more than subversive quotations and uncorroborated statements. The only co-conspirator produced was Rogge, in whose home the Center had been born. Referring to Rogge's Yugoslav government retainer, Marcantonio challenged prosecutors to prove that there was more than one foreign agent in court. No such evidence being produced, McGuire threw out the case.

DuBois continued his subversions during a recess of the trial; minister Donald Lothrop, introducing him in Boston's Community Church, recalled that one of the church's founders had also been an indicted criminal. "A great silence," DuBois told the congregation, "has fallen on the real soul of this nation. We are smearing loyal citizens on the paid testimony of self-confessed liars, traitors and spies; we are making the voice of America the babble of cowards paid to travel . . . But my words are not a counsel of despair, rather a call to new courage and determination to know the truth. Four times this nation has faced disaster and recovered. What we have done, we can do again." For him "the most frightening result of the trial" was that "most Americans of education and stature did not say a word or move a hand." Raised in Massachusetts to believe that "no one is ever

* Unless otherwise attributed, quotations on this and the next pages are from DuBois's *In Battle for Peace* (Masses & Mainstream, New York, 1952) and *Autobiography* (International Publishers, New York, 1968).

arrested without sufficient cause," he had long since discovered his error. But now he was doubly aware of the "thousands of innocent victims in jail because they had neither money, experience nor friends to help them"; they "daily stagger out of prison doors embittered, vengeful, hopeless, ruined," and "a frightful proportion" of them were black.

The idea that people must "loudly and angrily refuse" to support certain causes or groups "because they do not believe in everything these groups do believe in" outraged DuBois: if total unity of belief was necessary for any cooperation, he saw no possibility of progress. Yet "there is no path of human progress which a so-called 'free democracy' can advocate without adopting at least part of the program of socialists and Communists," since the two societies were both planned and only differed in the objects of the planning. As for Communism, "I believe in it wherever and whenever men are wise and good enough to achieve it." He ridiculed all claims to dominate other peoples on the ground of bringing them freedom and justice, but questioned how much justice America had to bring. "Americans may kill, steal, cheat with certainty of a fair trial or none at all; they may lie, betray, slander and inform with a chance of money, professorships and Book-of-the-Month Club selections; but let any man study or praise anything connected with the Soviet Union and he may be starved or imprisoned without facing his accusers or knowing the accusation." Meanwhile, "Blessed are the peacemakers, for they shall be called Communists."

The media almost ignored the trial, and the State Department replied to DuBois's passport application with a request to "state whether you are now or ever have been a Communist." He replied: "It is none of your business what I believe so long as I transgress no law. I absolutely refuse and repeat my demand." For nearly six more years he would dwell in the larger jail of the ghetto, and for another six—until the day came for the glowing obituaries—he remained a dead American for the media. The ghetto, in 1952, gave him the highest honor it could bestow: the annual TU award for services to education. Half a decade after his death, learned studies of his work would begin to appear, and the *Times,* reviewing his posthumous *Autobiography,* would call him "one of the country's greatest Negroes . . . a scholar of repute [who], largely ignored by the white community, had cause to be embittered" but to the end wrote of "this beautiful world, this wonderful America."

In the months preceding the trial, Chicagoans reacted with three days of mass violence and arson to a Negro's presumptuous renting of a flat in a white neighborhood, and two Norfolk (Virginia) citizens seized a black clergyman who had preached against segregation, threw gasoline over him and set him on fire. In Groveland, Florida, the county sheriff shot two Negroes while driving them to court, handcuffed together, to appeal against death sentences on the traditional rape charge (see p. 107): one survived for his last confrontation with the law, and the sheriff was exonerated on the ground that they attacked him. When the local NAACP man, Harry Moore, tried to do something about this a bomb was planted under his house and he and his wife were blown up. (An Orlando, Florida, journal commented: "Communists, bent on destroying tranquil relations between the white and colored people of Florida, could well have plotted it.") Citing such episodes as these, and protesting that America's refusal to enforce its own laws was sentencing 300,000 citizens a year to death because they were black, CRC charged its own government with genocide in a memorandum to the UN.

The Tuesday following the DuBois trial was gubernatorially proclaimed Herbert A. Philbrick Day throughout Massachusetts: 800 of the flower of the Commonwealth attended an American Legion banquet for its famous son. On Wednesday, New Yorkers ran for cover at a wail of sirens heralding the first atomic disaster rehearsal. Newsmen were allowed to remain on the streets provided they had signed loyalty oaths. Evaluating the Korean police action in the fifth month of truce talks, the *Times's* Baldwin wrote: " 'Operation Strangle,' the attempt of air power to isolate the ground battlefield by cutting enemy communication lines, so far has obviously failed to strangle . . . There is good reason to believe that the enemy is as strong as, if not stronger than, he was when the interdiction and isolation campaign started. How can this be? In part the answer is that we have deluded ourselves . . ."

XV

1952: Swift Death
at the Orphanage

Truman's proposal to spend nearly 90¢ of each taxpayer's dollar for past, present and future wars brought a *Wall Street Journal* prediction of the economy's "total collapse" if the escalation continued. At the same time the *Journal* reported mild panic on the commodity and stock markets after Stalin's latest gambit in "the Kremlin's peace offensive": he had remarked that "a third World War is no closer today than two years ago." Crusade leader General James A. Van Fleet, who felt that Korea had "been a blessing—there had to be a Korea either here or some place in the world," escalated his aerial pyrotechny to a crescendo on the war's second anniversary, by which time 17,000,000 pounds of napalm had been shipped from America. To newsmen distressed about napalm a Pentagon spokesman explained: "That it burns a body horribly no one denies, but tests show that death is frequently swift." A British war correspondent described a case where it was not: "He had no eyes, his body was covered with a hard black crust, he had to stand because he had no skin." Defense Secretary Robert A. Lovett irritably told a press conference, "I cannot take these complaints as anything more than a tiresome form of propaganda," and a *Times* man confirmed the swift-death theory with this report on a napalmed village: "The inhabitants were killed and kept in the exact position they had held when the napalm struck—a man about to get on his bicycle, fifty girls and boys playing in an orphanage . . ."

Yet the 5,000,000 gooks killed, crippled or dead of starvation and exposure had cost America $15 billion; and the survivors still would not yield an inch of ground to South Korea, where prices had risen 60 times since 1948 and Rhee kept afloat by black-marketing American equipment. The same obstinacy prevailed on South Korea's Koje Island. There America was employing Rhee's and Chiang's experts to persuade North Korean and Chinese prisoners that they would hate to go home—described in the media as "screening." Methods tried on the island included hanging inmates upside-down to tattoo them with free-world slogans. A massacre of no small proportions followed; but the survivors chanted barbaric songs and fashioned spears to defend the right to return behind their curtain, while their right to choose Rhee or Chiang hung up the truce parley for months.

Considering its non-embarrassment about napalm, America was oddly shy about Russian charges in the UN that it was dropping infected insects on the foe. The Chinese showed a convincing collection of such insects to Europeans who were invited to investigate, and bacteriologist Rosebury, a former employee at Fort Detrick, where for years "vast sums" had been spent on biological warfare experiments, challenged Truman to dispel the rumors by ratifying the international anti-BW convention. America contented itself with scoffing denials. Skeptics concluded that, if BW had indeed been given a trial run in Korea, it had not worked; but the rumors gave a useful lead to refurbished politicians and generals in Germany. A Dr. Mende observed that Germans were still behind bars for acts in World War II "no different from those committed by UN troops in Korea," and it was time to erase the misunderstanding which labeled them "war criminals." Generals Heusinger and Speidel, now being groomed for NATO leadership, said that unless this was done they could not adequately rebuild the German army to defend democracy.

The next step in Asia was more uncertain. MacArthur began talking strangely about "a dreadful fear in patriotic hearts" of "scuttle in the Pacific . . . when victory was within our grasp." The scuttle would force California, Oregon and Washington to "assume the hazards of a defense frontier"; at the same time the general saw the external threat as "pure nonsense" and America as facing a real threat: "a military state . . . geared to an army economy which was bred in an artificially induced psychosis of hysteria." If MacArthur's confusion was rising, I. F. Stone's was not. Developments since he called the war "a plain case of Russian-abetted aggression" had embarked him on the kind of research in which he was unexcelled, and in *Hidden History of the Korean War* he dazzlingly documented the fraudulence of the UN police action, causing French editor Claude Bourdet to wonder if "we are in the presence of the greatest swindle in military history." MacArthur's foghorn about a "military state" based on Pentagon-industry partnership did, however, reflect the distress of old-fashioned business circles. With airbases around the planet, America was now pledged to protect 37 lands from heresy and giving military aid to nine more. All this inflamed generals with a dream of immense annihilations, yet still failed to wrest the political initiative from Russia.

On the home front four concentration camps were being made ready, ostensibly for heretical aliens from whom the McCarran-Walter law definitively withdrew the Constitutional umbrella in June. (The law disentangled deportation cases from due-process courts and installed Immigration officials as judge, jury and prosecutor.) But while fear of American Buchenwalds had persuaded the CP to do what it was always accused of doing—set up a clandestine apparatus—the camps did not open for business, and this despite the availability of guards with the finest European training who had immigrated since 1945 and sworn to uphold democracy.

The Establishment still did not need Fascism, and New York's Ellis and California's Terminal islands sufficed for the assorted bodies being returned whence they came. No major flaw had appeared in the American system of inquisitors acting within a framework of law which they could break at whim, of unconstitutional laws performing their function during the period of years necessary to have them so declared. The general public accepted that the treatment of heretics did not threaten the rights and protections of anyone else. The system's great virtue was that the bulk of punishments—professional and economic ruin, social ostracism, nervous crises, broken families, suicides—was hidden iceberglike beneath the surface. The world's most sanitary jails held less than a hundred political prisoners on whom no physical violence was practiced, and who by definition were

not political prisoners.* A few hundreds facing a similar fate struggled on through
the legal bog to avoid it; a few hundreds more had been or were being deported;
two had been sentenced to die; and heresy had been reduced to an all-time low
in a country which could prove in writing its citizens' freedom to think and say
what they pleased. Fear, in which the media played so vital a role, had done the
rest. Press and radio had reduced Americans to a cataleptic state, convincing them
that they made up their minds from all the facts and viewpoints whereas what they
got was a small selection endlessly repeated and limitlessly magnified. Now the
magic TV picture box lent new magnification and digestibility to the same selection by every fireside. With this role being so skillfully played, only a few "cases"
were necessary: nationally inflated to bring the lesson home, each one was worth
a thousand in Torquemada's day.

The intelligentsia showed signs of anguish as the truce-talk holocaust proceeded and "McCarthyism" became the domestic conversation piece. The mounting death roll of "our boys fighting Communism over there" had removed nearly
all legalistic shackles from the inquisition, but the device of separating "extrem-
ist" McCarthy from his colleagues was balm for many a sensitive soul. In Cultural
Freedom circles, now benefiting from mysterious foundations which had proliferated since the birth of CIA, it was felt that while the inquisitorial "job done"
was laudable "McCarthy's methods" deserved reproof. Max Eastman, the mouthpiece for old-guard penitents who insisted it was "anti-McCarthyism" that needed
denouncing, spoke from an exceptionally undignified position as "roving editor"
of *Reader's Digest,* a monthly compendium of American platitudes circulated by
the ton throughout the world. *Commentary* contributor Irving Kristol, who found
McCarthy a necessary evil while conceding praise for his "unequivocal anti-
Communism," spoke for the main body of intellectuals. They had no patience
with liberal liberals like Henry Steele Commager who still thought America
should worry about America and leave Russia to the Russians. They agreed that
Communists desired an "Orwellian" world but were beginning to wonder if
America, in the grim necessity of resisting, was not moving down its own track
to the same station. MacDonald, writing about movies and shunning politics as
much as possible, only "chose the West" on the morose note that one could depend
on Russia to be worse. Mailer, preoccupied with the relation between sex and
violence, was equally dim in his Western loyalty. Hook had been obsessed for so
long by the "total error" of Communism that there was no room for criticism in
his "critical support" of America. *Partisan Review's* ex-Marxist Philip Rahv, who
saw a widening need for "ideological struggle against Communism on a world
scale," grimaced at the respectable prosperity of an intellectual "lumpen-bour-
geoisie" which had embraced anti-Stalinism as "a total outlook on life" in the
arms of "a political bum like McCarthy." Contemplating this, Rahv was nostalgic

* Marzani dedicated himself to proving that they were, after serving his full term in
Danbury where he had illuminating chats with Parnell Thomas. The embezzling inquisitor knew in advance, and said so, that he would be promptly paroled and would not
even have to pay his fine; but it was made clear to the heretical inmates (Marzani, Lardner, Cole, JAFRC's Dr. Jacob Auslander) that parole was not for them as long as they
"had the same ideas." The audience available to Marzani when back in circulation consisted of fellow impenitents who did not need his demonstration.

for "the old anti-Stalinism" of the 30s and 40s which had "true pathos and conviction."

McCarthy spoke near Princeton in February, five students went to evaluate him, and a *Princetonian* editorial resulted: "McCarthy a Threat to Individual Dignity." The shudders about "McCarthy's methods" arose from his consistently superior, yet embarrassing, mastery of demagogic arts. Newspaper polls showed that 60% of Americans had "no opinion" about him but, although he still had no committee of his own, he was steadily climbing in popularity. He easily persuaded Wisconsin's electorate to renominate him by a landslide vote. Rival inquisitors strove to incorporate in their work his refinements of traditional techniques, not very successfully in the case of HUAC, whose exposures of uncapitalistic unions and scared show people sagged into monotony. The pioneer committee's Rep. Harold H. Velde made a bid for the stolen limelight by summoning Edward Condon a year after he resigned from the Bureau of Standards and asking why he had "hung around known Communists and espionage agents like flies hanging around a pot of honey." Velde gave Condon an "unfavorable" rating but did not have what it took to parade him persuasively before the public as an A-spy, nor to frighten away his fellow scientists. Although semi-ghettoized for years, with his "clearance" limited or revoked, the "weakest link" was elected president of AAAS at the end of 1952.

Rep. George Dondero, whose campaign "to protect our cultural birthright" from "red art termites" got inches and seconds in the media where McCarthy got yards and half-hours, showed his respect for the master by calling him "a patriot of the first magnitude." McCarran's SISS colleague William Jenner, likewise out of McCarthy's league as a technician, beamed when McCarthy publicly embraced him for calling Gen. Marshall "a living lie . . . a front man for traitors." But SISS was onto good publicity with its UN probe, ushered in by a *Saturday Evening Post* article ("Sinister Doings in UN") and meshing in headlines with the almost continuous probe of IPR whose files had been "dramatically seized" from a Massachusetts barn. Lattimore spent 12 days trying to persuade the inquisitors that he too disliked Communism, only to face a recommendation that "this conscious, articulate instrument of the Soviet conspiracy" be indicted for perjury. Crediting a tip from a Finnish travel agent to a CIA man that Lattimore planned flight to Russia, the State Department ordered a ban on his departure. This had to be withdrawn when it emerged that "excessive drinking" occurred at the party where the tip was passed, but Lattimore had no travel plans at the time.

The UN probe brought a second contempt citation for Mrs. Keeney, to be followed by trial and conviction. She was one of five whom UN had already fired. The bewilderment of the UN staff, who had pledged a higher international loyalty, deepened as Lie announced he would fire anyone disloyal to his own government. Since several Czech employees who had fled from socialized Prague were evidently not included, the inquisition had now turned UN into its opposite internally as the police action had done externally. The challenge by the fired five of Lie's right to eject them without stated cause had eventually brought them back pay and compensation, and the Keeneys used theirs to open an art film club. This moved a grand jury to join the probe in October, subpenaing the Keeneys and their records to show that the club was a spy-ring headquarters planting reds in

UN. Most of the Americans at UN who received SISS subpenas would not talk and joined the Keeneys in the ghetto. In November, when 29 were known to have been fired (others had resigned), McCarran renewed his demand that UN "clean its own house of Communists . . . the sooner we resort to drastic methods the better." Next day the remains of UN counsel Abraham Feller were picked up beneath the window of his 12th-story apartment. Feller's motives for suicide were never determined. A former New Dealer but apparently not a suspect, he had been assigned by Lie to cope with the inquisitors, and the problem of purging heretics from an organization which by definition did not recognize heresy may have been too much for him.

At the year's halfway mark the media were featuring spy plots in France, Germany, Britain, Italy, Korea and Lapland with admonitions to overseas free-world authorities to take them more seriously. US Attorney Lane illustrated the correct approach at a New York communion breakfast by charging the Rosenbergs, as they fought from the death house for a new trial, with betraying secrets of the space platform as well as of the Bomb. Fuchs was reported to have smuggled from his British cell secrets hidden in the hollow leg of his bed—an incident about which his jailers learned for the first time from American media. The American spy diet had never been so rich. Chambers's *Witness* was a Book-of-the-Month and he was telling youth on TV what it purportedly wanted to know.* Bentley's and Budenz's confessions competed in bookstores not only with Chambers's but with Oliver Pilat's *Atom Spies*, Ralph de Toledano's *Spies, Dupes and Diplomats* and the works of other writers who, never having been heretics, could not aspire to the familiar's mantle. Movie theatres were offering *Walk East on Beacon* (FBI trapping spies in Boston), *High Treason* (spy rings in England), and *Red Planet Mars* in which a "US Defense Secretary" cried: "I don't want war but Moscow, Leningrad—every nerve center in the Soviet Union—must be wiped out." ** Yet public surfeit with the theme was suggested by languid box offices, poor spy-book sales apart from *Witness,* and the unprecedented death roll of newspapers and magazines after featuring the steamiest revelations.

---

* Reportedly getting over $54,000 in royalties on the first edition of *Witness,* and with paperback and radio-TV offers coming in briskly, Chambers wrote in *Saturday Evening Post* of the "tragedy" which his sacrifice for America had made of his life. Chambers had the imaginative powers and literary skill to make his exposition of a tormented soul read like a novel. Here and there he suggested awareness of the real nature of his tragedy, as in this passage about the informer: "He sits in security and uses his special knowledge to destroy others. He has that special information to give because he knows those others' faces, voices and lives, because he once lived within their confidence, in a shared faith, trusted by them as one of themselves, accepting their friendship, feeling their pleasures and griefs, sitting in their houses, eating at their tables, knowing their wives and children. If he had not done those things he would have no use as an informer. Because he has that use, the police protect him. When they whistle, he fetches a soiled bone of information . . . He is no longer a man."
** This was less imaginative than it might appear. Moscow was publishing photo-stated excerpts from the diary of America's ex-military attache there—a major general who had been brought home to a courtmartial for letting his thoughts reach the wrong hands—such as: "War as soon as possible! War now! . . . We must employ every subversive device . . . everything, truth or lies, to poison the minds of Soviet subjects!"

New York heretics rallied for their May Day ritual, a procession which took four hours to march into Union Square through an egg-tomato-ink barrage. Seeger marched in his army uniform, and the private inquisitor Vincent Hartnett this time filled Matusow's sidewalk role with a camera. In Tokyo some 400,000, of whom police killed nine, marched in protest against Dulles's Christian friendship treaty. In the same month Washington banned all travel to Iron Curtain lands, and the captive Robeson, unable to cross the border, sang from one side of it to 40,000 Canadians on the other. Proceeding westward, Robeson was as welcome as ever at Los Angeles's First Unitarian, but found nearly all Negro churches closed to him and performed mainly in parks. Back in New York he sang at the African Methodist Episcopal Church convention on the invitation of Bishop Walls, who balanced it by inviting America's newly appointed black delegate to UN, Edith Sampson. Sampson's theme, conveyed in lectures she had been giving in Europe, was that rumors about skin color influencing American justice were red canards. Walls wound up the convention by asking delegates to rise if they thought Robeson should have a passport; Sampson and an unidentified sympathizer remained seated as the other 2,998 rose. Her UN appointment had coincided with the denial of an entry visa to the English clergyman Michael Scott, white spokesman for Southwest African tribes whom South Africa had appropriated in defiance of the UN charter.

Later a plan would be worked out whereby alien suspects having business with UN received a pocket map of a few blocks of Manhattan in which they might circulate. But Washington was hard pressed to keep up-to-date the list of citizens barred from leaving and aliens barred from entering. On hand at every airport and seaport, the roster would soon rival in size an average city telephone directory. A maritime inquisition boarded approaching ships to probe the thoughts of their crews, causing disquiet to *Le Monde* when "this absurd investigation of seamen on their own territory" resulted in 269 crewmen of the *Liberté* being forbidden to come ashore. With more and more international conferences having to be canceled or held elsewhere, atomic scientists devoted their October *Bulletin* to the "indignities suffered" by their profession. Einstein and four fellow Nobel laureates headed a protest against new legislation "hampering the progress of American science, alienating our allies, comforting our enemies." The handling of world-renowned American scientists, whose heads bulged with secrets but who remained cold to the cold war, was a constant problem. Britain's Royal Society was dumbfounded by Washington's refusal to let Pauling come and address it on the structure of proteins, although Pauling swore he had Never Been and showed that some of his pet theories were tabu in Russia. He had written, phoned and wired to Truman and Acheson, and called at their offices, without result. A passport strictly limited as to time and place was later granted for him to attend other professional gatherings in Europe.

The fame attainable as a familiar kept attracting newcomers and, as competition with these stiffened, old-timers drew more heavily on their imaginations to remain in the field. Though they were automatically insured against perjury charges, this involved the risk of embarrassing the inquisition, and hence falling out of demand, if they failed to meet the not very exacting thespian standards.

Thus in the year of Matusow's ascendancy Bentley was lamenting to him that "no one will give me a job." George Hewitt, who fibbed too brazenly about the University of Washington heretics in 1948, died destitute under ironic circumstances: because his employer for most of his life had been the Party which he betrayed, he was denied any Social Security pension. Matusow saw the old "hard core of red baiters" like Matthews and Rushmore as lacking "the energy to keep up." Matthews nevertheless remained the familiars' grand old man, and the symbol of arrival for an acolyte was an invitation to autograph Matthews's coffee table. Budenz's indifferent acting ability did him little damage as long as he retained his excellent relations with God and the *Times*. John Lautner's only dramatic contribution in court or hearing room was an account of comrades subjecting him to indignities in a Cleveland cellar, but with something to tell about almost any heretic he would remain a Justice Department "consultant" for years. Rushmore's fount of original information was running dry but he remained on Hearst's payroll, writing "As Told To" confessions for Matusow and other new talent as it turned up. The fact that two heretics he named had committed suicide was cause for his pardonable pride. In the CP leaders' prosecutions now being undertaken in Los Angeles, Baltimore and around the country, and in the marathon SACB probe of the Party which ended with Budenz's testimony in April, most familiars old and new could count on at least a few days' employment at $25 and expenses. For Rushmore there was also—coinciding with Hoover's seventh roundup of Party functionaries—the grand jury probe and indictment of Browder for perjury in connection with his Russian-born wife's naturalization. For seven years a pariah to the Party he once led, Browder could not now raise $5,000 bail to avoid prison for himself and his wife: he could have surpassed Chambers in earnings as a familiar, but the profession did not attract him. As Rushmore explained the position of the jailed heretics' heretic: "He has constantly refused to cooperate with the government or to testify against his former comrades."

Unless, however, he could tap the literary, movie and lecture-hall side earnings, the familiar's work was shabbily recompensed considering the short career span to be anticipated; and the clandestine years before surfacing were generally still less lucrative. One Pennsylvania familiar, for example, would testify that starting at $15 a month he took ten years to earn $15,000; another, that his gross from Hoover for 13 pre-surfacing years amounted to $27,000. As for the testifying fees, if they were adequate for inquisitions they were hardly so for the nervous strain of trials where cross-examination was permitted. Among nonliterary familiars Crouch, with his unsurpassable Red Army reminiscences for hearings plus his Immigration retainer for helping deport heretics, would be rated in 1953 as the biggest earner. Yet Crouch never seems to have grossed as much as $10,000 a year. Generally rating low even with his employers, the familiar's lot is an unhappier one than that of the policeman, who by faithfulness to orders—whether to patrol, to arrest, to spy, to beat, or to feed into ovens—can reasonably expect to continue supporting his family until he retires on a pension.

Matusow saw Crouch, Cvetic and Budenz as the "stellar performers in the witness world" but underestimated Philbrick: an early McCarthy admirer, Philbrick would show better timing than any rival in turning against the master. On Cvetic's horizon no cloud had yet appeared. If Nelson's 20-year sentence was a victory for all Americans Battling Communism, it was a triumph for the ghosted author of *I Was a Communist for the FBI*. When this became a regular airwaves show Cvetic was an attraction as a lecturer with his picturesque accounts of Party life and statesmanlike conclusions; he could also touch the heartstrings with his allusion to "my brokenhearted mother who died thinking me a Red." He advocated "kicking the Reds out of UN" and ousting from schools all who "worm their way [and] mold pliable minds to their suiting. Academic freedom and freedom of speech are not involved at all . . . the Communist is not only plotting murder, he's plotting mass murder. Communists plan to liquidate one-third of the US population, mostly the oldsters." The *Times* devoted 12 inches to his SISS testimony that "all" Soviet-bloc UN representatives were spies, garnished by details of "homosexual parties given by a Czechoslovak Embassy official for the purpose of obtaining vital information." Matthew Cvetic Day was not enough for Pittsburgh to show its gratitude. In an emotional scene at the Pennsylvania Legionnaires' convention, their Americanism award was pinned on him by Governor John S. Fine and Miss America, Bebe Shopp, after cheers subsided for Senator James Duff's proposal that Communists be hanged. A month earlier Nelson had begun an eight-month stay behind bars without bail, not in a federal institution but in the county jail: first in a solitary Murderers Row cell, then with lunatics, bugs and rats in the narcotics-psychiatric division. The judge added a $10,000 fine and billed Nelson $13,291.98 for the costs of his sedition trial while he awaited his next one under the Smith Act. Unable in the darkness of his cage to prepare his own defense, he was fortunate in obtaining a heretical lawyer from Los Angeles who extracted him on bail in February 1953.

But 1952 was preeminently Matusow's year. As he would write later, "the craving for publicity plagued me" from the "frightening but wonderful" moment when Hearst newspapers blazoned his confessions and he found himself "rubbing elbows with the really successful people" in New York's 21 Club. Affectionate first-name letters from corporation executives arrived along with inquisitorial bids for his expertise, and in preparation for the second trial of national Party leaders at Foley Square he "poured over" Marxist books with Cohn for appropriate quotes about violence. Matusow used these tellingly—he "loved play-acting, so it came easy"—in courtroom combat with the shrewd California defense lawyer John T. McTernan. His first public HUAC hearing won him such headlines as "SAYS REDS USED SEX TO LURE MEMBERS" and a New York *Daily News* editorial on "the brutishly immoral strategies of the red traitors." Picking up $250 for supplying teachers' names to Saul Moskoff, he noted Moskoff's fake wall mirror through which suspects were "secretly observed by their accusers" while under inquisition, and returned with new banner headlines to Washington: "REDS REWRITE MOTHER GOOSE, TOTS INDOCTRINATED," "RED PLOT TO INFILTRATE BOY SCOUTS."

The Chief Scout rushed to news agencies an assurance that all scout chiefs had been alerted to take extra care in "scanning every applicant—we must be eternally vigilant." Matusow understudied for Bentley, who failed to show for SACB's probe of the Party, but he was "aiming for something bigger"—the SISS probe of Lattimore. He delighted SISS chairman Eastland with his testimony that Lattimore books were sold in the "Communist bookshop network" for use as "official

CP guides on Asia." (Headline: "CHARGE LATTIMORE BOOK IS RED.") "The happiest day of my blacklisting career" was when *Counterattack* put him on salary to gather data about actor John Garfield (a waste of time, as it proved, for Garfield "broke and was ready to talk" before expiring at 39). In August, after giving 700 pages of testimony at Foley Square about CP plans, Matusow was hired by the master himself. Honoraria for lecturing at McCarthy clubs were a generous $300, and he soon possessed a copy of McCarthy's book *McCarthyism—the Fight for America* autographed "to a great American." It was a diplomatic passport opening all doors: everyone who was anyone in the booming inquisition called him "Harvey."

Fear of the ghetto produced more recantations in the world of the theatre. To ensure that neither impresarios nor ticket buyers would miss it, director Elia Kazan published his confession in display ads in *Variety* and the *Times*. He named his heretical accomplices of the 30s including Odets, who followed him to the HUAC confessional naming Kazan's and Odets's dead friend Bromberg. Harassed and without work after insufficiently abject repentance, the young actor Canada Lee found himself in the same boat as Garfield: both succumbed to heart attacks in May. "How long," Lee was quoted as having asked, "can a man take this kind of unfair and unfounded treatment?" *Herald Tribune* critic Richard Watts noted that the American theatre had reached its "lowest point in creative vitality within living memory," and hoped this was "merely coincidence." Hellman, the next name on HUAC's list, offered to tell all about herself in return for exemption from the "inhuman, indecent and dishonorable" requirement to discuss her friends. The inquisitors could not oblige and she took the usual alternative of silence, denying them hoped-for details about her "closest, most beloved friend" Hammett.

Describing years later the near-disaster which ghettoization caused her financially, she said: "I used to wake up at least once a week and read in the paper something totally untrue that somebody had confessed to." She had considered writing something about the 50s but discarded the idea. "Black comedy," she said, "isn't my line. And you can't make a tragedy out of clowns."

Fever Chart

1952

Seoul: *AP* correspondent reports.

"When the 32nd Infantry Regiment adopted the skull and crossbones as its emblem, its chaplain was in a quandary. He didn't think the insignia seemed appropriate for a chaplain. His jeep now carries the emblem, with one variation. A halo is over the skull."

Toronto: *Globe & Mail* summarizes "Yesterday at the UN."

"LEGAL COMMITTEE: continued debate on definition of aggression, with statement by US that a definition of aggression was not in interests of peace but in interests of aggression."

London: New York *Herald Tribune* correspondent reports on new Moscow proposals for a German settlement.

"A settlement with Russia would upset the entire West defense program, especially NATO, and Western minds, after so many years of cold war, are hardly prepared for the idea of a settlement and all that would follow from it."

Washington: President's Commission on Nation's Health Needs reports.

"Americans last year spent on medical research about 3/10 of 1% of the defense budget and less than the amount spent on monuments and tombstones."

Abilene, Texas, and Washington, D.C.: Presidential aspirant Eisenhower tells press his position on critical issues.

On Korea: "I am not familiar."
On China: "I do not know."
On Negroes in his cabinet: " I don't know."
On China again: "Now I don't know."
On health insurance: "I'm not going to answer too specifically."
On reciprocal trade: "I must confess I am not in a position to answer."
On states' rights: "The whole thing has become so vast and complex that it would be idle to try to talk . . . I really have no information on the steel situation, on anything."

Los Angeles: Item in *Examiner*.

"HINT RED LINK IN NEW BIBLE—Amid claims that some of the translators have Communistic backgrounds, 700 Pentecostal representatives here yesterday voted to withhold endorsement of the new Revised Standard Version of the Bible. Instead, they voted to set up a committee to investigate translators' backgrounds."

Indianapolis: A Tokyo correspondent reports to the *Star*.

"It is reliably reported here that thousands of Chinese women are committing suicide because under the Communist regime they choose their own husbands instead of being forced to marry the husbands their parents select for them."

Memphis: *Commercial Appeal* reader writes about August drought.

"The real reason is the Reds in Russian planes have long nets stretched between the planes and turn back the clouds, and they also carry windblowers on each plane and blow the clouds over Russia where they have plenty of rain. This keeps the air over the US clear so we have drought to burn up our crops."

New York: Item in *Mirror*.

"When a passerby saw two men waving red flags yesterday from a rowboat in the East River, he called police. Four radio cars and a police launch responded. The men were Consolidated Edison workers signaling to surveyors on shore, preparatory to the laying of a cable."

New York: Cosmetic-counter item gets new box top.
             REVLON
             Face Powder
             "Dark Dark"
             (formerly "Russian Sable")

Washington: Dispatch to Pittsburgh *Post-Gazette*.

"People are noting the initials 'JRS' on the Benjamin Franklin half-dollars, and they call the Treasury to see whether the letters stand for 'Joseph R. Stalin.'" The initials are those of John R. Sinnock, nationally famous sculptor. On the Roosevelt dime he used the initials 'JS' and that caused a real flurry. On the Franklin half-dollar he included his middle initial thinking that would solve things."

Wheeling, West Virginia: City manager Plummer comments on the discovery that 50 chewing-gum vending machines emit pasteboard trinkets representing countries of the world, one of them inscribed with a hammer and sickle emblem and the words: "USSR, popn. 211,000,000, Capital Moscow":

"That's a terrible thing to expose the children of this city to. I have demanded a complete investigation. Names of store owners to whom the machines were licensed have been turned over to the FBI."

Buffalo, New York: Item in *Evening News*.

"Don't be surprised if on September 27—the day of Buffalo's mock atomic raid—you see hundreds of children munching on lollipops while the warning signal is on. Members of the Optimist Club, which has designated that day 'Sucker Day,' will give the confections to the children. The purpose, explained president Flicker, is to dispel jitters the youngsters may have and to make them feel secure in the belief that the adults of Buffalo know what they are doing."

New Haven, Connecticut: Cott Bottling Co. re-labels its bottled pop.

"Contains scientifically treated carbonated water . . . and US-certified color added. After an atomic blast, contents of this bottle may be used safely if bottle is thoroughly washed before removing crown. It's Cott to be Good!"

Washington: Civil Defense Administration studies atomic corpse-disposal problem.

"We will ask Congress for $2,100,000 to stockpile a million drab-plastic shrouds. Embalming would be entirely unfeasible. To permit relatives and friends to file past . . . in hope of spotting their missing loved ones would be impractical. If 40,000 bodies were laid out in two rows, the aisle between them would be 20 miles long."

Dearborn, Michigan: *UP* reports.

"Mayor Hubbard today mapped plans for a 'Dearborn loyalty day' on May 12, complete with mass loyalty-oath ceremonies, the crowning of a 'Miss Loyalty' and a street dance called the 'Loyalty Drag.' "

A Christmas selection (*AP, UP,* Boston *Traveler* items in December):

"Sen. Wiley said today that Iron Curtain countries in one of their 'most diabolic conspiracies' are flooding the US with Christmas-tree ornaments."

"John B. Keenan, director of Public Safety in Newark, New Jersey, suggested to House investigators today that Communists may be responsible for the 'filth' flooding the country in the form of obscene books, pictures and magazines."

"Russian antiques were barred today from the big Boston Antique Exposition . . . The director of the show said of the Reds: 'It is not beyond the realm of possibility that these vicious leaders would flood the antique market with stolen art relics . . . to kill American soldiers in Korea.' "

XVI

1952: "It's Like Dope"

Republicans and Democrats chose Eisenhower and Adlai Stevenson to lead them in 1952 in the quadrennial spoils-of-office contest required by the Constitution. In light of America's global pretensions, a French observer confessed himself "terrified by the aboriginal character" of the nominating conventions punctuated by "scalp dances, sirens, scuffles, elephants serenaded by pin-up girls, men and women stomping and shrieking." At a swan-song Progressive Party convention DuBois urged Americans to "crawl out of the caves of fear" by voting, through PP candidate Hallinan (then in jail), for no police actions and no inquisitions: "We cry aloud to those sleeping in the wilderness, awake, awake, put on thy strength O Zion, put on thy beautiful robes."

The Chicago *Tribune* voiced businessmen's pleasure at Stevenson's nomination because, whoever won, "they can feel assured that they have one of their own." Dulles's first foreign-policy speech for candidate Eisenhower proposed "liberating the people behind the Iron Curtain" as against "mere containment [which] is uneconomic and will lead to national bankruptcy." The *Wall Street Journal* found this unrealistic since, under still-escalating doses of napalm, the smallest of heretical nations (except for Albania) showed no signs of conversion. The concept that North Koreans suffered from mass insanity had been well assimilated, but Americans were tired of the police action and more concerned to know where they were going at home. Taking the longer view, the *Journal* began to relax in September: "The economy is adjusting itself to increasingly heavy infusions of military spending. 'It's like dope,' says one economist. 'It's a lot easier to start the habit than to break it.'"

With the inarticulate but impregnable Eisenhower in the Republicans' shop window, Truman's party had McCarthy to beat on domestic issues and Dulles on foreign policy; and although—or perhaps because—the intelligentsia flocked to Stevenson's banner, he was no match for either. His efforts to intellectualize inquisitorial, police-action America were gallant: he saw America's goal, "the triumph of spirit over matter," as opposed by an "abhorrent, implacable, sullen" monster who had "enveloped and enslaved hapless millions" with its "insensate worship of matter." He invoked "the Merciful Father of us all" before groups like the Legion, and pinpointed nursers of illusions about Communism as "in an alliance with the devil—you must act soon to save your soul." But the faultless sentiments lacked conviction for a McCarthy-oriented public recalling Stevenson's pale New Deal taint, his acquaintance with Hiss and involvement in the newly uncovered spy-nest UN. He could justly claim that his party had "instituted the federal loyalty system" three years before McCarthy's debut, "tightened espionage legislation" and prosecuted Communists aided by Hoover's "faithful and resourceful work"; but still cries of "I like Ike" rose from his audiences. Eisenhower needed only to imply that the Democrats had botched the police action and to promise, without specifying how, that he would end it.

As Republican "soft on Communism" charges swelled louder, Stevenson countered with even more winged phrases. By October Communism was "a disease which may have killed more people in this world than cancer, tuberculosis and heart disease combined; it has certainly killed more minds, more souls, than any corruption including the darkest days of Hitler." Hoover's performance had become "magnificent, superb" in "catching Communist agents like killing poisonous snakes or tigers," and Stevenson as President would "smash the conspiracy beyond repair." The aim of America's foes was "total conquest, not merely of the earth but of the human mind . . . to destroy the concept of God himself." Finally, America had received from heaven "an awesome mission, nothing less than leadership of the free world . . . If we walk through the valley of the shadow boldly and mercifully and justly, we shall yet emerge in the blazing dawn of a glorious new day . . . I shall ask Our Lord to make me an instrument of His peace." *

God was not listening. Dulles already had His ear, and Stevenson's shocked rebuttals of McCarthy's and Nixon's "systematic innuendo" about Hiss were unavailing. He insisted he only knew Hiss "briefly . . . he never entered my house and I never entered his." He had never (as Nixon charged) called Hiss's reputation "very good," only " 'good' so far as I had heard from others," and he "never doubted the verdict of the jury." Nixon, whose affection for his dog and whose resolve to jail Hiss were all the public knew of him, swept into the Vice Presidency on the coattails of Eisenhower, who saw a struggle "between anti-God and a belief in the Almighty" but pursued the thought no further. Only in the White House would Eisenhower discover that, although raised by a non-churchgoing mother, he was a Presbyterian. All of Stevenson's golden oratory could not keep the plum from going to the formulator of this résumé of the Asian situation: "In our efforts throughout the world, on outpost positions, I mean positions that are exposed to immediate Communist threat, physical threat, if we will help those people hold out and get ourselves back where we belong as reserves to move into any threatened danger point if they carry it to that point, carry it to that level, then what we will be doing it will be taking these 22 million South Koreans, pushing programs for getting them ready to hold their own front line." If the point was misty, this sounded more hopeful than any of Truman's or Stevenson's prescriptions.

Stevenson charmed liberal audiences by chiding and mocking McCarthy's "excesses"; but although circles reflected by Luce and the *Times* were beginning to fear that McCarthy might discredit the whole inquisitorial system, the time to laugh at him, much less to repudiate him, had not yet come. McCarthy organized an advertisers' boycott of Evjue's hostile *Capital Times* in Madison and called on its city editor to state "whether he was one of the leading Communists in the country." The editor of the Syracuse (New York) *Post-Standard* faced a $500,000 lawsuit for libeling McCarthy. Editor Hank Greenspun of the Las Vegas (Nevada) *Sun* produced a scatologically detailed dossier to show that Commu-

---

* Stevenson quotations may be found in *Major Campaign Speeches of Adlai E. Stevenson,* Random House, New York, 1953.

nists arranged McCarthy's career from the outset. According to Greenspun, McCarthy was probing State Department homosexuals to distract attention from the fact that he was one himself; McCarthy had himself started as a "pinko," witness his statement in 1946 that "Stalin's proposal for world disarmament is a great thing"; and "a close crony" had "admitted that McCarthy was a devoted student of *Mein Kampf,*" so that if he wasn't a Communist he was a Fascist (which was the same thing) or else "a lunatic." The master assigned Matusow to "dig up something" to show that Greenspun was a Communist, and smilingly watched Senator Benton—a Stevenson friend and patron who apparently fathered the "Communist McCarthy" theory—follow Tydings to electoral defeat. Money for all this was generously available, mainly from upstart multimillionaires challenging the hegemony of the traditional gentry. The retribution on hotheaded colleagues persuaded almost all congressmen to plead for McCarthy's electoral support. Columnist Drew Pearson complained in a $5,000,000 assault-libel-conspiracy lawsuit that McCarthy had not only called him a "Communist mouthpiece" but kicked him in the groin and lost him his TV sponsor, Adam Hats, by instigating a boycott of the hats.

An Eisenhower comment on McCarthy's exposure of Marshall ("By golly, un-American methods are never justified [but] I do support the uprooting of subversion . . . serious measures were necessary") inspired *Life* to set the proper tone for criticism of "the most extreme form of McCarthyism." The distinction was established between McCarthy's "ism" and others: it was merely a "venial sin" compared with the "mortal" one of Communism, a "Murder, Inc. [whose] traveling salesmen are men like Lattimore." To make this clear *Life* threw in Wallace as "a prize example of McCarthyism" and concluded: "Now that the case against McCarthyism has been so well made, we would like to recall all honest liberals and all serious Americans to the real danger—the terrible danger—Communism." In line with this formula, Eisenhower traveled through Wisconsin on McCarthy's electioneering train telling voters that, despite some "method" differences, they "saw eye to eye" on the "purpose" of eradicating "experts in treason" who had "penetrated virtually every department, every agency, every bureau, every section of our government." At the end of the ride McCarthy summed it up to newsmen: "I am not displeased . . . it was satisfactory."

With the electoral triumph McCarthy won a $200,000 initial budget for his own committee, which he would run by his own inimitable whim but with Fair Deal senators sitting beside him to lend respectability. Nixon was a heartbeat from the Presidency ("I think Dick will make a fine Vice President," commented McCarthy), and the House Public Works committee chairmanship lent Dondero new authority for his pursuit of red artists whose work adorned public buildings. The pioneer Dies was re-elected, but, despite his pleas that he had 100,000 heretical names, he was trampled in the rush of younger men for places on inquisitorial bodies. One McCarthy-backed senator, Harry P. Cain of Washington state, was defeated by a Fair Dealer, but this worked out positively: the Fair Dealer joined McCarthy's committee and Eisenhower appointed Cain, a man with the earmarks of a fine inquisitor, to SACB.

Approval of the Feinberg law "turning the school system into a spying project" (Justice Douglas, dissenting) stimulated the work of Moskoff and others;

but school inquisitors were moving so far ahead that teachers regarded the law as a comparative safeguard, for it provided a time limit on heresy and required some proof. Each New York school now had a special inquisitor to report on each teacher: "There is/ There is not/ evidence" of subversive thoughts and contacts. For Rose Russell the spying had become a "pyramid" since it had been arranged that superintendents should report on principals, Jansen on superintendents, and the Board of Education on Jansen. The *New Yorker* was worried about who would report on Feinberg: if the Attorney General, who would report on him?

With Bella Dodd—now baptized in St. Patrick's by her monsignor—as chief familiar, McCarran threw his weight into the New York teacher probe, promising that this was but the start of SISS's activity in the field. Six college professors and eight schoolteachers were first in a new series of firings for "insubordination" in not answering questions. Their competence was again unchallenged but ruled irrelevant. An Education Board man explained there was no need to prove they were Communists, for "formal non-membership does not prove non-dedication." Heretical widows' mites cascaded into a TU defense and aid fund for those who were being ghettoized for trying to open minds. But as Dodd pointed out to McCarran: "A mind which is so open is liable to be filled with the first evil thing which comes along."

The handful of lawyers defending heretics enjoyed the same consolation as teachers: the dissents by Black and Douglas to Supreme Court approval of the inquisition. In the appeal of the five CP defense lawyers against being sent to jail by Medina—decided adversely at the same time as Presidential candidate Hallinan's appeal—Douglas had "difficulty in determining" whether Medina had "used the authority of the bench to whipsaw the lawyers, to taunt and tempt them and to create for himself the role of the persecuted." Black thought Medina had shown "such bitter hostility to the lawyers that the accuser should be held disqualified to try them." The jailing of the five sharpened the lawyer famine when the need was greatest, with dozens more Communists awaiting trial around the country. A respectable labor lawyer who accepted a defense brief in the Los Angeles trial avoided jail but complained that his practice vanished overnight. Another defense lawyer there, Ben Margolis, was ready for anything since his experience at a trial in 1949, when he was ordered from attorneys' table to witness stand to say if he was a Communist, and was cited for contempt in holding this improper.

Margolis was among 100-odd Los Angeles lawyers and doctors who, along with film, radio and newspaper suspects, began getting HUAC subpenas in January for an *omnium gatherum* inquisition finally held in October. Some hospitals cooperated graciously—Cedars of Lebanon fired its top nephritis specialist and two other staff men on issuance of the subpenas—but the inclusion of lawyers, with their skill in the use of amendments, in this heretical goulash inspired an aggressive spirit to which HUAC was unaccustomed. Los Angeles's heretical community took the offensive to make the hearings a clamorous landmark, preserved for posterity in a clandestinely taped "Voices of Resistance" recording. ACLU's local chairman. A. A. Heist, a retired Methodist clergyman, presided at an inquisition-eve rally where the hat was passed for an "Abolish HUAC" movement. Scuffles outside the chamber between heretical pickets and loyal citizens produced minor casualties, and five members of the audience were forcibly ejected. The lawyers, and others whom they had coached in the maneuver, commented extensively on the inquisitors ("I hold this entire committee in contempt," Margolis concluded his peroration) before invoking the Fifth to avoid a citation. Over a rising babel of interruptions that they were giving "arguments," they insisted they were giving "reasons" for not answering. An NLG official managed to deliver to the end a lecture on precedents going back to Star Chamber and 17th-century Massachusetts. The tape-recording became a pandemoniac blur through which William B. Esterman—a heretics' defender in countless hearings and trials—could be heard shouting: "Get your hands off me—you don't have to throw me out because I'm walking out." An actor told the inquisitors: "I want to read the First Amendment because I'm not sure everyone in this room understands it. I would like to elicit from you evidence of whether you are still sworn to uphold the Constitution." "You are not here to question the committee," was the reply, "we're here to question you." "Is this a hearing?" "This is a hearing." "Well, I'd like to be heard."

At the probe of the Mine-Mill union's copper plot in Salt Lake City, where he denounced Jencks, Matusow gave a stimulus to the inquisition of journalists by telling SISS he could name some 200 heretics on *Time-Life* and the *Times*. Eugene Moy, editor of America's only Chinese-language journal which denied that Taiwan was China, was indicted for "extorting money" for Peking as part of an "international racket involving murder and torture." (The paper helped Chinese-Americans send cash to relatives at home.) *Compass* managing editor Tom O'Connor died of a stroke at 38, shortly after HUAC summoned him to explain his views on press freedom. The probe showed McCarthy's influence on chairman Velde, as in this passage:

VELDE: Are you a Communist now?
O'CONNOR: No.
VELDE: Were you a year ago?
O'CONNOR: No.
VELDE: Were you ten years ago?
O'CONNOR: No.
VELDE: I can draw only one inference, that you are not only a past member of the CP, but you continue to be a member and that you are an extreme danger to the country.

Chaplin left to present his film *Limelight* in London, learned on shipboard that he would be probed on his return "as a salutary lesson to the youth of our land," and decided to relieve the Attorney General of that duty. He confronted a press horde at Cherbourg nervously but, when they broke into applause, smiled and explained his politics: "I am an individualist, I believe in liberty." France recruited him into its Legion of Honor, and Lords and Commons banqueted him in London. His wife flew back to rescue $4,000,000 in securities from their safety-deposit box two days before the Treasury Department filed a $500,000 tax-arrears claim. Returning depressed by talks with the staff at their Beverly Hills home—there had been various FBI visits seeking evidence of political or moral heresies, with questions such as "Didn't he have wild parties and naked women?"—she soon formally renounced American citizenship. The Chaplin family retired to a Lake Geneva chateau, where he received celebrities of both free and curtained worlds and talked of the inquisition with deep sighs: "It's so bo-o-o-oring. America is so terribly grim in spite of all that material prosperity. They no longer know how to weep. Compassion and the old neighborliness have gone, people stand by and do nothing when friends and neighbors are attacked, libeled and ruined. The worst thing is what it has done to the children. They are being taught to admire and emulate stool pigeons, to betray and to hate, and all in a sickening atmosphere of religious hypocrisy." * A Legion campaign cleansed American screens of 30-year-old Chaplin comedies while Russia and China pleaded for his films at reduced rates. "You forget," he told them, "you're dealing with a capitalist."

Mann had likewise had enough and retired to a second self-imposed exile in Switzerland. Einstein's old Social Democrat friend Otto Nathan, an economic adviser to Germany's pre-Hitler government and an American since 1939, began a long fight with the State Department for permission to travel on Einstein's and his own business. Finally agreeing under protest to swear he had Never Been, he was asked at a series of hearings to talk about his friends and "disclose all discussions you had with them." A year and a half of this ended with rejection of his application, and he took the matter to court.

Before leaving, Mann joined in the appeals for the Rosenbergs which had become a downpour from overseas but remained to the end a drizzle in America. Urey made public his view "as a scientist" that the verdict "outraged logic and justice." Comfortable Jewish groups urged the faithful to "be on guard against the vicious Communist campaign to save the Rosenbergs"; Einstein appealed to Eisenhower on grounds similar to Urey's, and objections to the sentence without questioning the verdict came from 2,000 clergymen with uneasy consciences. NLG protested on civil-liberties grounds while the American Jewish Committee circulated a denial by ACLU counsel Herbert Levy, on ACLU letterheads, that civil liberties were involved. "This was a conviction for espionage," wrote Levy, "which we believe to be the proper way to deal with Communist totalitarianism." Max Lerner, dean of liberal Russophobe columnists, and Stone continued writing irately about the defense committee, but Stone would admit after the executions that, like almost everyone else, he never read the trial record.

The electrical ceremony at Sing Sing was again postponed after Czechoslovakia staged the last of the treason trials in Russian-bloc countries, inspired by Stalin's acute paranoia. In words they were forced to learn by heart, former Party secretary Rudolf Slansky and 13 top-rank colleagues—most of them lifelong heroes of the movement—confessed to an imperialist-Titoist-Zionist plot. The plot, as improbable as the one ascribed to the Rosenbergs, extravagantly flattered the subversive talents of the Dulles brothers. Unable to believe that socialists could resort to methods competing in obscenity with Hitler's, American heretics almost without exception sought to justify the trial and 11 executions. Yet could torture alone account for the defendants' performance, or was it such devotion as to persuade them that their abjectness and death could somehow benefit their cause? In any case few Americans could now deny that, even if both socialism and capitalism indulged in legal frame-ups, capitalism was more benevolent to the victims.

* Interview with the author, 1955.

America had more and better justice as it had more and better bombs: it had confined its heretical death sentences to two nobodies, who happened to be parents of prospective orphans.

Whether Americans should continue or stop killing Koreans was a question still unresolved. On the one hand publisher-editor Fleur Cowles returned from South Korea "completely enchanted,"* and even the anti-inquisitorial Justice Douglas, after visiting and praising Chiang in Taiwan, proclaimed from Korea that UN had saved Asia from Communism. But the price seemed excessive to GIs' mothers and wives in Argo, Illinois, who, gathering at the home of beauty-shop operator Florence Gowgiel, formed a Save Our Sons Committee to "end this senseless bloody war." A Quaker "working party" brought forth a global peace plan and expounded it in the short film *A Time for Greatness,* which drew a quick response from Philbrick in his *Herald Tribune* column. He exposed "secret instructions" issued by "underground Communist Party cell leaders" to boost the film, and revealed that the *Worker* had reviewed it favorably and given details for obtaining it. The film was in fact more of a secret than the instructions: TV officials to whom it was submitted rejected it as "socialistic, off-color, in poor taste . . . the context and overall effect is pro-Communist."

But if Yuletide was un-merry for Koreans and the Rosenberg and Sobell families, it was convivial for others. Parnell Thomas received a pardon from Truman, and Matusow spent Christmas night at the home of Sokolsky, "the philosophical leader of the McCarthy group." Cohn dropped in to wish the familiars the compliments of the season and drink with them to another fruitful year. Matusow's years of pining for popularity seemed finally over. He had just returned from a honeymoon trip to Miami and Nassau with one of McCarthy's backers, a wealthy Washington divorcee in whose home he would play host to the inquisitorial set. And ever since Thanksgiving, when he had dined at the Matthews's, his signature had adorned the coffee table of the familiars' grand old man.

---

* The editor of the defunct drawing-room magazine *Flair* found "even the little children and women looking happy": they reminded her of a painting by Braque. She coupled her report from the front with the announcement that Random House would publish *Flair* excerpts "as a bound book with a hole in the center . . . As you flip the pages an owl turns out to be a moth, which turns out to be a butterfly, which turns out to be an eye of a woman."

XVII

1953: In the Kitchen

with the Canapes

America moved into another cold-war year with millions of its families enjoying two or more cars and TV sets, while most families elsewhere had yet to graduate to a water tap. A minority of citizens noticed that a pall of see, hear, speak no evil hung over their accumulation of creature comforts. All but a handful had built walls between themselves and their neighbors in order to live with it, for any association with others might draw inquisitorial attention.

In such group activity as still persisted, the Party whose quarantining gave the inquisition its rationale was ever less significant: defense of its own legality claimed most of the energies of its dwindling forces. The "clandestine" leaders Gus Hall and Robert Thompson had been captured; the others were ready to give up, and the Party faced endless court battles and jail terms. To have his term raised to seven years, Thompson was brought to court with a metal plate in his head. He was recovering from the nearly fatal impact of an iron pipe wielded by a jailmate—an anti-Tito Yugoslav who thereby earned, in place of deportation, three more safe years as a guest of the Prisons Department. Few groups which would not purge their Communists could hope to survive. The arguments for obliterating such an organization as IWO, with its non-profit insurance policies, were compelling: a government lawyer pointed to "the losses of Latvia, Lithuania, Estonia, Poland, Hungary, Rumania, East Germany, Czechoslovakia, China and North Korea" and the fact that "war with Russia could come within a year." Eisenhower's Attorney General Herbert Brownell assured the Friendly Sons of St. Patrick that over 10,000 alien "snakes" such as congregated in IWO were being probed for deportation.

In selecting victims, the deportation mill reached far back into dossiers and made willingness to name names the acid test. Among those balking was Hollywood writer Reuben Ship who appeared at a hearing on crutches from an accident; he was dumped, crutches and all, in his native Canada where he would produce the classic inquisitorial radio-play *The Investigator*. The fifth attempt to deport Bridges failed, but Bridges predicted a sixth and would not be disappointed: his lawyer Hallinan having been returned to jail for tax evasion, he retained Telford Taylor, a liberal general who had been chief counsel at the Nuremberg trials. A more obvious non-Communist under threat of deportation was Chicago *Sun-Times* cartoonist Jacob Burck, who had arrived from Poland at age 10, contributed to the *Worker* in the 30s, and (according to familiars Crouch and Maurice Malkin) been seen in that decade at Party meetings. For years Burck's cartoons had been so hostile to Communism that they had won him a Pulitzer Prize; furthermore, he "regretted with shame" the *Worker* connection. The authorities were not impressed, but to protect a business asset Burck's employer Marshall Field gave lawyers a blank check to probe Crouch and Malkin. Malkin turned out to have been jailed for felonious assault and dismissed from a government job for forgery, and to have fraudulently obtained citizenship. On Crouch, the lawyers produced affidavits from respectable citizens he had claimed to know or have worked for, ranging from a managing editor's "This is not true" to a Texas judge's "I never met him in my life." With all this, Burck's deportation order would still stand in the fall of 1955.

Based on the old ACLU principles, an Emergency Civil Liberties Committee was born with Einstein, Pickett, NAACP's White,* architect Frank Lloyd Wright, Shirer and Princeton professor H. H. Wilson among its sponsors. (Some of them soon left.) North Dakota Senator William Langer—last of the maverick-isolationist school in Congress, who had opposed the legislative pillars of the cold war—came to address the founding conference along with Stone, Thomas Emerson of Yale Law School, Carey McWilliams, lawyer Leonard Boudin, Judge Hubert Delany, Meiklejohn, theologian Paul Lehmann, and authors Matthew Josephson and Merle Miller. Miller, representing the almost extinct species of intellectual who opposed heretics but would stand on a platform with them, said that liberty's main enemy resided in Moscow, Prague and Peking. Josephson agreed that things were bad over there but saw "a cultural depression, in fact a panic" in America and said: "The main job is here." Meiklejohn, about to accept TU's annual award at 81, keynoted the gathering with a rejection of the Supreme Court's "clear and present danger" philosophy: "The danger of political suppression is greater than the danger of political freedom. Repression is always foolish, freedom is always wise."

The prevailing trend among intellectuals with heretical pasts was to enter the confessional and name names. In February historian Daniel Boorstin, literature professor Gorham Davis, and the former *New Masses* literary guru Granville Hicks publicly performed the self-purification rite providing a passport to the media and to groves of academe. They appeared before Velde, whose approach to academic inquisiting was summed up in his widely quoted phrase: "The basis of Communism is education." Boorstin confessed that he had studied Marxism at Oxford, and Hicks and Davis explained how they came to join the Party and what and whom they found in it. At a time when "we were aware of the growing menace of Hitlerism," Davis recalled, the CP "did seem to be taking the lead," and he had joined a group of 15 who discussed Marxism, union policies, fund raising, anti-Semitism, etc. After the Party proved to be "politically and morally intolerable" he had resigned from the Wallaceite TU, joined the Hook-Schlesinger Cultural Freedom Committee and signed a manifesto exposing the Waldorf-Astoria conference plot. Complimented by Velde on his loyalty, Davis still confessed to twinges about the American "prejudice against informers" and the traditional honor system in colleges, but carried his "unpleasant duty" through to the end.

---

* White was protesting at the time that Negro veterans were returning from Korea to face "white" and "colored" Coca-Cola machines, and that "Do you have Negro friends?" had become a standard question asked of heretical suspects. Violence against blacks had, however, declined during the police action and some attention was now paid to their complaints. Coca-Cola chairman Farley assured White that skin-color tests would no longer be applied to buyers of his pop.

America's educational pace-setter was the Indiana Textbook Commission's Mrs. White, who called for removal from school books of information about Robin Hood or the Quakers. By robbing the rich to give to the poor, and by "not believing in fighting wars," both tended to support Communism. Temple University fired philosophy professor Barrows Dunham, author of *Man Against Myth,* who would tell Velde nothing but his name and birth date. Unreconstructed Judge Luther W. Youngdahl dismissed four of seven perjury indictments against Johns Hopkins professor Lattimore, but Lattimore would be re-indicted for denying he followed the CP line. Velde promised to probe Johns Hopkins, Harvard, MIT and Chicago for more "infiltrators into education, one of the most important weapons Stalin has for overthrowing our form of government." The National Council of Churches of Christ in America, claiming to speak for 35,000,000 Protestants, offered objections to "certain methods" of the educational inquisition. The rival American Council of Christian Churches, on behalf of a million Protestants who held that the King James Bible was heretical and that Jesus was a Prohibitionist, then asked HUAC to probe for reds in NCCCA.

At the beginning of the year America ushered in the H-Bomb era with a test at Eniwetok, but Russian capacity to match it with little delay was no longer underestimated. The new team in Washington called off the police action when America's death roll reached 54,246, but an admiral bolstered the morale of naval school students by reminding them that America "now confronts what amounts to running the world." With the slogan, "What's good for General Motors is good for America," GM's Charles Wilson emerged as Defense Secretary in an all-businessman cabinet which would further escalate arms production. A fuss about the cabinet members' holdings in corporations with which they would place war orders blew over quickly. Foster Dulles jetted about the planet with the Bomb in one hand and the Bible in the other, causing Britain's *Manchester Guardian* to ask if Eisenhower would "appoint an assistant secretary with the special function of explaining what Mr. Dulles is talking about." * Already alarmed by the military expenditures expected of them, and by Truman's nuclear threats before leaving office, free-world allies wondered where "what is generally known here as the American witch hunt" (London *Times*) was taking their leader and patron.

Stalin died in March,** but such headlines as "HEIR TO STALIN MAY NEED WAR TO HOLD POWER" warned Americans to expect no dilution of Russian aggressiveness. On a behind-the-Curtain trip the small steel magnate Ernest Weir found such hunger for peace everywhere that he wrote a pamphlet flatly contradicting the Establishment, arguing that negotiations were not only possible but alone could avert disaster. It was left to *Pravda* to afford Weir's views their

---

* *The Christian Herald,* at least, had no trouble understanding. A cartoon in that journal showed Dulles as a cook mixing foreign-policy ragout from a recipe featuring Moral Leadership, Religious Background, Christian Ethics and Churchmanship.

** Gathering in New York for a memorial ceremony, Stalin devotees—mostly elderly residents of Ukrainian and Russian origin—were targets of bottles, stones, chairs, and cries of "Jew bastards, Jew murderers, Jew Communists!" They described the aggressors as recently-arrived Ukrainian and Polish youths who had been "going about the Ukrainian community boasting of having participated in pogroms" during the German occupation of eastern Europe, "showing watches and jewelry they had stolen from Jews" there.

first newspaper airing, and the *Times* then published some excerpts with an admonition to Weir to consider "the awesome mushroom cloud" behind "Moscow's
honeyed words." Later in the year there would be revolts against Russia's heavy
hand in Poland and East Germany, and Stalin's chief policeman Lavrenti Beria
would be executed on the unlikely charge of having been an imperialist agent
since 1919. One of Stalin's last acts had been the arrest of six Jewish and three
other doctors for conspiring with one or the other Dulles, or both, to murder him—
a plot for which, if they were guilty of it, they might well not have needed the
Dulles encouragement. Russia's best Communists had been disappearing into concentration camps in such multitudes that almost everyone knew a victim, and the
country had become a network of informers on neighbors' or relatives' deviations.
Under the stimulus of induced cold-war fear, Russians were cooperating as faith-
fully as Americans in their style of purge and in the erosion of their popular
institutions.

But if some relaxation now seemed probable behind the Curtain, America's
inquisition was still gathering momentum. McCarthy's apogee and the Rosenberg case coincided with America's first failure to win a war, and the forces all
worked the other way. The names of the four Rosenbergs were on people's lips
all over the world during the last months of the legal dance of death. Their fate
was seen as a symbol of what America intended to become and to make humanity
become. The media buried the arguments which were front-paged overseas by
rejecting paid advertisements as well as releases of the defense committee, which
columnist Robert S. Allen exposed as being "financed from large Kremlin deposits
in Tangier banks."

The Broadway opening of Miller's *The Crucible*, a dramatization of good
folk sentenced to die for witchcraft in Salem, brought critics out in a rash of denials that any Rosenberg parallel was intended. "There never were any witches,"
pondered the *Times's* Brooks Atkinson, "but there have been spies and traitors in
recent days." Visas were denied to European sympathizers invited by the defense
committee, and all last-minute efforts for the Rosenbergs proved futile. The media
directed the public's attention to the plight of Judge Kaufman who, "vilified by
Communists," had been "forced by his doctor to take a rest in Florida" (New
York *Herald Tribune*).

With his usual explanation that shrinking CP membership made his work
harder, Hoover got $77,500,000 from Congress with a possible extra $5,000,000
for more agents to deal with the plot in the UN. He remained the nation's darling,
but McCarthy was catching up fast, his popularity poll rising by the year's end to
50% "favorable" and only 21% "no opinion." Velde's budget was raised to
$300,000, but he fell into blunders which McCarthy avoided. McCarthy's Perma-
nent Subcommittee on Investigations of the Senate Committee on Government
Operations had no restrictive mandate, and he chose his victims daringly, always
with an eye to the most headline-rich lode, traitorous New Dealizers in the government itself. His initial mistakes as a committee chairman were more in the
area of staff selections. Robert Kennedy (a future Attorney General), ex-FBI
agent Don Surine, Cohn with his Rosenberg prosecution prestige, the hotel magnate's son David Schine, Gerhardt Eisler's ex-wife and Matusow seemed good
choices at the time but the last four would produce headaches.

In New York's mass-circulation *Daily News,* which specialized in crime, sex, the flag and an editorial vernacular out-brazening McCarthy's, political commentator O'Donnell wrote: "Let McCarthy tear the boys apart in the State Department." Senators Wayne Morse, Lehman and Estes Kefauver gingerly asked for "changes of procedure"; George F. Kennan (the advocate of strangling Russia by "containment") saw "our established institutions whipped about like trees in a storm," and eggheads muttered about the peril of "demagogs, smears, undemocratic methods [to] our traditions of intellectual honesty and fair play." Soon even Hook would be chiding the master, who remained impervious to such puny barbs and aimed his arrows ever higher. He exposed Charles Bohlen, a Krupp relative nominated for the Moscow ambassadorship, as an associate of "the Hiss-Acheson gang." Chambers confirmed that as a Yalta participant Bohlen was an "unhappy choice," and McCarthy demanded a lie-detector test for the nominee and that Foster Dulles be summoned to explain himself. While Dulles and Eisenhower strove to appease him, McCarthy launched his probe of the State Department's "Voice of America" radio propaganda service before a huge, fascinated TV audience. VOA engineer Raymond Kaplan, expecting to be summoned, threw himself under a passing truck—the only suicide directly credited to McCarthy.

This probe led McCarthy into a spring and summer of intermittent "book-burning," as heretics called his inquisition of authors whose works were in United States Information Service libraries overseas. McCarthy sent Cohn and Schine to detect these un-Americana *in situ,* but Britain sneered at them as "distempered jackals" (*Financial Times*), "tightly shut minds like aborted rosebuds" (*New Statesman & Nation*), "agents of intolerance and totalitarianism" (*Church of England Newspaper*), "the best pro-Soviet propaganda recently found in Europe" (*Daily Telegraph*). Even West German media mocked them after they were heard asking an official, "What is European integration? What does Western orientation mean?" Frankfurt reported a quaint episode of Schine "batting Cohn over the head with a rolled-up magazine" in their hotel lobby, and a maid's later discovery of a litter of overturned furniture and ashtrays in Schine's room.

In Germany, however, Cohn and Schine got wind of the fact that recommendations by Cedric Belfrage and James Aronson had resulted in some Communists getting newspaper jobs in 1945, along with Social Democrats, leftist Catholics and the now-reigning President of West Germany. (The few Communist editors had long since been removed.) Summoned by McCarthy, Belfrage and Aronson suggested that Eisenhower—whom they admitted not having met, but whose orders they carried out—might be the best man to explain this. On everything except Germany they invoked the Fifth. McCarthy promised that if Aronson denied being a Communist "we would promptly refer the case to the Justice Department for perjury action," but apparently no familiar had yet been assigned to name Belfrage who, as an alien, was more vulnerable. An Immigration man in the hearing room was told to stir his Department's stumps, and next day Belfrage was led from his office to Ellis Island for deportation.*

---

* HUAC had already probed Belfrage a month earlier, and in 1947 he had spent two days before the grand jury probing Bentley's spy list on which he appeared. After a month in Ellis Island he was returned to limited circulation (curtained at the Con-

The Cohn-Schine tour yielded little for the book probe since the State Department, vowing it would never buy such titles again, had obediently supplied a list of all tainted volumes in its USIS libraries. The keynote familiar, Budenz, postulated that such books could not have got where they were without the cooperation of "a concealed Communist" in the Department. Televiewers enjoyed the spectacle of authors being paraded to defy or grovel. Asking if they had "engaged in espionage or sabotage" and "would serve your country in fighting Communism in Korea," McCarthy displayed his quick grasp of the Fifth Amendment as an inquisitorial tool. Its edge had just been sharpened by the American Bar Association which (confirming that the amendment was now a shield not for the innocent but for the guilty) had approved disbarment of any lawyer invoking it. McCarthy enjoyed compelling witnesses to spell out that they invoked it because "an answer might tend to incriminate" them. The authors' desire to speak positively about their work enabled him to play some of them like trout on a line as they answered certain questions after invoking the Fifth on others. When novelist Millen Brand answered "No" to "Have you ever engaged in larceny?" McCarthy closed in: "The inference is of course clear that the witness has been engaged in espionage." Yet by this time Fifth-invokers were two a penny at hearings, and jailing them had become a game for second stringers: McCarthy merely attached his "Fifth Amendment Communist" label and concentrated on big fish whom he could use the tadpoles to catch. The only citations went to Harvey O'Connor—a consistently heretical writer since the Seattle "revolution" of 1919—who invoked the First Amendment to defy all questions about his politics, and to Lamont who invoked it after denying he was a Communist. Huberman took Lamont's position but was not cited. Lamont was the most promising fish in the net since McCarthy was preparing to probe the Army, and the Army had bought copies of Lamont's book *Peoples of the Soviet Union.* *

William Gropper, for years a cartoonist for Party journals, was asked by inquisitor Henry M. Jackson: "If you are an artist, have you engaged in espionage or sabotage?" He admitted painting a folkloric map of America found in USIS libraries, but was an unsatisfactory witness:

GROPPER: I do not write books. I don't even make maps. I am a painter.

McCARTHY: But when you draw folklore maps, you are authoring the map.

---

necticut border) by an old-fashioned judge who insisted on witnesses to subversive acts. Also under inquisitorial fire at the time were the deportable editors of Yiddish, Lithuanian, Estonian, Russian, Finnish, Korean and Slovene journals.

* Lamont, a founder of ECLC, was about to quit ACLU which, in advertising for new members, was warning that "only those whose devotion to civil liberties is not qualified by adherence to Communist, Fascist, Ku Klux Klan or other totalitarian doctrines" need apply. Whether any civil libertarians in the Klan would have liked to join is not known. At an ECLC affair honoring him for defiance of McCarthy, Lamont said: "The clear meaning of the Bill of Rights is that all should enjoy full civil liberties—reactionaries, Fascists, liberals, progressives, businessmen, tycoons, workers, Socialists, Trotskyists, Communists, Catholics, atheists, and all the infinite variety of crackpots, fanatics and self-appointed saviors of mankind. As soon as we start making exceptions, we are lost."

GROPPER: No, sir.

McCARTHY: Before someone in the Information Service purchased your maps, did you contact any Communist in the Service and solicit them to have your maps purchased?

GROPPER: I have nothing to do with the sale of maps.

Probing James Allen of International—publishers of Marx, Lenin and Stalin, whose works fed bonfires throughout the land—McCarthy's colleague Everett Dirksen conjured a somber scene in Bombay: an impressionable young Hindu entering the USIS library and finding books which "are not an expression of the objectives of the free world at all." McCarthy enjoyed asking witnesses whether, if they ran the libraries, they would put such books in them: this forced the penitent to be "honest enough" (as Cohn phrased it), "even though you are the author of the books, to tell us you would not select them." The master inquisitor would stand no nonsense from lawyers and threatened to throw out and cite Boudin, who sought too zealously to guide his client Laurence Rosinger (Far East specialist, contact of Lattimore) through the Fifth-Amendment maze. William Mandel, a Moscow University alumnus who wrote about Russia, took the offensive with "This is a book burning. I am a Jew." Cohn said, "So am I"; McCarthy said, "Officer, I want you to stand by," and led Mandel into a discussion of the Rosenberg case. When Mandel called it "rather typical" that the inquisition's first two death sentences were passed upon Jews, McCarthy had his cue to appraise Jews as "a great race of people—each race has its traitors." To this Mandel, glancing at Cohn, riposted: "It certainly does."

Rosinger's refusal to say if he knew Hiss, Mao or Frederick Field irritated McCarthy's colleague Stuart Symington. "Why," he asked, "don't you state your position frankly as Professor Budenz did? That is what I cannot understand in these hearings." Symington led Budenz through a catechism of whether Russia would "risk attacking" if America had "inadequate defense." "Oh," replied Budenz, "I think we must have very adequate defense." But must not Americans "arm ourselves properly" despite Russian "peace feelers"? "Oh, yes, I think we must arm ourselves, decidedly, [but also] maintain internal security." "I agree with you. We should have internal security of course." What would be the effects of Stalin's death? "No change whatsoever—Communism is a philosophy which is determined to prove that God does not exist . . . Certainly not . . . That is correct . . . Yes, sir." With a request to the professor to name his anti-Communist book titles, McCarthy brought Budenz's literary-geopolitical reflections to a close: "Thank you very much," "Thank you very much, Mr. Budenz," "Thank you, Senator." McCarthy's affable disdain spoiled Symington's performance as a liberal statesman who had ruefully accepted inquisitorial duties. Turning to his colleague when Boudin asked that Rosinger be allowed to testify without TV cameras, McCarthy said: "We should not discriminate—what think you, Senator?" Such stage-management trivia did not belong in the world of Symington who replied on a peevish note: "I have no thoughts on it. I have never thought about it."

Cohn began questioning Hammett, who had just emerged from jail for contempt of HUAC: "What is your occupation?" "Writer." "You are a writer, is that correct?" Three hundred of Hammett's detective stories had been found in

75 libraries, but he would not say if he was a Communist when he wrote them, nor whether royalties from them ended up in Party "coffers," nor whether he was a spy or saboteur. McCarthy asked if he thought Communism "superior to our form of government," and the taciturn Hammett replied: "Theoretical Communism is no form of government. You know, there is no government." No, Hammett would not "favor adoption of Communism in this country . . . it would seem to be impractical if most people don't want it." Would he put heretical authors' books in USIS libraries if he were running them? "If I were fighting Communism, I don't think I would do it by giving people any books at all."

Cohn's introduction of Hughes ("You are Langston Hughes, the well known poet, is that right?") showed that the Negro writer had been pulverized into capitulation in advance. The $64 question was not asked, for Hughes confessed that "I had a complete reorientation roughly four or five years ago." He once thought that a black American could not get a fair trial, but now perceived that "one can and does." He had seen an "acceleration of improvement in race relations" in America while learning about Russia's "persecution and terror against the Jewish people." Readings from the "When a Man Sees Red" section of his sardonic *Simple Speaks His Mind,* written after a HUAC inquisitor called a Negro "a very ugly name," evoked a confession from Hughes that he was "not particularly proud" of this and other early works. Here McClellan, the only Southerner on McCarthy's team, interjected: "What interests me is that I want to commend anyone who will be as frank about their errors of the past as you are being—it is quite refreshing and comforting"; yet what had Hughes actually done to show "repentance or reformation?" Hughes obliged by quoting passages written later in which "I reaffirm the potentialities of our democracy." McClellan could "certainly commend you for the authorship of those remarks" but McCarthy, to make the cheese more binding, said he had "been asked to put into the record" Hughes's earlier poem *Goodby Christ* "to show the type of thinking of Mr. Hughes at that time." Hughes confirmed that he "no longer held any of the views expressed in it" and "certainly would not subscribe to it at this time . . . Thank you . . . I must say that I was agreeably surprised at the courtesy and friendliness with which I was received . . . Senator Dirksen was most gracious." McCarthy passed to the next customer with a "Thank you very much."

A peripheral problem of the book probe—one with which frightened heretics were already familiar—was how to get rid of the books. As Ray Bradbury explained in his well known novel, a temperature of *Fahrenheit 451* is required to reduce them to ash. The USIS un-Americana were burned in some places, but in Germany especially there was embarrassment about reviving the bonfires associated with Hitler. The *Times* reported that the volumes—including a recently purged professor's work on solid geometry—had been stored, crated or hidden away pending word from Washington on their final disposition. The matter did not come up again except in McCarthy's questioning of Dr. James Bryant Conant, America's new High Commissioner in Germany, as to what he would do with them if he opposed burning them. The ex-president of Harvard thought he could "make a deal" to sell them second hand, but McCarthy pointed out that this would still leave them available for people to read.

The intelligentsia, while broadly satisfied that if an author would not deny being a Communist he must be one, were dismayed by McCarthy's inquisition of James Wechsler, the New York *Post* editor who made the genuineness of his repentance crystal clear. "To keep the free press issue straight," he named for McCarthy 59 former comrades in YCL.

HUAC was matching McCarthy's energy but showing decidedly less flair in its choice of targets. It produced a Fifth-invoking ex-Congressman in a Dayton (Ohio) probe, but New Dealer Hugh DeLacy of Washington state had already been ghettoized too long—he was now working as a carpenter—to rate more than a few inches. A return date in Los Angeles did not repair the damage to HUAC's prestige of its lawyer-doctor hearing of 1952, even though subpena servers were sent with photographers to serve an estrogenic dancer during the show at a night club (she was fired on the spot). Results of a further show-business probe were spotty. Bandleader Artie Shaw said he had been a dupe, choreographer Jerome Robbins that he had been a puppet and that the Party was anti-Semitic. Songwriter Jay Gorney tried to undermine the dignity of the scene by rendering his musical version of the First Amendment, and gravel-voiced actor Lionel Stander by ignoring questions and continuing to elaborate his claim not to be "a dupe or a dope or a moe or a schmoe." Stander's oratorical crescendo drowned out the gavel and Velde excused him with relief to return to the ghetto, where he was engaged in selling stocks and bonds.

The deposed Mrs. Aldrich of General Foods' TV program made a desperate effort to escape from the ghetto by appearing voluntarily to compliment HUAC on its "fine and educational job" and confess some heresies. She had once "sent a greeting to the Moscow Art Theatre," contacted Stander, and given her name for an "Abolish HUAC" appeal in 1946. She explained the latter by comparing the coarse inquisitorial manners of that time with the refinement of the present committee. Velde "felt she was sincere" in this and in her explanation of how she came to lend her home for what turned out to be a Hollywood Ten fund-raising party: "Busy in the kitchen with the canapes," she had been "shocked" on emerging to hear the pitch being made. She left promising to let Velde know if anything "came to her mind" about "subversive activities in the entertainment field," but apparently still had not confessed enough to get off the blacklist.

Two incidents drew attention to the art termites detected by Dondero. At New York's New School of Social Research, an Orozco mural depicting Lenin and Stalin disappeared in the spring behind a monkscloth cover. This had happened once before, in 1951, but the mural had re-emerged with a plaque explaining that responsibility for its content was exclusively Orozco's. Asked to comment on the school's nervous relapse, the Metropolitan Museum of Art's director said it was "not any of my business" and a Modern Art Museum curator said: "I haven't heard." In San Francisco, where the New Deal had commissioned Anton Refregier to adorn the Post Office with a mural, loyal protests against this "Communist art" rose to a crescendo. The mural depicted such incidents in the city's history as the persecution of Chinese, the Mooney case and the 1934 general strike. A bill to remove it, backed by the Legion, DAR, VFW and Grand Parlor of Sons of the Golden West, had been introduced in the Congress with active support from inquisitors

Nixon and Dondero.* The Grand Parlor pointed out that one panel showed "the head of a family wearing a red tie, a boy reading a red-covered book. The predominating color is red: these murals are definitely subversive."

By June the Harvard *Crimson* tallied over 100 teachers suspended or fired for non-cooperation with Congressional committees. All opinion polls showed public approval. Lawyer Morris Ernst wrote unhappily to the *Crimson* that he thought most of the victims had balked only at talking about others: "We have taught our children not to be tattletales but are now publicly parading witnesses to testify against their upbringing. The parade may keep up for 60 years." He estimated that 700,000 Americans had at some time joined the Party and quit. The *Crimson* saw as a bright spot MIT's retention of three professors who told inquisitors they had been and no longer were, although Struik remained idle while MIT weighed his heresies against his erudition in non-Euclidean geometry and tensor calculus. In New York, school superintendent Jansen praised the committee as defenders of academic freedom while Moskoff, in his inquisitorial sanctum, asked a continuous stream of suspects: "Were you ever at the home of X . . . did you ever discuss foreign policy . . . what did your father do?"

SISS inquisitor Jenner took the spotlight from HUAC in the probe of Harvard, MIT and other Bostonian sources of infection. In exorcising the resurgent devil in Massachusetts, Jenner was competing on the ground with the state's Special Commission to Study and Investigate Communism and Subversive Activities and Related Matters, which had already exposed Struik as "conspiring to teach the overthrow" of Massachusetts in lectures at the Samuel Adams School.** Philbrick was on hand for Jenner's probe and added secretary Mary Knowles to the list of Adams School conspirators; but many of his names were no longer new, such as Harvard geologist Kirtley Mather ("one of the top ten academic collaborators of the CP" on Matthews's list), feminist-Wallaceite-trade unionist Florence Luscomb whose ancestors landed in 1720, and publisher Angus Cameron who, already ghettoized, had launched the heretical firm of Cameron & (Albert) Kahn. Harvard instructor David Hawkins, and Cornell physicist Philip Morrison who was researching cosmic rays at MIT, seemed more promising material. Both had been with Oppenheimer at Los Alamos, and both admitted heresies before they joined the Bomb project, but Hawkins said he "simply left" the CP and would invoke no amendment for declining to discuss his friends. He added that he told no one at Los Alamos he was a Communist because no one asked: he was asked there about "subversive organizations" but did not regard the CP as being such,

---

* Despite its distinguished backing the bill died in committee, and the mural remains. (Being painted directly on the wall, its removal would have involved outright destruction.) In a letter to Legion Post Commander Plant in 1949, Nixon had promised that as soon as the Republicans regained power "a committee of Congress should make a thorough investigation of this type of art in Government buildings, with a view of obtaining removal of all that is found to be inconsistent with American ideals and principles."

** A student of the thinkers who gave past luster to Massachusetts (see his book, *Yankee Science in the Making*), Struik liked to recall that Thoreau was jailed for not paying taxes in protest against the Mexican war. Struik ascribed his indictment primarily to his opposition to the Korean war.

and anyway understood that his employers knew he had been a member. "I want to say this is amazing!" Jenner exclaimed.

Morrison, who was still officially an AEC consultant despite his heretical contacts, presented an unusual problem. Hoover's men had been tapping his phone, intercepting his mail and paying him visits while he indulged an irreverent sense of humor in a battle against removal of all secret documents he possessed, mostly self-written. He kept sending AEC more such documents in face of their entreaties to desist; if he had an atomic idea important to American weaponry, he argued, he should surely not keep it to himself. But his name had recently emerged in the most scandalous of connections. He had been consistently amiable toward a neighbor, Alfred Sarant, who during the war had sublet his New York apartment to an acquaintance of the Rosenbergs named Perl. (In the Hoover version, the spy-ring used the apartment to microfilm documents; in the heretical version, the Rosenbergs spent some evenings there discussing guitar music with interested friends; Perl would soon get a five-year perjury sentence after a trial headlined "NEW ATOM-SPY ANGLE, PERL TIED TO ROSENBERGS.") Unable to purge Morrison's brain of its secret contents, SISS thought it unwise to cite him for contempt although his performance provided ample grounds. The high point of the probe came when atomic defense-drill sirens blew and he hurried into a corner to lie on the floor. From that position he explained that he had some knowledge of these bombs and advised the inquisitors to join him. They thought the urgent matter before them justified overlooking the drill, but he could not agree and remained recumbent until the all clear. In an ensuing year-long inquisition by Cornell authorities he would find, as did other heretical professors, that some former New Dealers were readier to ghettoize their colleagues than some old-fashioned Republicans. By a small majority of stomachs on Cornell's board of trustees, which revolted against tactics used to oust him, he survived at the university without recanting.

Shortly before the Rosenbergs' execution Einstein urged "every intellectual called before a committee to refuse to testify, [to] be prepared for jail or economic ruin, for the sacrifice of his personal welfare in the interest of his country's cultural welfare. The refusal must be based on the assertion that it is shameful for a blameless citizen to submit to such an inquisition . . . if enough people are ready to take this grave step they will be successful. If not, the intellectuals deserve nothing better than the slavery which is intended for them." But the agreeable possibilities of cold-war cooperation had broadened too much to afford Einstein the audience he sought. CIA had an increasing say in university appointments, scholastic grants, the choice of delegations to exotically located conferences, and publishing houses with strangely fat bankrolls; it was also sponsoring journals devoted to culture such as the London monthly *Encounter,* in which reformed heretic Spender was editorially teamed with America's Kristol.* *Encounter's* first issue appeared in time for a demonstration by Leslie Fiedler of the misplaced senti-

---

* Kristol explained later that he thought *Encounter's* bankroll came from a yeast millionaire who "would float over to London every now and then on his yacht," and complained that his $9,500-a-year job was "depressing and unrewarding" while other intellectuals were earning $25,000.

mentality of sympathizers with the Rosenbergs, whose guilt was "clearly established" and whom only Moscow could sincerely defend.

In their separate cells Julius and Ethel sat awaiting the end, writing each other letters as cheerful as the circumstances would permit. There was a clear offer to spare them if they would name some of their spy friends, but they insisted they had none. In Washington, patriots behind impassive police lines yelled "Fry the Jews, Burn the Rats" at the thousands who demonstrated for clemency. In Paris the American embassy was besieged by angry French multitudes to whom, said *Le Monde,* the affair had "restored the only unanimity they had known for a long time." London demonstrators far outnumbering those for Sacco and Vanzetti were told by a third secretary at the embassy; "They can save their skins if they squeal." Urey, the nearest the Rosenbergs had to an inquisitor-proof champion, listened in Kaufman's court to an eleventh-hour retrial plea based on new evidence brought to light by *National Guardian* and other heretics: the "hollowed-out console table" (a cheap item no hollower than when the Rosenbergs bought it at Macy's department store) and some illuminating memoranda about Greenglass's perjuries, filched from Rogge's files. Urey's doubts of the Rosenbergs' guilt changed to belief in their innocence (he told the *Times* court reporter) "after seeing what goes on in Kaufman's court . . . His bias is so obvious. I keep looking over at you newspapermen and there's not a flicker of indignation or concern. When are you going to stop acting like a bunch of scared sheep?" Next day's *Times* reported the denial of the motions without details of the new evidence and added: "Among those present was Harold C. Urey, noted atomic physicist." At the Supreme Court level Douglas (who granted a stay of execution till his colleagues could assemble to overrule him) said he had "perhaps unfortunately" read the trial record; Black said that none of the justices had. Outside the White House a rabbi and two Protestant clergymen stood with the children and Julius's mother praying that Eisenhower might extend executive clemency. On the basis that the case had been fully reviewed, and of the "thought of the millions of dead whose death may be directly attributed to what these spies have done," Eisenhower declined.

Standing beside the pit as Michael's and Robert's parents were lowered into it, DuBois said: "These people were killed because they would not lie." Bloch said: "This was an act of cold, deliberate murder." One of the defense committee leaders from around the country who formed the honor guard was Dave Brown of Los Angeles. "I heard the weeping of the crowd," he would say later, after attempting suicide; "I wept with the others and returned to Los Angeles and reported to my agent Stewart." Unknown even to his wife and children, Brown had for years been a paid FBI informer as well as an increasingly maudlin alcoholic. The New York Bar Association moved to disbar Bloch for his remark, and the following January Gloria Agrin would find him dead of a heart attack in his apartment. The thoughts haunting him in his last weeks are suggested in his words to John Wexley: "How could I dream that Justice Department officials would lend themselves to perpetuation of a complete hoax? I suppose that was my biggest mistake—having those illusions, underestimating the cynicism and power of evil in high places." He had spent the time since the execution trying to arrange a suitable foster home for the boys and raising a $50,000 trust fund to see them through school and college. Agrin's call to the police was answered by FBI men. They had her repeat four times her story of the discovery of Bloch's body, which they photographed and examined before minutely searching the apartment. Agrin asked if this was the normal procedure in a heart-attack case.

"We have to be sure," one of them said, "that someone on your side didn't bump him off because he knew too much."

Fever Chart

1953

Paris: Correspondent Harold Callender writes to New York *Times*.

"It is confusing that men like Maurois and Duhamel [anti-Communist writers] should sign their names along with those of Aragon, a Communist writer, and Picasso, a Communist painter, on a [Rosenberg clemency] cable to Eisenhower. This juxtaposition obscures the issues and colors humanitarianism with politics."

Paris: Sartre, idol of Western liberals until he attended a peace conference in 1952, writes to "Americans sick with rabies."

"The atomic secret is the fruit of your sick imaginations: science develops everywhere at the same rhythm, and the manufacture of bombs is a mere matter of industrial capacities. You have quite simply tried to halt the progress of science by human sacrifice. Magic, witch hunts, auto-da-fés, sacrifices—we are here getting to the point: your country is sick with fear . . . If we can have some hope, it is because your country gave birth to this man and this woman whom you have killed."

Washington: The columnist Alsop brothers consider America's first H-Bomb.

"The explosion at Eniwetok can conceivably presage a nightmare time, when the race of men will become wholly sterile or will breed only monster mutations. Perhaps the era when the praying mantis will rule over the earth may not be very far off."

Las Vegas, Nevada: *Women's Wear Daily* (New York) reports on "discussions of thermal radiation effects here by foremost authorities on atomic weapons."

"Atomic bomb attacks on our cities would place new responsibilities upon the lingerie industry at every level, it was revealed. Strapless and sleeveless designs will have to be eliminated as well as designs with tight-fitting front sections. At least one scientist thinks slips with loose, made-in panties would be needed to afford the fullest protection."

New York: Former Postmaster General Farley speaks at Communion breakfast.

"The atom bomb has more or less brought people back to realize there is a God. Certainly nowhere and at no time has the Catholic Church so prospered."

New York: *Daily News* and *Brooklyn Eagle* editorialize on proposal to ban heretics' peace parade on May Day.

"These rats should be allowed to put themselves on exhibition. If they get pelted with eggs or wetted down and colored up with squirt guns by patriotic young Americans that's their tough luck."

"A reckless horde that makes no bones of its main purpose: vilification of the United States. While we do not advocate throwing ripe tomatoes at anyone it is small wonder that disgusted onlookers give vent to their disgust. The shabby display of traitors and potential traitors is no longer amusing."

Ann Arbor, Michigan: Organ of VFW speaks.

"That the UN should be uncovered as a nest of subversives, commies, pinks, and other subversive factions was as inevitable as government taxes. What better brooding place could the mother hens of Communism find to nurture their young than in an organization which reaks [sic] with international flavor and has as its motivating force peace in the world?"

Inglewood, California: After arrests of Jewish doctors in Moscow, *American Nationalist* (journal devoted to exposing Communism as a Jewish conspiracy) protests against charges that Russia is anti-Semitic.

"These charges are an elaborate propaganda hoax launched by the Jews. The effect has been to condition the public mind for the inevitable conclusion that if Communism is anti-Semitic, then anti-Semitism must, by the same token, be Communistic. In other words, we as Nationalists face the prospect of being branded Communists for our anti-Jewish, anti-Communist activities."

Moscow, Idaho: City Council resolution forwarded to Soviet Embassy, Washington.

"Whereas the citizens of Moscow, Idaho, believe they have a prior and superior right to the name . . . the city officials of Moscow, USSR, be requested to change their name from Moscow to some name that will not by association embarrass the citizens of Moscow, USA."

Madison, Wisconsin: *Capitol Times* man reports street responses to question, "What, in your opinion, is a Communist?"

"I don't know—I'm an American citizen."

"Well, they are always sneaking around . . . I don't know too much about them."

"I'm not exactly sure—the definition seems to be changing."

"A crook, I suppose."

"A person who wants war."

"I've been trying to find out myself but I've never been able to get a definition."

London: British columnist-MP Driberg reports on his visit to Fort Monmouth hearings:

"After 'taking the Fifth' several times to McCarthy's question if he ever 'engaged in espionage,' one Fort Monmouth employee finally said he did not. By saying this he played right into their hands, for when he tried to refuse to answer other questions, involving other people, McCarthy ruled that by answering this one question he had waived his right to claim shelter of the Fifth Amendment. He still refused to answer; a new monotonous ritual developed; McCarthy ordered him to answer, further refusal, finally: 'I assume you refuse to answer?' The witness nodded his head. McCarthy, helpfully eager that I should understand the procedure, turned to me with a wink and said sotto voce, 'We get him right away for contempt, see?' "

New York: Evangelist Billy Graham reports on return from Korea.

"I never saw such suffering or utter misery as there is among the Korean people. Our army there has been called, and rightly so, the most compassionate army in American history."

Illinois and Iowa: Thirty monitors, assigned by Chicago *Daily News* to inspect childrens' TV shows, list findings for four days before Christmas.

"77 murders, 53 shootings, 59 fistfights, 7 kidnapings, 5 robberies, 30 gunfights, 2 knifings, boy beaten by uncle, man thrown over cliff, man blown up in ammunition dump . . . Mass deaths, such as the burning of a native village, are not included [in the listings]."

Hollywood: Report in Washington *Star*.

"Hollywood's Kathleen Hughes, a bathing-suit wearer, offers her company for an evening to the first Chinese traitor who delivers a MIG to General Mark Clark."

XVIII

1953: A Religious Experience

In 20th-century America, the trouble caused by familiars in 16th-century Spain was compounded by the importance of the media image: too many court and tribunal contradictions could damage it, and by 1953 certain observers began to differ with the Justice Department as to what constituted too many. The Alsop brothers picked out Crouch, Budenz and Matusow as excessively imaginative and forgetful familiars who, in the patriotic interest, should be restrained. The three were consoled by a "Dear Friends" letter from Kohlberg, suggesting that they give him a ring if "inclined to do anything about" this calumny. But they were happy as long as the Department was, and its only sign of concern was to withhold Crouch from the appeal trial of "Scientist X" Weinberg: a wise move since both Weinberg and Oppenheimer, whom the Crouches had placed at a Berkeley CP meeting in 1945, could prove they were hundreds of miles away at the time. The judge expressed "amazement" that the Department's Immigration Service could employ Crouch, but it continued keeping him as busy as ever.

At the Smith Act trial of Nelson and his Pittsburgh CP associates, the plump movie-theatre manager Joseph D. Mazzei made his court debut. He jerked jurors and media out of a creeping paralysis of boredom by dashing to McCarthy's tribunal in Washington, between appearances on the witness stand, to expose Nelson's plot to murder the master inquisitor. Mazzei established himself as a witness who rarely erred on the side of probability and was never dull. His sex life was equally unorthodox but would cause problems. While he and his wife worked undercover for Hoover, a Yugoslav waitress had named him as the father of her child, and four months before the Smith Act trial he had pleaded guilty to "adultery and bastardy" and agreed to pay $8 a week. He would twice be arrested for nonpayment, but suffered from failing memory as to just what he did with the waitress. His version when she first brought him into court was that she was a Communist spy, and that his FBI agent had ordered him to woo her in line of duty; no "illicit relations" occurred, but the agent nevertheless told him to plead guilty to "a. and b." A few weeks later he told a deportation tribunal that they did occur: "It was the common practice to have sexual relations with members of the CP." Since his masters could only afford him protection by admitting they were accessories to his sin, thereby tarnishing the Hooverian image, Mazzei's FBI agent denied giving him such orders. Mazzei was stuck with the $8 a week, which he continued not to pay while busily naming heretics for ghettoization or deportation. Defense lawyers naturally cited the "a. and b." affair to show he was a loose fellow and a perjurer, but with the usual lack of effect until his perjuries achieved scandalous proportions. For example, early in 1954 he would ensure deportation for a Greek cook by pointing him out in court as a Communist he had known for eight years; 16 months later, when the cook's name came up in another case, Mazzei said "the name is familiar" but he wouldn't recognize the man if he saw him.

Mazzei illustrated the eternal dilemma with familiars: the more effectively dramatic they are at tribunals, the harder for them to recall what they said before.

The Justice Department also used Cvetic in the Pittsburgh trial which added another five years to Nelson's 20 for sedition. Cvetic told the jury he "always wanted to be a spy ever since I was a boy," and he enjoyed the work despite the stingy emoluments. He said he never topped $85 a week in his undercover days but was now earning $10,000 to $15,000 a year. At the year's end he was called to Texas along with Matusow, Lautner and Malkin to expose a plot to organize department-store employees. Cvetic was in chipper mood as they swapped shop talk over the free drinks and food. Lautner, perhaps believing himself to be professionally in decline, looked so woebegone that Matusow hardly recognized him from the old CP days. Matusow himself, unknown to the other three, had already given his career the coup-de-grâce and was struggling (as he had told McCarthy) "to tone down my temptations which made me dishonest."

Only eight months before, the inquisitorial world had been his oyster: when the Justice Department summoned him, he was too busy to go there and had the Department official "shown into my library" by the butler. With his wife in tow on an assignment to convict Jencks in El Paso ("this was big-league stuff and I was the star"), he occupied a $100-a-day Hilton suite while giving testimony which would get Jencks a five-year sentence ("EX-SPY VOWS RED BOSSES ORDERED COPPER STRIKE"). As a freshman on McCarthy's team he had attended strategy sessions in the Waldorf Towers suite of Schine's parents, which McCarthy used as a New York headquarters. There, what with constantly ringing phones, the bustle of reporting investigators and highball-laden waiters, and Cohn in the role of coordinating sergeant major, Matusow was reminded of a regimental command post at the height of battle. In Washington the team foregathered in the Hawaiian Sun Room of his wife's mansion.

Somehow his invention of heretics on *Time-Life* and the *Times* had started the first stirrings which he would strive to explain in *False Witness*. Feeling "false and shallow," he wrote McCarthy in August that he no longer wanted "to be part of the Communist question," and later to *Time-Life* and the *Times* assuring them that their red employees were fictional. He also informed the Justice Department that he was a liar, which may or may not have been news to it. No sign came that these missives were even received. The simultaneous breakup of his marriage took him to the Reno divorce mill where he thought of killing himself, changed his mind, and took a radio-station job. But invitations to serve as a familiar still pursued him and he "slipped" into accepting several while seeking strength to resist—and money to write a book—from Methodist Bishop G. Bromley Oxnam. He told Oxnam he was having "a 'religious experience,' but I don't think he [Oxnam] fully grasped it"; no money was forthcoming, and "I found myself on the witness stand" again testifying to SACB against VALB and NCASF. Perhaps his choice of a confessor was guided by the fact that Oxnam's own heresies were under multiple scrutiny; but as if the bishop did not have enough on his plate convincing both HUAC and SACB that he disliked Communism (his name was on old VALB, NCASF and other letterheads), he was now propelled into the brewing Matusow scandal.

The idea for the church inquisition in which Velde starred Oxnam in July had originated with Matthews, who announced in a magazine that he knew of 7,000 clergymen "infected by the 'social gospel' . . . supporting the Communist apparatus" and named as "top pro-Soviet propagandists" Harry F. Ward, Willard Uphaus, the Episcopalian Kenneth Ripley Forbes, Christian Ethics professor Joseph F. Fletcher and the Methodist Jack R. McMichael. (The Presbyterians were about to inquisite Claude Williams themselves; the Unitarian Stephen R. Fritchman was already in the courts, contesting an order to swear loyalty or lose his church's tax exemption.) McCarthy, who considered entering this field, retreated before a burst of clerical fury about Matthews's statistics. But HUAC's Jackson denounced Oxnam in Congress as serving "God on Sunday and the Communist front the rest of the week," and Velde walked in where McCarthy feared to tread.

Velde omitted Matthews from his friendly-witness team, but the familiars he hired made an unpromising situation worse by bumbling and imprecise performances. Gitlow named John Holmes (who had turned inquisitor in 1940) and two defunct Russophobe rabbis as having "carried out CP instructions or collaborated." Kornfeder thought 600 clergymen were heretical, corrected it to "three or four thousand" when inquisitor [Rep. Gordon H.] Scherer scouted the figure as too low, and was "fairly certain" that Ward "saw Joe Stalin" on a Moscow trip. (Ward presumably would have liked to but didn't.) Manning Johnson brought photostatic evidence that the CP infiltrated churches "on the basis of conditioning them for overthrow of the government," * but added little verisimilitude by naming theologian Reinhold Niebuhr, a long-standing Russophobe, as leader of a group following this program. Oxnam, while unable to deny studying theology under Ward and contacting McMichael and Struik, pointed to his record of withdrawing from heretical circles and wound up ten hours on the stand shaking Velde's hand for photographers. Manning Johnson named McMichael, a California parish pastor, as an ex-comrade, but McMichael denied ever setting eyes on him, and Johnson's deteriorating status as a familiar made further steps inadvisable. None of the other "Communist-controlled churchmen," as Ward and his acolytes were labeled in HUAC's latest brochure, were even subpenaed.

The probe was so unpopular nationally that Hoover himself announced he knew of no Communist clergymen, and HUAC's report on its findings was a mere whimper: the number of churchly reds, it said, was "minute." In Massachusetts, however, tremors continued for a while from the testimony of Philbrick, who had committed the uncharacteristic error of naming to Velde an apparently total stranger. Philbrick's "best guess" regarding Party clergymen was that "in the Boston area there were perhaps between 6 and 12 people in that particular cell";

---

* Noting the "sinister" implications of the word "infiltration," as used by inquisitors in the church probe, the Baptist *Watchman-Examiner* commented: "One side of the problem never seems to have been touched. It is that our Christian duty and practice is to infiltrate society and its organizations with the Gospel of Christ . . . to minister the mercies and providences of God in aid to the poor and underprivileged in their struggle to rise out of poverty and misery. Any man who undertakes it needs people who will work with him, whether Christian or not. We shall not be carried away by the nonsense about 'infiltration.' " This was always the line of the *Catholic Worker*.

and while he had "no legal evidence," he was "sure in my own mind" that the Community Church's Reverend Donald Lothrop "is operating under Party discipline." Lothrop read this in the *Globe* and wrote to inform the paper that he had Never Been and that Philbrick was a "coward" performing a "weasel trick." Yet in the prevailing climate he might have expected it: not only had he provided a platform for DuBois, but (as he said in the letter) his church's program included "Marriage Problem Consultation, Group Psychotherapy [and] a Sunday School rooted in nonsectarian religion."

Challenged by an ex-president of the Bar Association to "ask the Committee for the opportunity to appear and rebut" Philbrick's statement, Lothrop replied that he would do no such thing but if they subpenaed him he would answer all questions. He would not betray the principles of the pioneer Lothrop who reached Massachusetts in 1634 after two years in an English jail "for the freedom of conscience and assembly." Philbrick accepted a $300 invitation to address a Boston group on the menace, and told his audience: "I spoke from the platform of Dr Lothrop's church several times as a Communist." Since Lothrop insisted he never heard of Philbrick till the Communist trial headlines, and there was no record of such an event at the church, the church board wrote to ask Philbrick if he would kindly supply the dates. Philbrick replied on *Herald Tribune* stationery: "I have already started to drop a reply to you. In the meantime I would appreciate it very much if you would let me know the names of those who are on the board." The board twice repeated its request but the reply, if dropped, was never received.*

Autumn developments in Plymouth Meeting, near Philadelphia, drew attention to Quaker heresies which—especially in view of Pickett's peace film and activity in ECLC—had been oddly bypassed by probers. The 300-year-old community needed a librarian and reached out to Boston to hire Mary Knowles, who in accordance with "the moral and ethical principles by which I try to live" had invoked the Fifth to SISS in 1952. The "quiet dignity" with which she had suffered ghettoization impressed the Quakers, and she assured them she now belonged to no "so-called 'subversive' organization." Protests came fast from the Legion and DAR; a "Citizens for Philbrick" movement pointed out that in hiring her, the Quakers had "repudiated the long, agonizing ordeal [of] the dedicated patriot" Philbrick who named her to SISS. Soon an Alerted Americans Group had 561 anti-Knowles signatures from "long-time friends and neighbors [who] surely deserve more Christian love than one lone Fifth Amendment User who has deliberately gone out of her way to create and foster this bitter strife."

William Penn's City of Brotherly Love, where the Founding Fathers signed their subversive Declaration, only lacked a Musmanno to equal Pittsburgh as an

---

* In a pamphlet about his "case" Lothrop reported an incident at the height of the activities of Massachusetts's Special Commission to Study Communism, etc., indicating the longevity in his state of the spirit of 17th-century Salem. The commission persuaded an expired heretic's parish clergyman to deny burial rites, whereupon Lothrop accepted the family's invitation to perform them. Efforts had previously been made to persuade the undertaker that he should evict the heretical corpse and refuse the use of his premises for the funeral. Lothrop recalled the denial of normal burial to Massachusetts witches. In the 1690s, according to a contemporary chronicler, a certain Burroughs was thrown into a shallow grave with two others, "one of his hands and his chin, and a foot of one [of them], being left uncovered."

inquisitorial center. Its Smith Act trial was delayed pending the discovery of lawyers who would defend Communists, but meanwhile TU activists were obstructing the state's efforts to cut the school budget and a teacher probe was overdue. As one teacher, Mrs. Goldie Watson, would later report, HUAC emissaries appeared in advance to assure suspects that "everything will be all right" if they would inform on their colleagues; follow-up phone calls promised promotion in return for "cooperation." Against a background of anti-Semitic street demonstrations, Velde's hearings got under way in a glare of kleig lights and banner headlines about the disloyalty of 26 non-cooperating teachers. When the time came to fire the teachers the Education Board assured them that there was "no charge of disloyalty," although Mrs. Watson, who invoked the First Amendment and was indicted for contempt, was told she had "extremely unsatisfactory ideals." Six more teachers resigned or retired. Their arrival in the ghetto was brightened by recently fired philosophy professor Barrows Dunham, who played Santa Claus to their children, and by Quakers who invited the children as summer-camp guests for the vacations.

The global preoccupations of America's exemplary churchgoer, Foster Dulles, did not keep him from again adverting at home to Christian principles. He reminded National War College graduates that, while the military establishment was "splendid," the "role of power is to give moral ideas the time to take root . . . Where there are many who do not accept moral principles, then that creates the need for force to protect those who do." He recommended a return to the spirit of "our forebears [who] had a decent respect for the opinion of mankind . . . sought to practice the golden rule by doing to others as they would have others do to them." In August CIA overthrew the popular Mossadegh government in Iran, which had nationalized that country's oil, and installed a free-world dictatorship.

This was so neatly done that a year later—after the process had been repeated in Guatemala, whose President was giving land to starving peasants— *Saturday Evening Post* would run an admiring series on the techniques used. Taxpayers learned that Allen Dulles's unvouchered expenditure on bribery, assassination and other black activities was "several" times greater than all of Washington's grants and loans to Latin America. Among other projects, CIA was said to have subsidized "a Nazi-type organization in West Germany which had marked leaders of the Social Democratic party for liquidation" and a Chiang army in Burma (about which Burma was vainly protesting to UN) "to make forays into Red China." The articles included Allen Dulles's home address, photographs of the identifying sign outside his headquarters and of the "master spy . . . puffing a final pipeful of tobacco before bed after he has read the voluminous reports," and anecdotes illustrating his professional acumen. "Sitting preoccupied in an Army General's garden one night," he had "suddenly blurted: 'Look at that. There it goes again!' In a window across the way a bright light shone briefly, went out, came on again. 'Signaling!' Dulles exclaimed. Investigation showed that the light was coming from an unshaded bulb hanging from a bathroom ceiling of a house where a noisy Saturday night party was going full tilt." The *Post* said Dulles was drawing recruits "from people in the field of letters, science, business, labor, agriculture or the professions," and stressed the careful security training they received—for "it might be signing one's execution order to pose as a European while wearing a pair of American red galluses." The implication was, however, that even if some red-gallus amateurishness still lingered in CIA, the bottomless well of dollars made success for its enterprises fairly certain. By October all important pro-Mossadegh Iranians, running into indeterminate thousands, were in jails, torture chambers or cemeteries.

While Eisenhower in his baroque press conferences explained America's far-flung problems and duties, the number of Russian megadeaths achievable by the Pentagon's improving Bombs was regularly re-computerized. The Russians' own H-Bomb explosion in the fall left the uneasy feeling that they could kill just as many Americans; but the goal from this point on was capacity to liquidate Russia's entire population more times over than Russia could liquidate America's. To the welter of pronunciamentos in the media as to when this ideal situation could be expected, confusion was added by McCarthy's discovery of treason within the armed forces themselves. Thoughtful generals fumed but were aware that McCarthy still enjoyed Dulles's and Eisenhower's support. The fact that the late Julius Rosenberg had once worked in the Army Signal Corps's radar center at Fort Monmouth made such headlines as the Los Angeles *Times's* "ROSENBERG CALLED RADAR SPY MASTER—RING MAY STILL BE WORKING FOR RUSSIA, SEN. MCCARTHY SAYS." Army Secretary Robert T. Stevens denied the ring's existence but, after a lunch with McCarthy, announced that he only meant the Army had not found it and perhaps McCarthy could. Fort Monmouth scientists' morale sank below zero as McCarthy revealed that Sarant, who had rented the apartment to Perl who had entertained the Rosenbergs there, had also worked at the center during the war together with his now divorced wife. The ex-Mrs. Sarant, remarried to a naturalized alien and in her seventh month of pregnancy, was among the scores of past and present employees questioned through October and most of November. She promptly had a miscarriage, and her new husband lost his job and was threatened with deportation.

Practically all America was now poised over TV wondering how far the master intended to go. McCarthy teased the media by barring them from less fruitful sessions on "security grounds," then giving his version of what occurred. Thus a witness who invoked the Fifth turned up in afternoon papers as "a leading espionage agent." From a technical standpoint McCarthy was at his best. "At the time you married your wife," he asked one witness, "did you have any reason to suspect she might be a Communist sympathizer?" (Answer, No; threat of perjury prosecution.) Another, who denied stealing secrets, was asked: "If you wished to steal such material could you have done so?" McCarthy put it to another: "What would you answer if one of your students were to ask whether murder was justified?" For Madison's *Capital Times* McCarthy had "begun his march to the Presidency"; but the Establishment was considering how best to curb its runaway Torquemada.

Long cold in his grave, Dexter White became the center of a contest between HUAC and SISS to match McCarthy's monumental publicity. The media scare-headlined charges by Hoover via Herbert Brownell that Truman had appointed White to the International Monetary Fund while knowing him to be a Russian spy. Truman's explanation was that he had known about Hoover's dossier on White in 1945 and had retained and promoted White as a decoy to aid Hoover. Since Eisenhower approved of the Hoover-Brownell bombshell, Velde miscalculated the possibility of successfully subpenaing Truman and his 1945 Secretary of State James Byrnes and Attorney General (now Supreme Court Justice) Tom C. Clark. Velde lacked power to make any of the three accept his invitation. SISS took an early lead by issuing an "Interlocking Subversion in Government Departments" report on the New and Fair Deal years; but laurels would clearly go to the committee which could stage a personal appearance of Hoover, and it was on SISS that Hoover smiled. Jenner, McCarran, Eastland and the media treated him with the honors due to a tribal totem. He recalled how, in the course of "his efforts to block the Communist conspiracy of the Roosevelt-Truman era to overthrow the government," * he had told Truman that White was a spy and Truman had refused to act. Not even the ex-President could impugn Hoover's loyalty and veracity, but Hoover could and did impugn those of the ex-President who (as D. F. Fleming notes) had "spent more than $100 billion trying to enforce his global anti-Communist containment doctrine." Hoover hardly needed to point out that all of his "thirty sources" establishing White's perfidy were "reliable," including Bentley whose testimony had been "subjected to the most searching of cross-examinations and found to be accurate." Indeed, Eastland interpolated, Bentley had been "flawlessly truthful." (Only ghetto journals raised the question of why Bentley, now teaching in Coteau, Louisiana, was consistently unavailable for hostile cross-examination of her charges, none of which had been or would be substantiated by a conviction for spying.)

HUAC's moment of glory in the contest was its production of copies of notes allegedly in White's handwriting, allegedly found in Chambers's pumpkin in 1948. The inquisitors again introduced Canada's foreign minister Pearson and UN delegate Norman into the melodrama as White's contacts, rousing angry Canadian editors to suggest that the whole uproar was bogus and so was Hoover. Canadian treasury officials who had known White well snorted at the notion that he was a Communist. Asked as he left for golf in Georgia whether he thought this inquisition was reprehensible "McCarthyism," Eisenhower did not "particularly understand the term" and "hadn't another word to say about the matter." The affair left HUAC in a mess of internal disagreements (Francis E. Walter saw the foolishness of subpenaing Truman) and put Velde on the road to oblivion, but further solidified Hoover's prestige. At budget-request time Hoover would list the red conspiracy's "principal activities during the past year" which kept escalating the cost of exposing it: "Its peace objective, geared primarily to raising a nation-wide appeal for settlement of the Korean war; recall of American troops from abroad; a five-power pact including China; resumption of trade with Iron Curtain countries."

Although McCarthy had nothing to do with the White affair, which particularly distressed free-world allies, "McCarthyism" was now the word for what caused the distress. McCarthy was pursuing his exposure of the Pentagon in a probe of an Army intelligence report on *Psychological and Cultural Traits of Soviet Siberia,* which had cited a book by Lamont and concluded that Siberians

* From the report of the occasion by New York *Daily News* columnist O'Donnell.

were unlikely to rise against Communism in the near future. Within three weeks the major general commanding Intelligence was fired. At this point Princeton professor H. H. Wilson posed the question of whether democracy could "survive rule by informers, political police and delinquents in government," * and Establishment fears of an out-of-control inquisition were indicated by a $15,000,000 Ford Foundation grant for a Fund for the Republic—a "wholly disavowed subsidiary" of the Foundation according to its director Robert Hutchins. The Fund proposed to study aspects of the inquisition and gave $15,000 to Quakers for use in "freedom of conscience" cases, $24,000 for counter-racist education in Dixie.** The Legion denounced the Fund for "discrediting our security programs."

If Eisenhower was distressed, he did not show it. In December he invited McCarthy and Velde to join him in discussing the shape of inquisitions to come. Among problems reportedly up for review was how to block "certain loopholes" through which heretics were escaping, such as the Fifth Amendment and the law against wire tapping which had aborted the Coplon trial. Velde found the conversation "very congenial"; McCarthy was "not displeased." Eisenhower then summed up the civil liberties situation as he saw it:

"In this country, if someone dislikes you or accuses you, he cannot hide
behind the shadows, he cannot assassinate you or your character from
behind without suffering the penalties an outraged citizenry will inflict."

* A late-comer to heresy, Wilson had been isolated at Princeton since he protested the jailing of Hiss. To his colleagues' indignant "Don't you know you never defend Communists any more?" he had replied: "I never defended a Communist in my life, but I was brought up on the Bill of Rights. If a man is accused of something, he should be tried for it and convicted or absolved on the evidence. I wouldn't convict a dog on the word of Chambers."
** On the race front, a milestone was passed in May 1953: for the first time in the city's history a New York policeman was indicted for beating a Negro (the Negro had to be operated on for bloodclots). In Florida, dynamitings and assorted violence against blacks continued more or less normally. After the usual Supreme Court refusal to intervene, North Carolina executed two youths, Bennie and Lloyd Ray Daniels, in connection with the murder of a taxi driver about which they claimed to know nothing. They said that police gave them a choice of confessing the deed or "we'll blow your brains out."

XIX

1954: The Brinkmen

If "brinkmanship" was an apt term for Foster Dulles's global cold-war methods, it was equally so for the domestic methods of McCarthy who shared front pages with Dulles in 1954. But while the inquisitorial brinkman took greater personal risks, the human race was suspended by a hair over Dulles's brinks. In January, as *Time* crowned Chancellor Konrad Adenauer its first German "Man of the Year" since Hitler in 1938, Dulles listened for the nth time in Berlin to the Russians' pleas for disarmament and a demilitarized, neutralized Germany. In October Eisenhower gave a hero's welcome to the "diplomatic magician" who had completed Germany's rearming into a NATO ally. (The *Christian Science Monitor* reported "dancing in the State Department.") Dulles was taking the well calculated risk that the Russians, who he said broke all their agreements, would keep their pledge not to throw the first Bomb. His theme was "massive retaliation" if their armies moved to enforce allied agreements of 1944–45.

When the catastrophe at Dienbienphu cured France of trying to convert the Vietnamese, Dulles had to sit down in Geneva with all interested parties, including some men from Peking who claimed to represent Vietnam's Chinese neighbors. Outside the conference room where he must hear their protestations that "the way to ensure peace in Asia is to end colonialism," Dulles absolutely denied the existence of Chou En-lai and his colleagues. They seemed, in any case, to prefer the company of Chaplin, who received them cordially at his chateau.* The British and French had been as queasy about Dulles's proposal to introduce America's Bomb into the Vietnam scene (perhaps he really meant it—and what then?) as the Vietnamese and Chinese were unperturbed; and it was agreed that pending election of a national government in 1956 Vietnam be divided into a socialist and a capitalist half. Since "Indochina war fears" had been "heartening factors" for American business (*Journal of Commerce*), the stock market sagged until Washington made its intentions clear.

While the North "concentrated on its internal development" and ordered sympathizers in the South to "engage only in political struggle," America picked South Vietnam's ruler as it had picked South Korea's—with Washington experts to guide his steps, including refusal to allow the elections—and sent in CIA men to organize sabotage in the North and form the nucleus of American military intervention.** The Geneva encounter had no effect on America's refusal to admit

* Chaplin accepted the 1954 World Peace Council award, moving the *Times* to comment: "He has allowed himself to be used by a sinister conspiracy . . . He shuffled off leftward to Moscow [which] moves us to tears."
** See *Pentagon Papers*, Bantam, New York, 1971. The South Vietnam President who was "the anchor of American policy for nine years" established so embarrassing a dictatorship that America became an "accomplice" in overthrowing and murdering him in 1963. South Vietnam now celebrates his assassination as an annual National Day.

the men of Peking into the UN. Senate majority and minority leaders William F. Knowland and Lyndon Johnson said they would demand America's abandonment of the UN if Chiang did not continue to speak for China. Nixon, who before the Geneva conference had proposed "putting American boys" into Indochina to continue France's crusade, added Korea and Vietnam to the bill of indictment against the Fair Deal; he reprised the "Acheson lost us China" motif with paeans for massive retaliation and scorn for negotiations as appeasement. But the formula of Korean crusader General Mark Clark for future Asian wars was more popular: "The ROK [South Korean] troops should have been built up. They died readily. They hated Communism and the more we can build them up the cheaper it is, in my opinion." As the future President and the general spoke, UN analysts suggested some connection between the general unrest and the fact that two-thirds of humanity suffered "endemic daily hunger": in some areas "approximately five children in ten die before reaching adolescence."

Dulles's domestic contribution was to instruct all members of his State Department to cooperate as informers with Scott McLeod, a friend of McCarthy's who had been entrusted with its security. (In November, after nine loyalty hearings, veteran China hand Paton Davies joined the unemployed for "lack of judgment, discretion and reliability" in having anticipated Mao's victory over Chiang. The case brought many diplomats to "despair," said the *Times,* citing one ambassador who "admits he no longer dares to report the brazen truth because of present hysteria.") * In the task of ensuring that—except for residents who were deported—only persons meeting free-world standards crossed American frontiers in either direction, Arthur Miller was forbidden to attend the opening of his own play in Brussels. Entertainer Maurice Chevalier was grounded visaless in Paris when his name turned up on the Stockholm peace petition. "I have never been in any politics," he lamely explained, "I was just not for anything atomic falling on the world." A British feminist and educator, Bertrand Russell's ex-wife Dora, was among several observer delegates for UN-affiliated organizations who, while they could not be excluded, were handed a map limiting their movements to a section of Manhattan putting out of bounds the west side of Central Park West. The Psychologists Congress was shifted from New York to Montreal after heretical delegates were refused visas. Two contestants for the "Miss Universe" crown were barred as security risks from coming to compete: Miss Greece, who had "once designed a cover for a Communist author's book," and Miss South Korea who, not having left North Korea till she was 18, was suspected of having interests other than her bust development. Dulles, however, chivalrously overrode the bar on Miss Greece at the eleventh hour. Pauling found a rare key to the door by winning a Nobel Prize with the usual invitation to Oslo to receive it from the King of Sweden. This drew uneasy attention to America's possession of a heretic who was also a great chemist, and his passport was restored for the trip.

In another phase of the heretic-movement-control program, an American journalist was taken from her home in Kandy, where she lived with her Ceylonese husband, and propelled up the ramp of an intercontinental American airliner. Rhoda deSilva, author of a friendly book on Poland and of a Rosenberg pamphlet,

---

* Davies's dislike of Communism was finally accepted upon his rehabilitation in 1969.

had been confronted with a presumably FBI dossier which said she once worked for the red publication "New York Guila." (A New York Newspaper Guild member in its heretical days, in 1943 she had been elected chairman of its annual ball while working for *Time*.) "Where are you going?" asked an American at the head of the ramp in Colombo. "I have no idea." "You're going to New York." "On whose order?" "The American embassy and the government of Ceylon." "In that sequence?" He laughed. Prevented from leaving the plane at stopping points, she reached New York on a bitter March day in gauzy attire without the money for a ride into town. Her letter of protest at being kidnapped—sent without result to Eisenhower and several dozen Congressmen—was published around the world and buried by American media. After 19 months of pleading for permission to live with her husband, who was barred from America, she would be allowed to depart while her lawsuit against the airline trailed on. The airline cited her invocation of the Fifth on her politics as ground for dismissing the suit, but would settle out of court in 1958.

The cuckoo in the intellectual nest, Einstein, showed rising impatience in a message to an ECLC affair honoring his 75th birthday. "The strength of the Constitution," he said, "lies entirely in the determination of each citizen to defend it. A duty is imposed on everyone which no one must evade, notwithstanding risks and danger to him and his family." This applied especially to intellectuals because "they have, thanks to their special training, a particularly strong influence on the formation of public opinion. This is the reason why those who are about to lead us back toward an authoritarian government are particularly concerned with intimidating and muzzling that group." No rise was observable in recruitment of intellectuals for the voluntary ghetto. Everyone was staring at McCarthy's super-inquisition on TV, the intelligentsia with a blend of disdain and determination to avoid "controversy."

McCarthy achieved an audience rising well into the millions but landed himself on a toboggan which he could not stop. Yet in January he rode high on a speaking tour denouncing the Democrats' "20 years of treason," pausing in Boston to expose the "privileged sanctuary" for heretics at Harvard and, on the eve of union elections, the subversive aims of the United Electrical, Radio & Machine Workers. *UP* reported that a UE man who rose in the hearing room to shout, "McCarthy, you're a menace!" was "mobbed" and rushed into the street by seven US marshals. When a "Trade Union Veterans Committee" found an obscure New York hall in which to "try" the master, Philbrick revealed how the CP planned it at "secret meetings." The "verdict" condemned McCarthy, who was about to achieve immortality in standard dictionaries,* to "historic and political oblivion." With its last breath ASP held a conference on "The Artist and Professional in the Age of McCarthy" and sank out of sight.

While Cardinal Spellman joined in an ovation for McCarthy at a Communion breakfast for 6,000 New York policemen, Sauk City editor Leroy Gore began collecting signatures to recall the senator under Wisconsin law. Gore described himself as "a thoroughly respectable, smug Republican." Neither Wis-

---

* "McCarthyism" first appeared in the American College Dictionary in August 1954. It was defined as "(1) Public accusation of disloyalty . . . unsupported by truth, (2) unfairness in investigative technique."

consin Democrats nor unions would touch his "Joe Must Go" movement; loyal
neighbors threatened (as he would write) to murder him, kidnap his children,
blow up his newspaper and "ship us to the Russian salt mines"; but in the 60 days
prescribed by the recall statute 335,000 Wisconsinites—65,000 short of what was
necessary—mastered fear sufficiently to sign his petition. The response was surprising considering how far Gore had strayed off the reservation. He had rejected
the idea that inquisitions were acceptable "so long as you don't do it like Joe":
it had corrupted the whole government, he thought, and Velde and Jenner were
"more dangerous and worse than McCarthy himself." A local restaurateur, craving eminence in the Legion, launched a "Door for Gore" movement advising readers of Gore's paper to "keep their noses clean and they'll be all right. Expressing
political opinions in small communities isn't the thing to do." Indicted under the
Corrupt Practices Act, Gore was found guilty, sold his paper and eventually started
afresh as a public-relations man.

McCarthy's discovery that the heretical dentist Irving Peress had been promoted from captain to major gave him "the key to Communist infiltration of our
armed forces," and he used Peress to humiliate publicly a general and the Army
Secretary. The immediate impulse for his fatal army probe came, according to the
record, from familiar Crouch, who could vouch for the presence of "over 1,000"
Communists waiting in the armed forces to disrupt any war against Russia. The
first Pentagon response was appeasement; Eisenhower, on the golf course, said he
favored "fair play"; but spring developments showed that the wind was changing.
The army spurned McCarthy's threatening demands that Schine be spared from
the draft; Peress got honorable discharge; Nixon turned openly surly; and the
master's own colleagues Symington, McClellan and Jackson went on strike against
his hogging the spotlight. CBS allowed Edward R. Murrow, a cautious survivor
of the great radio-TV purge, to attack McCarthy head-on. But the undying faith
of a large public, even as the Establishment put out the plank for McCarthy to
walk, was reflected in the experience of the bit-player in the show, dentist Peress.
Obscenities cascaded into the mailbox of his suburban home and into the ear of
anyone answering the day-and-night-long phone calls. Rocks hurtled into his
children's bedroom as they slept. School parents and assorted strangers jammed a
Parent-Teacher Association meeting to challenge Mrs. Peress's right to corrupt
their minds as editor of the PTA paper. Her attempt to reply, "I think a terribly
frightening thing is happening—McCarthyism is . . . ," was drowned by yells of
"Don't you say anything about McCarthy!" "Throw her out!" "Take the loyalty
oath!" "The oath, the oath, the oath!" Vowing she had written no "un-American
word" in her three editorial years, Mrs. Peress resigned from the paper. A few
neighbors remained friendly but the mail obscenities became an avalanche, many
of them citing the Rosenberg case as a model of justice for Jews. "It would be a
pleasure," wrote one correspondent, "to help string you and your little rats up
to the nearest pole."

The grandiose staging of the probe of McCarthy's army probe—2,000,000
words were spoken or shouted during the 36-day proceedings—confirmed the
Establishment's decision that it needed someone like him but not him, and that
"anti-McCarthyism" was to be certificated as loyal in the proper context. How far
it was from being a probe of the inquisition as such, *Newsweek* would indicate in

a retrospective piece 15 years later. The journal quoted lawyer Roy Jenkins, who was employed to question the inquisitor, as still thinking "both sides were guilty of the charges preferred against them." McCarthy had been "reckless" but "did serve his country" since "Communism did at that time pose a threat to US security as it does now. Senator McCarthy exposed it [and] I feel the country owes him a debt for so doing." The new "anti-McCarthyism" hemline in public relations was but slowly grasped by the media. No American network would take Reuben Ship's *Investigator* when the Canadian Broadcasting Corporation broadcast it in May, although two entrepreneurs reaped a bonanza with bootlegged, tape-recorded discs of it which sold out as fast as they could be produced. For his inquisitorial dialogue Ship borrowed from his own HUAC appearance in 1951, adding typical McCarthy touches. He had McCarthy dying in a plane crash and joining Judge Jeffreys, Torquemada and Cotton Mather in a heavenly committee probing "1,000 years of treason" by Socrates, Milton, Luther, Jefferson, Voltaire and various Karl Marxes all of whom were sentenced to go "from Up Here to Down There." A symbolic nonentity named Schmink replaces Galileo, Chopin, Schiller, Shelley, etc., after they are deported, but finally Schmink himself walks the plank and then the Investigator insists on probing God.

The shadow over the "McCarthy Era" inspired an attempt in August to get a "Roy Cohn Era" off the ground. A Joint Committee Against Communism dinner drew 2,000 to the Astor Ballroom to see veterans' groups shower Cohn with plaques and awards and hear him lauded in turn by the leading inquisitorial rabbi Schultz, Sokolsky, Fulton Lewis and Fordham and Notre Dame professors.* Senators were then debating a resolution to "censure" McCarthy, with Republican leaders openly disapproving and Democratic leaders "completely inert" (*Times*): they reached a compromise to refer the matter to another committee. In the same week a confetti-showered Syngman Rhee received, on New York's City Hall steps, a Medal of Honor and a scroll describing him as "the world's symbol of resistance to savage aggression." Mayor Robert Wagner asked Waldorf-Astoria lunch invitees to "look upon [the] dedication, devotion and love for freedom which are the fiber and soul of our guest"; and in the afternoon Columbia University bestowed a doctorate on the Korean symbol. In reply to all toasts Rhee urged America to go to war again "soon" on the most colossal scale possible.

Madison Square Garden was only half filled for a November "God Bless McCarthy" rally where generals, admirals, state governors, Legionnaires and Daughters of the Revolution joined in exhortations about America's "long and perhaps bloody fight" against a "hidden force." The force was variously identified with Roosevelt, Truman, Eisenhower, Acheson, etc. A *Life* photographer snapping the audience from the aisles roused cries of "She's a Communist!" "Hang her!" The evening's heroes included Dies, MacArthur, Sokolsky, the newly deceased McCarran, Pegler, and Cohn, a guest in Pegler's box; Woltman was off the list with other fair-weather friends who had decided that McCarthy did anti-Communism more harm than good. A month later the Senate, as a shy alternative to general "censure," picked out two occasions on which McCarthy's "conduct" toward fellow senators deserved "condemnation." Eisenhower struck McCarthy from the

* In 1969 Cohn would be indicted and tried for bribery, conspiracy, extortion and blackmail; he was acquitted.

White House guest list, and McCarthy publicly apologized to the public for having backed him in 1952. Inquisitorial traditions were reinforced when the Dixie small-town lawyer McClellan—a Bible-quoting Hoover aficionado sternly for law-and-order except in the matter of lynching—succeeded to McCarthy's chair.

McCarthy never recovered from what he felt to be the nation's ingratitude: if the job needed doing, assigning it to anyone less expert would be like putting a nun in charge of Treblinka. Yet his inquisitorial expertise had not been officially disparaged, and retribution upon his victims continued as sternly as if any other inquisitor had initiated it. In the month of McCarthy's condemnation indictments came for two Harvard professors whom he had cited for contempt in invoking the First Amendment and whom Harvard had refused to fire. McCarthy's favorite spy, Lattimore, had been re-indicted for perjury and Lamont indicted for contempt in October. The long, solemn Senate debate on the Lamont citation had yielded only three votes against citing "this man of fine family with a silver sickle in his hand," as a government lawyer dubbed Lamont. Heretics were grateful that guns had been turned on men like him and Edward Lamb of Ohio, who had both the determination and money for the long struggle.

A founder of NLG whose disbarment for defending strikers had been attempted in the 30s, Lamb had garnered several millions in newspaper publishing, manufacturing and radio-TV enterprises and could hardly now be classified as dangerous. Yet his prewar dossier was imposing—he had even met Stalin in Moscow—and, when his radio-TV license needed renewal, the urge to expose him was irresistible to an FCC which included a McCarthy appointee. It was indicated that his license could be renewed without fuss for a $60,000 payoff, but he preferred to spend eight months and some $900,000 exposing the exposers, hiring an ex-Attorney General to head his defense team. At an FCC hearing more bizarre than any of McCarthy's, he swore he had Never Been against a chorus of familiars swearing that he had. These ranged from Lautner and Budenz, who had Lamb on his list of "secret Communists permanently etched on my mind," to "51-year-old Miami Beach grandmother" Marie Natvig and William Cummings, who emerged as a proven bigamist and was actually arrested for perjury (in denying on his second marriage license that he already had a wife) during the trial. One familiar was a convicted murderer.

Lamb would express pride that his hearing "probably ended Budenz's profitable career as a government-sponsored character assassin." It did not end Budenz's—nor even Cummings's—but it dashed any hopes Natvig may have had in the profession. She not only recalled Lamb proposing armed revolution in CP huddles where they "ate caviar and drank gin," but as having had a "liaison" with her at a hotel—"my first infidelity" which led to the loss of Mr. Natvig. She added that in a Washington bistro the night before, a man had offered her $50,000 to withhold these memories from the court. A vigorous little lady who at one point attacked a lawyer with a water pitcher, she got excellent headlines. "Let Comrade Lamb start paying for his sins!" she told reporters. While she was filling 800 printed pages with her testimony, Lamb's lawyers learned that she had been arrested for soliciting and charged with embezzlement and "probably" never was in the CP. When one familiar began testifying, members of the audience chanted his lines before he could get them out: the defense had supplied them with a script from a tape recording of government lawyers coaching the witness. The hearing ran far into 1955 when Natvig would admit that her entire testimony was fictional, but Lamb's license would not be renewed until mid-1957 despite the exceptionally rank odor of the case which won him respectable support. In his *Trial by Battle* (Center for Study of Democratic Institutions, 1964) he wondered how "such a thing could happen in these United States." One thing he had learned was that "to blame it all on McCarthy is like blaming the temperature on the thermometer"; another, that defense costs were "far beyond the reach of the hundreds of minor officials, hapless intellectuals, college professors and innocent bystanders" caught by the inquisition.

The Lamb case spurred important clergymen and rabbis into petitioning Washington about the deadly imaginations of Attorney General Brownell's familiars, the record of which had been painstakingly assembled by Donner in the *Nation*. Nothing resulted.

The legislative year was as active as it was confused. The Chief Justice appointed by Eisenhower in 1953, ex-governor Earl Warren of California, had a sound pro-Establishment record but showed signs of less conservatism than inquisitors had anticipated. Dixie delegations in Congress were aghast when the Supreme Court outlawed separate white and black schools, although this decision could not prudently have been postponed much longer and it was accompanied by an assurance that there was no hurry about implementing it. (The embattled professor Lee Lorch, now at Fisk and noting that local schools continued as before, sought to start the ball rolling by placing his daughter in an all-black school. He was soon summoned by HUAC, indicted for contempt, and back on the unemployed list.) The high court had already upheld loyalty tests for tenants of federally aided housing; now it ruled that unproven allegations of heresy at any past time were grounds for deporting resident aliens, and that the McCarran Act was Constitutional. It reversed the disbarment of lawyer Sacher arising from the first Smith Act trial (and, six months later, of Isserman), but in the same month a Miami judge disbarred Paul Newman for invoking the Fifth starting him on the same weary road to high-court rehabilitation. Among the proofs against Newman was his membership in NLG, which at its November convention raised $17,000 to fight in the courts Brownell's threat to list it as subversive.

A stiffening of old-family Pennsylvania spines was noted when nine Bar Association Republicans agreed to defend the Philadelphia Smith Act defendants, and to back any lawyer who was attacked for taking such briefs. Their intrepidity was in vain, for there as in Pittsburgh all defendants received jail sentences, the appeals court confirmed them, and the journey to the summit had to be completed for a reversal. But in January New York lawyer Victor M. Rabinowitz had argued successfully with Pennsylvania's Supreme Court that, since state subversive laws were superseded by the federal Smith Act, Nelson's 20-year sentence for sedition must be reversed.* This decision, reached without regard to the eccentrici-

---

* With his five-year Smith Act sentence still standing, Nelson was far from out of the woods. Three months later his name returned to the headlines in the Oppenheimer probe, and in October SISS called on Lautner and Cvetic to repeat their reminiscences about him. Lautner gave an unusually mechanical performance and, when he forgot some of his lines, was grateful for the help of SISS counsel Richard Arens and of Idahoan in-

ties of Nelson's trial, set the precedent of Washington's exclusive right to jail Americans for heresy. Jealous of their prerogatives, 27 state Attorneys General asked the US Supreme Court to reverse the ruling. There was no reversal, but, as the Braden trial would show within a few months (see Chapter XX), state inquisitors proceeded as if the ruling had not been made.

Prospects for heretics' defense looked brighter with this reduction of the fronts on which they must fight, but the ghetto suffered the loss of one of its most stubborn and effective lawyers, Vito Marcantonio;* and as the year progressed, a goulash of new, even less Constitutional thought-control bills engaged Congress's attention. They were topped in July by a Virginia solon's proposal of the death penalty for "lurking with intent to spy." Eisenhower offered through Brownell a comprehensive package including elimination of the Fifth Amendment by compelling testimony under "immunity," power to liquidate trade unions, legalized wire tapping, widening of the definition of perjury, and death for peacetime spying. AFL and the *Wall Street Journal* both suggested that some of the proposals went too far, but Brownell assured the nation on TV that there would be no "McCarthyist taint." He introduced the package by announcing the discovery in "nooks and crannies" of 20,000 documents on spies-in-government "lost" by the Democrats.

Humphrey led a Fair Dealers' stampede to make CP membership per se a crime—a provision already existing in the Smith Act; it had not been used (presumably in recognition of the CP's indispensability) but, before the new legislation was passed, the Justice Department began selective prosecutions under the Smith Act "membership" clause. The Communist Control Act package went

---

quisitor Herman Welker. One of Welker's questions to Lautner was: "And was Steve Nelson one of the leading espionage agents and saboteurs of the Communist Party in the United States dedicated to the overthrow of this government by force and violence, and that he had been a member of the Lenin School, which taught Mr. Nelson manners and means of destroying this country by bombing, by poisoning, by killing, by ruining, or any other methods possible?" The answer was in the affirmative.

Cvetic, who reconfirmed to SISS that Nelson was "this Moscow-trained espionage agent," was still not hitting the bottle hard enough to spoil the lecture tours which he interspersed with his inquisitorial engagements. In January the Kalamazoo (Michigan) VFW billed him as an "undercover agent for the FBI in Soviet Russia for nine years" who had given Hoover "reports on more than 4,000 secret Soviet meetings." Cvetic's seven years in the CP had become nine, Pittsburgh had become Russia, and even in Russia CP meetings had become "secret."

* Marcantonio dropped dead in pouring rain on a New York street, aged 52. After representing the CP before SACB, he had joined Abt and Joseph Forer in a Supreme Court plea for reversal of the order to the Party to register, heavily based on recent exposures of Crouch (who had contributed 387 pages of SACB testimony), Manning Johnson (163 pages) and Matusow (118 pages). Marcantonio was also defending the Fur Workers' Ben Gold in a perjury trial; Gold had resigned from the Party to sign the Taft-Hartley oath but had not repented.

Also lost to the heretical community in 1954 were 83-year-old "angel" Anita Blaine, successfully screened off from it during her last year by relatives who implied she was mad, and Washington's emissary to the Bolsheviks in 1917, Raymond Robins. Crippled since 1935 by a fall from a tree on his Florida estate, he had survived to reach 81, but had been able to do little for heretical movements (which he identified as American and Christian) except give them most of his fortune.

through by acclamation with little change. One of the two Representatives opposing it reported that "nearly everyone" thought it "badly drawn and unwise, but was afraid if they voted against it their opponents would call them pro-Communist. You could almost reach out and feel the fear in the chamber." Eisenhower was "in cheerful mood" (*Times*) after signing the law, but if he understood what he signed he was among the few Americans who did: the *Times* said that a day earlier not even a complete text was available.* The CP said it would carry on.

A further source of public confusion, after America set off its biggest H-bang at Bikini in March, was the attempt to make Americans both comfortable with the Bomb and scared of it at the same time. Said retired Admiral William F. Halsey, now serving on the board of numerous corporations, in April: "I hate to see people appearing to be jitterish—I can't see any difference between being killed by an A- or H-bomb and being killed by a hand grenade. There is too much hysteria in this country and too much talk." Sokolsky reminded his countrymen that they were "a people who do not scare readily. If the H-Bomb came along, some speculator would probably put up grandstands and hope to make an honest dollar." West German deputies visiting America in May were reportedly "startled" by the information from their hosts that in case of atomic war 65,000,000 Americans would die but "the remaining 100,000,000 would go on to win the war." Little noticed was an AEC man's remark to an Atomic Industrial Forum in New York, scouting the thesis that Russia got its Bomb "sooner than we thought" by espionage: "Neither the A-bomb nor the H-bomb was stolen from us by spies." But problems lingered for Civil Defense, which had acquired its own Administration in Washington. Nationwide highway signs, advising against use of certain roads in the event of atomic attack, were ruled out-of-date by experts and removed. The new policy, said Civil Defense Administrator Val Peterson, was to let Americans flee down any road they could—to "run for the hills"; but another

---

* Amid the Congressional and national confusion about the new legislation a writer in the Fellowship of Reconciliation magazine *Fellowship* proposed this clarification of the horse-thieving laws, which he insisted was necessary to drive horse thieves from public life: "Sec. 1, DEFINITIONS: (a) 'Horse' means each and every animal which can be identified as a horse, including plough horses, saddle horses, cow ponies, milk horses, race horses, burros, asses, donkeys, colts, nags, mustangs of any size, weight, age, creed or color. (b) 'Horse thief' means any person who steals, attempts to steal, or aids in the stealing of a horse, or advocates, abets, advises or teaches by any means any person to steal, attempt to steal, or aid in the stealing of a horse, or in the commission of any act intended to facilitate the stealing of horses or who is a member of or affiliated with any horse-thief front organization. (c) 'Horse-thief front organization' means any organization, corporation, company, partnership, association, trust, foundation, fund, club, society, committee, political party, gang or group permanently or temporarily associated together for action or advancement of views on any subject or subjects one of the purposes of which is advocating, abetting, advising or teaching the desirability of any action, advocacy, abetting, advice or instruction, which will advance or facilitate the stealing of horses ... Sec. 4: No person shall hold any office of trust or profit or be employed by any agency of the state, or by any agency receiving tax exemption from or paying taxes to the state, unless he shall take the following oath: 'I swear that I am not now and never have been and will not be a horse thief, a crypto-horse thief (Footnote: One who, if he had seen a horse and could have stolen it, would have liked to—Webster, 3rd edition) or associated in any way with any agency heretofore or hereafter designated as a horse-thief front organization by any federal, state, county or municipal official."

school of thought held that they should rush into convenient places where "SHELTER" signs were being feverishly erected—especially in New York where evacuating 8,000,000 people in an hour was said to "stagger the imagination." Atomic scientists in their *Bulletin* leaned toward the Peterson view provided that the public could have "two, or better four, or still better six hours of warning." Yet they saw this as unlikely since radar, able as it was to detect an approaching object, could not determine which city was the target nor whether the object was a Bomb.

Some felt that the best solution had been found by the councilmen of Coventry, Britain's Lady Godiva city, who seemed to recognize nudity when they saw it. They voted to end all civil defense against nuclear bombs because, in their view, no such thing could exist. In America, however, the protection of "secret" formulas for atomizing the enemy still headed the security agenda. The announcement that AEC would probe Oppenheimer, in whose head the secrets already resided, brought more audible groans from the intelligentsia than any inquisition in years. Leo Szilard, a nuclear research pioneer with a sense of humor, thought it would be seen abroad as "a sign of insanity which it probably is." Nobel peace laureate Albert Schweitzer wrote to the press of "anguish in my heart." The prime question to be resolved was whether Oppenheimer's lukewarmness to the H-Bomb showed lurking heretical hangovers. The testimony of 40 witnesses, covering 992 pages of fine print, showed that it did and that he could be trusted with no further secrets. On the eve of the probe Einstein again repeated his plea for non-cooperation with inquisitors in an interview calling the H-Bomb "the very essence of evil," but Oppenheimer bared his soul or all that he could remember of it. His explanations of the heresy that led him to "lie because I was a fool" and tell "pure fabrications" in the Los Alamos years were uncomfortably hazy.

As he plunged deeper into contrition one point was clear: neither he nor his wife could achieve the degree of inhumanity that the new morality required. The former Kitty Dallet insisted that she "always felt very friendly" to the chief villain of the show, Nelson, who had been "very kind." Oppenheimer had hired Philip Morrison and sent him to Japan knowing he was "probably a Communist," but still considered Morrison and Chevalier as friends.* As for the "terrible moral scruples" he had had about atomizing Hiroshima, he had "set forth arguments against" it but had not "endorsed" the arguments. Although neither he nor Kitty disputed the need for an inquisition, this was far too little to save the father of the Bomb. The hearing suggested either that American security officers had been shockingly lax or that they should have been clairvoyant, and were not, during the strange alliance. At that time, testimony showed, they were able to chat quite rationally with and about heretics. Among hundreds of other names, all those on ASP's letterhead in 1946 (when Oppenheimer quit it) were recited and publicized in the media.**

---

* Chevalier could not return the compliment. In his *Man Who Would Be God* (Putnam, NY, 1960), a novelization of the friendly years in San Francisco, he depicted Oppenheimer as a man who sacrificed family, friends and principles to an obsession of the scientist's absolute power over nature.
** The ASP vice-chairmen and directors on the letterhead were: prewar Moscow ambassador Davies, Brig. Gen. Evans Carlson, Norman Corwin, Mayor La Guardia, Oppen-

By National Weak Link Day of 1954, Condon had also come to the end of the road pending alterations which would let him proceed. He had taken the post of research director to the Corning Glass Corporation, but such was the spread of military contracts that even glassmakers now needed loyalty clearance. Without it he felt his performance in the job could not be adequate, and he resigned. Within two years, however, his brain would again be called upon to function for a salary: as a University of Colorado professor and, for the Air Force, as director of a probe of flying saucers.

---

heimer, Robeson, Shapley, Frank Sinatra, William Rose Benet, Leonard Bernstein, Charles Boyer, Eddie Cantor, Joan Fontaine, Marion Hargrove, Moss Hart, Hellman, John Hersey, Walter Huston, Gene Kelly, Florence Eldridge March, Pauling, Walter Rauchenstrauch, Quentin Reynolds, Hazel Scott, Carl van Doren, Orson Welles.

Fever Chart

1954

Jacksonville, Florida: Headline in *Times-Union*.
CONFECTIONERS TOLD RUSSIA THREATENS 5¢ CANDY BAR.

Los Angeles, New York and Erie, Pennsylvania: *Mirror, Post, Dispatch* comment on Big Four talks in Berlin and atomic talks in Washington.

"It is still far too early to tell what the Soviets plan or want. Perhaps Moscow wants to embarrass Secretary of State Dulles, who can't be in Washington and Berlin simultaneously."

"It seems nobody expected the Russians to be that flexible. The result is that we are over a diplomatic barrel. Unless we become more flexible and roll with the barrel, we will be inside it by week's end."

"A diet expert said Monday he may cable Dulles in Berlin to watch out for a dangerous Russian secret weapon—sturgeon pie. Diplomats should be warned that the Soviets can use food as well as vodka as a political weapon, Martin Lederman said."

New York: Reverend McComb preaches in Broadway Presbyterian Church.

"Those who still imagine world peace can be achieved by the nations sitting down together and talking over their differences are naive indeed and disregard what the Bible teaches."

Chicago and Los Angeles: Mazur of Lehman Brothers investment bankers, president Gross of Advertising Association of the West, and economist Hoadley look ahead.

MAZUR: "Americans must buy much more than they need in the next 10 years or face a possible economic setback."

GROSS: "The job of advertising is to create the demand to live beyond our means and thus we make a real contribution to the economy."

HOADLEY: "The H-bomb may create a tendency of many individuals to adopt a shorter-term outlook on life. This may lead to spending more for immediate comforts and to saving less for the future, which in turn would stimulate production."

New York, California, Pennsylvania: Advertisements following success of new Bomb.

"HYDROGEN BOMB NEWS has caused me to realize how short life is—whether through natural or man-made causes. SO WHAT? So I'm going to enjoy life now. I'm fixing up with Sam Klein Carpet Broadloom. It makes me so proud and happy to have friends and relatives admire my beautiful floors!"—New York *Post*.

"OUT OF H-BOMB RANGE! New desert homes 1-2-3 bedrooms for as little as $100 down. A Safe and Healthy Place to Live."—Los Angeles *Mirror*.

"The bomb's brilliant gleam reminds me of the brilliant gleam 'Beacon Wax' gives to floors. It's a science marvel!"—Pittsburgh *Press*.

New York: Rev. Dr. Bonnell in Fifth Avenue Presbyterian Church, and Civil Defense director Lieutenant General Huebner, face the religious and philosophical implications.

"Easter dawn broke upon the ancient world with a might, majesty and power like that of the Hydrogen Bomb."

"With the H-Bomb, of course, more people are going to get killed. It can't be helped. So there is nothing to get excited about."

Keokuk, Iowa: *Gate City* headline of report of American Anesthesiologists' convention.

IF YOU CAN COUNT TO 5 AFTER H-BOMB THEN YOU'RE SAFE.

Los Angeles: Display ad in *Mirror*.

"LET'S SPEAK RIGHT OUT ABOUT FLASH BURNS—World conditions being as tough as they are, it's time to be frank and realistic with ourselves. A-Bombs play no favorites. That's where KIP comes in. If we do become a target, we'll have burns. Just spread it on, that's all. KIP doesn't mean perhaps—it's SURE."

Washington—*Wall Street Journal* and New York *Times* correspondents report.

"One problem gives the federal fiscal men headaches. They wonder what would happen if a bomb hit the Capitol, they had to borrow money to finance a war, and Congress couldn't convene to boost the debt limit."

"The Army's germ warfare authority said today it would be an 'act of barbarism' to deny American troops the use of biological weapons in a war."

Coast-to-coast authorities consider the Communist enigma and its implications:

"Two Russian émigrés, Karl Marx and Friedrich Engels, sat down together in a Paris attic to draft a blueprint for world domination . . . the Communist Manifesto."—Rep. (and HUAC inquisitor) Jackson, California.

"HASHISH DENS OF ORIENT NOT WICKED AT ALL—'If these people were not dreaming from hashish, they would be making trouble on the streets,' the guide explained. 'Remember this: No hashish addict ever goes Communist.'"—AP report from Beirut.

"Commies are the enemies of gun lovers."—Definition offered by *Gun & Cartridge Record*, Chagrin Falls, Ohio.

"There remain many enemies in our midst. We pledge to report to the proper governmental agency any person or persons who may be engaged in any subversive activities in our establishments."—Resolution passed by New Jersey tavern owners' convention, Atlantic City, New Jersey.

"The Payette high-school song has been expurgated of the word 'comrade.' The student body . . . agreed it had become part of Communist usage and was therefore unfit for use by patriotic American youths. As a substitute, 'colleagues' was selected."—*UP* report from Payette, Idaho.

"Mrs. Elsie Coia Allred won permission from Judge Brofman yesterday to change her name to Allgood. She told the court her surname was 'distasteful and gradually becoming more so.'"—New York *World Telegram* report from Denver, Colorado.

"We need legislation making it possible for the Attorney General to authorize wire tapping and make evidence thus obtained admissible in court. Only thus will we protect our citizens' right of privacy."—Blake Clark in *Reader's Digest.*

"The Soviet Embassy is preparing to establish a special school for the diplomats' children. A special schoolmistress is being imported from Russia. An official of the AFL American Federation of Teachers intends to challenge the Russian boast about Communism being the greatest friend of trade unionism. He plans to send a union application blank to the new Russian teacher to see whether she will be permitted to join. The challenge will be particularly interesting because the AFL union bars Communists from membership."—*Labor's Daily,* Washington.

"It may come as a shock to readers of this newspaper that one of the very first results of Communist domination of any nation has been the en masse rape of the conquered nation's female population. By 'female population' we mean girls and women from 12 to 72. In Czechoslovakia, Latvia, Lithuania and Estonia the sight of women from 12 to 72 walking the streets with their skirts split from waist to hem, so that rape might be less painful, was common . . . Will UN ambassador Henry Cabot Lodge wait to bring it up until we have to split the skirts of the children and grandmothers in New England?"—Boston *Post.*

XX

1954: Fewer Higginses,
More Plots

McCarthy's decline and fall came at a time of such uninhibited probing as to provide small cheer for the Higgins tribe. The Rosenberg affair, galvanizing them into a supreme effort which failed, had been a kind of watershed. More than ever dedicated to the pursuit of life, liberty and happiness through personal acquisition, the mass of Americans had become, for Higgins, strangers speaking a strange tongue. This would have been bearable if his organizations could have survived, but now he felt a new aloneness as leaders deserted from necessity or frustration. American popular institutions, in which he had believed with reservations about their frailty, were being irreparably burlesqued and torn. The words remained, but the reality was that an entire body of opinion had been excommunicated. There was no longer any bridge between it and the mass.

Physicians of the tribe had become accustomed to cases of mental and physical collapse in which the patient was convinced that FBI men were dogging him even though he might be too insignificant to be worth an inquisitor's time. Sometimes he distrusted even his doctor, for word had spread that doctors too received FBI name-gathering visits and that some—especially if they had guilt feelings of their own—were not above obliging. Parents lost the trust of children too young to grasp what was happening. Friends turned cold and vanished in fear of guilt by association, or would defy inquisitors one day and say on the next: "I decided to go down and tell enough to get them off my back."

For heretics who did not succumb to such fantasies, the only escape hatches involved a complete change in their daily routine. They tended to be of mature age with family responsibilities and little hope of employment in their own field, but they found that America was large and opulent enough to absorb even outcasts in some job somewhere within its borders. In "insensitive" business divorced from war production, employers were happy to hire an able and industrious Higgins at half the salary he could command if he were not in Hoover's dossiers. If on the other hand a Higgins scraped up capital to launch a small enterprise of his own, his organizing competence could bring him such prosperity as he never cared to dream about when the cause was the thing. Higginses excommunicated from trade union, school or journalistic functions succeeded in businesses ranging from laundromats to trade and technical journals; they advised investors how to make more money for less work and merchants how to package gadgets, cosmetics and prunes for the most stupefying effect on the shopper. Many such neophyte businessmen could only survive initially by taking in each other's washing, but in major cities the ghetto was big enough to maintain a viable miniature economy through the stormiest years. If they ended up doing nothing except make money, the inquisition substantially achieved its goal.

The bell tolling for McCarthy spurred Hoover, Eastland, Walter and their local competitors to greater efforts. The inquisitorial arm was long, as John and Jane Smith and their three toddlers discovered when they sought in Tiffin, Ohio (pop. 19,943) surcease from harassment in their own eastern city. Tiffin's mental health clinic had been seeking a psychiatric social worker for 18 months, but life in Tiffin attracted no suitable man except Smith and he was innocently hired. The Smiths' home-town dossier showed that, when Hoover's man had called to ask for their friends' names, the door had been slammed on his foot. Probably Hoover would not have pursued them further had not factories in the Tiffin area been about to hold union elections which UE threatened to win—a fact unknown to the Smiths until they arrived. An outside agitator was called for by the script, and Smith was excellent casting for the role. Duly alerted Ohio agents called at the Smiths' new home and hinted at grand jury treatment and renewed unemployment if they still declined to discuss their friends. Although Tiffinites had never seen a Communist and would not have known what one looked like, they read their papers and rumors spread fast that Moscow had sent a man to overthrow Tiffin. The Smiths made friends in the community but, to protect them from guilt by association, soon had to pull down the blinds when they called.

Loyal postures were struck vis-à-vis the Smiths by the Lions Club and Chamber of Commerce. The clinic director adjured Smith to "clear himself": if Hoover wanted names, Smith should supply them. A group of mothers who had successfully kept a pro-UE woman off the school board mobilized to repeat the process with Smith, sending a delegation to the state capital to press mental hygiene officials for his dismissal. A priest barred his parishioners from attending the clinic, a manufacturer held up his donation to it until Smith should disprove the rumors. No charge having been made, Smith had nothing to disprove except his obduracy about names. His staff colleagues avoided him and the advice of the least hostile one was: "In a town like Tiffin you must conform." Offering to come and discuss the matter with state officials, Smith was asked in reply for his resignation. He phoned for an explanation and was told: "You know very well." There would be no hearing; he should resign, and if he did not his job would be abolished.

When the scandal hit the headlines, Ohio's Attorney General said he was probing not only Smith but the whole state mental hygiene system for "Communist infiltration." Smith brought suit against his employers and, with a few friends sticking by him, took a factory floor-sweeping job while awaiting his day in court. His consolation was that his oldest child, aged 5, was prouder of him working in a factory than in a clinic. The last word from Tiffin was that the factory had fired him as ideologically unfit to sweep its floor; and 15 uncowed Tiffinites gave the Smiths a farewell party as they moved to a midwestern city for another new start—"at the end of our rope financially and emotionally," according to Mrs. Smith.

While Tiffin purged itself of the Smiths, Miami put to flight dozens of families in the greatest of local and state inquisitions. Inspired by Crouch who—

still professing genuine heresy—had settled there after the war, a vigorous inquisitorial team was led by two judges, the State Attorney for Dade (Miami) County,
and journalists William Baggs and Damon Runyon, Jr. During the New Deal
and Russo-American honeymoon, weeds of anti-racism, anti-Fascism and trade
union militancy had grown in Florida, a state ranking high for the frequency
of its lynchings and implacability of its chain gangs. Several hundred adherents
of these doctrines survived into the postwar inquisition years, mostly white
Miamians of exotic northern and eastern backgrounds who had settled there for
the climate, some 60 of them being Party members. The capacity of these to overthrow Dade County—and much more—was never lost sight of by the patriotic
team.

Early in 1948 a Miami hotel meeting for the CP's Elizabeth Flynn inspired
the first tocsin from Baggs: a page-one report with photos of the 150-odd persons
present, which set off a week of scare headlines featuring as chief subverter the
New York-born founder of the state CIO. Subsequently Baggs introduced Crouch's
confession-reminiscences under the scarlet head, "MIAMI BARED AS COMMUNIST
HUB"; HUAC moved into town for a probe; and the CIO man, "sought" and
briefly arrested, was "FIRED FOR RED POLICY" by penitent Michael Quill. A raid
on the CP treasurer's home yielded more names, and she was tried under the state
law against "assembling to promote, advocate or teach." Recalling "what happened when Hitler marched into Germany," and praying God it was "not too late
for the last Democratic nation to defend itself," Judge Holt set her bail at
$100,000 (she earned $1,175 a year) until maverick Florida lawyer John Coe
came to court to get it reduced.

By 1949, when Miami's 2,800 city employees were confronted with a
loyalty oath, only one—a park attendant—dared refuse to sign it. During the next
years, as bombings of Negro homes mounted throughout Dixie, one state after another ruled that heretics must "register" or go to jail. The harassment in Miami
was sporadic but enough to make the unscared remnant see the point: they could
only meet clandestinely, and that at their peril since the normal quota of informers was emulating Crouch. Baggs, becoming editor of the *News,* hired Runyon as
heresy expert to expose (with names and addresses) vast ramifications of the
Miami plot: it was aimed at subverting the whole continent down to Tierra del
Fuego. In 1953 heretics won a rare but pyrrhic victory when, owing to Crouch's
ineptitude before a jury, airlines worker Armand Scala whom he had named as a
Red won an out-of-state libel suit against the Hearst press, syndicators of the
Crouch-Baggs material.

But in 1954 inquisitor Eastland stormed into New Orleans to probe SCHW-
SCEF and galvanized the Miami patriots into furious action. With Crouch as star
familiar only two months before the Justice Department began repudiating him,
several Miamians along with SCEF leaders Aubrey Williams, James Dombrowski,
Myles Horton and Clifford and Virginia Durr were made to walk the plank. In a
performance that rivaled McCarthy's best, Eastland dramatized the anti-racist
plotters' "affiliation with a power abroad that has killed and maimed thousands
and thousands of American boys." Crouch outlined the impending Russian invasion of America and, naming various Miami conspirators, identified lawyer Paul

Newman as the Party's "secret tsar" to command sabotage forces when the Reds landed.*

In a turbulent hearing room Crouch linked Mrs. Durr with a "White House spy plot," and Durr rushed at him with raised fists crying, "You dirty dog, I'll kill you." Back in Miami, the Fifth Amendment stance of a contractor who had built some schools there so heightened the fever that inspectors began ripping out the school walls in search of bombs. An official disbarment move greeted Newman on his return, and Runyon collaborated with newly surfaced "ex-Communist" Al Spears in a series exposing infiltration of the local Unitarian church and a plot to turn the disused naval base, Opa Locka, into a "Soviet village." Panic gripped some heretics as they received subpenas to come and explain themselves to county prosecutor George Brautigam and a grand jury. The flight from Florida began, and with those who remained—already tried and found guilty in the News—a standard procedure was followed. Brautigam asked questions sure to be unanswered, the grand jury passed the victim along to Judge George E. Holt, and Holt ordered a year in jail without bail for not answering. With the aid of familiar Mazzei, who was brought down from Philadelphia, the Opa Locka affair was expanded into a plot to make the base the Russians' landing place for seizing America. This thesis in the media was not questioned in so much as one letter-to-the-editor. Thirty-six victims spent up to a month behind bars before Florida's Supreme Court (which showed more spirit than Washington's) upheld their right to invoke the Fifth. But the public was hostile or silent, the media violently hostile locally and silent nationally, and most of the victims saw no alternative to leaving the state and starting their lives anew.

Miami's second juridical scourge of heretics, Judge Vincent Giblin, disbarred Newman for his invocations of the Fifth without even listening to Crouch, who was in court waiting to testify. The judge had "earnestly prayed" that Newman would confess, but realized he was one of "those who regard themselves as 'intellectuals' . . . pygmies on stilts waving their masters' degrees" as they planned "to undermine our form of government." But with Coe leading the argument for a lawyer's right to the Fifth and ABA backing Giblin and Brautigam, the State Supreme Court ordered a new trial for Newman. Crouch having died, Brautigam now used Mazzei as star familiar. Between the two Newman trials, HUAC on a return visit to Miami introduced some new turncoats, one of whom blew up disastrously in Velde's face when the man's record of 22 arrests and trials for drunkenness and assault was dug up. On Mazzei's word Newman was again found guilty, but when the Justice Department itself impugned Mazzei's veracity the decision

---

* By way of credentials for Eastland, Crouch listed among other "major positions" he had held as a conspirator: "Head of the CP's department for infiltration of US armed forces, CPUS representative to the Executive Committee of the Communist International in Moscow, honorary regimental commander of the Red Army, member of a commission in Moscow to draft plans to infiltrate and subvert all the armed forces of the world." Mrs. Durr expressed "total contempt" for Eastland and in retrospect (to the author, 1969) compared the Crouch of 1954 with "a dirty piece of Kleenex about to disintegrate—such a wreck of a man that even while he was destroying you anyone would feel sorry for him."

had to be reversed. It took Newman more than five years of court struggles to win back the right to practice his profession.*

Throughout the land in 1954 the prime source of fear remained the Rosenberg case; and after Bloch's funeral, at which Robeson sang and heretics wept, it was still not over. Sobell, his second plea for a trial review rejected, was now serving his 30 years with the cream of America's professional criminals in Alcatraz. During the year Hoover's men visited him three times there to suggest he might get leniency if he named some spies, but he wrote his wife: "A person must live with himself. There is no slightly soiled dirt, all dirt is dirty." As Michael's and Robert's custodians under their parents' will, Bloch had found the children permanent foster parents who were, of course, heretical. In their home Robert, who since the age of three had seen his mother and father only in the death house and in coffins, gradually stopped the nightmares which woke him up screaming. But New York's Welfare Department notified the Society for Prevention of Cruelty to Children that the boys were being "neglected," and on the society's petition they were seized and placed in an institution under court custody. The judge denied the Rosenbergs' right to name a guardian. The children's paternal grandmother Sophie, who had had them before but could hardly cope with them, saved the day by appearing in court, traveling other than on foot on the Sabbath for the first time in her life. The judge, in view of Sophie's full set of orthodox Jewish beliefs, could find no breach in her respectability; and one of them holding each of her hands, Michael and Robert trooped off to be later restored to their foster home. The campaign to remove them slowly petered out, but in October the Treasury Department entered the game with a $124,000 tax claim on the Rosenberg defense committee, which was "not a non-profit organization." The committee dissolved itself and became a committee for Sobell.**

On the religious front, Presbyterians set up their own inquisition in De-

---

* The sequel to the Miami inquisition was interesting: the tables were turned and Holt, Brautigam and Giblin—but yesterday cited for conspicuous public service—became the community's hate objects. Giblin publicly accused Holt, who had recently been fined $200 for recklessly driving his Jaguar into a motorcycle, of "thievery" in administering rich Floridians' estates. Holt's reaction was an indignant "REDS AFTER ME, JUDGE ASSERTS" interview, but the grand jury, despite Brautigam's efforts to prevent it, called for Holt's impeachment. The successor grand jury, taking the same view of Holt, added a call for Giblin's impeachment on similar charges including overimbibing. The impeachments were narrowly defeated in the state legislature.

Of all the team, Holt was the only one to survive. A heart attack felled Al Spears after his Runyon collaboration, and cancer removed Crouch, elaborating his exotic plots to the last breath. Brautigam fell dead soon after his defeat for re-election; and Giblin died later, the obscurity of his last years broken only by a reckless driving incident in 1959. Runyon, who had written a book about his family's alcoholic history, plunged off a high bridge in 1968. Baggs died at 48 after an apparent change of heart: he joined Hutchins's Center for Study of Democratic Institutions and, touched by the plight of America's human bomb targets in Vietnam, had just returned from a second journey to Hanoi to try to stop the war. Meanwhile most of the victims, men and women of the same generation as most of their persecutors, prospered in their new settings.

** Bearing their foster parents' name but mindful of their identity, Michael and Robert would attend the best universities; both married and produced grandchildren for Ethel and Julius.

troit to probe Claude Williams, who used the Bible to teach of-one-blood-all-nations and the-poor-shall-inherit-the-earth heresies to the Dixie disinherited. After three days a charge of Communism was "dismissed on technical grounds," but he was unfrocked for his unbecoming views on the Trinity and Virgin Birth. He said he resented the dodging of the Communist issue since, if he was guilty, the Church should have "spelled out where I have violated the Son of Man's teachings"; but he "did not feel nude," and returned to Alabama to continue his work on such funds as brother heretics could contribute. The State Department, confronting applications from Iron Curtain clergymen to attend the World Council of Churches Assembly at Evanston, Illinois, "thought" that Hungary's Bishop Peter was a Russian spy but issued visas on the precautionary condition that the theologians must not talk to the media. Brooklyn's pastor Melish, appearing before SACB in its NCASF probe, had set off a minor headline flurry by testifying that it was possible to be both a Christian and a Communist ("startling, incredible"—Brooklyn *Eagle*). Christian Ethics professor Joseph F. Fletcher was invited to discuss this in another Brooklyn church and said that "the greatest living Protestant theologian, Karl Barth, has often replied to the same question in very much the same way. The real issue is Christianity versus atheism, not Christianity versus socialism." The *Eagle* disposed of Fletcher by recalling his attendance at the Prague peace congress. HUAC felt it could briefly reopen the religious Pandora's box to warn free-world WCC delegates of the company they would be keeping at Evanston. It called refugees from Hungary to testify that the Church had "gone underground" there and was holding "secret services," and a "Madam X" to relate from behind a screen how Russians raped her in 1944. Ten specimens of what clearly could not exist, including Czechoslovakia's Joseph L. Hromadka and Hungary's Bishop Berezcky, turned up for the Assembly. They spoke of troubles with their governments but Hromadka said that, while "every sermon I preach is a criticism of Communist ideology," Christianity and Communism could and did coexist.

In the NCASF probe Melish admitted being a Christian but denied Budenz's assertion that he was a Communist. NCASF's name being itself a declaration of heresy, the months consumed in establishing this were a tribute to the inquisitors' patience. Budenz undertook to sort out NCASF sponsors who had repented from those who had not, and each of the second group was examined in turn. The prosecutors lent the proceedings an informal air by chewing gum. One circumstance protracting the probe was that a cacophony of vacuum cleaners, pneumatic drills, and guffaws and altercations from adjoining offices, penetrated the partitions of the Immigration Building hallway used as a hearing room, so that inquisitors had to keep knocking and demanding quiet. Chairman David Coddaire was wearied by contending lawyers' arguments as to whether NCASF publications, which would have shown how respectable it once was, should take a place in the record.

On a possibly typical day* Arthur Upham Pope, 73-year-old Persian art expert, sat before the tribunal. As a former NCASF vice-chairman he wished to join Melish and others in calling Budenz a liar. His dossier was on hand and was consulted to ask if he had known heretic X or said Y to Z; what about this item

* The day the author visited the hearing.

in the *Worker,* and how often and why had he visited the Russian Embassy? (Pope was a friend and biographer of Litvinov.) Did he ever contribute to Spanish war veterans? Yes, because he thought they had fought "for American ideals." Coddaire: "That may be struck from the record." Who were the incorporators of the China Aid Council? Pope could not recall all the names but remembered one, "the famous physician who attended the Shah of Persia when he was here." Coddaire: "Strike that part about him being famous." What were Pope's relations with Intourist? He had visited Russia three times and Intourist arranged all such travel. "Isn't it a fact that Intourist is an agency of the Cominform?" What was Pope's relation with the New School for Social Research? "Isn't it a fact that this school is used by the CP to disseminate its propaganda? . . . Are you familiar with the CP line?" Pope: "To some extent." "Where did you get your information about it?" "I got a lot of it from a long conversation with Mayor LaGuardia." "Mayor LaGuardia has been dead how long?"

When it was implied that Moscow had provided a plane for Pope's visit to Russia after World War II, defense lawyer David Rein asked Pope if in fact the War Department had not provided it on Truman's order. Pope said that was correct. Rein: "Who else was on that plane?" Gumchewer: "Objection." Coddaire: "Objection sustained." Would Pope have supported NCASF if he knew the Attorney General had listed it? "I regard the Attorney General's list as irrelevant and without legal validity." When Pope tried to protest that a question was unfair, Coddaire: "Strike that out." Pope: "Must I sit silent while he impugns my honor?" Coddaire: "One more remark from you and I'll move these hearings back to Washington." Some elderly ladies, still under the impression that America fought on the right side in World War II, thinly populated the public section of the room: they could help only by supplying witnesses with paper cups of water and brave smiles. One man, perhaps from *AP,* sat at the press table taking routine notes, but weeks of testimony passed without anything being published except heretics' names.

New areas probed during the year included Americans employed abroad by the UN and "a diabolical conspiracy [for] furtherance of socialism in the US" by scholars working on tax-free foundation grants. The conspiracy's aims were no less than to revive the New Deal, and the suspicions of the special House committee probing it fell on the Rockefeller and Carnegie foundations. Congressmen saw the same conspiracy reflected in a Veterans Administration release on the tenth anniversary of the popular GI Bill of Rights, describing the bill as having been "signed June 22, 1944 by Franklin Roosevelt." The wording was changed to "signed June 22, 1944." In Paris a roving loyalty board confronted UN employee David Leff with a questionnaire which he would not fill out. Leff declined a grand jury invitation to return home and be probed, and a judge issued a warrant for his arrest.

Heretics on the UN's staff cheered prematurely when an Appeals Court reversed the contempt conviction of Mrs. Keeney; she would be tried again and not cleared until 1955. The UN had tried to cooperate with inquisitors, but the requirement of loyalty clearance for all American employees severely strained its personnel office. It complained that clearances had been asked but not received for 16 plumbers and carpenters, the need for whose services was becoming critical. An American security officer explained: "It's much harder to check a plumber than a professor." A few weeks earlier the UN's Trusteeship Department chief Ralph Bunche—one Negro whom the black community thought above suspicion—had been probed about heretical allegations made against him by Manning Johnson and another black familiar, Leonard Patterson. The probe brought out that Bunche had referred to America in a speech as "actually a colonial nation itself," but Bunche established his loyalty to the discomfiture of Johnson. In view of the barbs from certain columnists, Immigration removed Johnson from its payroll and thenceforth only provincial inquisitors and NBC found any use for him. UNESCO publications were exposed as subversive and banned from schools by Los Angeles inquisitors. Teachers found that any instruction to the young about the "controversial" UN imperiled their jobs.

Look surprised the thousands of teachers on whom Hoover had dossiers by publishing in March a Hutchins commentary on the Hook line that "only a few have been fired." "The question is," wrote Hutchins, "not how many have been but how many think they might be. You don't have to fire many to intimidate them all. The entire teaching profession is now intimidated." Celebrating Academic Freedom Week in April, Hunter College fired a psychology, a mathematics and a music professor named by Bella Dodd: they had repudiated their heresies but "concealed facts" about former comrades. Students and faculty expressed either agreement or inertia. An undergraduate paper pleaded for more conformity, accepting the theory of guilt until innocence was proved. Equal apathy reigned at neighboring Queens College where the undergraduate paper noted that the once "despicable" activity of informing had become "part of 'academic freedom.'" A Queens faculty member said that students there were "decent but not given to controversy. They don't even argue in the lounge about music and art the way we did. This is a generation that grew up in the cold war." New Hampshire Attorney General Louis C. Wyman won a jail sentence for economist Paul M. Sweezy, co-editor of *Monthly Review*, while Boston's District Attorney sought to have "burned or otherwise destroyed" two police-vanloads of books seized from the home of sculptor Otis Hood, a Mayflower descendant whom the CP had run four times for governor of Massachusetts. Along with the books and five other heretics, Hood had been arrested amid a babel of headlines about "arms depots," "pistol-whippings" and "female lures."

On a visit to Moskoff's bureau in Brooklyn, Denver *Post* reporter Lawrence Martin was told by the academic inquisitor that his "fat file" contained 905 more names for immediate probing. Martin had been assigned to survey "Faceless Informers in Our Schools" by his editors, who felt that while schools must be protected from "infiltration," "classic police state methods" must be avoided. Wherever Martin went, educators agreed that Communists must not teach but agonized over how to detect them in an "American way." The methods he found in use—based either on anonymous local accusations, or on Hoover's "raw file" information which he "never evaluated," or both—were perhaps not classical but were effective. Many schools were firing suspects wholesale rather than be labeled as "coddling subversives." One administrator said that if he received any charges against a teacher he acted "just as fast as if somebody yelled fire—I dare not wait to find out whether it's a false alarm."

Concluding Martin's report, his editors conjured an ideal situation in which, with all charges stated in writing, both "faceless informers" and teachers who "escape through First and Fifth Amendments" would be balked. Schools would thus be "protected by proof against Communists and fellow travelers" and thus freedom and justice would reign. The *Post* seemed unaware that it was touching the heart of the democratic inquisition's problem. Almost all Communists had now been exposed, and a viable due-process definition of the fellow traveler—rated by Hoover as even more dangerous—could not be devised. Concerning Hoover, the *Post* conceded him "well deserved acclaim" but said he was "treading dangerous ground"—for if he could do this to teachers, "preachers, authors, editors, doctors and street sweepers" might get the same treatment "conceivably within a few years." The *Post* had not noticed that they were already getting it. In November a Washington used-piano dealer was denied renewal of his license as an unfit person to sell pianos, having been "identified as associated with the CP" and failing to explain himself.

Editors, however, retained (even if they did not exercise it) the liberty to oppose the inquisition provided that their mothers had observed geographical proprieties when giving them birth. Alien journalists were not only prominent among victims of the deportation mill, but also received more immediate retributions. *China Daily News* editor Moy was sentenced, along with three Chinese laundrymen accomplices, to two years and a $25,000 fine for running Hong Kong bank advertisements about remittances to Peking. A ten-year sentence rewarded editor Kurt Heikkinen of a Finnish journal for "willful failure to apply for travel documents" after a deportation order. Carrying on under intense fire, ACPFB concentrated on stalling deportations to countries like South Korea, Greece and Taiwan where heretics' lives would be at stake. Overall deportations in 1954 reached 26,951—an all-time high according to ACPFB*—under the Immigration commissionership of Eisenhower's West Point classmate General Joseph M. Swing, who had two more generals to assist him. The McCarran-Walter law provided him with almost 700 grounds for deporting an alien, one being failure to report for fingerprinting within a month of his 14th birthday. Swing won a certain prestige for his dawn raids, carried out with military precision, on deportable Mexican-Americans whom he seized in bed or ran down in fast cars.

The Matusow front was temporarily quiet, but in April and May the Alsops resumed their aspersions upon Crouch—not mentioning his extraordinary performance for Eastland in New Orleans, but citing a new lapse of memory in his testimony at the Philadelphia Smith Act trial.** Brownell saw no alternative to announcing that he would "investigate" Crouch, although "this doesn't mean he is guilty" of perjury. With a little patience by Crouch the scandal might have blown

---

* Apparently no one calculated the year-by-year percentage of deportations that were directly political, but 295 were pending in 1956.

** The top lawyers who agreed to defend the Philadelphia Communists were incredulous and offended when their clients told them to be ready for suborned witnesses and displays of FBI corruption and blackmail, but left the courtroom sadder and wiser than when they entered it. They were particularly shaken by the appearance as a government witness of Crouch, whose recollections of previously given testimony were dimmer than ever. He described conspiratorial meetings with defendant Dave Davis, a UE official, forgetting that in 1949 he swore he never met Davis.

over. Instead, he came to the boil in a threat of a $1,000,000 libel suit against the Alsops and a reminder to Brownell that, "if my reputation could be destroyed, 31 Communist leaders could get new trials, 20 immigration proceedings would be reopened, the registration order against the CP would be reversed, with a cost to the government of many millions." In June he called upon Hoover to probe the loyalty of some of Brownell's aides; a week later he formally petitioned McCarthy's committee to probe Brownell who, by suggesting a Crouch probe, had "given considerable aid and comfort to enemies of the US." The *Times* reported that, with Crouch attacking the Attorney General himself, workers in "the anti-Communist field . . . could not see how the Justice Department could continue using Mr. Crouch." Before the year's end Crouch was parked in Hawaii where his adventures had begun, writing a never-published book *Red Smear Victim*.

Matusow was writing his memoirs for Cameron & Kahn, and heretics' lawyers were preparing new-trial demands in dozens of cases in which he had testified. His most recent victim, Jencks, stood in the shadow of jail for contradicting Matusow while *Salt of the Earth,* in which Jencks re-enacted his real crime of organizing Mexican-Americans, opened at an obscure New York theatre. The star of the film, Mexican Rosaura Revueltas, had been deported while still engaged on it in New Mexico, but neither arrests nor Congressional threats nor local vigilantism had prevented its completion. Revueltas went to Karlovy Vary (Czechoslovakia) to receive an international grand prize for the film, confirming its heretical nature although she described it there as "pro-American, showing courageous people fighting for equality as guaranteed in the US Constitution." Some 10,000 persons saw the film in four days at the drive-in movie in Silver City, New Mexico (population 5,000), but a Legion campaign to prevent its showing around the country kept it in the *succès d'estime* class. Its producers would end up $250,000 in debt.

Heretics for the first time saw their May Day parade (banned in 1953) replaced by a Loyalty Parade, which Mayor Wagner led and Harriman reviewed from a Fifth Avenue stand with ten-year-old "Little Miss Loyalty." In Union Square there was free pop for the kids and entertainment by Edgar Bergen and Milton Berle, but after the loyalists dispersed some 10,000 heretics assembled in the square to cheer Robeson, Elizabeth Flynn and the absent Sobell. In a December probe of the United May Day Committee the Painters Union's Louis Weinstock said the committee did not exist, against Lautner's assurance that it did; Weinstock, already facing three years under the Smith Act, was indicted for perjury. Battered Party leader Thompson learned from the Veterans Administration in jail that, under a clause excluding persons guilty of "mutiny, treason or sabotage," his war-casualty pension had been stopped.

With Vincent Hartnett's and Fordham professor Godfrey P. Schmidt's AWARE Inc. nosing out *Counterattack* as top ghettoizing agency, show-business blacklists took a new spurt. On the eve of voting in the American Federation of Television and Radio Artists to decide whether to fight the blacklist, AWARE exposed the anti-blacklist slate as a "Communist front apparatus," citing members' contacts from its dossiers.

Black Americans had had other things than McCarthy to worry about when the master rode high, and still did after he fell. Some were comforted by the Tuskegee Institute's discontinuance of its annual tally of lynchings, but by dictionary definition this exercise had lost its point: the number of Negro exterminations performed other than by representatives of the law was now hardly worth tallying. Inquisitorial heat still focused on advocates of bringing blacks into the Constitutional orbit, and Patterson, author of CRC's genocide complaint to the UN, went to jail in July for withholding names of contributors to defense funds. He emerged after three months to receive another subpena for his lists, which he told the judge did not exist. The judge was skeptical and indicated that until Patterson could prove it he would continue trips to jail. After 69 days of his second incarceration he was freed on an appeals-court ruling that the government must prove the lists' existence. At this point SACB began a probe of CRC, which had already been almost beaten to death around the country.

During the summer two white journalists set off a scandal in the Dixie border state of Kentucky. Already heretical before their marriage, and more so since beginning to raise a family, Carl and Anne Braden thought that skin color should not determine eligibility to live in this or that part of Louisville. Their black friends the Wades being unable to buy the house they wanted, the Bradens bought it for them. The Wades were welcomed on moving in with gunshots and rocks and a press campaign to block the "black beachhead" in an all-white zone; a bomb blew up beneath the house, but the Wades escaped intact apart from being fined $100 for breach of the peace. The discovery of heretical books in the homes of the Bradens and some of their skin-color-blind circle confirmed for state prosecutor Scott Hamilton that the purchase of the house was a red plot. With bail fixed well beyond their means to get out of jail pending trial, a grand jury invoked a state sedition law to indict the Bradens and four others including Vernon Bown, a Lincoln Battalion veteran who was pinpointed as planter of the bomb.

For Hamilton a simple issue overrode considerations of whether the Wades had rights and if so whether these had been infringed: "Sedition is Communism, Communism is sedition." The damning proofs were the books in the suspects' shelves. With the aid of HUAC emissaries Hamilton imported Gitlow, Leonard Patterson, Manning Johnson, Cvetic, Maurice Malkin and other experts for a political trial of Braden which had many highlights. Wade, slightly but not seriously scared by the pressures upon him to denounce Braden, was challenged to deny having said, "This is a hell of a country." Between readings from the seized books, dialectical materialism was demonstrated in court with a glass of water. A total of nine prosecution witnesses who never set eyes on the defendant probably set a new record. Defense lawyers quoted Manning Johnson's statement that he would lie under oath if higher interests so required, but had to admit that their source was a report in the *Nation;* Hamilton proposed that the *Nation* be added to the subversive list "if it isn't there already." Braden swore he was not a Communist, an FBI man swore he was, and his possession of a "secret" edition of the Soviet Constitution clinched the matter. With a 15-year sentence and a bond of $40,000 which he had no hope of raising, Braden settled down to six weeks of solitary confinement while Hamilton prepared Anne's and Bown's trials. ACLU offered to enter a friend-of-the-court brief as soon as it could find out "which offense Braden was found to have committed," an obscure point in the trial record. After seven months the bond money was raised by ECLC, but Braden's paper, the *Courier-Journal,* had fired him after his conviction.

In Philadelphia one of the Smith Act defendants, poet Walter Lowenfels, was permitted to wonder before being sentenced to jail why the prosecution, which "wheeled out carloads of books to cite from," had not read one of "the quarter-million words I have published." In a Boston hearing to decide whether Hood's jailed books should be consigned to the flames, State prosecutors argued that if this were not done the books "could be used" to advocate something, but the judge reserved his decision and they were allowed to survive after 236 days under lock and key. (Hood, whose saints and madonnas adorned various churches in the region, survived by sculpting Santa Clauses and giant hamburgers for window displays.) By this time Thoreau's *Walden* had been banned from USIS libraries as "downright socialistic," and a proposal had been rejected for USIS to buy world rights to *The Old Man and the Sea* which earned Hemingway a Nobel Prize. Hemingway, as reported in the *Nation,* appeared with some 7,000 writers, artists and musicians on USIS's "gray list."

A son of refugees from Hitler took the floor at a December forum for students in New York high schools. "I am told," he said, "that Hitler got power by frightening people with the danger of Communism. People followed him to be saved from Communism, and while we weren't seeing what we were looking at he took our freedom away . . . You fear Communism but you should also really fear people who try to save you from it." Among those in various jails who found this consoling was Elizabeth Flynn. On her 65th birthday she had received "loving greetings" from the blind and deaf humanitarian Helen Keller: "May the sense of serving mankind bring strength and peace into your brave heart." The consolations were the more touching for being so few.

PART FOUR:
THE RECKONING

XXI

1955: "A Hideous Dream"

Eisenhower set the tone for 1955 by asking Congressional authority to atomize Chinese if need arose, and announcing that "we shall continue to ferret out and destroy Communist subversives." Congressmen sinking "deeper and deeper into somnolence" (*Times*) endorsed both, but Leo Szilard wrote to the *Times* wondering when "the Government or anyone else" would "present even the principles" for a settlement before stumbling into the ultimate holocaust. He suggested that groups of experts might foregather to "think through the problems." Cleveland's eccentric industrialist Cyrus S. Eaton responded by arranging to bring together American, Russian, Chinese and other atomic physicists at his Pugwash (Nova Scotia) birthplace. Meanwhile MacArthur astounded a Los Angeles audience by urging America to take the initiative to abolish war, since no one could any longer win and the money spent on it might "abolish poverty." According to an *AP* report in *Le Monde*, "20 women fainted."

It was a year of tenth anniversaries of events dimly remembered. The anniversary month of Yalta brought ratification of Germany's brotherhood-in-arms with NATO and, from Washington, a tome of Yalta records to root Roosevelt's grand betrayal in history books. While the media overflowed with praise of this thesis, sound trucks toured Bangkok blaring, "No naked children allowed on streets this week. Thieves! Pickpockets! Please stay indoors." Foster Dulles was in town rousing enthusiasm for the freedom-preserving pact which Thailand, Pakistan and the Philippines had signed with five white governments. At home, AEC reported that it was turning out more than four times as many atomic devices as in 1950, and officials and the media began referring to the Hiroshima Bomb as "tactical."

Hardly anyone except Joe Polowsky of Chicago (who was there) recalled the April day 10 years ago when the triumphant American and Russian armies met in Europe and closed the ring on the Fascists. He was still trying, as he had every year, to arrange a commemorative reunion. Heretics' hard-dying faith in socialism revived as thousands streamed home from Stalin's camps and a global assortment of "imperialist agents," ranging from Tito to Anna Louise Strong, received Muscovite rehabilitation. But the CP could not bring itself to apologize to Strong, thereby increasing the exodus from the Party. Many members were leaving because, with Russia no more militarily vulnerable than its enemy, they no longer felt they should keep their criticisms of it to themselves.

While American arms spending soared, David Oistrakh and Emil Gillels were booked for concert tours: *Variety*, calling their appearances "biggest hypo to concert biz in 50 years," noted that ticket buyers could thus "show sympathy" for better Russo-American relations "without risking the accusation of being subversive." Ten years and a day after Potsdam the Russians returned to the conference table in rare concession-making mood; but since Dulles was convinced he had "positions of strength" in an obvious military stalemate, the conference could only produce a "euphoric hangover" (New York *Post*) from the fact that it was held. Later he would set forth to *Life* readers his "brink of war" philosophy—using the atomic threat—which had "saved peace" three times, in Korea, Indochina and Taiwan Strait. In fact America was already taking over France's "conventional" Indochina war, which would cost scores of billions and save nothing.

The UN's anniversary was marked in its birthplace by a sixth failure to deport Bridges, due to absent-minded witnesses, and in all America by a giant H-Bomb drill in which the government itself fled "31 ways" (*Wall Street Journal*). Eisenhower was rushed to a special hideaway and Dulles sheltered in New York's 21 Club. In Yankee Stadium the Yankees-Detroit Tigers game was interrupted for 23 minutes while crews pointed fire hose nozzles at the customers. Performing his "Operation Lemon Juice" duties of clearing the streets, a policeman asked a recalcitrant Bronx woman: "What would you do if it was the real thing?" "I wouldn't do anything," she replied, "I'd be dead." Muste, Dorothy Day and 27 other *Catholic Worker,* Fellowship of Reconciliation and War Resisters League heretics sat with "End War" signs on benches in City Hall Park. They would not budge and were arrested. A Mrs. Beck, one of their number whom the magistrate asked if she had ever been committed to an insane asylum, said: "No, have you?" She was led off to Bellevue's psychiatric ward and the others were held for trial in $1,500 bail.

Einstein saw humanity facing a "stark, dreadful, inescapable problem: Shall we put an end to the human race . . . choose death because we cannot forget our quarrels?" He joined Bertrand Russell and non-socialist scientists in a plea for the only way out—"to learn to think in a new way"—and died shortly after his friend Mann. When an appeals court ruled that Dulles could not deny Einstein's executor Otto Nathan a passport without specifying why, Dulles issued one rather than identify informants; but other heretics—and some people who were completely bewildered by the ban—were still grounded. Rockwell Kent became ECLC's right-to-travel test case along with psychiatrist Dr. Walter Briehl: Kent swore he was not a Communist to get a passport to paint in Ireland, and was told he might not go "to any country for any purpose." Twice investigated, he was as beyond intimidation as Scott Nearing, who at 71 remained America's most obstinate socialist. The Nearings grew a year's frugal food supply in six months on their Vermont farm and spent the other six writing and speaking to any American who would listen about the "folly, inefficiency, corruption and violence" of capitalism.

To mock the American Curtain, *Pravda* published cartoons of Lincoln being fingerprinted and books being burned and pointed out that Russia had neither fingerprinted William Randolph Hearst, Jr., nor asked if he was a capitalist on his recent Moscow visit. It did not mention that most Russians could neither travel abroad nor move freely around their own country. The travel bans sparked a special issue of the atomic scientists' *Bulletin* surveying aspects of the loyalty program, introduced by a repudiation of "Communists and fellow travelers" and a complaint that the inquisition "flings its net too widely." Taking the State Department as one example of the multipede inquisition, director Hans Morgenthau of the University of Chicago's Foreign Policy Study Center found that America's "series of ritualistic performances requiring human sacrifices" were "completely divorced from reality and reason." The "State Department clique deliberately working for the triumph of Communism in China" had never existed; and as the author of many foreign-policy documents, Morgenthau could recall none which a foreign power would have benefited by seeing—indeed, some might have helped Washington by deepening the foreign power's confusion. Spies might well seek to secure such documents but "the typical information obtained is either phony, irrelevant or public property"; in any case Morgenthau did not think the place to look for traitors was among ex-admirers of Roosevelt, or homosexuals, or people who had met Communists.

The *Bulletin* fixed as an American watershed the moment when almost everyone confronted with the first loyalty oaths agreed to sign them, thus conceding the principle of guilt pending proof of innocence. From that point the progression had been a natural one to 1955 when (as Spokane's *Chronicle* reported) loyalty oaths were required of "veterinarians who test cattle for Bang's disease." Other loyalty highlights of 1955 were a New York probe of children's summer camps, many of which were "maintained for clandestine meetings for high-level conclaves," and Massachusetts's extension of heresy-protection to dogs and cats: an animal hospital hired a ghettoized teacher—a direct descendant of Nathan Hale—and fired her on learning she had invoked the Fifth.

Post-McCarthy inquisitors indicated they had only just begun to fight the dragon. Communists in or out of jail, and the legless Trotskyist Kutcher, learned that their Social Security and war-disability pensions had been canceled. (The Veterans Administration requested the return of $9,781 already paid to the severe war casualty Saul Wellman, thoughtfully adding that "if it will cause you undue hardship to remit the full amount, you may liquidate the indebtedness by monthly payments.") Under the "membership" clause new Communist victims were arrested, old ones re-arrested as they completed sentences for conspiring to advocate. North Carolina Party chairman Junius Scales, descendant of a governor of the state and a wealthy banking family, was sentenced to six years for membership. At a trial four blocks from his birthplace two Chapel Hill professors and a local clergyman braved the McCarthy-style darts of the prosecution as Scales's character witnesses. His conviction was, however, assured when Lautner, who confessed he never met the defendant, took the stand to relate far-off subversive events when Scales was a child; and when an FBI man who had joined the local Party recalled one "Bob" demonstrating "how to kill a man with a pencil," and Scales remarking: "After the revolution we will shoot them."

The last attempt to deport Bridges was followed by a five-year sentence on Hugh Bryson of the defunct Marine Cooks union for Taft-Hartley perjury: he was not guilty of CP membership but of "affiliation," defined to the court as like "a man and woman living together without being married." For a first major application of his powers under the Communist Control Act to outlaw "Communist-infiltrated" unions, Brownell picked Mine-Mill, whose successful strikes had maintained an 80,000 membership despite inquisitions and loyal unions' raids.

Crouch's death eased the inquisition's task of tidying up after familiars who marred its image, but then Natvig followed Matusow into the contra-confessional. Quoting government lawyers as having told her, "All right, kid, let's murder the bum" (Lamb), she said she had "suddenly got out of the daze I was in" and now wondered how anyone but an idiot could have believed her testimony. Her reward was eight months for perjury in saying the government told her to lie. Matusow was a trickier problem, since his recantations affected the Lattimore, Sobell and other primary cases. Brownell promised a "vigorous inquiry" while the inquisition pondered two possible lines: that Matusow had "always been a Communist" and the Party planted him as a familiar, or that having been a truthful witness, Matusow then "fell into the hands of Communists" who plotted with him to obstruct justice by perjuriously saying he was a perjurer. SISS opted for the second thesis; HUAC's new chairman Walter was "thoroughly convinced" of the first but, when Matusow wired demanding the right to call himself a liar before HUAC, too wary to bite. The media were hesitant, especially the *Times* and *Time* which had been sitting for over a year on Matusow affidavits of having lied about their staffs. The Washington *Post* commented that, if Walter's theory was correct, a youth of "no great intellectual prowess" had "succeeded in completely defrauding the top Red investigators of both the legislative and executive branches of the Government."

To publicize his book Matusow invited to a press conference media heresy experts whom he had supplied with raw material, and who now felt personally betrayed. Their heckling brought the curtain down in an uproar. Their consolation was that the book had to be published by Cameron & Kahn, showing how effectively respectable firms had been intimidated. The hot potato was finally seized by SISS, which listened for two days to Matusow's revised version before closing in. Matusow said he had been "ready to do anything for a buck," that the same applied to his colleagues Budenz, Bentley, Chambers and Crouch, and that during his four Party years no word of violent-overthrow talk had reached his ears. Asked if he thought the CP "a real danger," he said: "Frankly, no." Eastland threw in a subpena for Sacher, the lawyer for several persons whom Matusow claimed to have falsely accused, and cited him for contempt in declining to discuss his politics. Sacher would be convicted and given six more months in jail.*

The media now had to agree that the inquisitors' use of Matusow had been "shocking." He was handed over for action to a grand jury, which, in passing, found grounds to indict the lawyer and assistant publisher of the *Nation*. (Matusow had paid them a call and they had allegedly conspired to obstruct justice by destroying or falsifying records of the meeting.) The grand jurors indicted Matusow for perjuriously claiming that Cohn had coached him as a witness in New York's 1952 Smith Act trial. SISS withheld the report on its Matusow probe until after an appeals court had confirmed Jencks's five-year sentence on Matusow's testimony, and Jencks's lawyers had filed a Supreme Court appeal.** In 1956 Matusow would receive the same sentence as Jencks, and thus the storm blew over.

---

* Sacher was disbarred (reversed in 1958) as well as jailed, and when he resumed law practice heretics under the gun logically felt that retaining him might harm rather than help their cause. Thus he was forced to take commercial cases affording him little interest but handsome fees. As with other heretics whose dedication had kept them poor, his ability soon made him prosperous. He knew considerably more law than most judges.
** While Matusow was testifying at the Jencks trial, "almost nightly I left my hotel room shortly after midnight. I went to Juárez (Mexico), where I changed character from

Perhaps the percentage of trouble-causing familiars was no greater than any inquisition should expect, but there were too few Philbricks. Rushmore had backed the wrong horse while in McCarthy's camp as "research director": McCarthy had estimated him as "one of the greatest living Americans," but he had fallen out with Cohn, who might now have helped him, and was used up as a witness and even as a Hearst red expert. He moved on to exposing citizens' sexual deviations in the peephole magazine *Confidential* with the same enthusiasm he had brought to exposing their political ones, but when one of the exposed sued *Confidential* an old habit. returned: he turned informer against his employers. He then began writing for "girly magazines," a task in which he was only disturbed by his wife, who claimed that he beat and threatened to kill her. Cvetic was hospitalized early in the year as an alcoholic. Pittsburgh's Foreign Born Committee thought this justified reopening of deportation cases in which Cvetic had testified, but his first engagement after discharge from hospital was to expose another obstreperous steelworker for SISS. He did poorly, for every word he said was denied by the steelworker: the script called for named heretics to refuse to answer. Drawing the conclusion that his work in Pittsburgh was now finished, Cvetic went to open up new fields in the far west where his lectures had not yet been heard.

Of the important familiars from early days, Philbrick alone remained free from tarnish. A Massachusetts lawyer sued him for an allegedly agreed cut of his profits, but heretics could find no deviations from the all-American norm to help discredit him. His experience confirmed the wisdom of a dull, earnest performance on the witness stand, keeping all but minimal adornments for peripheral and more lucrative fields. He had told SACB that he never reported to Hoover (thus presumably never saw) any act of violence by Communists, nor any Communist possessing arms, but the depiction of Communist murderers lent color to the TV version of his *I Led Three Lives*. *Time's* critic Jack Gould, while conceding Philbrick's book to be "a valuable volume," thought that the show overdid the "corny melodrama": for nearly half an hour it showed Philbrick "walking up and down streets looking furtively over his shoulder and momentarily expecting to be done in by the Reds." Loyal groups, however, rained congratulatory messages into the stations, and the show won a Freedoms Foundation award, putting Philbrick on a par with Foster Dulles, Medina and Billy Graham. It was exported to Europe, but TV customers there could not decide if they were supposed to take it seriously. Philbrick's *Herald Tribune* column sometimes got page-one play, as when he revealed in December "Cominform instructions" to the CP to "come out into the open" and the paper viewed this with alarm in an adjacent editorial. His simple but flawless method was to read the *Worker* and expose whatever it reported as the Party's latest secret activity; now he showed the secretiveness with which it had surfaced. "Reds are being told," he reported, "to install telephones with listing in phone directories" in CP offices which had been "long closed to public view. The national headquarters will be located at 268 Seventh Avenue, New York,

professional witness to burlesque comic in a night club." (*False Witness*). At his grand jury hearing in May 1955 he interspersed testimony about his tribunal inventions with claims to have "invented the stringless yo-yo" and an exhibition of how to make poodles out of pipe cleaners.

tel. no. OREgon 5–9250." The Party pointed out that it had been thus listed in the phone book for some three years.

Such rebuttals did not ruffle the *Herald Tribune,* which continued publishing Philbrick's revelations from places he visited on lecture tours. "The Communists in California," he reported from Los Angeles, "are as vicious a lot as you will find anywhere. The record is strewn with examples of violence, death, blackmail and other crimes including the trafficking in drugs from Red China." Praising loyal movie folk who "fought back" against the menace in the Motion Picture Alliance for Preservation of American Ideals, he noted that "three presidents of the organization died in office, all of them ostensibly from heart attacks . . . ostensibly, I say, because it is well known that the MVD [Russian political police] knows how to destroy enemies by means brutally impossible to detect." He warned that some blacklisted show folk were being secretly rehired by "certain subversives, well hidden in the 'capitalist' and management level of the industry." In the journal of the New York Folklore Society he detected dangerously kind remarks about Will Geer ("identified as a Communist"), about Martha Schlamme who had sung at Rosenberg rallies, and about the play *The World of Sholom Aleichem* in which "some of the cast have been publicly affiliated with Communist and Communist-front organizations." Worse, the Society had published an article by Seeger ("identified as a CP member . . . his records have received featured play in the *Worker*").

In HUAC's probe of AFTRA, Seeger rejected questions without invoking the Fifth. It emerged before the probe that AWARE's Hartnett had visited Walter to show his picture album with a shot of Seeger marching in the 1952 May Day parade. Walter summoned 27 actors, writers, directors and producers after an AFTRA majority condemned AWARE's interference and Actors Equity passed a similar resolution. Most of them (including Zero Mostel)* invoked the Fifth, but since they were already blacklisted thanks to several of the more repentant members of their trade, Seeger's citation—yielding a one-year jail term—was the main dividend for Walter. Seeger said he had "sung in hobo jungles and for the Rockefellers," intended to continue doing so for anyone he liked, and would be happy to strike up there and then the song "Wasn't That a Time?" which had been often and darkly mentioned in the hearing. Walter declined the free concert.** A

---

* By the mid-60s Mostel would be in greater demand than any star on Broadway; in 1968 the *Times* critic estimated him as possibly "America's greatest actor." "Old friends," who for years had been out when he phoned, lined up to congratulate him after the first night of *A Funny Thing Happened on the Way to the Forum,* when it was clear that he had emerged from the blacklist era to new success and prestige. They had qualified for his blacklist and he had them shown out.
** The song Walter would have heard (its words were entered as an "exhibit") ran: "Our fathers bled at Valley Forge/ The snow was red with blood/ Their faith was warm at Valley Forge/ Their faith was brotherhood/ Wasn't that a time, a time to try the soul of man?/ Wasn't that a terrible time? . . . And brave men died at Gettysburg/ And lie in soldiers' graves/ But there they stemmed the slavery tide/ And there the faith was saved/ Wasn't that a time? etc.) . . . The Fascists came with chains and war/ To prison us in hate/ And many a good man fought and died/ To save the stricken faith/ And now again the madmen come/ And shall our victory fail? There is no victory in a land/ Where free men go to jail/ Isn't this a time to try the soul of man, isn't this a terrible time? . . . Our faith cries out, They shall not pass/ We cry No Pasarán/ We pledge our lives, our honor/ All to free our native land/ Isn't this a time to free the soul of man/ Isn't this a wonderful time?"

similar Fifth-Amendment chorus came from 17 NLG lawyers formerly on the staff
of NLRB (including Nathan Witt, David Rein and Frank J. Donner), although
Boudin, now the chief champion of travel rights for heretics including himself,
denied being a Communist. As the AFTRA probe closed, blacklisted actor Philip
Loeb, once the famous "Papa Goldberg" of a nightly radio show, was found dead
in a New York hotel room. He had overdosed himself with sleeping pills.

A heavy work load faced SACB—five unions to be probed as soon as VALB,
NCASF, CRC and ACPFB were out of the way—but in March the behavior of
Washington state's ex-senator Harry P. Cain, who was assigned to probe the
Washington Pension Union, began causing embarrassment. Before the hearings
he appalled Brownell and his colleagues by defending the Fifth Amendment and
calling the Attorney General's list "warped and wormy." In the hearing room he
ruled frequently in favor of the defense against government lawyers' expostulations, and his attitude toward chief familiar Barbara Hartle was almost hostile.
(Hartle, a former Seattle Party official who had repented in jail and was brought
out whenever needed to provide names, testified that efforts to improve pensions
were a Communist plot to "undermine" the state by "mobilizing people into some
discontent.") This was the more alarming since Cain had publicly labeled PU a
"notorious Communist front," on which ground PU had requested his disqualifica-
tion from the tribunal. Finally a magazine article by Cain came like a square-dance
caller's cry to change positions: Brownell invited PU to repeat its previously
ignored request, PU declined, and Brownell himself now moved to disqualify
Cain. Cain related in the magazine how he had "awakened from a hideous dream
. . . felt shame rising in my throat." Communism had "become a plague [which]
broke the lives of many decent little people convicted by malicious rumor and
plain dirty lies." As for PU, it had struck him in midstream that many joined it
"because it worked for free milk and pensions."

Considering the mileage obtained down the years from the Dexter White
scandal, inquisitorial circles were gratified by the success of SISS's 1955 revival.
Apparently the media could never have enough of it. As SISS released a second
booklet on White's "world-wide espionage system," *U.S. News & World Report*
featured a "photostatic copy" of "the White Plan to Carve Up Germany . . . prepared in the office of Harry Dexter White." The new sensation consisted of excerpts from the diary of White's chief Morgenthau, showing how White not only
"participated in forming policies toward China that paved the way for that country's fall to Communists" but "is believed to have originated the plan to turn
Germany into a 'pasture,' which would have left Europe defenseless before Russia." The stage was set for the International Organizations Employee Loyalty Board
to reinvestigate Henry Taylor, a Bentley spy-ringer who had entered the International Monetary Fund about the same time as White and had already been
probed 19 times in eight years. He consistently denied ever being a Communist
or a spy or meeting Bentley, and kept demanding an opportunity (which neither
he nor anyone else would be afforded) to cross-examine Bentley publicly on 37 of
her most readily refutable "discrepancies." Among these were Russian plots to steal
data about an explosive which had been in global use since 1899, and to counter-
feit Allied occupation money in 1945 from samples to be filched for them by
White. The money having been printed as a joint American-British-Russian en-

terprise, this seemed little more probable than Bentley's oft-told tale of Washington heretics slipping the Russians "advance word of D-Day" at a time when Eisenhower himself did not know when it would occur.

Bentley spy-ringers William L. Ullmann and Edward Fitzgerald, the first to be tried under the "immunity" law castrating the Fifth Amendment, got six months each for contempt; Supreme Court justices were unmoved by their contention that the whole proceeding could be started again when they emerged, so that perhaps only the undertaker could free them from durance vile. Both insisted that if they were being punished on Bentley's charges they should have been tried for spying, but the possible discomfiture of bringing Bentley into court had evidently made this impractical. Ullmann would eventually "purge himself" by answering the questions, but Fitzgerald thus summed up his position: "Granted 'immunity' he does not want, for crimes he did not commit, the witness is securely impaled on the horns of a dilemma. Should he truthfully deny his guilt, Brownell can trot out paid informers who will fabricate a perjury charge. The only way for a witness to avoid a perjury charge is in fact to commit perjury." Fitzgerald went to jail; Taylor was cleared in 1956 with no comment from Hoover, Brownell or Eastland who had all publicly called him a spy.

The media reaction (almost zero) to the jailing of Belfrage without charges in May*—he was escorted from jail to a Britain-bound ship in August—promised that 1955 would be a prime year for the pursuit of journalists. After an appeals court upheld Moy's conviction (his jail term was later cut to a year), Brownell pressed his offensive against foreign-language editors. Immigration again summoned Los Angeles editor Diamond Kimm, who for years had been denouncing Rhee and trying to go to North Korea, to prove that Rhee would harm him if he were deported to South Korea. With several more alien editors walking the plank, SISS's Eastland probed infiltrators into the staffs of *Time* and the New York *Times, Post, News* and *Mirror.* The *Times,* which employed most of the victims, supported in principle the right to invoke the Fifth and set up its own preinquisition to fire staff men who said they would invoke it.** The Newspaper Guild, now a recipient of CIA aid, sat the affair out. All Fifth-invokers joined the unemployed except *National Guardian* editors McManus and Aronson, who apparently got their subpenas because they had been respectively president of the pre-CIA Guild and editor of its journal.

These events transpired against a background of unusual liveliness in Mississippi. White Mississippians determined to resist school desegregation as long as possible were fortunate in the possession of Eastland, who not only shared their views but bid fair to become America's top inquisitor. In May, while Eastland

* Stone in his *Weekly* was the only journalist to rise in fierce defense of "free press" principles in connection with the case. Frank Scully, papal knight and author of the *Fun in Bed* books for invalids, had left his sickbed to appear as a defense character witness before Immigration inquisitors, and ridiculed the deportation in his *Variety* column. As in other political deportations, courts of law declined to consider the case: the McCarran-Walter Act relieved them of any obligation to do so.
** Perhaps by way of antidote to its submission to the journalists' inquisition, the *Times* brought into the open in the same month the unhappy subject of American concentration camps. It described the camps which were being held in readiness in Allenwood, Pennsylvania, Avon Park, Florida, El Reno, Oklahoma, Tule Lake, California, and

traced the "monstrous crime" of the school ruling to the influence of "Communist-front groups," 12,000 blacks gathered to celebrate it in Mound Bayou, northwest Mississippi. There, inflammatory speeches were made about organizing to pay poll taxes and vote in the next elections. A clergyman who had already qualified urged others to follow suit. As he left for home, shots from a speeding car tore his face open and he died during the night. Another black voting enthusiast had already been eliminated in neighboring Belzoni. In a montage of rocks and bottles hurtling through Negro windows over a wide area, the sheriff called the murder "puzzling" but was sure a Negro did it and was questioning several.*

In June Mrs. Mamie Bradley of Chicago sent off her 14-year-old son Emmett Till to visit with relatives 30 miles from Mound Bayou. In August Emmett's remains, trussed in barbed wire, were found in the Tallahatchie River after two whites had accused him of "wolf-whistling" at the wife of one of them. The Chicago undertaker to whom Emmett was shipped said the face was beyond rebuilding into human semblance, but Mrs. Bradley insisted that the coffin be opened so that "people can see what they have to fight." A woman peered in and fainted, and Mrs. Bradley cried to her sobbing black neighbors: "See for yourselves what they might do to your son and make up your minds to put an end to it." Back in Mississippi the county attorney protested the "outside agitation" which had moved even Illinois's governor and senator to demand justice. Nobel laureate William Faulkner sent a message from Rome: "Perhaps the purpose of this sorry and tragic error committed in my native Mississippi is to prove to us whether or not we deserve to survive. If we have reached the point in our desperate culture when we must murder children, no matter for what reason, or what color, we don't deserve to survive and probably won't."

By late September a white jury was ready to acquit the two whites who threatened Emmett, after a reckless black sharecropper had testified to seeing them drag Emmett from a cabin toward the river at night. They admitted the dragging but not the killing. The defense asked Mrs. Bradley if she were sure the body she buried was Emmett's. She was, but the murder was found to have been a hoax by outside agitators. The formality of trying and acquitting the two whites for kidnaping brought the case to a close in October amid a global pandemonium of anti-American sentiments. Thousands could not crowd into the Paris protest meeting chaired by Josephine Baker and addressed by eminent Catholics, socialists and Africans. Michigan's black representative Charles Diggs, who had sat in the appropriate section of the murder-trial courtroom (someone asked: "Who's he?" "A Congressman." "Is that legal?"), announced on return that he would challenge

---

Florence and Wickenburg, Arizona. The more unattractive ones, it reported, were in hot waterless desert where bloodhounds would be available to pursue straying inmates. Even among heretics the view prevailed that the inquisition would not need to open the camps for business in the foreseeable future. The concentration-camp law remained on the books until the fall of 1971.

* At the same time a young Montgomery, Alabama, Negro awaited death for rape after 20 witnesses swore he was in another town on the day of the alleged crime. Georgia denied parole to Rosa Ingram and two of her children (she had ten more) in the seventh year of their life jail term, but after another four years they were considered to have expiated their crime of defending themselves (see footnote p. 82).

the seating of every Mississippi Congressman on the ground that blacks could not vote there and lived "under a virtual reign of terror."

Word from Hoover that he was investigating the whole situation, including denial of voting rights, assured loyal Americans that it was under control and they turned to other problems. But Dr. T. R. Howard, Mound Bayou's black hospital director and NAACP leader, vowed to "stay in Mississippi, armed with the Constitution and with God dictating my every move," to see justice done to his people. He had hardly expressed these sentiments when, again in Belzoni, a third Negro who wanted to vote was shot (but survived) and a Tallahatchie cotton-gin owner drew his gun on a black filling-station attendant who gave him the wrong amount of gasoline. ("I'm going to kill you," he said.)* Howard, who had posted a 24-hour guard outside his home, wired a second appeal to Brownell to "deal with this dastardly dangerous situation . . . Are you going to sit there and see us all killed one by one?" This brought to the zone of agitation two FBI men who, asked by a reporter how they were doing, said: "We made preliminary inquiries on Sunday and then we quit." (It was Monday.) Shortly afterwards Howard sold his home and moved his family to California. He told a Harlem rally en route that he wished there could be less talk about man's inhumanity to man behind the Iron Curtain and "something done about it in Mississippi.** But the FBI, which can pick up the pieces of a fallen plane on a mountain and find who caused the crash, can't find a white man who killed a Negro in the South." *Look* published an interview with the two whites in the Till case in which they talked of the killing in detail.

The induced hysteria about Communism had left the national NAACP too divided and impotent to spark active popular resistance in Dixie; and heretical organizations which might at least have made a louder noise were dead or dying under inquisitorial pressure. But in December Mrs. Rosa Parks started a black wave of the future by sitting in the white section of a Montgomery bus and refusing to move to where she belonged. Bombings and other customary techniques failed to stem the movement she had begun.

At the same time there was a detectable turn of the tide in white America, ascribable partly at least to the feeling in circles as far west as the *Times* and

---

* The filling station attendant's five children still had a mother, but not for long. On the day before the routine acquittal of her husband's accused killer—in the same court as the Till murder trial—a car in which she was riding "ran off the road into a swamp" and she was drowned.

** After years of upheavals in black ghettoes from coast to coast, northwest Mississippi's immemorial living conditions would come to New Yorkers' attention in 1968. A US Public Health Service doctor in Mound Bayou described to the *Times* "a tiny new American" whom he was attending, with "arms and legs the thickness of a man's little finger" due to "chronic malnutrition compounded by acute dehydration," typical of "hundreds" of cases in an area where 70% of houses had no water and "few have toilets." Another doctor observed that, on the small and still diminishing funds available, starved babies were being "saved only to sicken again, or to grow up beyond hope, an unwanted surplus on the rich land," or to "live in the lower depths" of a city ghetto: the medical mission was something like building a health center for a concentration camp. Since 1958 the county's infant mortality rate had grown by 25% for blacks and declined by 33% for whites, and 73% of adult Negro men had work for a few months in the year or none at all.

ADA that the inquisition was making America look ridiculous in the eyes of its free-world allies. For example, when New York's Education Board officially adopted the inform-or-go rule, the *Manchester Guardian* headlined: "INFORMERS WANTED, MUST BE ABLE TO TEACH." Lamont, who set up a Bill of Rights Fund to help a cross section of under-the-gun heretics, made some headway toward rescuing the First Amendment when—without ruling on the propriety of invoking it— a judge exonerated him of contempt for McCarthy.* (The government appealed the decision.) The judge trying ECLC chairman Harvey O'Connor for contempt of McCarthy waved aside as "not relevant" O'Connor's offer to repeat what he said outside the courtroom—that he was not a Communist—and O'Connor went home with a suspended jail sentence. A costly lawyers' team finally brought Lattimore's five-year nightmare to an end. In deference to the recantation of Matusow who had testified against them, two convicted Communists, Trachtenberg and Charney, were granted another trial (the judge, in allowing it, cleared government attorneys of any part in the fraud). A new alarm about churchly reds, this time from the US Air Force, stung Boston Unitarians into shouting down a motion to unfrock clergymen who invoked amendments. In Brooklyn, Melish's congregation fought their bishop to another standstill after changes in the vestry enabled him to appoint a respectable minister. A disreputable Sunday scene in Holy Trinity brought the struggle back to front pages: the new man trying to conduct a rival service after Melish had begun, and abandoning the field in face of the congregation's mutiny. The anti-Melish faction in the vestry now went back into court at the bishop's urging, but this and two further efforts to dislodge Melish failed and he continued as minister until the Holy Trinity war reached its climax in 1957.**

Recalling that it was the 166th anniversary of the Bill of Rights, 360 intellectuals signed an *amicus curiae* brief asking the Supreme Court to declare the McCarran Act unconstitutional. Most of the signers had appeared on occasional dubious letterheads but never been summoned for probing. Signers of an Open Letter to the American People, which followed it, included such certified Russophobes as union leaders Jacob Potofsky and A. Philip Randolph, Roger Baldwin, Donald Harrington, Granville Hicks, Archibald MacLeish, B'nai B'rith president Philip M. Klutznick and NAACP's Joel E. Spingarn. The letter complained of

---

* In an *Assault on Academic Freedom* pamphlet Lamont quoted Meiklejohn on why people of scholarly tendencies became Communists: "Undoubtedly some are hysterically attracted by disrepute and disaster. But in general the only explanation that fits the facts is that these scholars are moved by a passionate determination to follow the truth where it seems to lead, no matter the cost to them and their families." With respect to group discipline, Lamont maintained that "the Audubon Society would not tolerate as a member a man addicted to shooting down birds," and CP discipline was no more severe than that of the Roman Catholic Church.

**During 1956 the pro-bishop faction in the Holy Trinity war had locks changed on the church, employed a private detective, summoned the police, and released a press report (a fabrication according to Melish) of a Melishite parishioner felling a bishopite with his fist. When a court finally granted the bishop's plea to fire Melish in 1957, the flock gave its new pastor so icy a reception that Holy Trinity had to be closed two weeks later. Melish and his father remained in the rectory until a court order ousted them in 1958. Melish became a salaried official of SCEF and, after ten years, would be permitted to preside over another parish.

"nine evils" ranging from the care and protection of familiars to loyalty oaths, passport denials and the guilt-by-association principle "now extended to family relationships." The 83 signers felt that "changes in world relationships" not only made it possible to stop "savage and sustained assaults at our traditional liberties" but presented an "opportunity to focus calmly." Muste persuaded Mrs. Roosevelt, Norman Thomas and Elmer Rice to join Commager and others in a Christmas amnesty plea for Communists in jail. The exercise (coinciding with a trial of 11 Communists in the Free Commonwealth of Puerto Rico, who complained of "inquisition without representation") had no effect, but on its repetition in 1956 hundreds more respectable names would be appended.

Some stirrings occurred among young Americans drafted into the army, who were confronted with forms listing all heretical groups of the past several decades, by now a formidable mass of print. Each newcomer to the armed defense of democracy must swear he never had any connection with any of them. The form advised him that he "may invoke the Fifth" to decline, but it was no secret that anyone accepting this invitation would never rise above private's rank. In any event if "data" came in about him or any of his family or circle while serving, the army's inquisition would cross-examine him before discharge. "Less than honorable" discharge, depriving him of all benefits and barring him from government employment, could result if he failed to disprove that he read the *Nation* ("infiltrated with Party policy") or "associated" with his own parents. Eight GI's brought suit against the Pentagon challenging the army's right to haunt them throughout their employable lives with such discharge papers.

In November there was a change of tempo in the Senate caucus room which had been the scene of many McCarthy melodramas. The upsurges of unrest had given birth to an *ad hoc* committee chaired by Missouri Senator Thomas C. Hennings, empowered to investigate whether anyone's free-speech or free-assembly rights had been infringed. The hearings perhaps reflected Establishment fears that other inquisitors had not learned the lesson of McCarthy's demotion. For the first time in years some heretics were heard respectfully with no threats of contempt or perjury citations. Brownell was invited to attend but was too busy. Meiklejohn and Chafee made strong statements to the effect that the Bill of Rights meant what it said. Pauling related his two years of being denied a passport, getting a limited one too late, never knowing if he could accept conference and lecture invitations from abroad; finally getting a flat denial, on suspicion of being a "secret Communist"; just before he won the Nobel Prize and Dulles gave in. He had sworn six times that he had Never Been, he told Hennings, and that was enough: "Nobody tells me what to think except Mrs. Pauling," and he would continue saying what he thought when he liked.

In the innocuous atmosphere of the hearing, all present permitted themselves laughter at the buffooneries of passport chief Mrs. Ruth B. Shipley and State Department security chief Scott McLeod. State officials made glum appraisals of the heretic registration law under which nobody had, and apparently nobody ever would, register. A Delaware police captain said he had listened to 30 hours of lectures by Budenz but still didn't know how to detect forcible overthrowers. Hennings asked how many he had caught and he said: "The net must be full of holes, we haven't caught any." On the question of sabotage cases during America's last two wars, a UAW lawyer said there had been none. An army private told how, having refused on religious grounds to swear a loyalty oath, he had been put in a room with an unknown GI and a year later accused of "close and continuous association with a Communist" (his compulsory roommate). Another had been caught in the Army's inquisitorial net because his mother-in-law was "reported lying low as a Communist"; the lady had died 15 years previously, he said, when he was 11 and his future wife 6. The Civil Service Commission chairman said he had 2,000,000 dossiers on heretical suspects who might some day apply for a government job, and that he had approved 3,865 firings under Eisenhower's security program. Pressed to define a security risk, he said: "Frankly I don't know."

From a remote stance on the sidelines McCarthy called the hearings "disgraceful and dangerous; [they] would open the floodgates to wholesale Communist infiltration of the government."* Nothing decisive came from Hennings' genial probe. The flood, though slightly abated, continued pouring through the gates in the same direction as before.

---

* Except for reports that he was drinking himself to death, little was heard of McCarthy in 1955. On one of his rare Senate interventions he denounced the conference with the Russians as another "tragic blunder like Yalta and Potsdam." Majority leader Knowland, confident that "the distinguished senator from Wisconsin" yearned for "a free world of free men," besought him to have more faith in an America which had Eisenhower, Dulles and the Bomb.

Fever Chart

1955

"The Communists are flooding Cairo newsstands with American 'girly' magazines in a subtle scheme to make Arabs believe all Americans are immoral. At the same time they are distributing Russian magazines emphasizing sports and science. An investigation revealed that it is one more phase of the Red plot to besmirch America and win friends for Russia."—Denver *Post*.

"GI's serving overseas are exposed to 'appalling' immoral practices in dope pushing, prostitution and 'shacking up,' the National Lutheran Council has been told in Atlantic City. The Rev. Dr. Carl F. Yaeger said military authorities were convinced the Communists were back of the demoralization of our overseas personnel."—New York *Post*.

"The Communist loves nothing better than to be arrested. But he is not like the martyr for the faith. St. Joan of Arc did not like being tied to a stake; a Communist does."—Bishop Sheen in Buffalo *Courier-Express*.

"C. B. DeMille is listening to taped speeches by General Van Fleet [US commander in Korea] with a view to using Van Fleet as the voice of God in Paramount's *Ten Commandments*."—Hollywood dispatch to *Newsweek*.

"In a resolution adopted by the delegates at the closing business session the Council called for 'immediate removal' of Dr. D. Elton Trueblood, director of religious information for the US Information Agency. It charged he is using his position to promote 'peaceful co-existence' policies."—Memphis *Commercial Appeal* report on American Council of Christian Churches assembly.

New York: Dr. S. K. Smith writes in *Annals of the NY Academy of Sciences* on "The Use of Reserpine in Private Psychiatric Practice."

"The intensity of recurrent compulsion has been diminished after the onset of medication. It would be difficult to express in medical terminology the nature of the sequence more tersely than did one patient, recently a State Department member. He remarked: 'Co-existence is possible now.' He was beginning to appreciate the value of tranquillity, insight and accessibility personally, if not internationally."

"Only an unusually 'moronic or imbecilic' businessman will fail to attain success under the conditions that will prevail in the next 25 years. All manufacturers of consumer goods and services just HAVE to prosper barring imbecility, according to sociology Professor Hauser. He said that the only serious threat to our economy is peacetime."—*Advertising Age*.

Nevada: *Women's Wear Daily* reports on nuclear test using dummy homes and people.

"In a story from 'Doom Town,' Nevada, which described the effects of a big atomic explosion on fully clothed mannequins, it was erroneously stated that 74 mannequins were supplied by the J. C. Penney Co. The L. A. Darling Co., Chicago, informs us that this company 'furnished at our own expense a great many mannequins to be used to dramatize the human element of life in homes under atomic attack.' About 60 were fiber glass (all children and misses), men models were of papier mache, and babies (one month and six months) were composition rubber. The mannequins were dressed in merchandise from J. C. Penney Co."

"When Santa made these up, he was in a generous mood indeed—for they're the biggest dollar's worth we've ever seen. The huge 24-inch red net stockings are joy-packed with toys! Boy's stocking has an H-bomb and target . . ."—New York Xmas gift catalog.

New York: DuBois speaks after new wave of black eliminations in Mississippi.

"To your tents, Americans! We have gone far enough into this morass of fear, war, hate, lying and crime. For the time being, never mind about the Soviet Union; forget China; ignore Germany. Come back home and look at America. What are we going to do about it? Set your own house in order before you try to rule the world!"

XXII

1956: "We Need

To Discuss Ourselves"

Events behind the Curtain in 1956 reduced to its lowest point the morale of American heretics. The gloom produced by Khrushchev's report on mass liquidations under Stalin was deepened when a rebellion in Hungary, a formerly Fascist country socialized 12 years before, was suppressed by Russian tanks. Heretics with a deep investment of faith in Russia found the details of Stalin's terror beyond belief. By the time they had adjusted to the fact that it was true, whole Party organizations had fallen apart. Fast wrote of Stalin's "paranoiac bloodlust" in a final column for the *Worker*. Some heretics decided that if this was socialism, almost any brand of capitalism was preferable; others, that the corruption of socialist arguments made them no less valid. Jailed and blacklisted screenwriter Trumbo reminded a *National Guardian* audience that, while the Left had been trapped for two decades in the Russian orbit, so had Establishment groups, for the Soviet's "mere existence has been the most compelling fact of modern history." He looked for the rising of a "New Left" which would be stronger on humility and logic, weaker on "emotion, invective and empty rhetoric."

Overthrow of the government, in any case, was more than usually improbable when America moved toward relaxing the inquisition; and the relaxation, reflected mainly in high-court decisions, was modest under the circumstances. The Supreme Court denied Sobell a new trial and upheld the "immunity" law enabling Fifth-Amendment invokers to be jailed, but agreed to re-weigh the Smith Act* and the State Department's firing of John Stewart Service. Other decisions carried a note of reproof for over-zealous inquisitors. Having used Matusow, Crouch and Manning Johnson in its probe, SACB was asked to re-evaluate with more sanitary witnesses whether the CP should register as Communistic. (SACB did so and reached the same conclusion.) An appeals court voided a jail sentence on UAW organizer John Watkins, a non-Communist who would not discuss his friends. The decision questioned "whether exposure of individuals to public contempt is a valid legislative purpose"—a hint that Congressional inquisitors should at least seem more concerned about their official purpose of framing laws.

A voice was heard proposing that the judicial authors of this admonition be probed and exposed. It was only McCarthy, but indignation was general in Congress against the trend, which, said former Secretary of State Byrnes, was "bringing joy to Communists." By May some 70 bills had been introduced to curb the

---

* Madison's *Capital Times* compounded its readers' confusion by a comment on this which echoed the Party line for the past 16 years: "The Founding Fathers believed in forcible overthrow of government, preached it and fought a war for it . . . Under the Smith Act, Washington and Lincoln would have gone to jail."

Supreme Court. Local inquisitors were up in arms against the nullification of all except federal heresy laws.

The trend showed, in fact, that the Establishment was withdrawing to previously prepared positions in the domestic cold war. Inquisitors had been given their heads up to a point just short of abolishing the Bill of Rights. But the national totem, albeit battered and bewilderingly reinterpreted, was the glory of the democratic inquisition and only needed the formulations of up-to-date ideologues to remain so. The Dulles ideology had done yeoman short-term service, and the more sophisticated long-term one was taking shape and root. John Galbraith's *Affluent Society* further developed his thesis that giant monopoly corporations were the best basis of democracy, even if they must fatten on heresy hunts, dollar-induced corruption and the preparation of holocausts.* The intelligentsia rallied overwhelmingly to Galbraith as against Wright Mills, the brooding dissenter who saw democracy being buried in American earth by *The Power Elite.* Mills was haunted by the power of the "corporate rich" to make such decisions as the atomization of a city in the name of a public who did not even know the decision was being made.**

But America had raised an army of inquisitors, and while there was no serious thought of abolishing them, they reacted predictably to the apparent threat to their economy and way of life. The federal heresy-prosecution monopoly alone aborted years of patient work by local men. In addition to relieving Nelson of his 20-year jail term under Pennsylvania's law, the decision compelled Kentucky to vacate the Braden convictions for sedition in buying a house. Kentucky persevered with the prosecution of Bown for blowing up the house, but failed again, dashing hopes of inquisitorial glory for Hamilton who could claim credit for one of America's most effective waves of community hysteria. The same applied to New Hampshire inquisitor Wyman, although his efforts to jail the religious heretic Willard Uphaus would succeed. Uphaus was running a rural World Fellowship resort for peacemongers with or without churchly connections, and invoked the still-unrecognized First Amendment in declining to give Wyman the guest list.

Massachusetts had to drop the sedition charges against Struik, but no one could deprive its Special Commission on Communism of the right to continue probing him after MIT decided he could be rehired. Convening just after Russia's intervention in Hungary, the Commission had a new have-you-stopped-beating-your-wife question to ask him: "Weren't you horror-stricken at what your comrades in Hungary were doing to the Hungarian people?" MIT's chancellor was summoned to swear he had Never Been, an FBI man to prove Struik's Communism from his NCASF and other activities, and Philbrick to recall how "very well" he

---

* Later Galbraith would indicate some doubts on this point.
** Mills disliked both the affluent society and Russian socialism—as a serious student of Marxism, the former more than the latter. Concentrating on the development of his theories almost alone, he was never detected in active heresy. A rare mention of his name occurred in Walter's 1956 report on the plot to amend the McCarran-Walter Act. He was also contemptuous of the intelligentsia for their harping on America's alleged moral superiority and disregard of Moscow's economic challenge: he thought intellectuals should behave like internationalists. His pessimism about democracy's future, slightly relieved by the Cuban revolution of 1959, stemmed from awareness of the problem of bigness as such, whether of capitalist corporations or of socialist administrative bureaus.

knew the Marxist professor. "Is this a circus?" asked Struik, who had long since made public that he was not a Communist and hardly knew Philbrick by sight. His question fell as flat as his comment on Philbrick's TV melodramas: "If anything of the sort were true the jails would be filled with Communists under accusation of arson, rape, counterfeiting, spying and so forth. As far as I know there are no Communists in jail on such charges." Philbrick's reminiscences of Struik filled most of the Commission's report in 1957, but Struik remained at MIT.

While the Supreme Court prepared to re-evaluate conspiracy-to-advocate cases, Brownell pressed on with "membership" prosecutions and won a five-year sentence in Buffalo for steel-union organizer and ex-Party official John Noto. An FBI man had heard Noto say, "The capitalist class is its own gravedigger," and Lautner was present to show that books read by Noto could only lead to such disloyal conclusions. Under the same clause former Johns Hopkins professor Dr. Albert Blumberg, whose wife was already in jail for conspiracy to advocate, was convicted in Philadelphia. This time Lautner was teamed with Mary Markward and a Baltimore teacher who recalled Blumberg advocating violence over lunch in 1941. Hoover had worked up fair headlines in the case ever since his men "seized Blumberg on a Manhattan street corner as an underground Red" *(Times)* in 1954. Blumberg, Hoover revealed, had been "working secretly out of the Party's national headquarters at 278 Seventh Avenue," having "started operating underground in 1949." Defense witness John Somerville, an independent philosopher-educator specializing in Marxism, patiently sought to unscramble prosecution sophistries about Marxian passages read in court, with the usual non-results. An attempt to shift the spotlight to Blumberg's own writings, which said nothing about violence, failed when the prosecution denied there was any proof that Blumberg wrote them.*

Where relaxations came, they came in grudging crumbs. Heretics' pensions were restored on pre-1952 earnings as a result of a press storm over nonpayments to the family of familiar George Hewitt (d. 1952). Untested tenants were allowed in government-aided housing projects after a four-year effort by Washington to prevent it. New York's education commissioner said that teachers did not have to inform on each other after all, and the Supreme Court denied Brooklyn College's right to have fired German professor Harry Slochower for invoking the Fifth in 1952. But Brooklyn president Harry D. Gideonse, a disciple of Hook, immediately vowed to resuspend Slochower, and Moskoff promised that his inquisition would continue as before. The Slochower decision seemed to be a precedent, but other Fifth-invoking teachers found it was not: even those who had answered questions about themselves were not reinstated. Many school boards around the country indicated they would emulate Gideonse and Moskoff. The purge had become a habit and it would take more than a few vague rulings to shake it.

TU went into its 40th fighting year with undimmed exhilaration and a commendation on its "stand against tyrannic stupidity" from the partially blind play-

---

* A bright farewell footnote on the use of Marxist books to convict American heretics: By 1967 International, preening itself as "prime publisher of Marxism-Leninism for over 42 years," would be advertising *Das Kapital* (of which Americans had burned thousands of copies hoping to allay Hoover's suspicions) in a full-page *Times* advertisement.

wright Sean O'Casey in Cornwall. "In a way," he wrote to Rose Russell, "it's amusing to think of the manner innocent people are harried while the greatest subversionist has to go free forever; for the greatest subversionist is life herself, changing everything as she goes through Time, cuckolding the McCarthys." Buds of resistance showed faintly green on some campuses after a decade of student silence broken mainly by "panty-raids" on girls' dormitories. Forbidden by the regents to write on political issues, editor Willie Morris* of Texas University's student journal was leaving blank spaces with the explanation, "This editorial deemed too controversial." Campaigns were reported at Williams and Allegheny Colleges to bring in "controversial" black and Jewish students, and at New York's City College against "screening" rules for campus political groups. Students chose a black campus beauty queen at Iowa State, and a ban on playing football against a team with a black fullback caused a riot at Georgia Tech. Campus support was widespread for Autherine Lucy's right to study at Alabama University.

Something in the climate was making American youth unhappy. Juvenile delinquency arrests had risen by 50% since 1945, and a Senate committee probing this was told that 1,250,000 young people were "in trouble" every year. Committee chairman Kefauver pointed a finger at black slum ghettoes and thought that "stresses and strains of the cold war and Korea," and violence breeding counterviolence, might be relevant to the problem. He could not suggest how anyone might actively oppose these trends without the brand of heresy. Soon after the committee disbanded, America reaffirmed its readiness for World War III with the annual holocaust rehearsal and in New York the little band of *Catholic Worker* heretics went to jail for declining to "take cover." Dorothy Day told the magistrate that next year she would repeat the crime, and her colleague Ammon Hennacy said he would consider the sojourn in jail as "penance for my and my country's sins." A peripatetic one-man picketer against the obligation to pay taxes for extermination devices, Hennacy claimed the broadest short-term jail experience of any living American, beginning with his refusal to fight in World War I.

Inquisitors learned that the problem of imaginative overflights by familiars was shared by colleagues in Germany, where for two years detectives had hunted dozens of spies named by a Frankfurt *fraulein*. She had begun inventing them to avert the consequences of arrest for not paying her night club drink bill. "They were all so eager to hear my fairy tales," she explained when the spy hunt proved abortive; "I wanted to keep them happy." But America's most wayward familiar Matusow, minus 80 pounds accumulated in the lush years, began a five-year sojourn in prison for his betrayal.** ("A high-ranking Government official expressed relief," the *Times* reported.) And at last the reluctant Bella Dodd was naming scores of heretics in organizations ranging from the CP to the Young Republicans. SISS's Jenner thanked God that she was "willing to pay the tremendous price"

---

* Later editor of *Harper's;* resigned from that post in 1971 in a "dispute between the money men and the literary men."

** On his release Matusow settled in London where, in 1970, the *Observer* ran a photo of a dimly lit girl standing on a wall-to-wall air pillow with this caption: "What the visitor cannot see: inside Dark Touch, an exhibition organized by Harvey Matusow at the New Arts Lab, in which the enthusiast enters singly a totally dark tunnel filled with objects and fumbles from one end to the other with the help of a guide rope."

of testifying, and McCarthy interjected a "compliment for her courage. She is going to subject herself to a great deal of abuse, and I think it is a wonderful thing."

A promising new familiar emerged in Pittsburgh's 73-year-old Alexander Wright, who could not only reminisce about 13 years in the movement (for which Hoover had paid him $27,856.25) but had the added advantage of being black. On his debut at the Cleveland Smith Act trial in 1956 Wright did well—although the Cleveland jury only found 7 out of 11 defendants guilty—and there was hope that he would rescue Brownell from his dilemma in the Pittsburgh Smith Act case. The dilemma was caused by Mazzei, who had given the most dramatic testimony against Nelson and his accomplices but began to look like a cross between a Crouch and a Matusow. The Pittsburgh Communists had acquired, especially from Mazzei's testimony at the Newman trial in Miami, deadly ammunition for their high-court appeal which was now pending. At the same time Mazzei's loose talk in Miami about his FBI days could hardly be allowed to pass unnoticed by his employers. He had not only repeated that they told him to plead guilty to a. and b. with the waitress, but claimed that they put him in the Army to spy on a Communist and paid him $1,000 a month expenses.

Mazzei seemed to realize that his days were numbered, for in mid-1955 he had testified in court: "If you notice, I developed the attitude that I don't give a damn about this stuff any more. Frankly, I was better off when I knew Communists—I thought I had more friends. I would rather be outside now walking in the rain and getting wet." In any case the Justice Department saw him as expendable for the sake of salvaging the last Nelson conviction. It decided to get in ahead of the Pittsburgh Smith Act defense with a plea to the Supreme Court listing some of Mazzei's inexactitudes. The plea, signed by the US Solicitor General, set forth that Hoover's organization had neither put Mazzei in the Army nor told him to say he committed a. and b., and that it had paid him a total of $172.05 expenses since 1942; nor could the Department "corroborate" murder, invasion and other plots outlined by Mazzei in Miami. The Department added that none of this diluted its confidence in the accuracy of Mazzei's narrations about Nelson and Company, but "the interests of justice would best be served" by a probe of Mazzei.

This was essentially the same hairsplitting exercise that had succeeded with Matusow and Natvig: up to this point the familiar was truthful, then suddenly he turned liar. But the plea so embarrassed the Supreme Court that in one afternoon it declared all 5,147 pages of Pittsburgh Smith Act testimony null and void. The Department had to start again from scratch, and Wright was the obvious man to use at a new trial. But ill luck continued to dog the case: before the retrial could be set, Wright too would blow up. At a SACB hearing in Pittsburgh, lawyer Hyman Schlesinger (whose disbarment had been under well-publicized consideration since 1950, virtually ghettoizing him professionally) would ask him to identify his writing on a handwritten MS. Wright did so, and the MS proved to be an "autobiography" of such alarming obscenity that SACB refused to enter it in the record. The hearing was abruptly canceled, the Pittsburgh retrial never took place, and Wright was left with unlimited time for his literary work.

In the Washington backlash against the relaxation, SACB inquisitor Cain, of course, had to go. He was the ugly duckling of a dedicated body of men who, patiently probing heretical groups one by one, had twice found the CP Communistic and could confirm by 1956 that NCASF favored friendship with Russia. Cain wound up his service ordering PU to register as subversive, but his heart was not in it. He did it in the last stages of "mental anguish," he said, and left urging repeal of the McCarran Act to which SACB owed its existence. After many efforts to get to Eisenhower through the White House entourage who "feed him only varnish," Cain had spent 45 minutes expounding his disenchantment with the inquisition to the President. Eisenhower, however, had already made his position clear in an April speech to newspaper publishers, calling for a return to the spirit of 1776. Cain moved into semi-ghettoized status in a small flat for which his wife worked to pay the rent.

HUAC's year was characterized by Walter's irritation at criticism of his and McCarran's immigration law, an omnibus document setting rules not only for ejecting bodies from America but for how many from what countries should be allowed in. In drafting the law the two inquisitors had shown common concern to "keep America white" by cutting immigration quotas from pigmented countries. But immigration quotas were also an issue involving the votes of white national-minority groups, and no less than 78 amendment bills were offered by Congressmen who needed the votes. McCarran having passed on, Walter bore the whole brunt of the attacks on their joint legislative masterpiece, and the unmasking of red influences behind them was a spiny task of which he remained mindful throughout his 1956 probing tours. His concern for an appropriately colored America was manifested in Los Angeles where, in the spring, he exposed a musicians' plot to bring black colleagues into their union local. Later he acquired for $16,000 a year the services of SISS's former chief counsel Arens who, according to certain columnists, was receiving $3,000 a year from a New York millionaire as "consultant" on researches to prove the genetic inferiority of Negroes.

Walter was also reported to be cooperating in these researches, but his work showed that he was less obsessed than Eastland with the black aspect of the conspiracy. In June he summoned Mrs. Florence Gowgiel of the Argo, Illinois, Save Our Sons Committee to account for her group's petition to Eisenhower in 1953 to end the Korean holocaust. An FBI man pointed out that this was the Party line at the time, and the beauty-shop operator invoked the Fifth on whether she wrote to her Congressman, what were her politics, what she read, whom she knew and why; but a Chicago *News* reporter found her "not well cast for her role as a villainess," and no citation resulted. The more notorious peacemonger Robeson was also called in to explain his remarks to international heretics in Paris in 1949. Robeson thought everyone should understand by now what he had said and continued saying: that the world's colored peoples were "not going to die" to keep whites affluent, only for their own independence. Walter's gavel was impotent against the black giant's crescendo of denunciations of the Mississippi murders and Eastland's "truly un-American activities." "You want to shut up every Negro who stands up for his rights," Robeson thundered; "you ought to be ashamed of yourselves." After an unproductive hour Walter said: "I've stood about as much of this as I can—the session is adjourned." Robeson said, "You should adjourn this forever," and was unanimously cited for contempt.

The Robesons were still passportless*—he was sending concerts to Europe by tape—and Negro journals otherwise cool to them ascribed this to the desire to prevent them speaking their minds abroad on Eastland and Mississippi. Walter's interest in the travel situation brought before him many grounded heretics whose testimony, he felt, added up to "a skillfully organized passport conspiracy"—presumably to obtain the denied documents on the plea that any citizen was entitled to one. Among those summoned was ECLC's Clark Foreman, who was cited for contempt. Connecticut businessman Henry Willcox was accused of treason for the action which lost him his passport, attending a peace conference in Peking. He said his ancestors came to New England in 1620 "dreaming of freedom and peace," and he had gone to Peking to see what hope there was.** Others involved in the plot were Otto Nathan and Arthur Miller—a delicate case since Miller had just married the international sex symbol, actress Marilyn Monroe. In view of this development Miller got a six-month passport in July, while the State Department continued banning his plays in USIS centers and in the American pavilion at Brussels fair. During a honeymoon constantly pursued by media sex-symbol experts, Miller learned that a 373-to-9 Congressional majority had voted contempt citations for him, Nathan, Seeger and actor Elliott Sullivan. Miller had answered 198 questions to HUAC's satisfaction but balked at two relating to other persons. He would not name his companions at a Communist writers' meeting he attended in 1947.

With understandable caution since this was multimillionaire territory, both SISS and HUAC moved into the scandal around Hutchins's Fund for the Republic. Hutchins, while an imposing enough figure to be entrusted with surplus Ford dollars, had long aroused inquisitorial suspicion by his actions, contacts, and statements which might superficially appear whimsical. (For example, he had suggested that all universities should be "burned down every 25 years lest they get in a rut," and that no faculty members should be fired "except for rape or murder committed in broad daylight before three witnesses.") His circle included people

---

* Eslanda Robeson had had her own session with McCarthy in 1953 in which the following dialogue occurred:

McC: Are you a member of the Communist Party?

ER: I decline to answer under the protection given me by the Fifth and Fifteenth Amendments [citizens' right to vote not to be denied or abridged on account of race, color or previous condition of servitude]. The committee is very white; as a Negro I am discriminated against and treated like a second-class citizen, so I need the Fifteenth too.

McC: All who testify before this committee are equal. The committee is white because there are no Negro senators.

ER: That's part of the discrimination. Most Negroes are in the South where force and violence prevent them from voting freely, if at all.

McC: Wouldn't you agree that Negroes have made progress since slavery?

ER: No, I think they've gone backwards . . . In my grandfather's time there were Negro senators. Grandfather himself was Secretary of State and of the Treasury for South Carolina.

** The ban on going to see what went on in China was absolute; the country continued to exist only on Taiwan. China offered visas for 15 American press correspondents in August but Dulles warned that anyone accepting could be jailed for five years. In December *Afro-American* correspondent William Worthy defiantly crossed the border from Hong Kong, the first American newsman to enter China since Chiang fled. He returned to trouble but was never jailed.

of similarly dubious stripe such as Stringfellow Barr and Scott Buchanan, former president and dean of St. John's College, who had introduced the "great books program" idea there in 1937 and in 1948 founded a World Government Foundation with $1,000,000 from Anita Blaine.

When the F. for R. issued a mild but liberally documented critique of the heretic blacklist, after awarding $5,000 to Plymouth Meeting for having hired Mary Knowles, the first salvos were fired by Winchell and the Legion. Budenz's testimony that all foundations were Communist-infiltrated and supporting "socialist trends" raised eyebrows in foundation circles dedicated, now as ever, to channeling their largesse to Establishment-strengthening institutions. The storm around Hutchins became cyclonic when he said he "wouldn't hesitate to hire a Communist if he was qualified." The New York *Post* found "murky logic" in his philosophy of hiring on merit rather than politics, and Woltman riposted on the air: "Would you also hire a Nazi?" Hutchins said America was "hiding behind a cliche curtain, a veil of slogans and illusions that separates us from reality"; the Bill of Rights too was joining the illusions since legal moves to apply it were so arduous and costly as to be "for all practical purposes useless."

Hutchins's scholastic prestige and sharp tongue would hardly have stopped McCarthy from subpenaing him, but the inquisitors in office felt more comfortable recalling Mary Knowles and probing John Cogley, former editor of the Catholic journal *Commonweal* and compiler of the F. for R.'s *Report on Blacklisting*. The issue in the Knowles affair was rhetorically put to Congress by Tennessee Rep. Carroll Reece: "What is going on in this country when we cite and award known Communists and traitors with praise and checks for $5,000 of tax-exempt money?" Knowles told SISS she was not a Communist, but still balked at "purely personal" questions and had nothing to tell about "subversion, sabotage, espionage or violent overthrow." She would be convicted on 52 contempt counts and sentenced to jail. Testimony to HUAC by *Counterattack's* Francis McNamara (which Walter found "refreshing—they have no axes to grind") and by AWARE's Hartnett and Schmidt made it clear that Cogley had reported on a hallucination. All that existed was "preclusion" of "hard-core Communists" from employment. Arens put it to Cogley that *Commonweal's* Catholicism was a heretical masquerade, that the *Report* was suspiciously kind to the blacklisted and that tainted persons had provided the material.

Cogley left the hearing with satisfactory stains on his—and, by more than implication, on Hutchins's—character; and Walter turned to Plymouth Meeting with an assurance that, although "Communists and their dupes" would doubtless so distort it, this was no "interference with the great freedom of religion." Four members of the Quaker community turned up to agree with Walter that Knowles was a menace, but its library committee chairman appeared without the records she was subpenaed to produce. All she brought were minutes of a majority vote to "deny" the order, since "it has no doubt escaped your attention that this is a religious society." Some Quakers later wrote HUAC that they found "utterly incredible" its "apparent intention to judge the actions of our Meeting, which we reserve to ourselves to judge," and that the probe, with its "deliberate cultivation of hearsay testimony which fitted their thesis," was "a mockery of the idea of inquiry." At their next annual gathering in Philadelphia the Friends would recall that their Society's radicalism had always aroused persecution, but that from earliest days they had ignored bans on their meetings and refused to take an oath directed against Roman Catholics, "similar to the loyalty oath directed against Communists today." They objected then and still to the oath "not only because of Christ's command against swearing but also because of its futility," and long before the Fifth Amendment existed they had refused to answer questions in court. Now they reaffirmed "every man's right to believe whatever he thinks is true," and expressed a "debt to those courageous enough to make the personal sacrifices necessary to strengthen for all of us the Bill of Rights." Plymouth Meeting retained Knowles as librarian after her jail sentence, and in 1957 reported an unprecedented rise in use of the library.*

As far as the media were concerned the Quakers were still talking to themselves, although heretical views crept into a few journals when expressed by millionaires. Some space was found for steel magnate Weir's suggestion that, since the Russians had for ten years been "making it clear that their methods will not include aggressive war," America might "assume they mean it" and show more faith in its own system by trying peaceful competition and "calm and moderate language." Eaton, the industrialist who was organizing an extended meeting of international scientists at Pugwash, told a Toronto interviewer that, notwithstanding American "swashbuckler" statesmen who "grimly arrange the destruction of mankind—goading, prodding, challenging China and Russia," capitalism and socialism must somehow live together. According to Eaton 600,000,000 Chinese not only existed but felt Communism had "improved their material well-being." In light of this, he thought his own dislike of Communism had little relevance.

The extravagances of Brownell's familiars aroused New York *Post* columnist Kempton** to criticize this aspect of the inquisition—the aspect that most fascinated and appalled Stone. Heretics turned increasingly to Stone's *Weekly* for bold and accurate facts; a few citizens outside the ghetto dared to have their names on its subscriber list, and it would soon achieve the apparently impossible feat for a heretical journal of earning a profit. To all except inquisitors Stone made obvious his dislike of Communists and what he regarded as their causes, while absolutely defending the right to be wrong. He scolded Bertrand Russell—a Russophobe of longer standing, but less bewitched by Moscow as a yardstick for Western behavior —for joining in "the strident and hysterical tradition of the Rosenberg campaign" as

---

* *Storm Center*, the first and almost the only Hollywood film about the inquisition, dealt with a librarian (Bette Davis) who balked at orders to remove heretical books. She became in the community a monster who would destroy baseball and other pillars of the American way of life, and a boy was driven to burn down the library; watching the flames with her few supporters, she said she would not quit but was "partly responsible—I didn't fight back." Author-producer John Blaustein conceived the film in 1950 and after a series of delays (the original star Mary Pickford never reappeared for work after the first day) completed it in 1956.

** Kempton wrote of these extravagances in a style that would have been more effective if it had been less precious. In the same style he recalled in March 1971 (*N. Y. Review of Books*) his "feeble efforts," as an ACLU board member in the 50s, "at advancing my personal obsession with the rights of Communists, and all except one failed." He assesses the feebleness of ACLU when it was most needed and concludes: "Its history throughout that period was so depressing that I pray it will never be honestly written."

a defender of Sobell. Russell presumably realized as did every American that defending Sobell was the supreme mark of Cain, but he had read the record at the urging of Sobell's mother and concluded that the trial was a hoax. His changed view about America—he now compared "FBI atrocities" with "Nazi atrocities"— had closed to him the once-welcoming door of American media and changed him from a sage into a senile crank.

Hoover was disturbed enough by the high-court trend to sound a warning, in his spring request for more money, against the CP's "legal maneuvers." He called for "a fearless and independent legal profession alert to the Machiavellian devices of the Communists [who] resort to methods of chicanery to turn our legal and judicial system into a mockery." High-court rulings and exploding familiars also put Immigration slightly on the defensive, but some progress was made in deporting foreign-born heretics who had become citizens. This was a complex task since the law required the preliminary step—denaturalization—to be taken in courts where minimal legal proprieties must be observed. The law required evidence that a heretic was already a violent overthrower at the time of naturalization and hence committed perjury in swearing loyalty. By the fall of 1956, 13 such denaturalizations had been accomplished. The latest case involved a Croatian miner who arrived in Pennsylvania at the age of two, began mining at 8, and now managed a Chicago Croat-language journal whose editor had already been denaturalized. He was scheduled for shipment to a country, Yugoslavia, which did not exist when he left Europe. Averaging 55 years of age, 38 in America and 31 as citizens, the 13 enjoyed such defense as ACPFB could provide. The media were not interested.

ACPFB was challenged on two fronts in the case of its Los Angeles director Rose Chernin, a three-decade citizen who arrived from Russia at the age of 11 and had already been convicted of conspiracy to advocate. Her denaturalization trial ran for months featuring Kornfeder, Leonard Patterson and Malkin. The judge kept familiars outside until called, and permitted Chernin one morning to sit in the audience between a woman and a man in a gray suit. Asked that afternoon to point her out after swearing he had attended Party meetings with her, Malkin pointed to the person sitting between the woman and the gray-suited man; but Chernin had moved to another seat after lunch, and Malkin gave up trying to identify her from the many women present. The judge threw the case out. The Fur Workers' Potash, whose deportation had been simpler since he never became a citizen, returned to America clandestinely but was caught and returned to jail for another two years. His excuse was that he had a right to be with his family—he had a daughter and three grandchildren born in America—and they were denied passports to visit him in Poland.

For Eastland (now chairing the Senate Judiciary Committee) the Supreme Court had already proclaimed its treason in 1954 by ordering school desegregation, and the new rulings merely confirmed his view. As uninhibited as McCarthy, he was, unlike the extinct senatorial volcano, patently moved by ideology: the idea of a society in which blacks would be other than wood-hewers and water-drawers for persons of his own complexion was deeply repugnant. Ninety-five Dixie Congressmen signed his declaration of war against the Court, including Fulbright who helped compose the document, and Stevenson's Presidential election teammate

John Sparkman. The school-desegregation crisis came to its first head in February, while reports of routine Dixie violence continued to accumulate on northern city-room spikes. The Mississippi cotton-ginner who allegedly shot the black filling-station attendant was acquitted. An elderly black physician who wanted to play golf on the city's all-white course was liquidated in an Atlanta shop. In Georgia a white poet, Don West, barely escaped from a town where he had been editing a Negro church paper and had backed a union organizing drive. The ex-Wallaceite church pastor left him to his fate after a HUAC dossier showed West's long record of subverting Dixie workers. Fortunately carrying a gun, West eluded two car-loads of pursuers by firing at their tires.

Headlines were unavoidable for the February excitement at Alabama University. An NAACP lawsuit under the Court ruling forced the university to admit a black sharecropper's daughter; but a few days after state troopers escorted Autherine Lucy on to the campus, they escorted her out again through a furious mob. The trustees voted first her suspension, then her expulsion for making "baseless, outrageous" charges in a suit for readmission. As Birmingham's *Post-Herald* explained, "UNIVERSITY STRESSES RACE NOT INVOLVED; SAYS 'ANYONE' GUILTY OF MISCONDUCT WOULD HAVE BEEN DISMISSED." Eastland urged a death-struggle against the Court to 10,000 cheering whites in Montgomery, where bus-boycott leader Martin Luther King was about to be tried. (It would take the judge four days to convict him, but the sentence was light. Negroes crowded the courtroom and disconcerted the judge by their insistence on sitting in the unoccupied jurybox.)

Free-world countries simmered with embarrassment, and *Life* asked novelist Faulkner for a Dixie intellectual's view. Faulkner pleaded the case for the "middle ground" he had always occupied on the race problem, but now saw a threat to make whites "the underdog" and said he would have to stand with them. He added in the *Reporter* that if the government tried to force integration he would "fight for Mississippi against the US even if it meant going out into the streets and shooting Negroes."

In April Eastland brought his team back to New Orleans and had lawyer Philip Wittenberg, who defended several heretics, thrown out so violently as to require hospital treatment. The inquisitor gave to other probes such time as he could spare from his big crusade. A general in Hawaii sent him word of an impending red revolt there, but, after 24,000 members of Bridges's union threatened to down tools if he appeared, he assigned the mission to colleagues. The high yield of the China theme justified his personal attention to Harvard-Cornell agriculturist William Hinton, who had gone to China with UNRRA after the war and stayed on for years to study the revolution. Hinton's trunkful of documents and notes,* seized as "foreign propaganda" on his return in 1952, had passed into Eastland's hands and Hinton had filed a $500,000 lawsuit against him. In a three-day second-round probe an inquisitor said SISS's problem was security and Hinton said: "I'm interested in internal security too, and I want to know when this committee will start investigating its chairman." Eastland still kept the documents, from

* Eventually appearing in Hinton's book *Fanshen,* Monthly Review Press, New York, 1968.

which he could read to senators timely excerpts substantiating the theme of treason.

State Attorneys General in Dixie cooperated with Eastland's crusade by exposing the subversiveness of local NAACP's which were thrust into the firing line. Mississippi, South Carolina, Georgia and Alabama led the field in such moves, Alabama preparing a law to bar its NAACP from fund solicitation and ordering it in court to name its 14,000 members on pain of a $100,000 fine. A temporary fine of $10,000 was imposed for its "brazen contempt" in refusing. Mississippi's Dr. Howard finally drew a comment from Washington on his repeated charges that Hoover did nothing about the terror in the Mound Bayou area. Not only were the charges "intemperate and baseless," said Hoover, but his Bureau had ended lynching and Howard ought to know it. Howard's request for clarification of this—for there was no anti-lynch law and he could not recall any federal prosecution of a lyncher—ended the exchange. He wondered why, if Hoover could act without such a law, he did not do so in the Till case. Writing in Negro History Week* which heretics observed each February, DuBois recalled that efforts to make Washington enforce its own charter in Dixie had always ended with "freedom lynched, democracy disowned by its own children," but refused to abandon the hope he had always placed in education.

When schools reassembled, troops often had to threaten mobs with rifle butts to make a path for black children. Dixie governors discussed open defiance of the Court order, and Negroes began storing arsenals in their homes. Some black clergymen asked Eisenhower, who had begun varying his golf game with quail shooting, to speak out against the violence used to prevent enforcement of the law. He said he had spoken out so often on civil rights that he didn't know what he could add.

The fact that some blacks were attending some white schools under armed guard showed, in any case, that the free world's metropolis retained democratic mobility as compared with some of its outposts. America's concentration camps were still unopened, whereas inmates of Greece's island corrals, in bottled messages cast upon the tide, graphically credited them with surpassing Buchenwald. South Africa was beginning a trial of 156 citizens, a cross section from illiterate black laborers to two white clergymen and a university head, with which nothing in American inquisitorial annals could compete. The crime was opposing the apartheid system, and a copy of the UN charter found in a defendant's possession was among proofs of treason to be used by the Hitler enthusiast who was to prosecute. In Saudi Arabia, which fueled the engines of democracy, recalcitrant workers and slaves were disciplined by a more ancient tradition: the former (the International Labor Office reported) were thrown into pits of scorpions, and the king had recently beheaded in the public market 14 of the latter who tried to escape.

---

* The object of Negro History Week was to recall that Negroes had a history and their share of heroes and great men and women. Journalistically the exclusive property of the ghetto during the main inquisition years, it would be enthusiastically taken up by the media after Negroes had fought their way into some limelight in the 60s. In 1969 the *Times,* for example, ran a page ad for Negro history books it was publishing, pointing out past "distortions of history to justify discrimination."

The horror stories of the year, however, were the Stalin liquidations and Russia's successful suppression of the Hungarian revolt—coinciding with Britain's armed intervention in Egypt, which failed.* Muste took the lead in an attempt to paste together the fragments which these events had made of the American Left: he saw some hope if each of the fragments would stop "regarding itself as the True Church." Muste's view of Communists was that one should "love" them while holding them guilty of much evil. (Hoover would tell SISS in 1957 that Muste had "long fronted for the Communists"; Muste deemed it worthwhile to write denying this, but to no heretic's surprise his letter was not acknowledged.) The reconciler's efforts resulted in the joint appearance at Carnegie Hall of Roger Baldwin, DuBois, CP secretary Eugene Dennis, and Norman Thomas who was reportedly discussing "something like a new Fabian Society" with Browder. The traditional altercation soon developed about Russia: Dennis said it was a socialist country despite Stalin; Thomas and Baldwin said socialism without individual freedom was a mockery. DuBois reminded them that the evening's topic was "America's Road to Democracy," and Thomas fumed at Muste, DuBois and Baldwin for trying to steer back to it. DuBois said America was in a state of "cultural disaster, almost cowering in the midst of wealth and comfort, desperately afraid yet scarcely able to name its fears. We know perfectly well that no nation plans to attack us; the utmost they plan is to resist our attack on them. We know well that there has been no plot in America violently to overthrow the government, [but] we have set up a secret police with power beyond anything of which this nation ever dreamed. The cure lies in ourselves, not in others. We need to discuss ourselves, not the USSR."

In November, when Stevenson made his second and last bid to outdo Dulles-Eisenhower in nuclear piety and loyalty to the inquisition, the CP recommended him as a lesser-evil President and the alternatives were to vote for Thomas, for one of two shades of Trotskyism, or not at all. Shock from the Matusow affair had made Thomas a fund-raiser for perjuriously convicted Communists while he pursued his program of advancing socialism by cooperating with the Establishment: he was now on amiable terms with CIA. His party hit bottom with 2,192 votes, one of the Trotskyist parties scored 7,805, the other an all-time high of 44,368; the combined total of the three slightly exceeded the Prohibitionist vote, but only in a few states were they even on the ballot.**

Sympathy with Hungary's "freedom fighters," whose rising Allen Dulles had not been able to crown with victory, became a new test of loyalty accepted throughout America but with grumblings from the black community. The *Afro-American* congratulated the Red Cross on its aid to Hungarian rebels but wondered why no one suggested sending surplus food to Port Said's starving thousands after the British bombings: "Why is it that State Department hearts bleed only for

---

* Egypt wanted to run its own Canal.
** The Socialist Workers Party, operating out of a loft near Manhattan's fish market with a linotype machine and a press bought secondhand in 1914, ascribed its 44,368 votes to the fact that it was "uncompromisingly revolutionary." It was contemptuous of America's trade unions, undismayed by the fact that no one prominent had ever joined it, and convinced of final victory. To the triumphant Montgomery bus boycotters it sent the message: "Now Negroes ride with whites—but where to?"

those oppressed and downtrodden people of the world whose skins are white?" In similar vein the Pittsburgh *Courier* mentioned the 10,000 reportedly killed (1,000 hanged) and 75,000 concentration-camped in the suppression of Africans in Kenya. A New York *Amsterdam News* writer, "pretty well fed up" with Hungarians, wanted "aid to THE HUNGRY in the rest of the world . . . I don't know, I suppose I'm just a maladjusted Negro. Americans can sit back and watch black people from Ethiopia to Mississippi get their brains beat out by anyone who has enough guns to do the job, without getting 'charitable' or excited."

HUAC updated and extended its *Cumulative Index* of mostly defunct organizations, and SISS listed Pauling as one of 82 "typical sponsors of Communist fronts" in its *Handbook for Americans.* In New York, ECLC produced a radio script based on optimism that high-court decisions might revive the Bill of Rights. The only station willing to sell time for it canceled the broadcast on finding the script "controversial."

Fever Chart

1956-57

"Grandmotherly Mrs. Hobart of Cincinnati, first president of the American Legion Auxiliary 36 years ago, calmly advocated bomb extermination for home-grown Communists in her talk to Legion women yesterday. 'We'll push them out and push them out,' Mother Hobart said, 'until we have them all in Russia. Then we'll have a circle of good bombers and every weapon we can find, and that will take care of them."—Los Angeles *Mirror-News*.

"Gloomy dispositions in Russia may simply be a matter of poor mattresses, according to mattress company executive Hubbell who just returned from a Soviet tour. He declared that 'Russia is not sleeping properly.' "—NY *Herald Tribune*.

"There would be no threat of World War III, says New York perfume importer Cournand, if Russian women used more perfume. [This] would keep the minds of Russian men on something aside from guns."—Spokane *Chronicle*.

"As is well known, this newspaper prints letters whether or not we agree with the letter-writers, so long as the letters do not libel anybody, are not obscene and are not written by Communists. This is what we believe freedom of the press means."—Manchester (New Hampshire) *Union Leader*.

"A Hungarian refugee plans to dive into Lake Huron Sunday to start what he hopes will be a record swim to Belle Isle. Why does he want to swim from Lake Huron to Belle Isle? It's simple—he says. 'I want to show the people in my Communist-dominated country that anything is possible in America.' "—Detroit *News*.

"A 15-year-old American girl with a scarlet Bible—it matches her hat and skirt—flew into London yesterday and announced: 'I have come to help England find God.' She has a special message for teen-agers: 'They are just looking for thrills. In Chicago we call it getting kicks. I want to show them how to get their kicks out of Christ.' "—London *Daily Mirror*.

"Fabulous Flamingo Hotel in Las Vegas staging lavish productions built around 16 girls holding doctorates in any subject from accredited universities. Slight dancing ability necessary and good looks too. Already have 3 Ph D's, 1 Dr of Anthropology, 1 Dr of Physics and 2 Drs of Home Economics. Girls with only masters' degrees not acceptable."—Ad in New York *Times*.

"WANTED, single man not over 25 to drive in head-on collision at Powell Speedway. We already have one man. Both cars must be speeding at 45 miles an hour at point of crash—a 90-mile-an-hour impact—and drivers must give an unconditional release in case of injury or death. Give price you want and all details."—Ad in Columbus, Ohio, paper.

"Technically, the economy will 'recede' or move sideways. But if the recession is defined even in the mild terms of the 1953–54 slump, it will still be a gold-plated recession."—*Time.*

"If the new capitalism sags on the agricultural sector the reason is, first, that the human stomach can digest only two quarts of food per day, and that agricultural products are the hardest to give away. If a means could be found for turning butter, eggs and grain into weapons, the problems would be solved. For there is never an over-production of weapons."—Dorothy Thompson's syndicated column.

"DEMOCRACY, a game for children 6–12, teaches fundamentals of democracy and American way of life. Game played by tossing dice."—*Toys & Novelties.*

"This is the best year in history for . . . atom-bomb watching. For the first time the AEC's Nevada test program will extend through the summer tourist season, into September. And for the first time AEC has released a partial schedule, so that tourists interested in seeing a nuclear explosion can adjust itineraries accordingly."—New York *Times.*

"Supposing the Soviets elect to make their initial attack where the radioactive fallout will not be wasted, as it would be at sea. So they attack US land targets, and the US counters against Soviet bases, and both are destroyed. At the end of this massive attack, who's left? We're left—the Navy."—Admiral Burke in *This Week.*

"Last year's air raid test jolted industrial mobilization planners. Initial reports didn't seem so bad. Only 25 million casualties and 2% of the aircraft production knocked out. 'But then we started going over the whole picture,' says Lloyd Mulit of the Defense Department. 'Counting up sub-contractors, we found we had no aircraft production.' "—*Iron Age.*

"$50,000 a day it costs to keep them nine little Negroes in that white school in Little Rock. Good money we could have spent for defense. I'm telling you people if it weren't for them nine little Negroes it would be our sputnik up there tonight and not the Communists.' "—Virginia Lieutenant Governor Stephens, campaign speech reported in *Newsday.*

"The Mason County Veterans Council is planning a hexagonal, 20-foot granite memorial column with one of six sides left blank for the names of future war dead. The memorial committee chairman said: 'This is a permanent thing and we must be prepared for the future.' "—*AP* report from Ludington, Michigan.

XXIII

1957: He Is Not Here,

But Is Risen

"He was an intrepid fighter against insidious enemies, malignant powers. Let us pledge ourselves anew to the struggle until this torn and tortured earth is made safe for decency, truth, honor and the pledged word."

The speaker was the Senate chaplain; a whisky-bloated body lay beside him in the Senate chamber on a bright May morning. The fallen fighter's colleagues bowed their heads as his soul was commended to God. In Washington's Roman Catholic cathedral, where a pontifical requiem was sung, thousands moved in procession past the flag-draped coffin.

Alien newsmen struggled to describe appropriately the national ambiance of McCarthy's passing. The London *Times* man reported that the chaplain had "echoed the general sentiment of the American press." The less laconic Toronto *Globe & Mail* recalled McCarthy's condemnation by his now-grieving colleagues in the same chamber. Not for his "brutal and slanderous attacks on private individuals" had they abased him, but for attacking *them* and thereby breaking the club rules: "Had he been more discreet in this respect, he might have continued at the head of the pack."

In fact the man had already been broken by the Establishment, and it mattered little whether the husk died or continued to live. On the whole he was better under ground, for once the usual hypocrisies were over it could be made to seem the burial of an era which neither started with him nor ended with him. He would take his place in folklore as a symbol, and even as the cause, of something that went wrong in America. But the operative part of the chaplain's eulogy was the call to continue the struggle against heresy until the millennium when Satan would no longer seduce Americans into sinful thoughts.

Lesser inquisitors heard the call sitting at their battle stations. A moving scene occurred in Boston when the life of the Massachusetts Special Commission to Study Communism, etc., was further extended in the same room where petitions to rehabilitate 17th-century witches were being favorably considered. While criticism of "McCarthyist methods" broadened among liberals, the fear temperature was maintained by new and old spy sensations and by contempt citations which had never been more lavishly dispensed. SISS opened the year with a massive report on master-spy J. Peters. He had long been beyond reach but it was not to be forgotten that his apparatus had included Hiss and Dexter White. In March SISS updated its information on the past heresies of Canadian diplomat Herbert Norman, now his country's ambassador to Egypt. The perpetual harassment so depressed Norman that he jumped from a Cairo roof, leaving a note for an ambassador friend: "I have no option. I must kill myself, for I live without hope."

Some weeks later SISS was vying with HUAC for names available from the show-business eccentric Boris Morros, who helped identify spies for a generously headlined melodrama. One of these, described as a Russian colonel, was named by a Finnish accomplice who testified, inter alia, that he (the accomplice) was a thief, a bigamist, a drunkard and a liar. The Russians had given him $5,000 to give to Sobell's wife, he said, but as he was unable to locate her he had buried it, then dug it up and spent it. The colonel was convicted and the Finn's testimony opportunely coincided with Sobell's latest plea for a new trial. The colonel, the Finn, and Morros all lived up to the established image of the kind of people Moscow employed as agents.

Morros introduced himself to spy aficionados as a piano and cello prodigy who had conducted the Tsar's imperial orchestra at 16 and, at 22, come to America as musical director of Balieff's *Chauve-Souris* for which he composed *The Parade of the Wooden Soldiers*. On a return visit to the old country in 1945, the Russians had asked him to spy for them and he had reported this to Hoover; in 1950 Hoover had sent him back as a counterspy and a Russian secret-police general had "wined and dined me for ten hours straight." The Roman-candle headlines for Morros flickered out after Balieff's widow said he had neither been *Chauve-Souris's* musical director nor composed the *Wooden Soldiers*. He confessed to the media that he was broke but had "signed up all the Nobel Prize winners in Europe" for TV and had "fabulous offers." His best spy names were wealthy Alfred Stern, a notorious angel for heretical causes now living in Mexico, and his wife, novelist Martha Dodd. Fined $25,000 each for contempt in absentia, the Sterns passed out of reach in the first plane leaving for Prague. They saw no chance of living in peace anywhere in the free world, but were only able to leave it by hastily acquiring Paraguayan passports.

In the fight led by Eastland to keep black Americans in their place, marathon oratory in Congress on white womanhood, Christ and kindred themes effectively headed off all contrary proposals. In Dixie the intervals became increasingly short between bombings of black homes and churches and of white schools where one or more black children had been enrolled. Alabama convicted a 55-year-old Negro handyman of stealing $1.95, for which he was sentenced to death. His court-appointed lawyer told newsmen after the trial: "The nigger was lucky he wasn't lynched, but the people held off lynching because we're bending over backward to please you folks up north." Alabama's Supreme Court confirmed the sentence but, in face of negative reactions in Europe, Asia and Africa, it was commuted to life imprisonment.

The governor called the national guard in September to bar the path of nine black 15-year-olds who had been registered at Little Rock high school. The defiance of law was so bold and widely publicized that Eisenhower "federalized" the troopers to curb the mob outside the school and let the children in. A white woman pressed through the jeering multitude to comfort one child who broke into sobs. She was Grace Lorch, wife of the mathematics teacher who for his active skin-color-blindness had been harried from one place and job to another ever since 1949; he now taught at an obscure Little Rock college. The Lorches were evicted from their Little Rock apartment for their habit of inviting Negroes to dinner, and SISS summoned Mrs. Lorch to appear before it in Memphis, explaining that it was not concerned about her action at the high school but about "the threat of Communism." Georgia poet West was among others subpenaed to a hearing which exposed a "Communist network" aiming to infiltrate practically everything in Dixie. Lorch was already under contempt indictment from a HUAC appearance in Ohio in 1954—a crime of which he would be cleared on the contention of his defender, ex-judge Delany, that HUAC was supposed to be probing subversion in Dayton and only on HUAC's invitation had Lorch ever been there. But by year's end southern state NAACP's were banned in Alabama, severely restricted in Texas, cut to two branches in Louisiana, and under constant assault everywhere else. As the bombings went on, Manning Johnson confirmed for Louisiana inquisitors that the "Communist Trojan Horse" was "stabled today with NAACP," and Matthews—equally discredited on the national level—gave Florida inquisitors a 99-page list of NAACP heretics. Matthews detected Communism in "every major race incident" of recent years.*

Hallinan was disbarred for three years on the tax-evasion charges for which he had been jailed, but a hard core of lawyers were still ready to risk defending heretics. Their Guild convened to name Florida's Coe as its president and Delany for its Franklin Roosevelt award. Wilson came from Princeton to offer the convention a modest analysis of America's ills, now so widely attributed to "McCarthyism" in liberal circles. As he saw it, McCarthy was a symptom of a symptom; the problem was public indifference. America's huge private collectives had installed government by public relations and image merchandizing, and on those techniques for stalling brains more was being spent than on anything but the arms program. If persecutions of the unstalled brain had perceptibly abated, they were less necessary as this phenomenon became rarer under a public-relations barrage ennobling a simpler ideal than humanism: acquire and consume, consume and acquire.

Looking ahead, Wilson submitted that while some form of collectivism was inevitable by technological definition, it could not serve human welfare unless individuals and groups accepted more, not less, social responsibility. But the inquisition had left only shreds of organizations with the desire, let alone the capacity, to challenge the image-merchandizing corporate society. CIO had merged with AFL under the leadership of AFL's George Meany who expressed pride in "never having walked on a picket line."** Muste cheerfully bent himself to mingling Communists, Trotskyists and other fragments in an American Forum for Socialist Education, and ran straight into trouble. The *Times* chided AFSE non-Communists for letting Communists into their discussions, thereby doing "both the country and the cause of socialism a disservice." A New York *News* editorial recommended: "LOOK INTO THIS MOB." Philbrick recalled in his column that he

---

* After Matthews's death in 1966, an $82,000 J. B. Matthews Memorial Library was built to house his dossiers by the Church League of America, a thriving inquisitorial enterprise at Wheaton, Illinois. Together with the files of ex-*Counterattack* publisher Keenan and other acquisitions, CLA claimed to possess "ten tons of original documents by actual shipping weight and nearly 7,000,000 3x5 indexed reference cards on individuals, organizations, publications, and movements."
** At a time when the government was beginning to insist on Negroes being employed on its projects, AFL-CIO used whites exclusively to build its Washington headquarters. The building trade unions only admitted whites, and no non-union help could be hired.

had been alerting his readers for two years to a secret Cominform plan to have its American agents "advance the cause of socialism." Roger Baldwin labeled AFSE "romanticist nonsense." Thomas endorsed the inquisitorial ghetto in a protest against giving AFSE Communists "the false impression that they could remain in the Party and still be accepted in the community." SISS arranged to probe AFSE, but Muste wrote that he would not answer any of Eastland's questions and, since he had too obviously Never Been, the probe did not take place. In his annual report ACLU director Patrick Murphy Malin said that his organization was "cheered" by the CP's reduction to "a puny crew"—"a big help [to] the police job necessary to internal security."

The F. for R., by no means exclusively benevolent to Quaker peacemongers, financed a prodigious research job in *The Roots of American Communism* (Viking, N.Y., 1957) by former *New Masses* and *Worker* contributor Theodore Draper. Draper omitted no available documentation of the thesis that socialism was "foreign" to America and that Moscow completely controlled his late Party. Fast made public his disgust for the Party in an interview with the *Times's* veteran expert in Russophobia, Harry Schwartz, an article in an investment-house magazine, and a book *The Naked God*. Heretics sympathized with his pain and fury at the treachery of his Russian writer friends, who had placidly lied to him about Stalin's liquidations, but were repelled by his choice of outlets. His denunciations of Party leaders' talmudry had a touch of arrogance for ex-comrades who recalled him as one of the most talmudic. In the context of the investors' magazine he pleaded for "total brotherhood" and objected to "anti-Communism as we know it in America." If, as he hoped, America would "act wisely, with a new tolerance, a new understanding, and especially a new effort to prove the good faith of the people of the East . . . it may well be that we will witness the peaceful cooperation of democratic socialism and democratic capitalism in the building of a better world."

Few writers, once in the Party, managed to leave it without opening themselves to contempt on both sides of the ghetto wall. For Richard Wright, however, and even for Hughes who had abased himself before McCarthy, their blackness saved some rags of dignity. Fast suggested that the Party had tried to destroy him as a writer; Hughes was more concerned about America's publishing establishment which, since long before there was a Party, had blacklisted writers merely for being black. Most journals had never published, most studios never filmed, a line from a black hand, and some libraries would not even stock a Negro writer's book. The few who were published showed a strong tendency to exile themselves, because, Hughes wrote, "the stones thrown at Autherine Lucy are thrown at them too." Wright, in Paris, felt he had fled from a double nightmare: the "absolute racist regime" in his native Mississippi and the "political dictatorship of the CP," which he had endured for 12 years and denounced. At the opposite pole was DuBois, still unalienated at 89 but ghettoized in his own land for his dangerous thoughts. In 1957 his most treasured dream came true with the rebirth of ancient Ghana as a black African republic led by Nkrumah. The master at whose feet Nkrumah had grown to revolutionary stature was invited to the celebrations as guest of honor. "Deeply regret no passport," was the reply. To congratulate the Africans on their freedom, America sent Nixon.

While the discoverer of Chambers's pumpkin inspected Ghana's festivities, the ups and downs of a familiar's life were illustrated in news items from Iowa and Pittsburgh. A *Labor's Daily* correspondent reported that midwestern audiences were paying $1,000 for lectures on the menace by Philbrick. Cvetic, on the other hand, had returned broke from his west-coast lecturing enterprise. He told the Pittsburgh *Press* that he had earned little gratitude for dedicating his life to "this fight against Communism. I know they plan to overthrow the government by force, stealth and subversion . . . they perpetuate themselves by forced labor and mass murder." His loyalty was unshaken although his share of the earnings from magazines, radio and the *I Was A Communist for the FBI* film, which "reportedly grossed $1,500,000," had been a niggardly $50,000. The rest had gone to various parasites, and this on top of the "constant harassment and smears by Communists" had caused him to "hit the booze pretty hard." He had been hospitalized three times for the "cure" and again for a broken shoulder when he "tripped on a step." For a man who had appeared 63 times against heretics, and named some 500, this was a sad denouement. Life was still hazardous since ex-comrades he met on the street gave him "dirty looks," and one had "come after me with a butcher knife; I pulled out my .38." But he had abjured the bottle and was writing a book revealing "for the first time how I trapped one of the top Nazi espionage agents."

The Justice Department still valued Malkin and Kornfeder as major-league material, and they justified its esteem at the six-week trial of James Matles, a UE leader who had once yelled "Liar!" at McCarthy. Kornfeder's recollection of knowing Matles as a Communist in 1925–26 prevailed against that of Matles's Rumanian mother, who said she only brought her family to America in 1929. The judge declined to recall Kornfeder for cross-examination after this contradiction emerged, thus opening the door for Matles's deportation by removing his citizenship. As in nearly all denationalization proceedings at this stage, higher courts would reverse the decision. Most of Budenz's appearances were now on TV to tell the public, in the matter of red spy rings, that "the surface has only been scratched"; but the press still published his longest communications *in extenso*. When the *Times* remarked that Russian barbarism was "combined with scientific prowess," he adjured the editor to examine more thoughtfully a system which taught that "the world began without God and will go forward without Him." With regular doses of Philbrick, *Herald Tribune* readers hardly needed—but received—Budenz's analysis of recent Supreme Court decisions as showing "the effectiveness of the line laid down by Khrushchev."

Lautner's lifeless routine would remain in inquisitorial demand for several more years. He repeated it at a HUAC probe of publishing and film heretics including 18 who were connected with foreign-language journals, two booksellers, International Publishers' James Allen, and publisher Angus Cameron who was running a Liberty Book Club for ghetto dwellers. The journalists were fully eligible to follow Belfrage back where they came from, but most of them would be let off with years of harassment in their adopted country.* A month later Laut-

* Hoping to explain the inquisition to his countrymen, Belfrage had just published his personal report *The Frightened Giant* (Secker & Warburg, London, 1957). As one of the rotating co-editors in London of the CIA-financed journal *Encounter*, Dwight MacDonald was available to review the book for the *Sunday Times*. He pointed out that

ner could not save from an unenthusiastic press HUAC's second probe of musicians, this time in New York. One of four musical witnesses who were friendly complained that he could never get work till he joined the Party, and that as an orchestra leader he had been compelled to hire Communist fiddlers regardless of competence. The chief target was a music school which wondered how it "could be subversive unless Bach, Chopin, Brahms and Beethoven are." Its president emeritus, 70-year-old composer Wallingford Riegger, invoking the First Amendment, said: "I fear the loss of my self-respect if I answered you." Robinson, the subpenaed composer of *Ballad for Americans,* relieved the tedium slightly by humming snatches of his songs. After Robeson's SISS performance HUAC thought it wiser to summon his accompanist Alan Booth rather than Robeson himself. (Still trapped but deluged with worldwide concert offers, Robeson was arranging to sing to a London audience by telephone.) Columnist Kempton, now a far-out critic of inquisitorial extremism, found that the musician probe had shown HUAC to be "tawdry, stupid and malignant." New York's ACLU called the hearing "grotesque, arousing a mounting sense of disgust."

Seeger and actor Sullivan were indicted*—and Otto Nathan, a TV man and three employees of respectable journals convicted—for contempt, but Jencks's conviction for perjury was reversed. Discreetly bypassing Matusow's testimony, the Supreme Court based the latter decision on Hoover's refusal to produce his documentation of Jencks's heresy. The decision affected many other cases, but Brownell and Hoover quickly devised a strategy to circumvent it: relevant documents did not "now exist as defined by law." Their list of labor heretics was far from exhausted and they proceeded to organize an enlarged and improved Taft-Hartley perjury trial. They had detected eight Clevelanders "conspiring to file" false non-Communist affidavits, six of whom never actually filed one.

The inquisition returned to headlines abroad—where it had long been inspiring yawns—with the trial of Arthur Miller whose play about the New England witch hunt had been widely performed. For the London *Times* the "six perplexing and rather somber days" leading up to the guilty verdict "in some respects smacked of the Star Chamber." The perplexity stemmed from the fact that Miller had ar-

---

support of Wallace, opposition to the Korean War, and defense of the Rosenbergs ("I don't see how there can be a reasonable doubt of their guilt . . . the trial was fair") showed the "consistent pro-Communism" of *National Guardian,* and that in the course of a "lengthy legal process replete with appeals" Belfrage had refused to say if he ever "engaged in espionage activities." Thus, while MacDonald "disapproved" of the deportation and thought the Rosenbergs' sentence "excessive," he found it "hard to blame a Government for deporting" such an alien. These reflections left MacDonald little space to discuss the book.

* Seeger was finally tried in 1961; the verdict was reversed in 1962 on the Lamont case precedent that HUAC had not shown its authority to ask the unanswered questions. Walter appeared as a witness but knew nothing about anything: he was "not familiar" with AWARE or any of its people, and did not even remember the Hollywood Ten affair. Seeger described himself to the court as "a very lucky man" at 42 with a wife, three healthy children and a beautiful house "built with our own hands"; then he asked, "Do I have the right to sing these songs—to sing them anywhere?" and got his answer of a year behind bars. After 17 blacklisted years he would be allowed back on TV "prime time" in 1969, the *Times* then commenting: "It is time to nail the lid on the blacklist coffin."

rived at so nearly impeccable a position on heresy as to draw his inquisitors' compliments: but he still would not name the names and, despite the appeals-court
decision in the Watkins case, the judge ruled this to be a crime. The appearance of
an ex-inquisitor—Cain—as a defense witness was an unavailing novelty. Cain's
views about heretical writers—that they should be judged by their works and that,
since the average American could not even define Communism, they were justified in trying to enlighten him—were duly noted. One defense contention was that
HUAC had summoned Miller to garner headlines after his capture of Monroe;
but HUAC's Arens scotched this by testifying that someone had named Miller as
a Communist. Party membership not being in the charge, Arens would not say who
this was, but under questioning he lifted a corner of the veil on HUAC's card-index
system. It comprised some 1,500,000 "items" on groups and persons, available to
any Congressman on request and cross-referenced to secret files with "a vast array"
of further material. The secret files contained not only anonymous denunciations
but even "an anonymous letter referring to another anonymous person."

Miller had hardly been pronounced guilty when the Supreme Court, by
affirming the Watkins decision, definitively abolished the crime of non-informing.
The Court also freed five Californian conspirators-to-advocate on a technicality;
reversed the conviction of *Monthly Review's* Sweezy; found that diplomat Service
had been improperly fired; and ordered new trials for Scales in North Carolina
and Uphaus in New Hampshire, both of whom would be reconvicted. (Uphaus
had been probed by HUAC in 1956 and consistently swore he had Never Been;
now he was fighting a jail order "until purged of his contempt"—theoretically
forever—in withholding his World Fellowship guest list.) The rulings were still
weak and contradictory but underlined the caution to inquisitors: as Warren said
for the Court majority, "There is no Congressional power to expose for the sake
of exposing." Urged on by ABA, Congressmen intensified their efforts to pass
Court-curbing legislation. Patriots demanded the impeachment of Warren, who
increasingly agreed with Black and Douglas as to what the Constitution meant.

After an October probe of Buffalo housewives to determine "possible infiltration into the YWCA," HUAC looked back on its poorest publicity year to date.
The headlines it earned in San Francisco in June were its biggest and also its least
positive. When Stanford University biochemist William Sherwood took poison on
inquisition eve, leaving a suicide note about the "Committee trail of blasted lives
and wreckage of youthful careers," the media reaction was cool. Sherwood was
suspected of Spanish Republican partisanship and attendance at a "Marxist study
group" in his youth, and had been visited three times by FBI men: they offered the
alternative of cooperation or an inquisitorial invitation, and he had chosen the
latter but could not face it. His widow came to read a statement to the inquisitors,
pointing out that Sherwood had been "out of politics for 10 years" and recalling 11
earlier suspects who had killed themselves or died of heart attacks under similar
circumstances. Walter refused to hear her and had her led out weeping. She brought
a desperate $500,000 damage suit against him but, since he enjoyed Congressional
privilege, soon withdrew it.

SISS took a more fruitful approach to the revived probing of scientists by
initiating the exposure of Pauling. Obsessed by the atomic arms race and radioac-
tivity from constant hecatomb-tests, Pauling had mustered some 2,000 colleagues

to demand that tests be stopped. "I don't know what his qualifications are," commented ex-Los Alamos chief General Leslie R. Groves, "other than that he has won a Nobel Prize. I would never ask a football coach how to run a major league baseball team." Eisenhower muttered to the media about scientists "out of their field of competence . . . it looks like almost an organized affair." Pauling had indeed dropped almost everything else to organize it, but since Moscow had long pressed for a test-ban agreement he was following the Party line. SISS invited him to come and tell whether "Communist organizations are behind" his petition, but Pauling had a lecture-date in Paris and could not accept.

The build-up for the postponed probe was copious. Philbrick's files contained so much data that he had to apologize to *Herald Tribune* readers for merely excerpting. Pauling had been a Waldorf-Astoria sponsor in 1949, and a bulwark of Fritchman's church; he had attended a Mexican peace conference, opposed the American arms program and the Korean war, sponsored CRC, protested the deportation of Hanns Eisler ("an admitted member of the Communist International"), objected to the McCarran Act, signed appeals for conspirators-to-advocate, "personally vouched" for a heretical Cal Tech professor. In brief, he was "one of the most notorious fellow travelers," "hailed" by the CP along with Mather, Shapley, Morrison and Struik, and to crown all he had signed a petition for Sobell "as recently as February this year." Yet as tests increasingly radioactivized the atmosphere, the humanitarian weakness of scientists brought thousands more signatures to Pauling's petition. Twelve years after the tactical Bombs were dropped on Hiroshima and Nagasaki, the media reported how survivors were getting on—some with no eyes, some with half-faces apparently not including mouths.

Eastland's preoccupations with the Supreme Court could not let him ignore the headline potential of Russia's sputnik, which went into orbit in October. America's first satellite, launched two months later, exploded four feet from the ground. The Smithsonian Institution's Dr. Fred L. Whipple told the media that America would continue falling behind in the rocket department—the new priority for successful hecatombs—"until the Phi Beta Kappa had the same social standing as the football player." SISS cut through academic persiflage to the core of the matter—spies. It disclosed that Julius Rosenberg had given Russia the secrets of satellites as well as space platforms and the Bomb: SISS counsel Robert Morris had visited Gold and Greenglass in jail to obtain this information. The Russians refrained from crowing or saber-rattling—Khrushchev was confident that America would "soon catch up"—but were accused of it because Khrushchev also said, "We will bury you," meaning (as he explained) that socialism would outlive capitalism.* Some circles suggested that American prestige would not have suffered this blow if Condon had not been "weak-linked" and Oppenheimer forced to emulate Galileo.** Condon remarked that the blow was no surprise since Washington was

---

* "We will bury you" became the media's favorite Russian quotation for some years, superseding the previously popular remark by Molotov, "No power on earth can prevent our people from going ahead on our chosen socialist path." The latter emerged in a New York *Herald Tribune* headline as: "MOLOTOV TELLS WEST NOTHING CAN STOP 'MARCH' OF REDS."

** In December 1957 the ultra-loyal *Reporter* published a comparison between the Oppenheimer and Galileo cases, finding that both scientist and inquisitor emerged with rather more credit in 17th-century Italy. Galileo was allowed to talk for a long time "committed by policy to the persecution of scientists." Cries rang out in high places to fire Dulles, and some of the media bore down hard on the maestro of massive retaliation. Journalists were already miffed by Dulles's ban on reporting from China. As the *Times's* James Reston saw it, it was just because the Chinese were "wicked" that reporters should go there, for "it is not the good that have to be watched but the wicked." China had no illusions as to the kind of reports American newsmen would send, but was willing to accept them because it wanted reciprocal correspondents in America. Except, however, for *Afro-American's* Worthy and the exiled Belfrage, no journalist moved in either direction between New York and Peking.

Russia was no longer excluding even journalists like Fischer, whose *Russia Revisited* (1957) described his return to his prewar station. Having found a "god" in Stalin's Russia, Fischer was now in the Philbrick fee-bracket for lecturing on his new god Gandhi, and how the first one "failed." Among his book's conclusions were that "there have been no basic changes but essentially conditions are different" in Russia; that demilitarizing and neutralizing Germany would be "neither Christian nor Gandhian"; and that "freedom must win." At the same time the heretical but still-employed professor Frederick L. Schuman tried again, in *Russia Since 1917*, to convince Americans that Russia had never considered an armed attack on the West, and had made large and frequent concessions; that it had had both "triumphs and tragedies," and that most of the latter could have been avoided if America's Russophobia had been less intense. He invited both countries to abandon their "fallacious, irrelevant and hazardous dogmas," and submitted that the "freedom-democracy" concept was meaningless to poor, ignorant, diseased people such as the Russians had once been and half the world's people still were. Within Russia a major topic was Dudintsev's *Not By Bread Alone* describing the grim bureaucracy and spiritual corruption under Stalin and reasserting socialist values which got lost after Lenin. But Washington still exhorted Russia to "deeds not words" for peace, and prepared a military budget equaling the peak Korean war year.

The only ex-Communist writer for whom heretical admiration grew in this anguished period was Isaac Deutscher, a Pole resident in England, who pursued his researches into Russian and Communist phenomena with relentless respect for scholarship, for socialism, and for old friends with whom he had come to differ. He had published a sober biography of Stalin in 1949, citing Cromwell and Robespierre parallels and appraising Stalin as "both the leader and exploiter of a tragic, self-contradictory but creative revolution." Now he was doing the same for Trotsky in a biographical trilogy. His prescription for oracles like Fischer, who traded one

---

before the mandatory groveling; Oppenheimer groveled before his trial began. Galileo tried to keep his trial to the real point—his theories—while Oppenheimer accepted the inquisitors' ground rules of endless probing into his private life. Pope Urban VIII's inquisitors turned a blind eye to the condemned Galileo's continued contacts with heretical friends. The AEC inquisitors accused Oppenheimer of "persistent and continuing association" with heretics including Chevalier "who had been intermediary for the Soviet Consulate in 1943"—an assertion about Chevalier which was never proved. Both men were essentially found guilty of "lack of enthusiasm" for what the establishment decreed to be true: in Galileo's case for the Church's astronomical fancies, in Oppenheimer's for the morality of mass exterminations and the loyalty judgments of J. Edgar Hoover.

religion for another while preserving inflexible self-righteousness, was a period of quiet reflection until they could make peace with themselves.

At the end of the year, HUAC was exposing a conspiracy to abolish it involving SCEF president Aubrey Williams, Meiklejohn, Pickett, O'Connor, Los Angeles's Frank Wilkinson, Trumbo, Wilson and others of the ECLC circle. Familiars brought the plot to light by buying tickets for the abolitionists' inaugural rally at Carnegie Hall, a lively affair at which stinkbombs were thrown and Hungarian Freedom Fighters headed a "Murderers . . . Traitors . . . Communists" picketline. The appearance of Trumbo, one of HUAC's first postwar victims, as a calumniator of the inquisition followed the award of Hollywood's "best screenplay" trophy to Robert Rich, author of *The Brave One,* who could not be located to come and claim his "Oscar." After Trumbo admitted two years later to being Rich, the Hollywood blacklist would slowly turn to dark and then paler shades of gray. Having lost neither his talent nor his sense of humor, Trumbo would by 1970 be rejecting offers of less than $250,000 per screenplay. But both HUAC and the committee to abolish it would still remain in business.

XXIV

1958: Laughter Beyond the Moon

After the jail sentence—promptly to be revoked—on the author of *The Crucible,* America's inquisition vanished almost without trace from foreign media. The 94 percent of humanity living *in partibus infidelium* gave up trying to fathom it. America had in fact proclaimed itself a special case ever since the birth of the term "un-American." Other lands had assimilated hot dogs and Coca-Cola with little pain but never managed to think in terms of "un-Dutch," "un-Swiss" or "un-Finnish activities." Students of old-fashioned jurisprudence were baffled by America's vast corpus of heresy laws and apparent indecision as to which of them to enforce. Older nations' thought-control experts were impressed by their American colleagues' bounteous budgets but mystified by the ratio of these to concrete results in the form of publications suppressed and bodies removed from circulation. Yet this paralleled America's method of fighting wars, uniforming and maintaining about six men for every soldier with a gun—and America had a high score of victories.

When Cleveland millionaire Eaton remarked that "Hitler in his prime never had such a spy organization as we have today," the *Press* of that city did some checking. No full count of inquisitorial personnel was possible, but the *Press* came up with 6,000 FBI agents out of Hoover's 14,000 payroll, 1,859 Justice Department agents apart from FBI, 22,059 agents employed by the armed forces, 16,000 Treasury agents, and 7,300 AEC, Labor Department, General Accounting Office and farm-control investigators. Government employees reporting on their colleagues amounted to over 1,000 in the State Department alone, according to the *Bulletin of Atomic Scientists.* The *Press* estimated that Hitler had employed "20,000–50,000" agents. Its survey did not include either the loyalty program or the "secret" CIA, but Yale Law School professor Ralph Brown found that the loyalty of at least 18,000,000 Americans working directly or indirectly for the government had been tested, and that this cost $37,400,000 in 1955 alone.* A conservative guess in 1959 was that CIA employed 14,000 Americans apart from "thousands" of foreigners mainly on piecework. In Germany it had taken over intact the team Hitler built for black operations against Russia, and in Washington it was building a $55,000,000 headquarters for the world's largest "cloak-and-dagger" organization.

The heresies which this multitude sought to frustrate were passing more and more into the hands of *ad hoc* groups, led by politically unaffiliated persons like Pauling and mainly concerned to "Ban the Bomb." Under this slogan thousands of Britons joined an Easter weekend march and hundreds of Americans marched

---

* A partisan of America's "death struggle" with heretics, Brown favored any way of uprooting them which would work. Although sent out to reviewers with the Yale University Press imprint, his book discounting the loyalty program's effectiveness went almost entirely unnoticed.

to the UN from points around New York. Pauling, who had presented to the UN his test-ban petition signed by 35 Nobel laureates and 9,200 other scientists, insisted that the issue "mustn't be confused by minor problems such as Communism vs. Capitalism," for atomic fallout was no respecter of ideologies and tests already made might genetically affect millions of unborn children. He sought a court injunction against further tests and in the same month accepted TU's annual award, calling it "the Nobel Prize of education."

The Russo-American thaw edged forward with the appearance of the Moisseyev Dancers at New York's Metropolitan Opera House and of American pianist Van Cliburn in Moscow, both earning ovations. Then Hungary executed its allegedly traitorous ex-premier Imre Nagy after a secret trial which only the most ardent Russophile could defend—a cue for Dulles to declare a summit meeting almost unthinkable, and to land marines in Lebanon just after a heretical-flavored coup in Iraq. Meanwhile two Quaker architects, ex-US Navy Captain Albert Bigelow and W. R. Huntington, were trying in their ketch *Golden Rule* to reach the Eniwetok area where America's latest H-test was scheduled. Bigelow disliked Russia but, after having as house guests two Hiroshima children who came to America for plastic surgery, disliked mass exterminations more. He thought most Americans agreed but were "benumbed, morally desensitized by ten years of propaganda and fear." The Eniwetok mission was hopeless since Bigelow announced a stop in Hawaii and that he would not resist attempts to halt the ketch by force. Muste, whose hand was visible behind the plot, flew to Hawaii to "see them off" but they ended their journey in a Hawaiian jail for contempt.

Presidential advisers surveying the power-balance were confident that, with appropriate billions added each year to the arms budget, America could control the globe indefinitely. President-to-be Lyndon B. Johnson saw a vision of America "controlling outer space," drawing the comment from DuBois on his 90th birthday: "Somewhere beyond the moon there must be sentient creatures rolling in inextinguishable laughter." DuBois was still sure that America could not stop socialism, only silence and jail its promoters. But "what is truth," he asked, "when the President of the United States stands up in public and says, 'The world thinks of us as a land which never enslaved anyone'? Everyone who heard this knew it was not true, but not even a Negro weekly has dared to challenge that extraordinary falsehood."

Hoover elaborated the documentation of his "fewer Communists, more conspiracy" theory in *Masters of Deceit* (Holt, New York, 1959) just as Congress was being asked to raise HUAC's budget to $305,000. Roy W. Wier of Minnesota, a 66-year-old Congressman who had begun life as an electrician, spoke negatively about HUAC in the House as he had done every year since 1954. The *Times* now estimated CP membership at a maximum of 5,000 (if correct, less than one to each FBI agent), but the Party's decline was precisely Hoover's point. HUAC's budget spokesman pointed out that "the hard core of the Communist conspiracy" was now to be found in ECLC, ADA and the Washington *Post*.

One visible product of the domestic thaw was a rush of heretics to Europe after the Supreme Court ruled against the passport ban in June. The *Wall Street Journal* had been suggesting that if America could not risk the free circulation of "a radical baritone" (Robeson), it had "built a foreign policy that is insecure indeed": "millions upon millions" had been spent on projecting a "land of the free" image and this sort of thing hardly helped. In the months before his liberation some halls had allowed Robeson to sing in them, and there had been overflow audiences, rhapsodical reviews and no violence. Heretics felt a sense of unreality reading in the *Times* of the "tremendous dignity" of the man who was a traitor at Peekskill and had just reaffirmed the same ideas.* He did not care what "Big White Folks" thought of him, he wrote, and insisted that neither "gradualism" nor reliance on whites would ever win Negroes their manhood.

Returning to England to play Othello at Stratford and sing in Albert Hall and St. Paul's cathedral, Robeson knew again the pleasure of walking streets freely and being recognized with affection and respect. When DuBois and others followed, Europeans received them with special friendliness as they had received Chaplin: they were astonished by America's systematic vilification of its own distinguished children. (The vendetta against Chaplin had been resumed in the spring with a three-part exposé of his sins in *Saturday Evening Post*.) During the summer Russia welcomed as guests the Robesons, the DuBoises and Anna Louise Strong. Robeson, whose Moscow stadium concert was sold out in a few hours, told the Russians: "Things are better for Negroes in America but there is still plenty to struggle for." Strong spoke to 15,000 at a Moscow peace meeting and went on to China where she would remain. DuBois received the only standing ovation at an Asian-African Writers Congress in Tashkent.**

Foster Dulles had moved to his most ominous brink over China's islands Quemoy and Matsu (next to the mainland, 100 miles from Taiwan), which Chiang still occupied under American protection and which Dulles called "essential to the defense of Taiwan." American and Chinese emissaries were finally facing each other across a table in Warsaw in an exchange of views which would continue barrenly and ludicrously for years. China offered to stop shooting at the islands if Chiang would stop the raids on the mainland for which he used them. Dulles, controlling the strait with his fleet, declined and sent more bombers into the area; Chiang hoped for a new chance to recapture his throne; and Khrushchev said that any attack on China would be an attack on Russia.

Even on the decisive medium, the airwaves, doubts began to be voiced about Dulles whose cold-war techniques failed to scare the right people. The thaw was moving toward an inevitable summit encounter, but for HUAC and Hoover this merely widened the area within which conspirators were to be smoked out.

---

* In *Here I Stand*, Othello Associates, New York, 1958.
** DuBois would delight heretics of almost all complexions with his final American gesture, joining the CP at age 93. He settled in Ghana to fulfill a lifelong dream of compiling an *Encyclopedia Africana* with his friend Alphaeus Hunton and died there at 96. A few years later his books and the entire 50 years' issues of his journal *The Crisis* were reprinted (the latter to sell for $1,450), and NAACP officials who fired him joined the media in ringing praise of the man they had quarantined and virtually buried. In 1969 his Massachusetts birthplace, Great Barrington, dedicated a park to his memory despite some residents' fears of "an influx of Negro visitors to the park" (*Times*). The plans called for a plaque with the DuBois quotation, "The problem of the 20th century is the color line," to be mounted on a granite boulder; but the *Times* said the plaque "would not be mounted until passions generated by the problem of the 20th century have cooled in Great Barrington."

Eaton's insinuations against the inquisition more than qualified him for a probe, and Arens announced that one would be held; but after signing a subpena, Walter lacked nerve to go through with it. Eaton said he would be delighted at their convenience to come and discuss America's "secret police" and Arens's and Walter's "despicable tactics." He was denounced by Cohn and inquisitor Scherer at an AWARE rally but found defenders in ACLU, in the *Times* which called the subpena "preposterous," and in Senator Douglas who found it "perhaps impetuous." On his F. for R. radio program Hutchins singled out for praise Eaton's deprecations of Hoover, confessing that he "didn't know why any governmental agency should become a national ikon." Hoover denounced "the carpings of professional do-gooders, pseudo-liberals and out-and-out Communists." Hutchins's radio performance included an interviewer's question as to what he thought would result in the educational field from "this jolt to our national complacency" that was Russia's sputnik. "Nothing," Hutchins replied. "The American people, no matter what they say, are really indifferent to education." It was a country where a child "just above the level of a moron" could obtain the necessary diplomas for a job and comfortable living.*

High-court cooperation having become low in the deportation sector, the Justice Department cut through red tape in the case of 52-year-old William Heikkila who had reached America at the age of three months. As a Communist in Minnesota, Heikkila had led unemployed and farm-foreclosure struggles in the 30s; he had quit the Party on moving to San Francisco in 1939, but the Department had been trying for 11 years to return him to Finland as an impenitent. The Supreme Court's refusal in another case to accept such ancient heresy as grounds for deportation persuaded Heikkila that he was out of danger, and his plea for a favorable ruling on this basis was pending. As he left work one day in April, agents dragged him into a car and rushed him to the airport; in an hour he was airborne for Helsinki and arrived there in a sleet storm with 30¢ and no overcoat. He had time only to yell to a fellow worker as he was seized, "Call Phyllis!" (his American wife). Noisy protests brought him back in a week. He was again ordered deported but died of a heart attack before his appeal could be heard.

In its new Taft-Hartley approach, the Department arraigned UE Organizer Marie Haug, her husband who worked for Mine-Mill, and six Cleveland Communists for "conspiracy to cause" false oaths to be filed. Nelson and seven more Communists were named as co-conspirators but not indicted; 14 present or past Mine-Mill leaders awaited trial in Denver for a similiar conspiracy. The device held out promise for wholesale jailing or rejailing of labor heretics, and seven of the eight were sentenced to 18 months on testimony of six familiars, one of whom had recently nominated his wife to walk the plank. Mrs. Haug was a suffragist's daughter who had joined the CP on graduating from Vassar and—with a lack of sincerity which was patent to the court—resigned to sign the inescapable oath in 1949. An *ad hoc* Haug defense committee warned that the case set a new inquisitorial precedent, but only heretics would lend their names.

* According to the St. Louis *Post-Dispatch* in January 1958, America had some 1,000 mail-order "diploma mills" selling college degrees for $20. Missouri, where a charter to start such an institution was as easily obtainable as a dog license "and doesn't cost much more," was especially rich in them.

Familiars continued to strut their long or short hour upon the stage and pass into limbo. Something in the profession served to shorten their life expectancy after they fell from demand, and when they died, often in sordid circumstances, their once-famous names were as forgotten as their perjuries. For Rushmore, now "outdoors editor" of *True War,* the end came in January shortly after his abandonment by his second wife, who had earlier joined Alcoholics Anonymous and tried to jump into the river. He entered a taxi in which she was riding, shot her and then shot himself. Lautner and Barbara Hartle were the most durable familiars, traveling extensively to help the Department get "membership" convictions. At the trial in Butte of John Hellman, the son of Montana pioneers, Hartle pointed to a distinguished record in her field: the 470 heretics she had already named included her ex-husband and ex-common-law husband. Hellman said he was a Communist but knew of no plans to overthrow anyone. The judge bowed to the Supreme Court by asking Hoover to prove that his documentation on Hellman, which the defense wanted to see, did not exist. This was expeditiously done, and Hellman got five years.

In his second trial at Greensboro, North Carolina, Scales was again sentenced to six years for "membership" although he was not a member: he had announced his exit from the Party due to "moral and ideological differences." With Lautner, Hartle and eight more familiars this time, Scales's feat in securing Telford Taylor as his defender proved unavailing. Lautner gave his usual description of the Cleveland cellar scene; black familiar Cummings repeated his line about "blood must run in the streets"; Hartle said the Party's aim was "to smash the bourgeoisie state" and that it had ordered her underground in Seattle. Her first underground project, she explained under cross-examination, had been "to crochet a bedspread," but she had "moved stealthily from town to town and from job to job."

Despite Taylor's efforts in a weeks-long selection process, Greensboro's most ardent anti-integrationists predominated in the jury; and the essence of the local Party over which Scales once presided was summed up by an FBI agent who had joined it. "I was taught," testified the agent, "that Communists in the South should persuade Negroes that they are oppressed and win favor with them as an ally." Dixie events of the year including the bombing of a Jewish center in Miami and another in Nashville, where anti-integrationists passed out "Jewish Marxists Threaten Negro Revolt" leaflets, and an unsuccessful attempt by 25 Georgia Negroes to register to vote. Many of them were school teachers but they were stumped by the registration board's whimsical questionnaire. One would-be voter was slugged on the head by a policeman and died after brain surgery. Asked for comment, the county police chief said: "Things have gotten worse since television—they hear what the Supreme Court has done and what the federal courts say and all about civil rights, and we've had trouble." In Mississippi a Negro trying to register at the university was removed to a mental hospital.

A week after publication of Anne Braden's *The Wall Between,** relating the 1954 events in Louisville to national race patterns, she and her husband were sub-

* Monthly Review Press, New York, 1958. In his dying *Southern Farm & Home,* Aubrey Williams wrote of the book that if 10 clergymen in each Dixie county would read it, "it might convict them of the sin of silence and galvanize them ito some sort of action."

penaed for a HUAC probe in Atlanta. On leaving jail the Bradens had taken over SCEF, the rump of SCHW which refused to lie down. They had two small children and, since Mrs. Braden would not go to Atlanta without them, the hearing for her was postponed. The probe became involved with the national "Abolish HUAC" movement through a former Los Angeles public housing official, Frank Wilkinson, whose Citizens Committee to Preserve American Freedoms was participating in that movement. Wilkinson flew to Atlanta to research the abolition project and was handed at the airport a subpena to be probed along with Braden. He gave his name, then challenged the inquisitors to cite him for contempt; they accepted, and he and the equally defiant Braden would both be jailed for a year. Walter assured the nervous that he was concerned not with integration but with "Communist penetration," but 180 black clergymen, editors and professors scoffed at this in a furious protest to every member of the House of Representatives. HUAC moved in to probe 40 heretics in Los Angeles and some more in Newark, New Jersey. In Newark ECLC chairman O'Connor came to help the subpenaed and, for the second time, was subpenaed himself. His contempt indictment for letting the subpena fall on the floor would still linger on the docket in 1960.

In October 12,000 students marched on Washington to demand that the school-integration ruling be respected. No White House secretary had time to receive them, and they assembled near the Lincoln Memorial to be told by black labor leader Randolph that they should not "embarrass" Eisenhower and that, above all, they must "completely reject and unconditionally condemn Communism." A marginal event in the racist sector was ILWU leader Bridges's attempt to wed a Nisei (American-born Japanese) in Nevada. After two denials of a license on the basis of a state law barring white-oriental marriages, he succeeded. At the time, 30 states barred white-black marriages, 15 barred white-oriental, 5 barred white-Indian; interracial cohabitation was a crime in eight states.

Of all the year's trials and probes only one produced more than a few lines in foreign media: the trial of a 9-year-old Monroe, North Carolina, black boy for kissing a white playmate. It was undisputed that the pair had been playing hide-and-seek around a drainpipe and that a kiss had been exchanged. The boy said she kissed him, the girl that he had exacted it as the price of letting her out of the pipe. Threats to lynch the boy by the girl's father and friends were foiled by six carloads of policemen rushing to the scene and arresting the boy. After six days in jail he was found guilty of "attempted rape on females" and sentenced to reside in a delinquents' home.

XXV

1959: An Un-American

with a Rocket

Khrushchev's visit to Eisenhower formally raised the curtain on the second or co-existence stage of the American Century, when the impossibility of an American-Russian war was publicly acknowledged; and Foster Dulles's death a few months earlier put a neat *finis* to the first, or pseudo-schizophrenic, stage in which America acted as if such a war was possible and indeed probable.

Dulles passed to his reward shortly after taking humanity to another brink over Berlin. The news evoked, as his theologian admirer Henry Pitt Van Dusen tells us ,"an outpouring of acclaim without precedent in our day . . . Not only throughout the length and breadth of his own country but across the world, tributes almost of reverence welled up."* Most of mankind had regarded him with horror thinly laced with pity, and what welled up abroad was the touching hope which springs eternal on such occasions: that the policy was the man and would die with him. In America, mass-circulation newspapers had praised him to the end and urged him toward ever more breathless brinks. Extreme toadies among his employees shed a tear for the man who had turned top diplomats into nervous office boys. The intelligentsia, who would have liked to see the same policy carried out more suavely by Acheson and/or Stevenson, had begun in his last years to lampoon his pious protestations in an attempt to transfer to him their own hypocrisies. The general public was hardly ruffled. In short order he would, in contrast to McCarthy, be little more than the name of an airport.

As long as the war-based economy required total inflexibility, Dulles had convinced the public that Russia would only respond to threats; but his style had been rendered obsolete by Russian rockets. Furthermore the success of Castro's bearded Cuban horde, who turned out to be obstinate socialists, provided Moscow with a thorn in America's side similar to the American thorn (the West Berlin enclave) in Russia's. The futility of the Dulles approach was underlined when Khrushchev entertained Harriman and Nixon in Moscow with chatty data about his intercontinental missile, which could atomize any American city in some 20 minutes. It was time to invite Khrushchev to America and grant that the Russians had a point of view worthy of discussion; but this was no reason to fear a slowdown in the American Century's advance. The fabulously costly hecatomb devices would continue to be produced on the basis that they were pillars of peace, for any unfavorable missile or other "gap" would imperil the delicate balance of stalemate. This would indefinitely prolong the distortion of socialist countries' economies,

---

* Introduction to *The Spiritual Legacy of John Foster Dulles*, edited by Henry P. Van Dusen, Westminster, Philadelphia, 1960, from which Dulles excerpts in Chapter V of this book are taken.

depriving them of the consumer goods for which they hungered. The new phase would call for greater concentration on small wars to prevent more Cubas as in Vietnam, and on the corrupting functions of CIA.

After several cautious years the relaxation brought from respectable publishers a sprinkle of books impugning more basic aspects of the domestic and foreign cold war. *Nation* contributor Cook's* *Unfinished Story of Alger Hiss* (Morrow, New York, 1958) threw uncomfortable doubt on Hiss's guilt and on the passion for justice of inquisitor Nixon. Ginzburg's *Rededication to Freedom* (Simon & Schuster, New York, 1959) not only queried the Hiss, Rosenberg, Lattimore, Remington and Dexter White cases but challenged inquisitorial bastions from HUAC to loyalty boards, Brownell's familiars and Hoover himself. A Voltairean preface by theologian Niebuhr, who did not doubt Hiss's and the Rosenbergs' guilt but could vouch for the author as "free of the taint of Communist sympathy," saved Ginzburg's book from media oblivion. With no bow to the inquisition a rare hysteria-proof historian, Wisconsin University's William Appleman Williams, traced *The Tragedy of American Diplomacy* (World, New York, 1959) to the obsession that only by copying America could other countries solve their problems.**

These straws-in-the-wind on the eve of Khrushchev's arrival were vigorously countered by inquisitors, whose task was to see that the head of the world conspiracy should not take home illusions that all was forgiven. With a budget raised to $327,000, HUAC was able to add to its *Who Are They?* series—already covering Tito, Ho Chi Minh and Mao (with whom DuBois lunched in March)—"a brief biography of Karl Marx," described as "a glimpse at the mysterious processes of a life which produced the ideological base for the most devilish and menacing force mankind has ever experienced." In a peak year for media apathy toward its work, HUAC had by March carried out probes in Los Angeles and in Pittsburgh, where Nelson was re-summoned but "told the Committee nothing except his opinion of them, which was low" (Pittsburgh *Post-Gazette*). One Pittsburgh familiar earned a VFW plaque as "citizen of the year," but the old spirit of rooting for inquisitors against heretics was lacking in the public sections of hearing rooms. In another probe of the passport plot, CRC's Patterson (now manager of the *Worker*) and Bridges could not deny obtaining passports without swearing they had Never Been. Bridges, who had been detected "participating in a number of conferences with leading Communists" in Europe, was asked if he would "advocate a strike" in the event of America aiding Taiwan in a war against China. "I would do what I could to oppose America engaging in such a suicidal enterprise," said Bridges, adding that Chiang was "a bum."

The thaw brought the Bolshoi Ballet to New York: media and public were too delirious about Galena Ulanova to make a probe advisable in that quarter, but

---

* Fred J. Cook, author of the best available work on Hoover and his Bureau, *The FBI Nobody Knows* (Macmillan, New York, 1964).

** An Annapolis graduate who took the war against Fascism seriously and whose combat injuries kept him in Navy hospitals for a year, Williams would fall under inquisitorial scrutiny in 1961 when HUAC subpenaed him along with the manuscript of his next book *Contours of American History*. An irreproachable law firm fended this off, but he experienced several years of "tax arrears" harassment, media blackout of his work, phone and mail threats, lost friendships, etc.

HUAC's card index showed that Ben Shahn, Philip Evergood and 20 more artists whose works were on show in Moscow "had a total of at least 465 separate connections" with heretical groups. Spokesmen for an American Artists Professional League described how heretics had "infiltrated the art world . . . to destroy all phases of our culture" so that "they can take us over without a hydrogen bomb," and confirmed that Communists used art as "a prime weapon [to produce] organized confusion to the mind." In America's current mood, Eisenhower merely directed that 25 additional paintings be added to the show "covering earlier periods in American art history." A probe of a new Party school, eliciting Fifth-Amendment intonations from the school's musical and other instructors, produced open yawns on all sides as did HUAC's charges that 67 Fifth-invoking lawyers had "assisted Communist operatives in circumventing the law . . . served in secret cells aimed at espionage."

HUAC inquisitors had run the same water too often over the dam, but now they mounted a coup-de-théâtre with every promise of restoring them to front pages: a probe of Khrushchev on the eve of his arrival. While they could hardly expect a green light to subpena him, here at least was a crystalline case of un-American activities, and there would be no amendment-invocations to deaden the proceedings. Since the probe clearly could have been stopped, we must assume a decision by the Establishment to give Khrushchev an unmistakably mixed reception. For one thing it would show him the multiformity of a free society in contrast to socialist totalitarianism. At one end of the spectrum Lippmann, fresh from a Russian visit, was conjuring Americans to "abandon the notion that the Russian and Chinese revolutions can be reversed" and talk politely to Khrushchev. At the other end AFL-CIO spokesmen were insisting that, even if Eisenhower could talk to Khrushchev, the toiling masses whom they led would not enter a room with so satanic a figure. They stood firm for massive retaliation.

It was an eminently American phenomenon, imaginable nowhere else, to invite a state guest and at the same time semi-officially depict him as a monster dripping with blood. This was done at the probe by former Moscow correspondent Eugene Lyons, who had been collecting statistics in his field ever since witnessing the horrors of socialism 25 years previously, and a series of postwar immigrants from the Ukraine. In two prewar years as "Stalin's trusted killer" Khrushchev had liquidated "an estimated 400,000," Lyons testified; in 1941 "the Soviet peoples, as is by now generally known, for the most part welcomed the German invaders as liberators," but after 1943 Khrushchev had conducted a purge whose victims "ran into hundreds of thousands." "What," Arens asked Lyons, "will be the effect of Khrushchev's visit on the subjugated people behind the Iron and Bamboo Curtains?" "It amounts to a body blow . . . a day of gloom and despair for tens of millions inside Russia." "I gather you consider the invitation a mistake . . . Based on your background and experience as a student of international Communism, tell this committee, Mr. Lyons, how late it is now on the Communist timetable for world domination." "Later, much later, than most people think . . . Khrushchev is one of the bloodiest tyrants extant. He has come to power over mountains of corpses."

To provide illustrations for HUAC's probe report, the Ukrainians brought photos from the period when corpse production unquestionably broke records in the Kiev area. On the question of the producers' identity, a former Vinnitsa news-paper editor said that in May 1943 "we discovered" dozens of mass graves and "the German government gave its permission" to dig up the bodies and prove that they owed their fate to Khrushchev. Another witness who "arrived in Vinnitsa in 1943 . . . after being arrested by the NKVD in June of 1942, accused of counter-revolutionary activities" had, "with permission from the German authorities . . . helped examine the bodies." Khrushchev's systematic massacres had been "repeated ad nauseum during his regime," and he had, inter alia, "poisoned medical capsules with certain injections of typhus" and "poisoned water for public use." "May I ask," asked Arens of a witness to earlier hecatombs, "if you observed instances of cannibalism?" The picture was rounded out by a Georgetown "professor in Soviet economics" who gave examples showing Khrushchev as "really the most infamous genocidist alive today." Arens asked: "These, of course, are not the only crimes attributed to Khrushchev?" "Definitely not," said the professor, proceeding with more.*

But most Americans neither knew nor cared where the Ukraine was and seemed more interested in the possibility that Khrushchev's visit might lift the nuclear nightmare; and perhaps also from lingering sensitiveness to vulgarity beyond a certain limit, the media again blighted HUAC's hopes of banner head-lines. Khrushchev introduced himself to America by having one of his rockets fired at the moon, hitting it the day before he flew in. He was insulted here, smil-ingly greeted there, but the welcome, however frigid, bore a note of respect. His themes, as expected, were wholesale disarmament and the promise that "in peace-ful competition with capitalism" Russia would within a few years lead the world in per capita and volume production. If this was somewhat over-sanguine, he could not hope to rival in boastfulness "the mad statements of American generals and admirals" (his own phrase) about annihilating socialism, which were far from having stopped. Industrialists were as eager to meet him as labor leaders were aloof—with the exception of Bridges, who embraced him in San Francisco. He and Eisenhower agreed that neither would do anything rash in Berlin. Otherwise the visit merely served as a *nihil obstat* for the view that nuclear war was not the formula for defeating socialism.

Before and after the visit, heretics were kept guessing as to the extent of the relaxation. Dorothy Day and her group went to jail for their standard refusal to take cover on defense-drill day. Muste was jailed again at 74 for demonstrating for peace at an Omaha missile base. Inquisitors awaited the return of Pauling from a 70,000-mile peacemongering tour to decide on a viable approach to so celebrated and combative a citizen. New York heretics flocked again to Union Square for a May Day peace demonstration with Seeger leading the entertainment, and in the

---

* These catechistic exchanges were fairly typical of Arens's technique when a familiar was on the stand. His approach to heretics is illustrated in these examples recorded by Donner: "Are you now or have you ever been a member (of a godless conspiracy based on perversion and deceit) (of the army of the Kremlin steeled to overthrow our insti-tutions and operating behind a facade of humanitarianism) (of any organization which is an atheistic organization, dedicated to the destruction of religion, the sterility of the individual, of all concepts of God)?" "Are you a dedicated zealot . . . who masquerades behind the Constitution of the United States and would desecrate the flag of this great nation?" "Are you a murderer?" etc.

same month the Supreme Court declined to prevent the rejailing of Party leader
Thompson. With continuing pain after three operations on his cracked skull, he
would die soon after getting out and be denied the war-hero's privilege of burial
in Arlington cemetery.*

Eastland and his colleagues Kenneth Keating (New York) and Thomas
Dodd (Connecticut) found an almost acceptable formula for curbing high-court
power over the inquisition but, failing to allay other circles' fears of a weakened
legal fabric, lost by one Senate vote. The Supreme Court was still dodging the
Constitutionality of heresy laws while often ruling favorably for heretics on tech-
nicalities. It reversed contempt convictions (as in the case of lawyer Sacher in
1958), on the ground that questions asked were "not clearly pertinent." In ruling
against the imposition of a loyalty oath on Fritchman's Los Angeles church, it had
granted California's right to impose the oath but said the state went about it in
the wrong way.** At the same time the Court upheld the contempt convictions of
Uphaus and Barenblatt, a former Vassar psychology instructor who had invoked
the wrong amendment at a HUAC probe in 1954.

In Dixie, the jail sentence on SCEF's Braden was followed by another old-
fashioned Mississippi lynching: residents of Poplarville dragged a Negro by his
feet down the jail stairs, clubbed him on a riverbank and disposed of him in the
water. In Alabama, on the other hand, a clergyman was stripped, strung from a tree
and chain-whipped but allowed to live. A second march to press for school desegregation brought 26,000 student demonstrators to Washington. When schools
reopened, integration had dawned in four of 2,095 school districts containing children of both colors, and 74 black children of a 2,600,000 school population
trooped into the same classrooms with whites.

* Robert Colodny, who like Thompson served against Fascism both in Spain and in
the Pacific, wrote in 1967: "When will we know that the crisis [of American policy as
seen in Vietnam] has been overcome? . . . When an agency of the US government will
be empowered by the Congress to go to Spain, and from one of the battlefields bring
back one dead American and put him as an unknown soldier in Arlington Cemetery—
where he has the same right as those who fought at Gettysburg or at Belleau Wood or on
the beaches of Normandy." But to have fought in Spain and not repented was still the
primary stigma of disloyalty in 1961, when Pittsburgh University professor Colodny became the target of a barrage from HUAC, SISS, Pennsylvania Supreme Court Judge
Musmanno, Legion, VFW and the Pittsburgh Press. "The Communist-led Abraham
Lincoln Brigade still tops the Attorney General's list of subversive organizations," the
Press pointed out, reporting that among other continuing heresies Colodny kept a
Spanish Civil War poster in his office at the university.
** This decision in June 1958 had cost the church over $50,000 in a four-year court
fight; $35,000 in property taxes which the church had to pay into escrow was returned.
During the fight the church recruited a record number of members and the congregation became increasingly militant. Looking back later on his embattled Los Angeles
years, Fritchman wrote of the functions of a Unitarian minister: "He helps people
accept the tragic factor in life amidst the banal superficialities of our prevailing culture
. . . He has the unpopular responsibility of reminding men they can die by a hydrogen
bomb or by mediocrity, or fraudulence, or vulgarity; by smog, by the gas chamber or
by the death of goodness in their own souls. He is perpetually aware of the cascading
power of inertia and ignorance, stupidity, hatred and fear in men's lives . . . He
declares there are no absolutes, no dogmas, and that man can live under an open sky
without fear of death."

In trials of 1959 the Scales pattern was repeated: heretics who had quit or disavowed the Party were sentenced to jail for belonging to it or following its precepts. The government's seventh assault on Mine-Mill since CIO expelled that union in 1949 brought a statement from its leaders that it "held no brief for Communism and was devoted to the American democratic system," but nine of its Denver organizers were convicted of Taft-Hartley perjury. Six more Denver citizens— of whom two were still Party members—were found guilty of membership in their second Smith Act trial.

Eisenhower, on a world tour in December, was noticeably moved by the multitudes everywhere applauding his invitation to Khrushchev. Nearing the end of his Presidential term, and with no Dulles at his elbow, he began speaking to ragged, hungry Asians strange words "in the name of humanity." The tensions that wracked mankind were, he said, "the creations of governments, cherished and nourished by governments. Nations would never feel them if they were given freedom from propaganda and pressure . . . Men and women everywhere [should] lift up their eyes to the heights that can be achieved together, ignoring what has been." The multitudes seemed to agree. Perhaps they expected practical proposals as to how a start toward brotherhood might be made and how the widening of the chasm between rich and poor nations could be reversed. If so, they expected too much at a time when America was presiding over the rearmament of Hitler's prosperous heirs. The profits of preparing for war, even if it could never be fought, soared higher than ever above any possible profits from preparing for peace.

XXVI

1960-?: A Not Unreasonable Hope

So rarely do great endeavors produce the results envisaged, or only those results, that morbid historians see the human species as condemned to perpetual frustration. All computers now agreed that America's nuclear and chemical devices could expunge Russia many times over or kill all the rice in China with a capsule; yet Korea had shown, and Vietnam would confirm, that the proprietors of this peerless electronically controlled arsenal could not defeat a small dark people armed with little but determination. Domestically, the artificers of the American Century faced a similar anomaly: 22 years of successful probing had fashioned an America which its own inheritors increasingly rejected.

The world marveled at the ingenuity of American contrivances to curb nature's enemies and harness its bounties, to make life easy and orderly for men; yet natural and human chaos rose with the ingenuity, while psychiatrists' waiting rooms were cluttered with the beneficiaries of material ease. Oceans, rivers, lakes and forests were dying, cities becoming a mink-lined and ghetto-pocked shambles with poisoned air, to make the American Century work better. The cry that the disease was in the system, and could only be cured by citizens less devoted to personal gain and more to social responsibility, had been suffocated—for those who raised it were notoriously conspiring to advocate violence. Yet with the near-extinction of the notorious conspiracy, America entered its most violent decade.

The new crop of Americans, grown up under the cleansing inquisition, proved to contain an even higher and more perverse percentage of weeds. Where their predecessors had found remediable faults in a basically acceptable America, "New Left" heretics denounced it as an almost total fraud. Their scorn, voiced twice as loudly, covered everything from the acquisitive and exterminative morality to sexual and sartorial mores, from the Establishment's democratic pretensions to the revolutionary and socialist ones of the "Old Left" and of Russia. Of the holy office itself, their opinion was that it did not even merit their contempt.

Although all signs pointed to indefinite inquisitions in some form, a sign of the times was the blank reaction in January to Philbrick's hour-long analysis for HUAC, responding to Arens's "Tell us about the importance to Communism of youth," of the schools' "apathy to the red threat." * Since heretical youth were

---

* As a device for suppressing the unruly in provincial areas, however, Philbrick remained serviceable. In 1967 he gave Daytona Beach (Florida) and Pikeville (Kentucky) residents "startling statistics on the number of people, roughly 85,000,000, murdered by the Communists . . . What we need is people who care. For goodness sake let's not be apathetical." Strip-mining coal companies were profitably wrecking the forested hills around Pikesville; SCEF had organized some resistance by destitute Kentuckians demanding at least some share of the profits; and SCEF leaders had been charged with advocating violent overthrow. For his statistics confirming this, Philbrick received a standing ovation from attenders at the Pikeville "banquet-lecture." The local paper reported that "practically all those present shook hands with him" and the Chamber of

now not merely shunning the CP but deriding it for what they saw as its weakness and failure, the traditional are-you-or-have-you-ever-been thought-control approach was plainly archaic. The shape of the future emerged at a HUAC probe in San Francisco in May, with 16 subpenas to picketers of stores which would not serve lunch to Negroes. A few hundred students with a scattering of old heretics gathered noisily outside and inside the chamber and were dragged, clubbed and swept with fire hoses downstairs into the street. Sixty-three were arrested for inciting to riot; next day the picket line swelled to some 5,000 protestants of whom few had yet graduated to a Hoover dossier.

Presumably the mastodon lingered long after the first signs of its anachronism, and so it was with the Dies-style tribunal. It would not expire until its natural food—the headline—was wholly cut off. San Francisco gave it headlines which, while not the most desirable, could be turned to dubious profit in exposures of the fracas as a Communist plot. Meanwhile media cooperation in SISS's delayed probe of Pauling showed how far the animal was from becoming extinct. The task of the inquisitors was far from done, or if it was they did not think so.

Pauling brought his case to a head by joining the San Francisco pickets and by resigning from the peace group SANE after its leader, *Saturday Review* editor Norman Cousins, began investigating members to assure that its pleas against the Bomb should remain hygienic. Cousins welcomed SISS inquisitor Dodd's help in purging SANE; Pauling thought that if anything needed purging it was the Senate, starting with Eastland and Dodd. A month later Pauling received his subpena. The *Times* joined so ardently in the weighting of coverage against Pauling that he wrote accusing it of "rapidly becoming an unreliable newspaper." To the media it was as clear as it was to SISS that Pauling could not have persuaded 110,000 scientists in 49 coutries to sign his Bomb protest without the aid of the international conspiracy against America. SISS demanded his fellow conspirators' names and did not get them.

The media headlined everything except Pauling's estimate—proclaimed around the world and now at home—of nuclear-age war as "so lacking in logic that it's hard to say anything sensible about it." At a resumed probe of his heretical contacts in October, he told Dodd that he "very much missed" ASP, wished he had more time to work for Sobell, and had enjoyed marching on the San Francisco picket line. When SISS counsel J. G. Sourwine quoted Hoover's identification of the picket line with the red plot, Pauling replied: "It is my opinion that he is mistaken." Perhaps fearing boomerang publicity from abroad, Dodd hesitated to cite for contempt the scientist who, by 1963, would be the world's first holder of

---

Commerce president, as master of ceremonies, said: "All of us will leave here as better people."

Not alone in the Kentucky hills, but in some intellectual circles, respect for Philbrick lingered long. In December 1969 the *Times* reported across three columns that USIS had paid the reformed heretic Burnham $950 for a critique of its overseas book catalog. Burnham, distressed by the inclusion of books by such "vicious opponents" of American policies as Susan Sontag, Wright Mills and Art Buchwald, had proposed rectifying this by inclusion of such "modern conservative writers" as Chambers, Budenz, Bentley, Cvetic, Bella Dodd and Philbrick. Of these and other recommended authors Burnham was quoted as saying: "By any objective test every one is well above the median of the book list as a whole."

two unshared Nobel prizes.* But the media would still be trying to silence Pauling when he won his second prize, the *Herald Tribune* then labeling him "a placarding peacenik with extravagant posturings" who had "made himself a dangerous nuisance." Pauling said he would go to jail rather than give names, called SISS "a cancer on the body politic . . . HUAC is probably even worse," and bought newspaper space to urge the abolition of both.

Control of the New Left called for more direct application of force, but inquisitorial tribunals were retained for the dwindling intimidations they could provide. On the other hand atomic defense drills had lost their power to instill fear and seemed ready for the undertaker. The 1960 drill in New York brought out not only the old pacifists but some 1,000 protestants of a new, mainly younger type. Even Dwight MacDonald had had enough and, by coming out to say so, eliminated all possibility of labeling the protest a red plot. Unsettled by this dilemma, the police filled their paddy wagon at random and left out Muste and Dorothy Day who had been protesting annually for years. Governor Nelson Rockefeller praised civil defense for its efforts in an "attack" which, according to computers, "killed" 3,935,490 New Yorkers instantly and 1,405,000 later; but it was decided not to invite the public to participate in further drills.

Harassment of old-school heretics perceptibly lost momentum but had much momentum to lose. MacLeish told a TV audience that America had no political prisoners as mathematician Chandler Davis followed Uphaus and Barenblatt into jail for incorrect non-answers to HUAC. Black CP leader Winston was going blind behind bars; at some point on the legal treadmill, trying to stay out, were 32 First-Amendment invokers including seven factory workers, four clergymen, four journalists, three teachers, two actors, two union officials, two radio-TV men, an author, an engineer and a folk singer. An appeals court, uncertain whether the abolition of the First Amendment was definitive, upheld six convictions for invoking it and reversed two (librarian Knowles and Philadelphia teacher Watson). Lower courts continued routinely handing out convictions destined for reversal higher on the treadmill. Ten years after the proceedings began, Pittsburgh lawyer Schlesinger was formally disbarred on Cvetic's and Mazzei's testimony that he was a Communist.**

* A solon rivaling Parnell Thomas in the crude faking of expense accounts, Dodd would merely be censured in 1967 by fellow senators who thought it unwise to jail another inquisitor. One of his last inquisitorial follies was a probe of British drama critic Kenneth Tynan, who in 1960 presented on London TV a negative portrait of America featuring heretics of old and new schools from Hiss and Trumbo to "beat" poet Allen Ginzburg and Mailer, a rising idol of marijuana-smoking "hippies." The burden of the show was that the new generation knew what it disliked but not what it wanted.
** Pennsylvania's Supreme Court (Musmanno tactfully "not participating") would reverse the disbarment a year later. It found that Schlesinger had been subjected to "shocking and flagrantly outrageous treatment"; the "Committee on Offenses" which tried him had acted as prosecutor, judge and jury; being a Communist did not necessarily reflect on a man's moral character; Mazzei had been "wholly discredited," and Schlesinger had been improperly denied the right to bring testimony that Cvetic was an alcoholic and recent psychiatric-ward patient.
    In December 1971 New York's Board of Education was "exploring the possibility" of reinstating 31 victims of the Moskoff inquisition. (Many others had not survived through the two blacklisted decades.) The *Times,* reporting this, called the teacher probe "especially obnoxious" since it tried to turn teachers "into informers against their col-

With Moskoff as prosecutor, New York's Education Board fired four more teachers for non-informing despite the state education commissioner's veto on this.* Clergymen for the second time drew the fire of the Air Force's inquisitorial apparatus. In an *Air Reserve Center Training Manual* it renewed its warnings that reds had "infiltrated our churches," citing as evidence ministerial pleas to let China into the UN and the National Council of Churches' sponsorship of a *Revised Standard Version of the Bible.* The Air Force had been too absorbed in the organization of megadeath to keep up with home trends, and the first thunder from the bishops forced it to withdraw. Walter leaped in to reprehend the Defense Secretary's "groveling apology" for the *Manual,* and summoned the Air Secretary to make him grovel in reverse.

By far the most serious challenge to Establishment strategists was the revolt of the descendants of black slaves. The connection between their and the Africans', Asians', and Latin Americans' plight, constantly pointed out by DuBois, was beginning to sink in. They had waited a century merely for equal educational opportunity, and six years after being granted it they were still waiting. "I see no way to stop racial integration," a realistic Florida Klansman told a reporter, but Eastland generaled his Senate allies** through days and nights of filibustering to prevent a vote on the Negro's right to vote. The bill which the Senate finally passed left the situation unchanged unless blacks themselves changed it, which they clearly intended using all available means to do.*** Four Greensboro (North Carolina) college freshmen, sitting-in at lunch counters where they were refused service, had started in February what would become a nationwide crescendo of black resistance through the decade.

In March and April 20,000 protesting blacks in South Africa, and tens of thousands of South Korean and South Vietnamese demonstrators against American-sponsored regimes of graft and torture, were suppressed with guns; nine months later, heretical Premier Patrice Lumumba was assassinated to keep the Republic of the Congo safe for the free world. Yet France's surrender of Algeria to heretically oriented Algerians showed how much remained to be done to persuade the inhabitants of ex-colonies that they did not want socialism. While force was theoretically applicable from America's 3,401 planet-encircling bases, its dangers and limitations were obvious and nonviolent absorption of leaders into junior Century partnership would remain a top priority.

---

leagues." Neither Moskoff, who conducted it, nor the *Times's* own sponsorship of its ideological father Sidney Hook was mentioned in the report or in the editorial calling the probe "a shameful chapter."

* Protests postponed the firings, and in 1961 the entire Board would be removed by the state legislature for incompetence and corruption. The new Board compromised by upholding two of the dismissals.

    The whole story of *The New York City Teachers Union, 1916–1964* is in Celia Zitron's book of that title (Humanities Press, New York, 1968).

** Including South Carolina's Johnston, who quoted Hoover on the red plot to extend the Constitution to blacks; Fulbright of Arkansas; Stevenson's 1952 running mate Sparkman of Alabama; and Florida's Smathers, just back from the Dominican Republic with bouquets for dictator Trujillo.

*** In the 1960s Negroes began to insist on being called "blacks," which they had previously regarded as insulting.

Eisenhower left the throne with an oddly explicit warning against the "military-industrial complex" which he and Truman had built up. New Left heretics and remnants of the old would cite this Presidential aberration for years in efforts to reverse the cold war and its economy; but with corporate war-production profits continuing to soar, a reversal seemed impossible short of a revolution. The escalating war budget would finally cause such inflation as to weaken the dollar, so that rumors of more war produced greater Wall Street headaches than rumors of peace; but unhappy businessmen who had no share in the bonanzas found themselves as impotent to stop it as heretics.

Kennedy inherited CIA arrangements to overthrow Castro in 1961, which proved so amateurish that a replacement was required for Allen Dulles to handle more smoothly the corruption, spying, torture, assassination and kindred elements of Century-building overseas. America, meanwhile, entered an unprecedented period of domestic assassinations, including black leaders who remained impervious to Establishment seductions. Some blacks smelled the possibility—especially after America began massacring wholesale in Vietnam*—of a Hitlerian "final solution" in which they would be obliterated as part of a white genocide program.

In the later 60s, as new suppressive forms arose to replace the lingering mastodon, much of the inquisitorial hoax—even the Rosenberg frame-up and CIA's corruption of intellectuals—would come to public knowledge; but the cynicism, fear and apathy it had engendered would triumph over all proposals to alter course. The suspicion would spread well beyond heretical circles that it had been a transcendent example of that ancient human blend, folly and tragedy. Yet its domination by clowns had been no obstacle to its success, and the Establishment had little cause to regret the promotion of patriotism from the last to the first refuge of scoundrels.

Although inquisitors owed a debt to Russia's non-achievement of an enviable society, they could claim most of the credit for defusing a generation of heretics by plunging it into dismay, isolation, and struggles to stay out of jail. None could assess the full cost in ruined lives, but statistics showed that human casualties had been few. The inquisition had been especially successful with the intelligentsia, upon whom the consequences of their surrender now began to dawn 15 or more years late.** With the rarest exceptions they had become fat and could be trusted, in the foreseeable future, to agree neither on any positive goal nor even on how to

* "Seymour Hersh, a freelance journalist . . . told how [his battalion in Vietnam] encountered no resistance at Mylai, yet how the blood ran. He told how old men were tortured and women raped and dying children thrown into a drainage ditch that made one think of Babi Yar and Treblinka. He told how chips of bone went whistling off the people and cattle that were used for target practice while GIs laughed."—*Times* Book Review, May, 1970.
** By 1967–68 MacDonald would be appealing as "a member of the Old Left" for support of New Left defiance, and accepting the risk of jail for it; a Vietnam trip converted Mary McCarthy to ideas she fought at the height of the inquisition; and Mailer would be ready with MacDonald and Lowell to lead (and write a brilliant book on) an invasion of the Pentagon and consequent procession to jail. Arthur Schlesinger, Jr., who had served as a top adviser to Kennedy, would decide that Pentagon policy was "disastrous . . . we have been fought to a standstill by 280,000 characters in black pajamas mostly armed, till recently, with rifles and mortars." Concerning the inquisition ("retrospec-

repair their damage. The Pentagon moved in with vast subventions for universities, where tens of thousands of scientists devoted themselves to perfecting devices for suppressing human beings and conquering the moon, and no area with megadeath potential was too recondite to be studied.* The 60s would be a decade of bounties for studying everything, not excluding the phenomenon of destitution amid prodigious wealth and the probabilities of uprisings against it by populations now deemed surplus. Concerning percentages of children who died of starvation or survived napalm burns, and comparative budgets and life-expectancies in America and the countries on which it fattened, doubts were scholastically set at rest in a new style of mandarin jargon. While America advanced far along the road to automation, an intellectual could achieve the good life, including a psychiatrist's regular services, by studying the effect on a family of not having a water tap—or a home to put one in if they had it, as in Calcutta, a city to win American fame in the pornographic title of an appropriately nude Broadway revue.

The New Left's contempt for the intellectual establishment was only equaled by its contempt for laws which the government so consistently broke. They inherited the driving conviction of the old Higginses that paper rights were paper, that only those agitated and fought for would be enjoyed. Seeking new avenues for action, they slew many a dragon of hypocrisy; yet the threat they posed might well not be serious for years to come. Their "revolution," openly so designated, took at least two forms—indiscriminate sex and the use of drugs—toward which the Establishment could afford indulgence: its laws against these cults could always be invoked to silence heresy without seeming to do so. The hair defiantly growing on heretical faces only made them easier for the police to identify. Policy in cultural fields would be abruptly changed during the decade: the burning of books, and jail terms for reading them, were outmoded. Political literature would be as little controlled as pornographic; and with discord becoming babel on the left as to the correct interpretation of Marx, in a nuclear-computer era when trade unions had a multi-billion-dollar stake in the status quo, this would predictably compound confusion. Painters and playwrights had free rein to develop an art and a theatre of the absurd but one by one gave up the struggle to outdo the absurdities of real life. Meanwhile the Establishment itself became the number-one propaganda machine, enormously extending the public-relations services of every government ramification. As for ideology, the Establishment found that it could get along well without a Satan, although Mao lingered in this role for some years.

---

tively so absurd"), Schlesinger would still recall it as having been the work of "one senator alone," and warn of a "new McCarthyism" arising from Vietnam frustrations.

Looking back with greatest anguish on the intelligentsia's performance was Christopher Lasch, who in 1967—the year of public disclosure that they had worked all along for CIA—described at length their "defection" which "goes a long way toward explaining the poverty of public discussion today." MacDonald, but not Schlesinger nor Galbraith, shared Lasch's embarrassment. Conceding that a few had offered resistance, Lasch found consolation in the thought that they were "self-serving": they indulged in "desperate acts of conscience [which had] as their object not truth or even social change but promotion of the individual's self-esteem." So much, e.g., for Einstein.

* In 1969 the University of Mississippi's psychology department would be "trying to train birds to take aerial pictures, fire guns, steer missiles and detect mines." (*Times*).

The conflict would increasingly be seen as one between "teams": "the other team" was a satisfactory formulation for what America had to beat.

The inquisition had decisively scared a generation away from disciplined organization, without which no change of course had ever been imposed on a government; and among the new heretics this aversion would remain strong for some years. Almost every one with his own ideology or anti-ideology, they were readier than their predecessors to face jail or bodily injury; the extent to which they defied orders to participate in distant massacres was something new in history, and their street demonstrations would multiply to many times the old size. But the new media style of fully—sometimes even accurately—reporting such defiances and their suppression indicated the Establishment's awareness of its resilience in living with trouble, provided that no organization arose which might be able to take power. Production of devices for physically crushing and eavesdropping on heretics shaped up into a new billion-dollar business.

Hoover looked backward contentedly at the "McCarthy era" of which he was the true father. Adherence to his apparently simple-minded doctrines had brought to many the rewards of power and would soon put an inquisitor in the White House; and despite all that now began emerging about his methods, fear of his dossiers kept his Bureau free of any decisive challenge. In his first 40 years he had paid the CP his highest compliment by concentrating his forces upon it—for if he knew little else, he understood that the threat lay where there were organization and strategic experience. Now the Party nursed its battle scars in eclipse; but whatever might turn out to be tomorrow's prime danger, he stood ready to escalate violence or whatever was necessary for its extermination. His ever-multiplying army of agents penetrated wherever two or three were gathered together in the name of change. To many this paragon of policemen seemed to be in a suicidal race with military-industrial brinkmen who, while fingering the button to blow up the world, shared with him the slogan of ultimate loyalty: "Better dead than red."

The problems of the 60s, about which America appeared to have most to say, boiled down to a question that appeared very simple: Does man have a future? A Dixie senator would express the hope in 1969 that "if we have to start again with another Adam and Eve, I want them to be Americans." At that point some scholars would be estimating man's chances of avoiding self-liquidation at "about 50–50" by the year 2000. The position of the Vietnamese, who had survived years of American technological marvels raining from their skies, was that man had a future but they would accept any sacrifice to reject the American Century version. Their feeling was shared by mounting millions of Americans, but how they could triumph was yet to be seen; for they who inveighed against violence were still violent in a mythology that remained inquisitorial and was generally accepted. Yet 94-year-old Bertrand Russell could still sound a bright note in 1966: "It is not unreasonable to hope that American policy may change before it has taken steps which will put an end to the human race."

Index

No attempt has been made to index such persons as Joseph R. McCarthy, J. Edgar Hoover, Harry S Truman, and Adolf Hitler; and such organizations as the FBI, HUAC, and the Communist Party, which appear throughout the book.